Critical acclaim for Icons in the Fire*:*

'Impeccably researched, written with considerable eloquence and thoroughly provoking . . . Required reading if you want to know how the film business works, and how often it doesn't, in Britain'
Evening Standard

'*Icons in the Fire* is a fitting tribute to the late Alexander Walker, veteran film critic of the London *Evening Standard,* whose shrewd and witty commentary is matched by a fine sense of moral outrage . . . Walker is tartly ironic about the various deluded visionaries, charlatans and egomaniacs who people his story, but his acute sense of comedy is countered by an undertow of genuine sadness at what has come to pass'
Sunday Times

'Walker's narrative is clear-eyed and merciless. His forthright opinions earned him the enmity of the so-called great and good, which only vindicated his thorn-in-the-side journalism'   *Daily Telegraph*

'With a honed, dry wit . . . each page shows his elegance . . . uncompromising and intelligent, this study requires some answers'
Scotland on Sunday

'He wrote like a dream . . . the glittering style which lights up this final, and posthumous, part of the trilogy'   *Academy magazine*

'This excellent, indeed exhaustive, new book from Orion Publishing represents the third and final part in the late Alexander Walker's history of the modern British Film Industry . . . a very well-researched and readable title . . . *Icons* deserves to sit atop any self-respecting film fan's book shelf'
Screentrade magazine

Alexander Walker was the revered film critic of the London *Evening Standard* from 1960 until his death in 2003. He was born in Northern Ireland, educated there; at the Council of Europe's College d'Europe, Bruges; and at the University of Michigan, Ann Arbor, where he did postgraduate studies and lectured in government. He was three times named Critic of the Year in the annual British Press Awards (1970, 1974, 1998). He wrote and presented many radio and television programmes on cinema and was the author of twenty-two books on various aspects of Anglo-American and European cinema. Walker was a member of the jury at many international film festivals, including those held in Berlin (1969), Cannes (1974) and Chicago (1995). He was appointed a Chevalier de l'Ordre des Arts et des Lettres in 1981. He died in 2003.

By Alexander Walker

Icons in the Fire: The Rise and Fall of Practically Everyone in the
British Film Industry 1984–2000
The Celluloid Sacrifice: Aspects of Sex in the Movies
Stardom: The Hollywood Phenomenon
Stanley Kubrick Directs
Hollywood, England: The British Film Industry in the Sixties
Rudolph Valentino
Double Takes: Notes and Afterthoughts on the Movies 1956–76
Superstars
The Shattered Silents: How the Talkies Came to Stay
Peter Sellers: The Authorised Biography
Joan Crawford
Dietrich
No Bells on Sunday: Journals of Rachel Roberts (*edited*)
National Heroes: British Cinema in the Seventies and Eighties
Bette Davis
Robert Benayoun, Woody Allen: Beyond Words (*translated*)
Vivien: The Life of Vivien Leigh
It's Only a Movie, Ingrid: Encounters on and off screen
Elizabeth: The Life of Elizabeth Taylor
Zinnemann: An Autobiography (*jointly*)
Fatal Charm: The Life of Rex Harrison
Audrey: Her Real Story
Stanley Kubrick, Director

ICONS IN THE FIRE

The Rise and Fall of Practically Everyone in the British Film Industry 1984–2000

Alexander Walker

Introduced by Joseph Connolly

ORION

An Orion paperback

First published in Great Britain in 2004
by Orion
This paperback edition published in 2005
by Orion Books Ltd,
Orion House, 5 Upper St Martin's Lane,
London WC2H 9EA

1 3 5 7 9 10 8 6 4 2

A CIP catalogue record for this book is available
from the British Library.

ISBN 0 75286 484 X

Printed and bound in Great Britain by

Clays Ltd, St Ives plc

www.orionbooks.co.uk

'When we are born we cry that we are come
To this great stage of fools'

King Lear

Contents

Illustrations

Ken Loach[1]
Mike Leigh[2]
Nicholas Hytner[1]
Michael Winterbottom[1]
Terence Davies[2]
Neil Jordan[1]
John Madden[2]
Stephen Frears[2]
David Leland[1]
Julien Temple[1]
Mike Newell[1]
James Ivory[2]
Guy Ritchie[1]
Bill Forsyth[1]
Richard Attenborough[1]

[1] Rex Features Ltd
[2] The Kobal Collection Ltd

Introduction

Alexander Walker 1930–2003: a personal memoir

Joseph Connolly

Dying, though: it was just so unlike him. I mean to say, this is Alexander Walker we are talking about: the best advertisement I had ever come across for being in one's seventies – fit, trim, active, and with a matching mind and pen, both of them as sharp as a sabre. I assumed, I suppose, that he'd more or less live for ever – that the same old Alex, great friend and peerless companion at lunch, would still be amusing me, and educating me, and banging on about Lottery funding for films for about another hundred years. Why else, over one of our lunches, would I have agreed to become his Literary Executor? I hate taking on any job at all, really, and I only said 'Well, OK, Alex; if you want' because (a) I was flattered to be asked (while not, in truth, having even the first idea as to what such an appointment might entail) and (b) for the very good reason that it was perfectly clear to me that I would never be called upon to do anything whatever – always my preferred situation – because people like Alexander Walker (and no – I can't think of one) ... well, they just didn't ever die. Did they?

'Well, OK, Alex; if you want. But what if I pre-decease you? Shall we have a glass of champagne?'

'Mm – well in that case, of course, you're no bloody good to me at all, are you, Jo? Yes – I think a glass of champagne: most agreeable.'

And then we'd order. We'd meet for lunch four, maybe six, sometimes eight times a year – most usually at the Villa Bianca in Hampstead, from time to time at the Ivy and latterly at one of his latest discoveries, the Brasserie Roux in Pall Mall. He would not always precede the meal with champagne (and two glasses, that was rare: he never did anything to what he perceived as excess); sometimes he would go for a Campari and tonic – not soda, he stipulated: made it too sweet. Prosciutto was a favoured starter, followed by grilled fish, maybe – Dover sole for preference – or chicken, or veal. Glass or two of red, usually; bottle of fizzy. Never a pudding and always a large espresso. The finest constituent of all, however, was always his easy and fluent conversation – perfectly phrased opinion and anecdote, sometimes in-house gossip, always witty and informed but by no means invariably concerned with the film world – and all woven together with eager and sincere enquiries as to the welfare of my wife, my children, and the progress or otherwise of my own writing and endeavours. Literature was an abiding interest – his library was enormous – and there was rarely a book of the moment that he had not already read. Contemporary art, too, was another great enthusiasm and again his collection was considerable. Largely prints and drawings – Hockney, Bacon, Freud, Warhol, Lichtenstein, Dine, Frinck and Bomberg among literally hundreds of others, all framed, and those not currently hanging (he alternated them) stacked eight-deep against the walls.

When we *did* discuss film, though ... well, we didn't discuss: I prompted, he talked, I listened. Despite, over more than fifty years, having met and written on just about every great film star and director you could mention, Alex was never remotely star-struck, but nor did he ever err in the other direction, as lesser critics have been known to, and sneer at all and sundry. He talked of their merits and prospects as actors and directors, and marvelled at their private lives and vanities – the meanness or the profligacy (because it always did seem to be either one thing or the other). His knowledge of the ins and outs of the business was, of course, both encyclopaedic and thoroughly up-to-date, his many books on Hollywood, British cinema, stardom and the biographies of the stars themselves pretty much immediately becoming established as instant and definitive classics of the genre.

Following lunch, getting out of the restaurant always took a fair bit of time because of Alex's quite extraordinary civility and elaborate politeness. If food and service were below par he could be very curt and impatient; it rarely happened, though, because he tended to patronise the same few tried and tested venues. So normally the scene would be, then, that there he was, being helped into his Burberry and thanking the waiter profusely, and the waiter would say, 'Oh no, thank *you*, Mr Walker.'

And Alex would say, 'No no no – I thank *you*; thank you so very much.'

And then the head waiter or the proprietor would come along next and Alex would say, 'Oh hello and thank you – thank you so *much*' and the head waiter or the proprietor would protest that all due gratitude this day must, he insisted, be upon his part and his alone – but here was not to appreciate Alex's absolute determination on these matters for then he would in turn insist that oh no no no, it was *he* who was so extremely pleased and grateful for the wonderful food and attentive service.

'Oh but *no*, Mr Walker – it is we who were so very pleased and grateful simply to *have* you here ...' I'm telling you, it could go well into the night, all this sort of thing. For myself, I just fixed an all-purpose and rictus grin on my face intended to convey not just a general and contented detachment but also a large delight at all this caper and rigmarole, and then I'd start counting up again the flowers on the wallpaper until such time as all this mutual felicitation would gradually simmer down into a sort of truce, and then at last we could get out of there.

Alexander Walker was born on 22 March 1930 in Portadown, Co. Armagh. Legend has it (and he was content to let the legend live) that at the age of four he was taken by his mother to the local cinema to see a cowboy film, *Buck Jones*, and from that moment on he was addicted to all things celluloid. Well, addicted he certainly became – but never obsessed, rather refreshingly: with Alex there was always time for all the other pursuits – skiing, which was a passion (God knows why; I could never understand it and he, quite properly, never troubled to explain); travel (though often work-related); research for books and visiting film festivals: this year would have marked his fortieth Cannes); reading; collecting and persecuting smokers. His answerphone message memorably concluded: 'And remember: smoking is the slow way to suicide' – and this was decades before the shaming and hounding of smokers became so fashionable and international a pursuit. Film, though, was of course his first and greatest love, and he once told me that he had an ambition to see every single film that had ever been produced. Of all men on earth – in the sixty-nine years of dedicated viewing since that first *Buck Jones* – he must surely have come the closest.

Alex Walker first swam into my realm of consciousness in the mid 1970s. At the time I owned the Flask Bookshop in Hampstead – a small shop specialising in antiquarian, modern first editions, art, literature and review copies: no new books at all. When I first heard his voice – it's inimitable, but if you know that intonation and gentle burr, you won't ever forget it – and I thought, oh, gosh, look, that must be that bloke from *Movie-Go-Round* on the radio: I'd know those polished tones anywhere. And so it proved; and of course I'd always read his film reviews every Thursday in the *Evening Standard* (were there Londoners who didn't?) and I'd even got a few of his books in the shop (he thought I'd priced them too cheaply; still didn't buy them, though). We seemed to hit it off, despite the fact that in those days I was a committed pipe smoker. I never actually blew it in his face, but the row of Dunhills, the detritus and the paraphernalia, were always there to see and sniff: he never once even commented on it, let alone berated me for killing myself slowly.

After that first encounter he came in just about every single Saturday morning. Alex would buy books on contemporary art, design and cultural phenomena: Sixties Pop (art and music), new movements such as Punk, street and popular fashion and photography (another huge interest of his). Often on these Saturdays he would invite me to lunch across the road at the Villa Bianca but this was, to my abiding regret, always impossible because I was very much a one man band and Saturday was the only day when I had an even chance of covering the rent, so closing for lunch was out of the question. When I finally shut up shop for good in 1988 (I was a full-time writer by then), he recalled all of that and Saturday lunch at the Villa Bianca became quite a regular fixture. Always, on those Saturdays, sartorially Alex was never less than perfect. The suits were Savile Row (sometimes from Rome, though, much to my jingoistic disapproval), the shirts from Hilditch & Key in Jermyn Street and there were always a tie with a bar and cufflinks – one of which had a tiny watch set into it. Only very recently did he take to wearing a standard watch round his wrist. What with all this and his thicket of grey hair – usually, much to his irritation, described in the press as a 'bouffant' – many thought him to be rather vain.

Well, he was certainly aware of and very careful about his appearance, but in the true sense Alex really was the most modest of men. When I congratulated him on winning the Critic of the Year Award for the third time in 1998, he simply batted all that away and said, 'Oh no no no – all it is is that my turn has just come around again, that's all.' He always had to be pressed to divulge details of his latest journalistic and literary successes (twenty-three books was his total), never alerted me to upcoming television or radio appearances – and should anyone approach him to praise a recent review or feature in the *Standard* he would enthusiastically thank them (about ten times) and then just shrug it away. Modest in his taste of transport, too: although he hated the Underground, he wasn't fond of taxis either. He would either walk or take the bus. He was involved in a car crash as a child and it put him off driving for life. He was involved in another accident as recently as 2002 – a car mounted the pavement near his home and knocked him over – and this shook him badly. The only time I have seen him stricken to his core, however, was when in the 1990s he broke his leg while skiing. He looked so forlorn, stumping about on his crutches; the then editor of the *Evening Standard*, the late Stewart Steven, had laid on a chauffeur-driven car, completely at Alex's disposal, twenty-four hours a day. He hated the mobile phone he was given in order to contact the driver (the only time he tolerated such a thing) and he hated as well simply having to make the call: he was embarrassed to be a burden and rather frightened, I think, by this unprecedented loss of independence, however temporary.

His loyalty to his friends was fierce; few of them ever met each other, though: he preferred his relationships to be neat and compartmentalised. The often-requested autobiography, therefore, was pretty much out of the question, rather sadly. The nearest he ever got to memoirs is the extremely entertaining book *It's Only a Movie, Ingrid* (1988) – the title taken from a withering comment in Alex's hearing from Alfred Hitchcock to Ingrid Bergman, when she was worrying him about her motivation, or somesuch. In a series of essays he trawls a few experiences in filmland; typically, he wrote the book as a favour to an editor known to him newly arrived at a start-up publishing company (now part of the mighty Hodder Headline) – and what's more he managed it in ten weeks flat. His personal views and foibles, of course, came through loud and clear in nearly everything he wrote. You could always tell if he approved of a certain actor – and certainly, by God, the means by which any given film had been funded and marketed. His tastes in humour, too, were plain to see: he loved Walt Disney animations and Peter Sellers – he loathed Norman Wisdom and Mr Bean. He bore with quiet fortitude forever being asked for his list of ten favourite films; he changed it occasionally, simply to prevent himself from dying of boredom, but *Citizen Kane* would always emerge triumphant. He rated *A Clockwork Orange* maybe rather more highly than was consistent with his views – it contained much more graphic violence than usually he would tolerate (sex, though, was fine) – but then it was of course directed by his good friend and most esteemed director Stanley Kubrick, about whom he has written both often and brilliantly. We had a few words about Kubrick's very last film, *Eyes Wide Shut* – Alex had been awaiting its release for ever so that he could finally write the last chapter of his Kubrick book. He greeted the film with rapture and awarded it his rare and coveted three stars in the *Evening Standard*; I think it one of the weakest and most risible films I have ever witnessed . . . so that was one of our briefer and less chatty conversations.

He loved writing books – on a manual typewriter until quite recently, when he bowed to the force of the computer. With a typewriter, he said, you can see all the pages mounting up nicely: this, he thought, was extremely gratifying and a great encouragement. That he wrote so much in his lifetime had a fair deal to do with his chronic insomnia. Whatever time he went to bed, he was generally up and about again by three in the morning, writing away. Neighbours have told me of his wandering out before dawn to get all his letters posted. And my God, did he write letters! Anyone who wrote to him – an academic, an institution, a fan, a lunatic – they would each receive a thoughtful and perfect reply. 'Why do you respond to the nutters?' I asked him.

'I respond to the nutters first of *all*,' he replied. 'It's being ignored they cannot bear – if you answer, there's a good chance they'll leave you alone.' He was wrong about this – most of them simply assumed that they'd now found a pen pal for life and they kept on writing and writing. And Alex, to give him his due, just kept on replying.

One of the very last films that Alex reviewed in the *Evening Standard* was the adaptation of one of my novels, *Summer Things* (two stars!). It was a French film, rather oddly, directed by Michel Blanc and starring Charlotte Rampling, Carole Bouquet, Lou Doillon and quite a few more rather gorgeous actresses, all of whom were due to attend the post-British première party last year at the French Institute in Kensington. Quite by coincidence, my wife and I found ourselves standing behind Alex in the queue to get in to the party. In view of the Frenchness of the occasion, Alex was wearing in his buttonhole the discreet little ribbon that denoted his status as a Chevalier of the Ordre des Arts et Lettres. This distinction, however – worn by the doyen of British film critics – was cutting no ice with the French girl on the door. Apparently the problem was that the ticket to the première screening had been in a cardboard wallet that doubled as the invitation to the post-film party. Alex (typically) apologised for having inadvertently thrown away the

wallet. The girl remained firm: no wallet, no entry. Alex did not pull
rank – instead, he turned to me and said to the girl. 'Look, I'm with
him: this is Joseph Connolly – he wrote the novel, he wrote the film.'
The trouble was I, too, had inadvertently thrown away the cardboard
wallet that had held the ticket and so there was no way on earth she was
going to let me in either.

There the matter rested for quite some considerable while – the queue
behind us stretching out into the pouring rain, wailing and swearing,
sometimes in French, sometimes in English – until eventually a slightly
older and more authoritative girl sashayed along to us (must have been
getting on for about twelve, this one, thirteen maybe) and she apparently
did know who at least one of us was (Alex, needless to say) and so I said,
'Look, I'm with him' and in we went.

We left the girl on the door in a state of chagrin – shrugging like mad
and protesting to the other one, '*Mais merde* – zey ad no *valets* . . .!'

So now we were in and packed among seemingly thousands. We
fought our way down the endless staircase to check in our coats, and
manfully struggled back up again: another battle of the shoulders to
secure a glass of champagne. Then the band started up – so utterly
deafening as to render all speech an impossibility – then another few
thousand revellers crammed their way in (no sign at all of even one of
the gorgeous actresses) and so what we did next was we fought our way
down the endless staircase to collect our coats and manfully struggled
back up again. Another battle of the shoulders to get out into the rain
once more and then a swift taxi to Chez Max, in Knightsbridge. We
had a wonderful meal, Alex, my wife and myself – for which, wholly
characteristically, he insisted on paying, in order to celebrate the première
of the film. We all then got into another taxi and he got off at his block
of flats in Maida Vale in very fine spirits indeed. I was never again to
share a meal with Alexander Walker.

He died, wholly unexpectedly, in the early hours of 15 July 2003, one
of the hottest days in England's recorded history. He had told no one
that he was booked in to the London Clinic for 'tests', but clearly he
expected to be there for only a few days. He suffered a totally unforeseen
and instantly fatal brain haemorrhage in the middle of the night. I was
contacted and just stood there, sweating through the heat and disbelief.
I was stunned by shock and sadness, though clearly I was far from being
alone in this. The midday edition of the *Evening Standard* was full of

photographs and tributes, Alex's friends and colleagues there – the editor Veronica Wadley, the arts editors Norman Lebrecht and Fiona Hughes – having responded so swiftly, professionally and really rather brilliantly in the face of their own stark amazement and grief. Two days later, Alex's very good friend Victoria Mather contributed a heartfelt and personal memoir to the paper. And so began the task I thought I should never be called upon to perform: that of Alexander Walker's Literary Executor.

I had not been that often to his flat, but God how very strange it was to be standing there now. Although it was not a particularly tight space for a single person – hall, living room, study, bedroom, bathroom, kitchen – Alex's unstoppable devotion to the acquisition of so many books, pictures, pieces of furniture and objects did rather tend to overwhelm it. One has read so many times of walls being 'covered in pictures'; in this case it was quite literally true – the frames were touching, side to side, top and bottom, from floor to ceiling. Each side of every door was closely hung with pictures; the only walls not given over to the display of contemporary art were covered in bookcases – and should a few of these stop short of the ceiling, they were topped by row upon row of unique pieces of Italian coloured glassware and sculptures. Alex loved the primary colours: it remained a secret until the pictures were eventually taken down that the walls throughout the flat were painted red, yellow and blue – and, in the case of the living room, all three.

The furniture was modern, mostly 1950s and 1960s classics: Joe Columbo, Castiglioni, Magistretti, Jacobsen, Eames, all these and more – Alex deplored antiques of any description. The result of this mass of rather glorious possessions was that there remained only a few well-worn and tortuous avenues through which one could (gingerly) make one's way. There was a circular steel rod and glass coffee table designed by Warren Platner piled high with 118 art books (I counted). A long leather sofa was also strewn with art books, but only a few dozen. In the kitchen was a small cooker, its four electric rings stacked high with art books – the oven was full of Christie's catalogues (Alex did not cook, as will be gathered, but he did grind fresh coffee; the fridge was reserved for fruit and champagne). Apart from the thousands of books there were hundreds of multicoloured ring binders, each of them dated. These were chock-full of newspaper and magazine cuttings – not his own work but any interview, feature, news, fashion or design piece that he thought particularly pertinent to the year in question and might one day form part of his meticulous research. Then there were the piles of magazines such as *Screen International* and *Vanity Fair*, and of course all his own files containing research material for his past biographies, as well as financial records going back decades. Despite the impression I might be giving here, however, the whole flat was ordered and scrupulously tidy: Alex, I am sure, would have known instantly where to put his hand on any tiny detail. For me, however, it wasn't so straightforward.

The reason I was there was to locate the manuscript I knew he had been working on. The first two volumes of his personal survey of British cinema – *Hollywood, England* (1974) and *National Heroes* (1985) – had been published to great acclaim, and he had been hard at work on the overdue third and final volume. Alex never spoke in any detail about a work in progress and so I had no idea how far it had progressed. The book had been commissioned by Ion Trewin at Weidenfeld and Nicolson, and it was he who told me that he believed the book to be very well advanced, if not complete. Thus encouraged, the quest was on: I found the typescript in his study – this sounds easy, but it wasn't. Alex's study was one big floor-to-ceiling typescript. Alas, the opening page following the title read 'Chapter Three'. Chapter Two was eventually turned up after an awful lot of searching over two and a half days in an airless room during the hottest English summer I can remember (it didn't seem to me to be in a logical place, but then what did I know?). Chapter One was found among his personal effects in the London Clinic where he spent his last hours – the ending, thank heavens, was in place. Later, on an ancient computer, Ion turned up the Preface and has since managed with his usual professional aplomb to piece the whole thing together seamlessly, having unearthed a series of links and interpolated references referred to on the typescript as marginalia, but located in separate notes and on the computer. Given time, of course, Alex would have presented to Weidenfeld his customary immaculate typescript. This concluding volume, then, takes us to the close of the year 2000, and it would appear that he had always intended the end of the millennium to form a natural and convenient conclusion to the history.

As the title and subtitle suggest – *Icons in the Fire: The Rise and Fall of Practically Everyone in the British Film Industry* – Alex did intend this book to be something of a cat to be flung among the pigeons, though by no means simply for the sake of causing controversy. Alex did not censure lightly though, when he felt it was due, he did not shirk or stint – as this book will amply demonstrate. He never lost his enthusiasm and anticipation of a newly released film, although there were times – and ever more increasingly lately – when he would moan in genuine despair at all that he had had to sit through on any given Tuesday at the weekly screenings. To the finish, his exhilaration when he saw a fine film was as total and as genuine as his sadness and anger over what he perceived to be a shameful waste of talent and the squandering of a fortune. All this is very evident in this third and final volume of his survey of post-war British cinema. Of all his works it is likely that these three books will prove to be his most lasting and landmark contribution to the literature of film. The trilogy forms a fitting, if premature, end to the life and career of Alexander Walker, this country's most eloquent and knowledgeable film critic and historian.

Joseph Connolly
April 2004

NB: Alex bequeathed many of his prints and drawings to the British Museum, where a year after his death they were shown in an exhibition entitled *Matisse to Freud: a Critic's Choice.*

Preface

Icons in the Fire is the last part of a trilogy about the British film industry from 1960 to 2000; but it can be read satisfyingly as a separate account of a wholly unprecedented couple of decades – roughly 1984–2000 – during which a once thriving, respected and socially relevant entertainment industry was turned into a chaos of competitive and incompatible elements; once great film corporations crashed, new saviours came forward regularly, only to collapse under the weight of their own ambition; stars, directors, writers and other creative people continually promised renewal of the talent bank or redemption of the idea of a national cinema, but seldom delivered on those promises; and, in the final years of the period under review, endless Lottery money was fed into the production machine in financially prodigal but artistically doomed initiatives, until the public benefit had been all but forgotten in the political attempt to impose a bureaucratic pattern of control on an entrepreneurial structure of risk capital.

Like its two predecessors, *Hollywood, England: The British Film Industry in the Sixties* (1974) and *National Heroes: British Cinema in the Seventies and Eighties* (1985), *Icons in the Fire* attempts to illustrate the immense diversity of talents and human motives, social and economic changes, historical accidents and occasional achievements throughout these years, and to link them to the famous (sometimes notorious) names, movies, national trends and media manipulation that have formed our view of the industry and the people in it.

But this is a more turbulent story, if only because the connecting theme is an industry falling into disorder and disrepute – often dramatically so, sometimes deservedly and occasionally fatalistically as an unforeseen result of the very attempts to salvage it from its own promoters and, yes, predators.

Consequently, the schema adopted by me, in tracing the multitude of events, is one drawn, however fancifully, from that offshoot of contemporary philosophy known as 'chaos theory'. In particular, the economic metaphor dubbed the 'Chinese butterfly' (or the 'Butterfly Effect'). Suppose a butterfly flutters its wings once, as butterflies do; it could just as easily have fluttered them twice, causing slightly different perturbations in the air around it. This makes the difference between a hurricane devastating the coastline of (say) Florida two months later, or, in the earlier case, that same hurricane dying out over the Atlantic.

The moral of the story for 'chaos theorists' is not about the randomness of events, but about how minute differences in the initial starting conditions of change can lead to massively different consequences down the line. In short, tiny changes, even in the natures of the men and women precipitating them, can have huge results. Prediction is thus rendered foolish, indeed impossible. *Icons in the Fire* derives its tragi-comic impact from the attempts of the main players – governments and individuals – to prove otherwise.

Unlike its two predecessors, *Icons in the Fire* is also a very personal story: I have known, sometimes at a safe distance, often quite intimately, occasionally indiscreetly, almost all the characters and participated in some of the events. I acknowledge that it involves a large amount of subjective judgement. But I believe that in surveying such a period of change, one should not restrict one's search for evidence too narrowly. The perpendicular pronoun – the 'I' of authorship – has to intrude into the story in the appropriate places. It is this which I hope gives the human face, the colour, comedy and drama, to a chronicle of events, facts and figures that is the tragic history of the decline and fall of practically everybody in the British film industry.

Alexander Walker
July 2003

Before the Title

The Chinese Butterfly

The phrase 'corridors of power' was applied by the novelist and bureaucrat C. P. Snow to the metaphorical channels of influence in government. But for civil servants at the Department of Trade and Industry in the mid 1980s it had a more flippant conversational use. 'Millionaires Row' was their nickname for the corridor where their political masters had their offices.

The Rt Hon. Paul Channon was Secretary of State for Trade and Industry and his deputy, the Minister of State, was Alan Clark. Channon inherited his millions from the Guinness brewing dynasty; Clark received a considerably smaller but still comfortable family patrimony via his father, Lord Clark, the aesthete, art collector and godlike populariser on television with the early influential series called *Civilisation*. Alan Clark, a more worldly man, added to his parliamentary income by speculation in vintage automobiles, taking advantage of a little-known loophole in the tax laws which relieved 'connoisseurs' of paying capital gains tax on any profits they made. Clark was a chancer, a 'card', a compulsive womaniser, faux landed gent with an inherited castle in Kent. He was a habitual rule breaker. Channon was (and is) an authentic Tory grandee. With access to wealth came a sense of responsibilities and a cautious approach to the world that his father, Sir Henry Channon, a social adventurer from Chicago who married into the Guinnesses, described when he wrote the splendidly bitchy series of social and political diaries about his contemporaries by which he is remembered today by the affectionate clubland nickname of 'Chips' Channon. Paul Channon's political mentor had been his father's old friend R. A. ('Rab') Butler, second in command to Prime Minister Harold Macmillan, an economist and one-time Chancellor of the Exchequer, whose particular Victorian values were impressed on Paul Channon, his Parliamentary Private Secretary, as a vaccination against any raffish virus his father might have passed on to him.

It is worthwhile, for irony's sake alone, to dwell a little on these two neighbours in office, since it was to one of them, around mid 1986, that the task of deciding the fate of the British film industry of the time was entrusted. Its destiny – and this book – might have been very different had Alan Clark, rather than Paul Channon, been the man to take the decisions. Clark's bohemian nature, his fondness for sailing close to the wind, his need of ready money (no matter how much he had, it never seemed enough) and his general suspicion – usually well founded – of the motives of foreigners (especially those from the Levant) might have prejudiced him against the 'upstarts', two Israeli cousins, who headed Cannon Films. Menahem Golan and Yoram Globus were also known as 'The Go-Go Boys'. This world was not Paul Channon's; in another life it might well have been Alan Clark's.

In 1985, Cannon Films was poised – 'crouched' was nearer the predatory stance – to acquire the assets of roughly half the British film industry. The deal then in the making comprised the ownership of Elstree Studios (the second largest in Britain after the Rank Organisation's Pinewood) owned by the ailing Thorn-EMI conglomerate; the 287-screen EMI cinema chain (also the second largest, after Rank's Odeon circuit), the EMI film library of about 2,000 movies, including such classic Ealing titles as *Passport to Pimlico, Kind Hearts and Coronets* and *The Lavender Hill Mob*; and the Pathé newsreel collection, a unique spectrum of British life exemplifying the nation's stamina in the war years. A huge prize. Whoever owned it would be an instant 'player' in the Hollywood sense of those who are 'movers and shakers' of events. But the approval of the Secretary of State for Trade and Industry – Paul Channon – was needed: the deal included such economic power in the entertainment world that it might constitute an unacceptable monopoly.

Film-making in the 1980s was not regarded by politicians, Tory or Labour, as an opportunity for populist branding that could remake a party's image, make it appear 'cool', attract 'youth' and allow the word 'culture', that word which British politicians of all parties wiped from their lips after the rare occasions when it slipped out of their mouths, to seem the heart and soul of the social contract. That era was to come.

Mr Channon, who had been a Minister for the Arts and was one of the few Tories to have sat through Wagner's *Ring* cycle, had to approve or reject the Cannon takeover bid – but on business grounds only. He would have no notion of the drama that was to come, and be played out over years, bringing businesses to bankruptcy, and causing ever more unlikely characters to pose as saviours, in one case leading to criminal investigations: in short, the whole machinery of grand opera in which the main players had sung their final arias of triumph or despair, pocketed their money and demurred about taking their bows, leaving one much diminished figure waiting in the wings – the British film industry.

All this industrial and cultural chaos arising from one simple yes or no? Such is my thesis in this book. It is an account of how and why things go wrong. It is an account of chaos tempered by occasional bouts of hope and glory but ultimately unable to produce order out of multitudinous characters and events contributing to the decline and fall of the British film industry. In such circumstances, turn to the Chinese for a guiding principle. The one I have adapted carries a nuance of 'fortune cookie'. But its use and truth will soon be evident. I shall quote the guiding principle of the account that follows: 'The flutter of a butterfly's wings may cause a thunderstorm.' Philosophy students will recognise this oft-quoted maxim of chaos theory.

'Suppose a butterfly in China flutters its wings once, in the way butterflies do,' one such philosopher, Dr Barry Smith, has written. 'It could just as easily have flapped its wings twice (although it didn't), causing slightly different perturbations in the air around it. This makes the difference between a hurricane devastating the coastline of Florida two months later, or, in the other case, dying out over the Atlantic. The moral of the story for chaos theory is not about the randomness of events, but about how minute differences in the initial starting conditions of a dynamic system like the weather lead to massively different consequences down the track.' In short, small changes have huge consequences – and not only in the weather. 'We then have an outcome that was determined, but unpredictable, and hypersensitive to the minutiae of the initial conditions.'

Perhaps, then, one shouldn't blame Paul Channon for precipitating the downfall of the British film industry by one tiny decision in the summer of 1985. It may have been 'unpredictable' but the huge consequences were 'determined'. To understand more fully Channon's choice one must go back a year or so – 1984 is now an auspicious date – and take stock of what was at stake in the film community.

1

Alive and Kicking

The British film industry's mood at the start of 1984 was one of hope without elation. Everything seemed to be holding its breath. *Variety*'s headline summed it up: 'UK FILM ON A ROLL, BUT WILL IT LAST?' More movies were getting made; yet much of the talent invested in them felt an apocalypse coming. An unlikely figure was responsible for both buoyancy and pessimism: the tax man.

From August 1979, individual film makers were allowed to write off production costs in full in the first year, instead of over a period of years. This concession was immediately abused by people investing in films simply to reduce their tax liabilities; so, in 1980, individuals were disqualified but not companies. The result: companies not directly involved in films began investing in them. In theory, a film could be 'in profit' – from tax concessions – even before it was released. Some, maybe, didn't have to be released at all. It worked thus: a bank (or finance company) buys the project (the film), then writes off its production costs against its own profits, then leases it back to the producer, sharing tax-deferred benefits with him. The producer has already sold the film to the distributors and all rights on terms that make him a profit. With fifteen years – the usual term – to exploit the film in cinemas, TV, video, in-flight entertainment; all that's necessary is to cover the yearly rental, which in turn is written off.

Films are not made to produce a profit – some do, most don't – but to generate income. A profit has to be declared; income can be 'diverted'. In an industry that's systemically dishonest, income is the aim and leasebacks are the means. The loser is quite clear: the public exchequer. That's why the film community in 1984 was nervous. Would this 'gift' last? To qualify, films had to be British. But, as usual, Hollywood quickly exploited the concession. British subsidiaries of Hollywood companies claimed the tax write-offs intended to help the native film-maker. An even older concession had been almost milked dry by similar ruses. The

Eady Levy, a 12 per cent tax on box-office tickets that was returned to producers of British films in proportion to their success, had been set up by Harold Wilson in 1949 when he was President of the Board of Trade. Wilson never lost a chance to boast of his cunning in 'selling' this tax to the Treasury, which traditionally opposed such taxes ring-fenced for specific beneficiaries. 'Wilfred Eady was a vain old Treasury mandarin,' Wilson would relate. 'At first he said no. "Pity," I said, "I'd like to have named the levy after you, Wilfred." '

For years the Eady Levy was the modest but useful 'tip', worth several millions, that supplemented British producers. Then the Americans used their box-office leverage to divert it. One example: a major US-owned distribution company bought a twenty-minute British-made short about skateboarding for £25,000; then released it in the same bill as a John Travolta 'blockbuster'. Shorts paid double the Eady Levy money. So the big Hollywood film 'piggybacked' the little British one and the skateboarding short put £200,000 of British subsidy into American pockets.

By 1984, though, the Eady Levy was feeling sick. Cinema audiences were down to 64 million the year before and falling. Not really a surprise in a nation with 3.2 million unemployed – 13 per cent of its work force – and 18 million Britons estimated to be living on or below the poverty line. With the European Union's Value Added Tax on cinema tickets at 15 per cent (and set for a rise), box-office prospects in 1984 looked glum, even alarming. And yet the optimism of the film-makers held up, tax-aided investment was higher than ever: thirty-one British films were made in 1983, the highest total in years. Television had an unassuageable hunger for movies, old and new. 'Cable' and 'satellite' broadcasting were the buzzwords. The hot money was on cable – 'Who wants satellite broadcasting, anyway?' asked Peter Fiddick in the *Guardian*. 'Cable TV will be on offer by 1986.' The government had just issued licences for new cable channels: one a dedicated movie channel.

By 1984 Channel 4, which started transmissions two years earlier, had kept its promises to the film industry by co-producing twenty-odd features for the new slot that was to earn the industry's blessing under the name 'Film on Four'. A C4 film could take more risks in theme and style than cinema movies. Among the early co-productions was *The Ploughman's Lunch*, one of the few overtly political attacks on Thatcherite Britain. A C4 film was much cheaper than conventionally produced movies. The latter could cost £3–4 million or even more; the typical

C4 film had a budget of £500,000–600,000 tops. Tax write-offs made 'Film on Four' attractive, though producers and directors could be a headache. They had soon begun agitating to have their films shown in cinemas, which delayed their TV premières. David Rose, C4's astute commissioning editor for fiction, was feeling that an eighteen-month, or two-year 'window' for theatrical release, which some film-makers demanded, did not help him build TV audiences. Still, overseas sales of some C4 films, like David Puttnam's experimental 'First Love' series, had returned welcome revenue from the US. How much? Rose's business manager, Larry Coyne, would only say, 'The best price, which is as much as you can get.'

This philosophy was close to the heart of the Association of Independent Producers, an agitprop lobby of Young Turks, mostly twenty- or thirty-somethings, that had come into being in February 1976 through generational frustration with the film-making Establishment and fear that their own potentially fruitful years would lie barren. By 1984, the Association had over 400 members. They energetically solicited more government aid, instead of tea and sympathy. Tax breaks sustained their hopes. In AIP's January Newsletter, Martin Auty acknowledged that 'future archaeologists of British film will date the "new age" from 1982–3'. He meant the means of production – leasebacks – rather than the content of movies. *That* 'showed little change in twenty years'. Too many films, though confidently crafted, had low aspirations. Few illuminated contemporary British life and manners in the 1980s: a *Ploughman's Lunch* was exceptional (and would remain so for decades). Television did today's social scene better and more cheaply. Even here, the retro pull of 'heritage' cinema, nostalgic, privileged and safely in the past, was strong. On TV, 1984's big 'event' was the fourteen-part *Jewel in the Crown*, successor in ratings success to *The Forsyte Saga*. In the cinema, *Gandhi* in 1982 and *Chariots of Fire* in 1983 were forerunners of David Lean's forthcoming *A Passage to India*.

No one had a good word for the Rank Organisation. It was now clearly pulling out from domestic film-making, judged too risky by the ultra-cautious accountants, grey men, bourgeois in dress and outlook, haunted by the corporate memory of the huge bank overdraft incurred in the late 1950s, when Rank's former chief, the ebullient boardroom despot John (later Sir John) Davis, had allowed the elephantiasis of his accountant's ego to inspire a grandiose attempt to 'crack Hollywood' with costly, star-packed British-produced flops. Film-making means crisis management: Davis's successors did not want crises. It seemed wiser to buy into films ready-made by others – the Americans. Even safer to distribute and exhibit films in Rank's 200 circuit cinema screens. Safest of all was to sit back, do nothing, but enjoy the lucky strike the company had made buying a huge block of Xerox shares. Though this was a wasting asset – Rank's pre-tax profits in 1982 had fallen from a 1981 high of £102 million to £61.5 million due to reduced Xerox yield – it was a tidy little earner which should see the executives into their pension years. Such was the shrunken scope of the once great Rank empire, an asset of enormous potential if properly managed, one of the last entities with invaluable 'vertical integration', owning the means to produce, distribute and exhibit films. But all it was inclined to do was sit tight and do nothing. Twenty years on, this 'fail safe' policy would spell the end of Rank as a film-making power. But for now it was a non-player.

Who filled Rank's void? Thorn-EMI Screen Entertainment (TESE) had suffered a near fatal debacle under its twin production chiefs, Michael Deeley and Barry Spikings. With the backing of Thorn-EMI's chief executive, Lord (Bernard) Delfont, they had applied the 'blockbuster mentality' to film-making in the US. American mercenary talents were hired to make British-budgeted Hollywood-packaged movies with US stars and scripts: *The Deer Hunter, Convoy, The Driver.* Only the first enjoyed critical and commercial success. Delfont beat a retreat from the US beachhead when TESE's parent company, the electrical and music conglomerate Thorn-EMI, suffered severe financial setbacks with its medical scanners and its stock price collapsed.

Now TESE was regrouping on home territory under Gary Dartnall. It had six more modestly budgeted films (four British, two American-financed) set to go. To head production, Verity Lambert was recruited from Euston Films, a Thames TV subsidiary successful with cutting-edge TV programmes such as *The Sweeney.* But caution was the watchword. Lambert, pressing the accelerator, was to find a dismaying number of other people had hands on the brake. Lord (Lew) Grade, Delfont's brother, was by now out of films. *Raise the Titanic!* had carried his own grandiose ambitions to the bottom: 'It would have been cheaper to lower the Atlantic,' he commented, with game ruefulness: at least he gave the world a quotation for the dictionaries. ('Gave' is perhaps not the word: it cost him $34 million.) Ironically, once he had ceased to be a player, some Grade-financed films in the pipeline, *On Golden Pond* and *Sophie's Choice*, went on to win Oscars and earn good box office – for others.

If these former leviathans couldn't be counted on to give reality to talk of a 'film renaissance' in 1984, who could? The tentative answer was a mixed bag of so-called mini-majors. The thirty-six-year-old National Film Finance Corporation, backed by a frugal government subsidy of £1.5 million annually from the Eady Levy with powers to borrow £5 million more, was trying valiantly under Mamoun Hassan to run a commercial set-up and pursue a cultural policy – to be 'art' and 'commerce'. A schizoid venture at best. More and more of its time was consumed in boardroom hand-wringing over what constituted a 'British' film. Government had never been willing to admit cultural content as a requirement. 'No culture, we're British' might have been the watchword. This often let films that were American in every way that mattered slip through the legislation network to consume the crumbs of finance provided for home-grown talents. Barbra Streisand's *Yentl*, conceived as a Hollywood blockbuster, shot in Czechoslovakia and set in Poland, but registered as 'British' by virtue of studio work here, had taken £67,721 from Eady Levy funds by October 1984. 'Hanging on' would best describe the NFFC's status in 1984.

The best hope of a film 'renaissance' at this date seemed to lie with the Goldcrest company. Goldcrest had been hatched by a Canadian called Jake Eberts who dabbled in films as relief from his boring job heading the London office of the Oppenheimer private bank.

Eberts was a bilingual Canadian, distinguished by his tall, rangy, tennis-playing frame, with rimless glasses, a trim moustache and a lean, sharp face, with a temperament marked by an equanimity that he brought to the business of selling films, a hatred for office administration. He owned a farm in Quebec, to which he retired for weekends between deal making and which helped bring his feet back to earth. He put his faith in his forthrightness: a hard bargainer, but an honest broker who didn't shrink from sensible risks, but worried endlessly even about them.

Eberts was happily free from commitment to 'culture', sizing up a proposition for its money-generating potential. He spoke the language of finance and frankly acknowledged he didn't have the slightest experience of actually making a film; it's likely that, if he had, his pitch to investors wouldn't have carried such conviction. At first he used relatively small sums in the low tens of thousands hazarded by corporate and private sources for a 'flutter', in order simply to 'develop' films – bring the idea (or the gleam in the eye) to the point of production, then take shares in whoever took the risk of producing the film. Eberts had had a fluke success with the animated cartoon *Watership Down*, based on the Richard Adams best-selling novel; it eventually returned to investors 5,000 times their stake.

Goldcrest really spread its wings in 1987, when Eberts persuaded Pearson Longman Enterprises, the publishing group which owned a shopping basket of mixed investments including Penguin Books (and saw a synergy between its books and films), and Electra Finance Co. to form a joint venture, with tax breaks as an inducement, which at first was intended to pursue only film development. Soon they discovered you cannot be just a little bit pregnant. Getting into the business of *producing* films seemed inevitable, even though at this time no one on the Goldcrest board, not one of its directors from financial investment companies, had any practical experience of film-making save David Puttnam in whose production, *Chariots of Fire*, Goldcrest had put development money. It was left to 20th Century-Fox and an independent company, Allied Stars, whose chief executive, a young man called Dodi Fayed, son of Muhammad al-Fayed, soon to be the boss of Harrods, to put up the production cash. Success, as genuine as it was unexpected, followed *Chariots of Fire*'s Oscar wins and a US box office which, though modest by twenty-first-century standards, was more than respectable for its day and almost unbelievable for a 'period' British film about class, anti-Semitism and running.

Goldcrest put development money into other British films, among them Richard Attenborough's *Gandhi*, Bill Forsyth's *Local Hero*, Pat O'Connor's *Cal* and Roland Joffé's *The Killing Fields*.

By 1983, in fact, new film investments by Goldcrest had dried up. *The Killing Fields*, *The Dresser*, *Another Country* and Puttnam's latest, *Cal*, were put into production in the summer months: each drew on the company's cash flow. After that, fresh capital became imperative, just at the time Eberts quit the company and a huge reserve of energy had to be diverted to maintaining investors' confidence and calming management unrest.

The Goldcrest board allowed the undertow of Oscar awards, box-office success and the sheer contagious 'glamour' of 'the business' to pull the company inexorably into *producing* movies. By which time Eberts had quit. The cause of his departure is still unclear. Money played a part; personalities probably played a bigger part in his returning to the US to do what he admitted he did best: making deals. He remained at heart a financier, at home with figures, blessedly unseduced by fame. This probably saved him from the overwhelming catastrophe that was awaiting Goldcrest as its chief executive, a Scottish-born financier, Harvard Business School graduate and former McKinsey high flyer named James Lee, yielded to the temptation (and, at the time, what seemed sound sense) and gradually became a film-maker. By 1984, under James Lee, Goldcrest was emboldened to leave the nest of development funding and take to the higher and headier zones of film production. By 1983 it had made a £900,000 trading profit, owned a £24.6 million portfolio of shares in seventy movies produced by others, had £12 million in the bank and a £10 million credit line: all of which seemed sufficient capital to become a force in British film-making.

Eberts had been replaced by Sanford Lieberson, a genial, laid-back, London-loving American – the same Sandy Lieberson who, at the end of the 1960s, co-produced for Warner Bros one of the most influential (and demonised) British films of the decade, *Performance*, co-directed by Nicolas Roeg and Donald Cammell, a dark journey into psychedelia in which Mick Jagger as a reclusive rock performer who has lost his creative daemon solemnises a compact with James Fox's East End gangster who has lost his criminal grip in a marriage of Pop world and underworld. Lieberson's career had then zigzagged, in partnership with David Puttnam, into productions like *That'll Be the Day* and its sequel *Stardust*, tuneful studies of working-class Pop idols. Since then he had been production chief of 20th Century-Fox for about nine months, admitting ruefully, when he left, that you could only do such a job if you felt you were worth what they paid you. His job now was to transform Goldcrest from a bank financing other people's 'inspirations' into a production company generating its own projects. Already Goldcrest was eyeing more distant fields than Eberts had had in his cautious perspective. 'We have to do things which can penetrate the American market,' Lieberson announced on taking up his new job; but lest this raise the spectre of Lord Grade's ignominious lack of penetration, he added, '... in order to support making material for the UK.' So *that* was all right. Along with Goldcrest board members Attenborough and Puttnam, Lieberson was prominently featured in the *Observer Magazine*'s issue of 20 October 1984, all three of them pictured as colossi, confident and smiling like 'Talking Heads' pitching projects to Hollywood executives for production coin, above the title of a super-production called 'The Industry'.

'Probably the most powerful man in British film and probably the best paid' it called Lieberson. 'A level head in control of important purse strings, Lieberson can be expected to curb the wilder excesses of the younger generation.'

James Lee, by now Goldcrest chairman, did not rate a mention: but then he was a financier, though one who was discovering quite quickly that the more he knew about the film business, the more he liked being in it. The *Observer*'s pantheon of contemporary promise is worth a closer look, in order to see the standing that some of those who will feature in the present narrative enjoyed at the time, at least according to its author, Mary Killen's, somewhat flippant but usually shrewd rating.

In 'The Oldsters' enclosure was the veteran film-maker Lewis Gilbert ('He Stayed the Course'), whose film *Alfie*, with Michael Caine, had defined the burgeoning 'swinging' cinema of the 1960s. He was now directing *Educating Rita* for an American, Herb Oakes, a Chatanooga-born stockbroker who could rope in film-struck partners as various as the National Coal Board's pension managers and the Sheikh of Sharjah, and who looked, for a moment or two, as if his Acorn Films might produce important seed money for The Industry. It was not to be: this little Acorn didn't grow, but Gilbert went on making movies and was still behind the camera in the new millennium.

Under 'Middle Age' were producers Davina Belling and Clive Parsons, who helped create Bill Forsyth's hit, *Gregory's Girl*, and were now backing his new comedy, *Comfort and Joy*, a darker-hued work about Glasgow's 'ice cream' gangster wars. David Puttnam was there, of course ('the most lauded ... Knighthood seems inevitable'), with *The Killing Fields* due to première in November 1984.

In 'The Young Ones' holding pen was thirty-five-year-old Jeremy Thomas ('bounced on the knee of his godfather Dirk Bogarde'), head of the Moving Picture Co., credited with producing such Nicolas Roeg films as *Eureka*, *Bad Timing* and Roeg's new one, *Insignificance*.

Jeremy Thomas's production of *The Hit* (1984) was one of those thrillers that confounds speculation about who will be the last man (or woman) in the cast to be left alive. Two hit men, one grim-faced (John Hurt), one a cockney kid (Tim Roth) arrive in Spain to abduct the criminal, played by Terence Stamp, who grassed on his confederates ten years earlier and deliver him to vengeance in Paris. The prisoner, who's embraced existential philosophy, surrenders meekly, but the story makes him the master of everyone else's fate. Nearly twenty years later Thomas had another 'hit' with an almost identical plot, now called with come-hither lubricity, *Sexy Beast*, in which Ben Kingsley is the hit man sent out to abduct a retired British gangster with similar consequences. Never throw away a good plot: reuse it. It was the most sustained role Stamp had had for years: he was to become an almost continuous global traveller, playing parts wherever the script was set. Tim Roth, soon to depart for America and reinvent himself as an American star, played the cheeky cockney kid out of his depth in these Spanish latitudes. But the film belonged to Hurt. His killer's face seemed to have died on him hours before his body does.

Other Young Ones included Simon Perry, forty-one ('The Nob', due to his Eton and Cambridge education), who was producer of the film *1984* opening just in time to catch the last weeks of its eponymous year; and Steve Woolley ('He Wears a Ponytail') was the 'youngest of the Brit movie brats', a smooth-faced boy from tough South London, ex-usher and later programmer at London's Scala cinema, then in partnership with Nik Powell, a sharp-tempered individual, abrasive where Woolley was emollient, in their youth-orientated company, Palace Pictures.

Palace was unusual. Its production, *The Company of Wolves*, financed by conscience money from ITC, Lew Grade's former organisation, confirmed that its director, Neil Jordan, whose *Angel* had impressed the critics who caught it at the Cannes film festival in 1982, was a confident, highly original talent, with a painterly eye and a novelist's sensibilities. It was that very rare thing in British film-making – a movie for the senses, which recalled in some ways the flamboyant stylisation of some Powell and Pressburger productions. It was a story-essay in the ways we make ourselves conscious of our own sexuality, how we condition our children through myth and fairy tale to fear sex, yet often simply stimulate desire.

Angela Carter's story, set in and around an enchanted wood brilliantly constructed by Anton Furst, who was later to turn a disused Thames Estuary gasworks into a plausible Vietnam for Stanley Kubrick's *Full Metal Jacket*, situated its several story lines at the point where cautionary fairy tales overlap with uninhibited desires. Sequences were brilliantly designed and devised to exhibit the unconscious side of sexuality: a child witnessing the primal scene of parents making love; a granny's scarlet embroidery thread suggesting menstrual stirrings in the watching child; a father crying proudly 'That's my boy!' as his son takes a girl into the woods, while a mother, voicing the female's vigilant concern for chastity, cries, 'Keep on the path!'; a farm boy drinking an elixir and growing a veritable forest of manly hair; a child in a Red Riding Hood cosying up to a 'granny' with a suspiciously long tongue – and enjoying being seduced. *The Company of Wolves* established Powell, Woolley and Jordan – though it was a 'one-off' for Palace and the impact it made concealed the touch-and-go nature of the producers' set-up.

Palace had no funds of its own, but its twin heads depended on whipping up enthusiasm (and cash) from other sources to allow them to produce the movies. What they brought to the table was first-hand understanding of the 'youth market' and, even more attractive, money from clever marketing of the films in circuit cinemas and – increasingly important – on video. Video became Palace's front-line financing; it was, ironically, to become its downfall, too. Video release of the films through record stores allowed them to part-fund a more varied collection of movies than any other mini-major, from demi-art-house fare (Nagisa Oshima's *Merry Christmas, Mr Lawrence*, sweetened for youth by David Bowie's casting) to chic trash (Jean-Jacques Beineix's parodic *film noir*, *Diva*, a tremendous hit) to pure fun pulp (Sam Raimi's *The Evil Dead*). 'Of all the young producers,' Killen's commentary continued, with what proved to be remarkable clairvoyance, 'Woolley looks like the one who understands the bluff that is movie-making, the one best able to execute the three-card trick.'

Virgin's production of *1984* just sneaked under the wire of that year. It was one of three films – *The Killing Fields* and *The Company of Wolves* were the others – on which, *Variety* said, industry confidence uneasily rested. Written and directed by Michael Radford, produced by Simon Perry, it translated the very bone and marrow of Orwell's prophetic novel on to the screen, not just a skin graft of the book's narrative. It eschewed futuristic sets, going in for a vision of the future that showed it didn't work – in a word, everything in this Brave New World looked like many things in contemporary society, only irredeemably dated, like a vast time slip that imposed one era on another. So that the Ministry of Truth looked like the BBC and the COI united in sinister collusion and pushed to authoritarian extremes. London, capital of Airstrip One, resembled today's Beirut.

John Hurt, the martyr figure of contemporary British cinema, was Winston Smith, a Giacometti-like sculpture whose flesh has been austerely eroded down to snapping point to expose the essence of a minimalist existence. Richard Burton, already visibly touched by his own imminent mortality, turns his debauched looks into a mask of inflexible masochism that relives the pain he causes others. 'For twenty years I've had the most famous voice in the world,' Burton told *Newsweek*'s Edward Behr, 'and I want to do at least one movie without it.' In mortal sickness he at last found a kind of greatness; by abandoning his pretensions he regained his power.

Virgin Films was funded by Richard Branson's records company millions (courtesy of Boy George and Human League); it was headed by Al Clark, an Australian movie buff, who ran it with Branson's brother-in-law Robert Devereux. Virgin had struck lucky with a short, *A Shocking Accident*, based on a Graham Greene story about a young man's embarrassment at his father being killed when a pig fell on him: it had won an Oscar. Virgin was about to release Michael Radford's film of Orwell's *1984*. While undiscriminating customers at Virgin record stores produced the funding for such ventures, Clark wanted to spread the appeal. 'To make a film which isn't just a "youth movie", but has a range of elements which are just automatically attractive to that age group is very appealing.' 'If only ...' one hears a chorus of other producers. Virgin was hoping to reach this nirvana with an adaptation, with music, of Colin MacInnes's novel *Absolute Beginners*, about what being young was like in the 1950s in Notting Hill and Soho. Steve Woolley would produce and Julien Temple, a young director of Pop-disc promotional films, would direct. 'There is an audience that hasn't been fed into,' Temple asserted, 'a few films that hit that could change the structure overnight.' That was the aspiration among many young but not quite 'absolute' beginners of the film industry in 1984.

Another company that had emerged in the late 1970s was HandMade Films, an eccentric outfit run by the Beatle George Harrison and an American 'hyphenate' – a lawyer-accountant-producer, Denis O'Brien: these two had called it into being in order to 'rescue' Monty Python's *Life of Brian*, which Lord Delfont had wished to banish from Thorn-EMI's roster on grounds of possible blasphemy. Possibly his own sensitivity as a Jew played a role in not wishing to give offence to Christian film-goers. Bought for $2 million by HandMade, it was sold on a country-by-country deal and made them a pile of money. *The Long Good Friday* was also rescued when Delfont wanted to censor its violence into bland acceptability. But their quixotic Python films became Hand-Made's house style, though with diminishing returns when the Pythons passed into the American orbit, making *The Meaning of Life* (1983) for

Universal, though individual Pythons, like Michael Palin with *The Missionary*, returned at times to HandMade.

HandMade was capitalised in Luxembourg, presumably primed by Harrison's royalties from Beatles recordings. It claimed it could make films for 60–70 per cent less than a major studio would spend. Their *Time Bandits*, made for less than £2.2 million, grossed £6.7 million in the US alone. The company stubbornly maintained its right to be eccentric. After spending six months trying to negotiate a £10 million financial deal with two finance houses, O'Brien abruptly broke off talks when the potential backers claimed the right to vet not only co-productions with their money in them, but HandMade's own-money movies. Better than any other company, HandMade had a feel for the often comic complexities of the English class system, derived from Harrison's and O'Brien's appreciation for the Goonish side of the British character: O'Brien had been Peter Sellers's manager for a short, traumatic time in the early 1970s. With the exception of Thorn-EMI, Rank (out of the production game anyhow) and the merchant bankers of Goldcrest, these mini-majors had one or two things in common: they were in touch with young people's taste. Their managements were themselves young. The films they backed were irreverent, transgressive, con-temporary (if not in period then in generational feel). Their marketing departments – Palace's in particular – aimed the product squarely, but with subtlety and wit, at intelligent if as yet undiscriminating young people in the fifteen–thirty age bracket, weaned on the TV satire shows of earlier decades and nourished afresh by the present-day Pythons.

This group's independent views and restless search for novelty were being served more and more by Sunday broadsheet supplements and magazines, now written and edited, and in some cases managed, by those who had themselves been adolescents in the 'Swinging Sixties'. This generational buoyancy in turn kept film-makers afloat, for good commercial reasons, of course, but for ideological ones, too: they gave hope to those who still hadn't acquired power. All of which helps explain the paradox of the industry, simultaneously in a state of vague expectancy and anxious uncertainty. One film company, however, possibly saw things clearer than most, since its policy was based on rapid and predatory aggrandisement. Cannon Films was the least British of the film-making groups, which gave it an advantage, since its chiefs were ruthless analysts of the national character flaws that made the industry vulnerable to those with cash and chutzpah.

Yet, in 1984, not much attention was being paid to Menahem Golan and Yoram Globus, Israelis who were disposed by temperament (if not talent) to think unsentimentally in Hollywood terms and define power as something for the taking rather than the earning. Cannon believed in bulk, not quality. In 1984 it had fifteen films in production from Los Angeles to Hungary, running level with the Hollywood majors like Columbia and Paramount. Budgets were generally rock-bottom: the average £2 million or under, whereas an average Hollywood feature cost £5.3 million. All costs were covered in pre-sales to exhibitors before a single film was made. Lord Grade tried this out, too: it worked the first or second time, but if the films didn't perform, it was harder to ring the bell again and get a welcome. Cannon, however, took a self-absorbed view of this territorial blitz. 'It doesn't matter to us whether a single ticket is sold,' Golan, the 'accountant' cousin, was quoted in the *Sunday Times* as saying. 'All you need to make a profit is to make sure you have a beginning, a middle and an end.' By 1984 their budgets were growing with their ambitions. In mid 1984 they had *Space Vampires*, an Agatha Christie mystery.

In 1982 Cannon's British company paid £7 million to acquire the 150-screen circuit of Classic cinemas owned by Lord Grade's empire before it hit the *Titanic* iceberg: that sum exactly covered the loss Grade's company had announced in 1981. The advantage this gave Cannon was cash flow, the most vital (and least easily monitored by fiscal authority) of a film company's operations. Independent film companies had hankered for this cash flow; with that circuit as the base for financing and exhibition, they might have given Rank and ABC (Thorn-EMI-owned) cinemas a run for the customers' money. But it was Cannon that put the money down – ask not where it came from, yet. Now the chance was lost. Even then, no one spotted the danger signs to the British film industry of having a predator like Cannon in the midst of the pile. 'From a commercial angle [their] record seems more than acceptable,' wrote one commentator, '[but] scarcely any movie that Cannon has yet made will figure in any serious history.' This was to be true. But Cannon would have been the last to care about this. It was about to shake the film industry and alter its shape for ever. Its bosses would have thought this compensation enough.

However, the first blow that damaged fragile confidence in the film community came from those it depended on. On 12 March 1984, leaning on the Despatch Box, Chancellor of the Exchequer Nigel

Lawson proposed in his budget speech to withdraw the 100 per cent capital allowances from film-makers in March 1985 – effectively ending the tax break for investors. The Treasury move was aimed at putting film financing on what Lawson termed 'a proper commercial footing': he hoped to recover £150 million annually in tax for the Treasury. It brought home to everyone how much the industry had existed on the Treasury subsidising them with lost tax revenues. Everyone had thought the allowances safe until 1987 at least. This was crushing news, except to those few industry alchemists with time and aptitude to find loopholes in the small print of tax legislation the world over that will benefit someone, somewhere. Big companies were in gloom; small ones in panic. Even as the Chancellor spoke, the British Academy of Film and Television Arts (BAFTA) was posting embossed invitations to a conference, at £165 a plate, to celebrate the 'fundamental revival' of the industry. Projects began falling, or at best stalling like flies in winter's first nip. The NFFC claimed that two thirds of the films in production could be abandoned or go abroad. Virgin, with £20 million committed annually, started trimming film budgets and hinted at quitting – full stop. Only Channel 4, which was debarred from applying tax-shelter write-offs, thought the reform overdue. Like a physician putting a hard-drugs case on methadone, a spokesman for the TV channel said, 'Film funding could take on a new lease of life if the unhealthy reliance on tax shelters is broken.'

Another blow, not as savage in its unexpectedness but causing more blood loss, fell on the industry in mid 1984. A hint had been given the year before when Iain Sproat, Minister for Information Technology, suspended the 1927 Quota Act compelling cinemas to show a minimum percentage of British films. This wasn't ruinous: the antiquated act had simply promoted a spate of so-called 'quota quickies', cheaply made films whose only value – apart from a one-off sale by their opportunist producers – was their 'Britishness'. The act totally failed to 'protect' British cinemas from Hollywood domination; in fact, many cinemas in 1984 were desperate for more 'domination' by the folk who had brought them *Rocky* and *ET*. But an alarm bell rang more shrilly in 1983 when Kenneth Baker, who had taken over as Technology Minister when Sproat lost his parliamentary seat in the general election, announced a major economic review of the film industry.

Baker's proposals, entitled 'Film Policy', were published as a White Paper in mid 1984. They effectively knocked the legs out from under the industry. Away with the Eady Levy, to begin with. Not everyone wept to see it go. The AIP ginger group said, 'Eady sapped £4.5 million from cinemas, the section which could least afford to pay it.' Much of it went out of the country, into the pockets of US producers of 'British' movies; it didn't encourage films of merit; it was an anachronism amid a booming audio-visual industry – TV, that is. Its abolition wouldn't be so bad if something better replaced it. But Baker's idea of 'something better' was self-help by the industry. The NFFC, to whom even the £1.5 million Eady money a year was like an intravenous injection, saw the death warrant in the government's proposal to privatise it and replace it by a company financed jointly by Thorn-EMI, Rank, Channel 4 and the British Videogram Association. This new body was striving – and failing – to prevent the insidious Video Recordings Bill, which required all films on video cassette to be classified by the censors, from being passed into law – the most Orwellian piece of 1984 legislation. The Tory government promised £1.5 million for five years for the NFFC 'replacement': each component would contribute £1.1 million annually – for an unstated term. To try to sweeten the deal, the NFFC's assets – primarily £200,000, its income from past and present films it had co-financed – would be made over to the new body. Two rival film companies, a TV company and a video lobby: how, asked the NFFC's Mamoun Hassan, could members of such a mongrel entity ever agree on anything – 'even the time of day'?

It was a shabby cover-up for the Thatcher government's policy mantra: privatise, don't subsidise. Its effect would have been comical, if not so tragic. Rank, which had pulled out of producing films after losing a fortune five years earlier, and Thorn-EMI which had lost so much shareholders' money trying to crack the US market, became two of the heirs to the longest sustained and most honourable output of British film-making. Even though Rank had to put money into an industry it spurned, its acceptance of the plan called off the guard dogs from the Office of Fair Trading that was even then attempting – and failing – to break Rank's and the Thorn-EMI ABC cinema chain's unfair hold on film distribution. The government needed the goodwill of these two; once more the vital issue of the big boys' duopoly, which cut out the small 'independent' fry, was shelved.

Mamoun Hassan resigned in June, announcing, 'In my five and a half years at the NFFC, I have had over three years of being reviewed, by Norman Tebbit and now by Kenneth Baker.' AIP backed him up: 'The

NFFC will have little more than a token independence, subject to trade-offs and pressures from the duopoly whose own performance in financing British films has been little short of deplorable.'

Twelve AIP firebrands issued a 'Call to Arms' in their November bulletin and planned an activist campaign. With courtesy, they withheld the opening of hostilities until 12 November, the day after Armistice Day. It took a rather touching, indeed positively English, form. No one raised the barricades; instead the AIP, in this dark hour, announced a 'British Film Year' to begin in March 1985. A relieved government took off its flak jacket and promised financial support – for the very industry it was even then 'ruining'.

The alarm felt in many quarters might have been alleviated – or sharpened, according to your industry status or political stance – had what later came to be believed by insiders been then brought to light, namely, the warm and increasingly 'special' relationship between Tory party luminaries, even inside the Prime Minister's office, and individuals of power, charm and money in the US film industry. The Eady Levy had long been a thorn in the latter's side: it had been a small prick up to then and some of Hollywood's 'made in Britain' films had exploited Eady; but Hollywood imports now had the European VAT tax – 15 per cent at the time, soon to be 17.5 per cent – to pay on top of every ticket sold. Wouldn't it be helpful if one tax could go? As VAT was here to stay, Eady was the candidate for the chop.

The quid pro quo which Hollywood emissaries like the American industry's 'elder statesman' Lew Wasserman are said to have offered Downing Street was a commitment to expand cinema circuits in Britain by building the multiplexes that had revolutionised US box-office receipts. The gain to the British Treasury – which had always hated the Eady Levy subsidy being ring-fenced for film-making – was clear. At a single handshake it would abolish one tax that brought nothing into Treasury coffers and simultaneously gain huge new revenues from profitable North American-built multiplexes. To date, no one has admitted that this was the deal struck: the 'visitors' book' at No. 10 Downing Street remains closed to enquirers like myself, interested in seeing which of Hollywood's power-brokers passed across the welcome mat. But even if the usual suspects are innocent, the coincidence of timing and effect, the perfect equation of the Tories' entrepreneurial dogma, isn't easily dismissed. Cinema audiences, which fell to the lowest point ever of 55 million a year in 1984, were to rise and rise phenomenally over the next decade and a half alongside the expansion of 'the multiplex experience' in cinema-going.

At the mid point in the 1980s, anyone looking at the British films then in production, or on release, would have had the impression of a country that was not at ease with itself. There was not the same synergy that the generation which came of age and cultural influence in the 1960s had fostered: but malaise was palpable in the governance of the country and its reflection on the cinema screen.

A paranoia strain was perceptible in film-making after revelations of Whitehall duplicity in the trials of Clive Ponting, Sarah Tisdall and Cathy Messiter, all civil servants accused of secrecy breaches; in the government management of the media during the Falklands War; in the (still unsolved) murder of Hilda Murrell, a spinster lady and anti-nuclear campaigner who may have had access to classified (and embarrassing) Admiralty communiqués on the naval war with Argentina; and in the policing of the miners' strike, which disclosed the role of MI5, the counter-espionage service, in the surveillance of civil disturbances. This sense of change, of mistrust of official appearances and suspicion of illegalities and deceptions were fed into *Defence of the Realm*, a sort of 'All the Prime Minister's Men', which sowed its screenplay with seeds of treason.

Scripted by Martin Stellman, who wrote that prophetic parable of punk Britain, Derek Jarman's *Jubilee*, and directed by David Drury, it caught the grey texture of duplicity in the 'secret state'. A left-wing, ex-Communist MP taken in adultery in a West End call-girl's flat where the East German military attaché is another client; an East End escapee from a borstal prison who's discovered they have been already thirty-six hours dead when a bus knocks him down; connecting the dots revealed a miasma of nuclear policy blunders. In a US film such cover-ups would be vulnerable to constitutional (if not exactly institutional) transparency: when Gabriel Byrne's reporter actually telephones the Pentagon for information, the ready answers he elicits are like gale-force winds compared with the stale air in our own corridors of power. Unsavouriness rather than villainy is the British disease here: a moral crumminess that eats away at the once solid integrity of a society where nothing any longer works – the film was the last to reflect the terminal seediness of a pre-electronic age in Fleet Street newspapers where it seemed even the industrial revolution had scarcely arrived. The squeaky lift cages, dim-lit reading rooms, ugly and uncomfortable flats, even the St James's gentlemen's club full of 'one of us' types, as Margaret Thatcher sub-divided society, and which look like museums that have seen better days – all this evoked the state of the realm better even than the far-fetched plot. Produced by David Puttnam's Enigma company, it was the best film to date showing how civil liberties were being picked off, one by one. It was also the last of its kind for many years.

Defence of the Realm had been preceded by *Another Country* (1984), Julian Mitchell's West End play, directed by the Anglo-Pole, Marek Kanievska, a lesson in the genealogy of treason set among the ethos of the public school system of the 1930s, a sort of *huis clos* which bred traitors by a form of natural selection among the boys. Status protected by a paranoid fear of losing it and revenge exacted by stealth and deceit; the homosexual English traitor of the 1960s, Guy Burgess, was played in the bud of boyhood by the newcomer Rupert Everett; the role established him. But political thrillers found television was a cheaper, quicker, more direct channel of communication with the viewing elect-orate. A series of the 1990s, like *House of Cards*, putting a highly melodramatic spin on the rise of a leading Tory to become Prime Minister through blackmail, bribery and even murder, dramatised politics to the disadvantage of the cinema screen – which ignored them.

The British cinema, *circa* 1985, reflects, in John Boorman's words, a malaise ravaging the Brits: 'There is no grace or dignity in these people, no harmony in their dress, no art in their play. Here is a tribe gone sadly wrong, mutated. Worst of all, they seem to have lost the knowledge of what they have lost.' Boorman, a visionary talent happier in the Celtic mists than the London pollution, was soon to leave for Brazil to shoot his ethnographic parable, *Emerald Forest*, in the depths of the jungles: what he saw of the primitives there no doubt reinforced these home thoughts.

One would have thought British cinema at the time had enjoyed its fondest if not finest hour in the 1950s. Two films in particular illuminated the crimes committed by English repression. On one case, mortally so: *Dance With a Stranger*, directed by Mike Newell and based on the case of Ruth Ellis, the last woman to be hanged, in 1955, for the murder of her toyboy – Rupert Everett again – whom she shot with her spectacles on, so as to be sure not to miss the target. Miranda Richardson played Ellis as both a 1950s and a 1980s woman, a trampish blonde whose every detail of dress, hairdo and showiness stamped her with the most pejorative adjective of her time, 'common', and yet a woman determined to live life on her own terms and no other's. The next year, 1956, the debacle of Britain's armed expedition into Egypt to protect the Suez Canal split Britain open at the socio-political seams. Newell's film failed to reflect the fabric tearing; otherwise, it focused on how little had changed – it was as if Sixties permissiveness had never happened. The first shot, of Richardson's heavily lipsticked mouth, signified her sexual appetite.

A Private Function, set even earlier, in 1947, was also about appetite: eating was this comedy's most powerful metaphor for a Britain starved of the emotions. Written by Alan Bennett – shamefully, his only cinema screenplay – and directed by Malcolm Mowbray, it was a sardonic, sour, black social comedy set in a Yorkshire town, but generating an almost Gallic feeling of small-town malice, envy and denunciation. The plot was about pignapping in a country still accepting austerity, but seeking black-market ways round it: he who has the side of bacon – Michael Palin and Maggie Smith, a married couple in the purgatory of the petit bourgeoisie – can call the tune. The sight of Palin failing to entice the abducted porker into the oven and Maggie Smith grabbing the carving knife like a terrace-row Lady Macbeth marked a high point in the social comedy of the period. And, though set forty years before 1985, it still delivered the shock of the contemporary.

It was much more effective than David Hare's *Wetherby* (8 March 1985), though Bennett's talent for humouring the self-punishment of the English found an echo in Hare's film that turned tragedy in a country cottage into a *Heartbreak House* where people lie to each other amid the jumble of the Sunday supplements. Pinter, anyone? Not quite: Pinter's pauses refresh; Hare's wordiness wearies. The quiet desperation that well-bred English films invariably do well was thinned into minimalist misery.

Misery was transfigured in *A Letter to Brezhnev* (1985). It became a political climate as well as a social one, enveloping two Liverpool girls (Alexandra Pigg, Margi Clarke) – one stuffs chickens, the other is unemployed – who fall for Russian sailors (Peter Firth, Alfred Molina) they trawl into bed for a one-night stand; for one of them, this becomes a determined pursuit that, she hopes, will take her to Moscow if only Brezhnev grants a visa. A night's fantasy, maybe, yet director Chris Bernard and writer Frank Clarke root it in the actuality of inner-city decay, youth on the dole, a general air of Merseyside downbeatness.

Liverpool, once the pride and a great part of the profit of 1960s Beatle-mania, is now a city ousted from its place in Pop mythology by the depression of the 1980s.

For the first time in mainstream British cinema a film dared to judge the Soviet Union to be a better bet for workless, but far from shiftless, youth than Britain under Margaret Thatcher. The feminism of girls paying for their night with the men is justified by the likely poverty of Russian sailors in port; while the wisecracking couple, unintimidated by men, their wit like sparking plugs and their wisdom summed up by their opportunistic grab at any and all passing pleasures, said something new in British cinema. It was one of the early co-productions between David Rose, executive producer for Channel 4's film-making venture, and Palace Pictures. Such a film created an optimistic buzz among critics, public and film-makers that countered the industry's pessimism.

The scent of change in the air was reinforced a week later by one of the era's seminal productions, *My Beautiful Laundrette* (1985), a view of the British Asian community from the inside, written by Hanif Kureishi, whose own relationship with his Pakistani family and community had the edginess of a social renegade without the obduracy of a revolutionary. He made a social comedy out of race, class and politics in Tory Britain that stood the old imperial order on its ear: a nation of shopkeepers was mutated into a nation of Asian shopkeepers; words were used that the English were usually too mealy-mouthed to utter. It was about the unlikeliest of friends and lovers: Omar (Gordon Warnecke), a diffident, charming Pakistani teenager and Johnny (Daniel Day-Lewis), a punk with a Day-Glo blob of hair and a face like a tomahawk who wants to live down his past as a Fascist with the National Front, earn some loot and get some love from someone of his own sex.

Directed by Stephen Frears, a director with something of his mentor Lindsay Anderson's eye for the realities of the social scene, though without Lindsay's rage to change, *My Beautiful Laundrette* marked an important coming of age in the Asian community's relations with itself as well as with the country that was once its ruler and was now its next of kin. Homosexuality was still a discreetly handled theme; interracial gayness was even bolder then; and a movie that said a former British Fascist could get on with a same-sex lover was provocative – even though the white lad now dances to the monkey tune piped by his Asian partner as he discovers that in today's Britain it's no longer who you know that counts, but simply how much you got. The two boys were original characters; but almost overshadowing them was a performance by Saeed Jaffrey as a genial Asian uncle with one hand 'squeezing the tits' of the Welfare State while the other did the same for his white mistress (Shirley Anne Field). Jaffrey blended the drive of a landlord shark like the late Peter Rachman with the bonhomie of the sort of ageless clubman featured in Peter Arno's *New Yorker* cartoons. *My Beautiful Laundrette* was a porthole into the swirling dirty linen of contemporary Britain.

New stars of a match for the 1960s constellation of Finney, Courtenay or Alan Bates suffered from the lack of films to nourish them; but Daniel Day-Lewis's appearance had that innovatory authority: different in temper as well as talent, unpredictable in a part, or the pitch he brought himself to, until you saw him on the screen – and then, maybe, may not immediately have recognised him. A Method actor by instinct, rather than training, but both by self-torment, Day-Lewis, just twenty-eight in 1985, son of the late poet laureate Cecil Day-Lewis and Jill Balcon, daughter of Sir Michael Balcon, had made his movie debut as a car vandal in John Schlesinger's *Sunday, Bloody Sunday* (1971) and went on to incise a different personality into each subsequent role that showed a temperament nearer Robert De Niro than Albert Finney. He had a hunger then that later turned obsessional and neurotic in a way that intensified interest in him (or his fate). The 'damaged' personality, too, was more American than English: in Day-Lewis's case, a school runaway who eventually spent a short spell in hospital recovering from a break-down that had family roots, and the sense of a player using roles to exorcise traumas, or exteriorise aspects he wasn't comfortable about discovering in himself, lurked within his screen characterisation. (On stage, he had less chance: and quit his Hamlet role at the National Theatre in mid-play, apparently finding the obligations laid on the young prince too close for comfort to his own unresolved relationship with his father, Cecil Day-Lewis.)

Day-Lewis wrote to Frears about the part in *My Beautiful Laundrette*, 'Don't be fooled by my polite education. I've got some very unpleasant friends.' The underlying 'threat' may have been only a joke; but threat never cost an actor his audience. It got Day-Lewis the part – and the film that opened just a few months later, *A Room With a View*, enforced the sense of revelation.

For his performance as Cecil Vyse, the insufferably priggish aesthete of the E. M. Forster novel that the Merchant Ivory company had turned into a film – the unexpectedly profitable hatching in Goldcrest's nest of addled eggs – was unrecognisable as the punk with antisocial armour protecting his aching core of insecurity in the earlier film. Pince-nez sat on his nose like a spirit level, always in beautiful balance with the world and even chastely impressing themselves into an engagement kiss (to Helena Bonham-Carter). He walked like a supercilious tuning fork, tingling precisely to each tiny cultural shock, making marriage a form of mental hygiene and social discourse a display as ordered as a piece of artistic table setting.

In two roles, released virtually back to back, Day-Lewis revealed himself the most promising young actor of his generation: the sort of talent that causes one to register shock at first seeing it, then to sit back, enjoy and admire it. Unfortunately, life, art and temperament rarely run so perfectly in sync with each other as they did in Day-Lewis's star 'double'. Like Finney who, once satisfied, allowed his drive to dwindle and lost momentum, Daniel Day-Lewis was to tread a path as unsettled in its choices as Brando's and eventually, with lengthy 'retirement' spells, seemed to seek personal salvation from whatever demons still inhabited him rather than the fulfilment to which his talents still entitle him.

2

Self-congratulatory Trumpet Flourish

They were not the first names one would choose. But they were available, and able (a couple of their owners with difficulty) to go on their knees and impress their palms into the soft cement of what had been designated the 'Star Pavement' in London's Leicester Square: Alan Bates, John Mills, Anna Neagle, Charlton Heston and Omar Sharif – three Brits, an American and an Egyptian.

British Film Year had officially begun, in March 1985. Almost as it ended, a set of stamps was issued in October. As no living person could share space on a stamp with the sovereign's head, the five chosen were all dead: Peter Sellers, David Niven, Charles Chaplin, Vivien Leigh and Alfred Hitchcock. All five were British-born. Hitchcock, though, became an American citizen; Chaplin worked almost all his life in America; Peter Sellers never felt at home in any country; David Niven, like Sellers, paid his (reduced) taxes to the Swiss. Alone of the five Vivien Leigh made Britain her permanent home, though she, too, owed her greatest successes to Hollywood films.

The individual who had the clearest right to be commemorated, British-born, British-domiciled, the best-known British producer, a patriot whose films 'projected Britain and the British character' was shamefully omitted: Sir Michael Balcon. Apparently the nation had a short memory of the man who thought so much of the nation he portrayed in his Ealing Studios films. One only hoped that people who spared a lick for their film favourites in British Film Year spared a thought for him.

British Film Year was decidedly a low-key event and slightly mis-named. Cinemas, rather than films, were the intended beneficiaries: the aim was to increase cinema-going, which had fallen to an all-time low of 84 million in 1984, compared with 250 million just fifteen years earlier. David Puttnam, always the boy who did his homework, recalled that the United States had one screen per 10,000 people, whereas Britain had only one per 44,000. 'The basic aim', he said candidly, 'is simply to raise average attendances to a level at which a moderately priced British movie has a chance to recoup its costs in the home market. If [it] can obtain a 5 per cent increase, [British Film Year] would be a success.'

Amid such admirable self-help, the word 'art' slipped out almost as an afterthought, in a letter from Norman Lamont, the then Minister of State for Industry, who spoke of 'the cinema's unique and magical contribution of technology, skill and art'. Such 'art' was represented by an official selection of twenty-one films made since the late 1970s, dubbed with prudent vagueness 'The Revival Years', augmented by eight Oscar winners dating way back to Olivier's 1948 *Hamlet*. Hugh Hudson's *Chariots of Fire* and Richard Attenborough's *Gandhi* made both lists; but of Derek Jarman, John Schlesinger, Mike Leigh, Terence Davies, Ken Loach, Nicolas Roeg or Lindsay Anderson there was not a mention. The critic David Robinson commented, 'The common factor is that they are all nice, bright entertainment with nothing to rock the boat, such as [Leigh's] *Looks and Smiles* or [Anderson's] *Britannia Hospital*, or [Franco Rosso's 1980 docudrama about black culture] *Babylon* or [Jarman's] *Jubilee* might do.'

Fourteen of the twenty-one were set in the past, commemorating a nostalgically imperial stance; all the Oscar winners were historical pieces; no ethnic factor was visible in the selection. A purpose-built 'space age' module showing clips from past films and trailers for forthcoming ones toured Great Britain (but not Northern Ireland). The two main cinema circuits, Rank and EMI, pledged to spend £1 million each on refurbishing their theatres (and incidentally consolidating their duopoly hold on the market). The slogan was 'Cinema – The Best Place To See A Film'. Money wasn't going to be wasted on art while there were seats to be filled. However, those who doubted, or jeered, at this pragmatism were proven wrong: British Film Year would later claim to have succeeded and rightly so. But it is doubtful if it was as simple as *post hoc, propter hoc.*

Before the Year opened, even before Rank and EMI had repaired cracked toilets, put in more buttery popcorn machines and repadded their outworn seats for those bums that so often figure in the eloquence of exhibitors, cinema-going was on the up and up: a 65 per cent increase over 1984 in the 1985 January–March quarter for Rank; 51 per cent for EMI. How to explain this? The multiplexes had just started laying their foundations; the first sizeable one, the Point, at Milton Keynes, dubbing itself 'the McDonald's of the film industry', did not open until October 1985. So what indeed was to prove a cinema-going revolution had yet to have impact. One reason, maybe too simple to be noticed at the time, was a new, sharp hunger for film.

Few recent films got shown on British TV at this date: the main circuits were still trying, with weakening resolve, to operate a bar on any film whose distributors didn't guarantee to keep it off TV screens for three years. Only those that failed in cinemas were granted dispensation. Channel 4, one of the few new hopes of finance for independent production, felt particularly frustrated by this anti-trade practice. It had put up the whole of the budget, £950,000, for the Julie Walters comedy *She'll Be Wearing Pink Pyjamas*, its biggest investment so far in a feature. It intended to release it theatrically, but also wanted to televise it – at which point its cost could be written off – as soon after as possible. To hold it back from TV for three years was unacceptable. The only compromise permitted by the cinema trade was shaming: it had to be seen to fail in the cinemas before a *nihil obstat* was granted to show it on the small screen. However, video was rapidly undermining this restrictive practice.

The increasing availability of films on video, for hire or sale, which was fast putting money into the pockets of a thrusting young company like Palace Pictures, whose chiefs, Nik Powell and Stephen Woolley, had the foresight to see video marketing as a supplement to film-making, was encouraging households to buy or rent VCRs. The growth would be phenomenal in Britain, outstripping all European countries, far outstripping North America. By the end of 1986 more UK households owned a VCR than owned a car, or life insurance, or even their own homes. From 42 per cent penetration in 1985, the figure rose to 54 per cent in 1988, then reached near-saturation point as video shelves appeared in village shops along with *Playboy* and *Penthouse*, and a new magazine named *The Face*, launched by Nic Logan in May 1980, whose intelligent coverage of Pop culture had quickly won over a teenage readership that could be transferred to the newly built cinemas. For this and a slightly older age group, the novelty of newish films on video helped sharpen an appetite for brand-new films on the big screens – precisely at the moment when multiplexes were mushrooming.

British Film Year may have been only a self-congratulatory trumpet flourish; but it announced a real recovery. The irony was that its attempt to put the cinema back at the centre of the local community succeeded largely through the booming video industry that seemed so divisive to film-makers that they were still agitating for a levy to be slapped on all videotapes, pre-recorded and blank. The House of Lords actually voted an amendment to the Finance Bill that would have done this, but it was annulled when the Bill went back to the Commons for its final reading in the spring of 1985 just as British Film Year was getting under way.

If video indirectly lured audiences back into cinemas, enriching the new multiplex exhibitors, it did so at the very moment the government remained intent on robbing the producers of what they considered an already bare subsistence. This see-sawing imbalance was to be one of the most constant factors shaping the industry over the following decades. Kenneth Baker, Minister of Information Technology, insisted: 'our policy is to free the industry from an intrusive regulatory system dating from the days of the silent films'. The argument of monetarists down the ages, of course: he and Norman Lamont were denounced as 'ingenues' by the Association of Independent Producers. The truth was, the Tories did not think of films as an art to be supported, rather they mistrusted them as a business to be rescued. The frustration was palpable; even the government-appointed Midases were flayed, as Melvyn Bragg put it in early February, 'for selling the arts down the drain of dogma'. His *j'accuse* finger pointed directly at Lord Gowrie, Arts Minister, and Sir William (later Lord) Rees-Mogg, chairman of the Arts Council, for 'broken promises, failed principles, the disruption of the bungler and the ugly debris of the demolition: these are the marks of that duo'. Both went along with 'The Mistress's Voice', aka Mrs Thatcher.

'Grey' Gowrie may well have sympathised: the money-pinching policy took its toll on the Arts and Libraries Minister. Before the year was out he had resigned, saying he couldn't live on his £30,000-a-year salary. The *Guardian* sarcastically commended him for exposing the Dickensian poverty that hadn't yet been eliminated from London life. 'If the noble lord's courageous decision to "come out" leads to others coming forward so the full depths of the problem can be revealed, then it will not have been made in vain.' Ten years later Gowrie would be chairman of the Arts Council with huge National Lottery funding available for films: he still bungled the patronage.

Film industry leaders were especially incensed by the abolition of the National Film Finance Corporation and the new plans now taking shape to replace it with the British Screen Finance Corporation. This 'bank' for part-funding independent films was to be supported by the industry as a quid pro quo for putting £3 million back into the box-office tills by doing away with the Eady Levy which had been terminated with effect at midnight on 25 May 1985. Channel 4 and Thorn-EMI Screen Entertainment were divvying up £300,000 annually for five years; Rank £250,000; and the British Videogram Association an (unconfirmed) £250,000: chicken feed for such corporations, but resented all the same. The government would put in £1.5 million over the period, but this was to be treated as 'income', not a 'grant in aid', and therefore subject to tax. The NFFC's stablemate, the National Film Development Fund, to be run by Colin Vaines, had £500,000 a year, which was better than anticipated, but was not permitted to lend more than two thirds for projects in the admittedly riskiest section of film-making where there was only an average success rate of one developed project in twenty becoming a fully fledged film. Faced with such parsimony, one was uncertain whether to laugh or cry – both, probably.

The resentment had deeper roots than simply a waiter receiving an inadequate tip in his outstretched palm. It was considered unlikely that these four 'funders' of independent film-making could agree on anything between themselves: two of them, Rank and EMI, were already responsible for rigging their film exhibition policies against the very same small-budget, independent films they were now supposed to succour. Mamoun Hassan, the ex-NFFC chief executive, said, 'It's a shotgun wedding with no chance of a pregnancy.'

The pessimism would have been deeper still had the film community been aware of what was happening in the boardroom of Goldcrest, the company that, as its founder, Jake Eberts, said, was often talked about as *being* the British film industry. This was, for a time, the best-kept secret of the year. A secret that, as Richard Attenborough, a non-executive Goldcrest director, said later, left the company 'filled with dread'. In short, Goldcrest was about to run out of funding, having put too much money into too few projects, some of which were in trouble or out of control. By the second week of February 1985 it was about to overdraw its £10 million facility at the Midland Bank. At the end of June it had no more money to its credit and not even enough ready cash in the bank to go on trading. As Jake Eberts and Terry Ilott wrote later, in an 'in memoriam' account of this catastrophe which is the best primer ever on the subject of running a film company, 'Goldcrest had come to a stop ... It could not cover its coming week's expenses. It could not sign cheques. It could not make any more movies.'

Three films had helped bring the flagship of the industry to disaster: *Absolute Beginners*, *The Mission* and *Revolution*. They had been announced at an extravagant party launch at Maxim's London restaurant in December 1984. All started filming in the March–April 1985 period. Each was plagued with difficulties. Some were within the makers' remedy, others were due to the makers' creative ambitions. None was completely under the control of the parent corporation. All were injured by the falling value of their dollar contracts with their American investors, the pound sterling fluctuating wildly in the early 1980s.

By 1984, Goldcrest's very success with *Chariots of Fire* – although they put only £25,000 into it whereas Fox and Allied Artists each invested £50,000 – and *Gandhi*, had stimulated other companies to go for the 'niche' market then represented by intelligent films, offbeat in treatment or subject, aimed at discriminating film-goers. Hollywood studios were going into production with *Amadeus*, *Sophie's Choice*, *Falling in Love*, *The Color Purple*, *Out of Africa* and others. Goldcrest's very success – or perceived success – had bred that most flattering but unwelcome thing: imitators. Audiences for such films were no longer as hungry as they had been for a 'testing' or 'different' experience. Puttnam noted, with well-founded apprehension, that the US box office for *The Killing Fields*, his well-received account of Pol Pot's cruel regime in Cambodia, had 'softened' and concluded that the film was viewed as too serious, too male-orientated and too harrowing. By then, though, the pull of a not dissimilar story of barbarity and exploitation, *The Mission*, was too strong to resist.

Production costs were soaring, too. *Chariots of Fire* had cost £3 million; *Gandhi* £9.5 million; by contrast, the initial budget for *Absolute Beginners* was £6 million; for *Revolution* £9 million; for *The Mission* £11.5 million. The budgets of all three were revised upwards as shooting got under way and concepts or conditions altered, and the first two were to exceed even the panicky, 'final final' estimates; dreadful reviews – 'some of the worst notices in living memory', Goldcrest's founder, Jake Eberts, recalled when *Revolution* finally opened in New York on Christmas Day 1985 – killed any hope of recoupment in time to save Goldcrest from its fate. None of them should have been made: they represented a great financial risk for an under-capitalised company, even one with the huge fortune of Pearson Longman, financiers and publishers, behind it. Each had a different reason why it was a bad risk at that time or price.

Absolute Beginners, based on Colin MacInnes's novel about late-1950s youth culture, was set in Soho and Notting Hill, and directed by Julien Temple, an experienced maker of promos for Pop groups and music companies. This made a kind of sense: they recast MacInnes's story as a 'street' musical. The project had been brought to Goldcrest by Palace Pictures, where its promise of 'buzz' and 'event' excited Palace's young founders, Woolley and Powell. (Powell, don't forget, had once been one of Richard Branson's partners in Virgin Records.) These two were assumed to have youth culture on tap, to be able to set music trends in partnership with Virgin (a co-investor in the film). The book was viewed by Goldcrest's middle-ageing executives as a talismanic part of teenage culture, like *Catcher in the Rye* – it was not. The film promised 'scale and impressiveness' and 'a strong visual element'. It actually delivered extravagance, muddle and waste, and if it has since become a sort of camp classic, though very little seen since 1986, this is a retrospective benefit of no compensation for the company it helped put out of business.

The Mission, produced by Puttnam and directed by his partner in *The Killing Fields*, Roland Joffé, appeared a shrewd follow-up to such 'serious' epics as *Gandhi*: an international subject (the predatory invasion of South America by nineteenth-century Spanish and Portuguese slave traders, the exploitation of the tribal communities, the resistance of the Jesuit order); unfamiliar and spectacular locations; brutality, but a liberal message. But script problems remained unresolved; the budget was to climb, partly due to the casting of Robert De Niro. Attenborough warned Eberts that when you had an 'A' list star like him, you added $200,000 to your prospective cost right away: a good guess, for in fact, a provision of £3,000 for De Niro's per diems finally totalled £103,000. And a film that looked magnificent ultimately ended up curiously passionless.

However, it was arguably *Revolution* that effectively did Goldcrest in. It had been presented to the Goldcrest board as a small, intimate family drama set against the background of the American War of Independence. As Chris Burt, its associate producer, remarked wryly later on, 'It was a [John] Ford script which Hugh [Hudson] shot as a [Gillo] Pontecorvo movie, and the two just didn't meet.' Hudson and his American producer, Irwin Winkler, gradually changed emphasis and scale: so that the characters were subsumed into the events, the revolution became the foreground, and crucial financial decisions were made on location in

Norfolk and the West Country, doubling for the American north-east, apparently without knowledge or approval of Goldcrest's executives in London.

Elephantiasis of the creative will seemed to rule Hudson's ambitions; just as Julien Temple's similarly obdurate vision for *Absolute Beginners* seemed to determine the inflation and incompetence that characterised the finished product. The same hard-headed executive observed, 'The production team didn't know what they were doing ... the whole project was out of control.' Final responsibility, of course, lay with Goldcrest management. Even twenty-five and more years later, it is a matter of controversy who was most to blame, though the Eberts–Ilott book, *My Indecision Is Final*, pins it squarely on James Lee, the company chairman whom they characterise as having 'gone Hollywood' – which is to say that Lee, who had come from a sound business career with Pearson and had an impeccable background in Harvard Business School, could not resist the ego-feeding temptations of film-making. According to Eberts–Ilott he was felt to resent the advice, even the presence, of Sandy Lieberson, David Puttnam's former partner, who had joined Goldcrest as head of production in 1984 when Jake Eberts had departed to join Embassy, an American company that would pay him what he (rightly) considered himself worth.

Lieberson came with a Hollywood background – for a short period he had headed 20th Century-Fox's production in Hollywood – but as only one film out of every twenty ever gets from concept to production in a Hollywood studio, this experience was of little use in the edge-of-the-seat operation of a British company. Lieberson's brief was to find and develop new talent: the opposite of Eberts's, who worked with tested and proven talents who could be trusted not to depart from script or budget. He found his chairman, James Lee, taking decisions which Lieberson felt should have been left to him and which overruled his budget-trimming orders to the *Revolution* producers who found Lee more accommodating to their views when he visited the location. Lieberson suspected Lee wanted to be both company chief and production chief.

Goldcrest under Eberts had acted primarily as a financier, looking for profit from one shared investment at a time that scored big; Eberts, an ultra-cautious man who worried endlessly, always kept a distance between his own talent for raising film funding and the passion to make the films. Lee, however, wanted to be involved, 'build the company', and the temptation to turn it into a major producer got to him personally – fatally, in his colleagues' view. But running a film company requiring hands-on interference at all levels was very different from taking a chairman's lofty perspective, which Lee had done extremely well at Pearson Longman.

The wrong man was in the wrong job and acting in the wrong way at the wrong time. Colleagues noted a significant change in his appearance. He abandoned sober town suits and bow ties for a more florid style of dressing and a beard, characteristic of the deal makers of Beverly Hills. In May 1985 he had moved Goldcrest from cramped offices in Kensington to a palatial headquarters in Wardour Street, with atrium and fountains, whose rent was £500,000 a year. Perception is an invaluable asset in an image-making industry like films, but even this extravagant relocation had the opposite effect on the film community. In such grandiosity it detected the first sign of catastrophe.

It is astonishing to consider, when all the dust settled from Goldcrest's collapse, that the company had only two experienced film-makers as non-executive directors on its board, Attenborough and Puttnam. Both had to be absent at times shooting their films on the other side of the world. Puttnam was much the better informed – 'in that company,' Eberts commented, 'his expertise was not far short of dazzling' – and certainly the more involved board member; after all, Puttnam's Enigma production company accounted by 1984 for 34 per cent of Goldcrest's film and television investment. The company very reluctantly co-financed (with Warner Bros, which contributed to Puttnam's overheads as part of a 'first look' deal) three Enigma films: *Mr Love* (total budget £486,000), *The Frog Prince* (£896,000) and *Knights and Emeralds* (£1.1 million), which Puttnam hoped would be training grounds for new talents. All three were unsuccessful; Goldcrest lost over £1.4 million in humouring Puttnam and keeping in with Warner to whom the company was offering equity stakes in seven films (including the cursed trio of *Absolute Beginners*, *The Mission* and *Revolution*).

One of David Puttnam's strongest talents was convincing others, as successfully as himself, that things should be done his way. By mid 1985, however, associates were noticing a change in the man who, at this time, was considered with reason to be the most successful producer in the British film industry. Success had taken its toll: the immense effort involved in producing two films, *The Killing Fields* and now *The Mission*, in faraway places, coupled with the feeling that things were falling apart at home, had made Puttnam seem, well, mellow to some, pessimistic to others. When Goldcrest finally collapsed, he bitterly regretted having put 'ten years of my life into the company'. Naturally, perhaps, but a more profound change was at work. He was then forty-five and had invested more than a decade in the British film industry as a whole. It seemed in no better shape now than when he'd started out as an independent producer. British Film Year had evoked, in his view, mainly 'apathy and scepticism'. His remarks in Los Angeles the previous year, unreported in the British press, should have been forewarning enough. What they did not explain were personal worries.

His own company, Enigma, had become bigger than he could comfortably administer – while continuing personally to produce movies. Debts were piling up. He had been offered a boardroom-level appointment at the advertising agency, Saatchi & Saatchi. But as he told Dominique Joyeux in the autumn of 1985 (Puttnam's remarks to foreign journalists are notably less guarded than the ones for home consumption): 'I still think of myself as a marketing man who happens to produce movies, not as a film-maker who happened to have an advertising background.' But for someone who had begun as an ad account executive, it was like a step backwards as well as upwards.

Puttnam, whose schooling had ended in his mid teens, hankered after the chance to see the world in a broader aspect than a viewfinder. He was already dickering with the notion of a year at Harvard, studying ethics, law and moral philosophy. Maybe even lecturing. Like many autodidacts, academia seemed a world in which they did things differently ... better. Maybe his forebears' Russian-Jewish background, his intellectual restlessness, his uncertainty that perhaps he wasn't asking himself the 'right' questions about his purpose in life, the value he attached to, well, *values* was all asserting itself in this mid-life, mid-career period. He had often alluded to Diaghilev as his 'hero'. The connection between a film producer and the Russian entrepreneur is too obvious to develop; yet what Puttnam particularly admired in the great impresario was his success in putting together the Ballets Russes, twice, after it had collapsed once. Looking at Goldcrest, as the crisis overwhelmed it, Puttnam must have felt even Diaghilev could not have worked a miracle. In his mind, if not yet in his destination, David Puttnam was already putting considerable distance between himself and his team at Goldcrest despite the fact that he (and Attenborough, the other working film-maker on the board) had spent at least as much time out of the country as round the boardroom table. (If they had been, as Eberts and Ilott shrewdly guess, conflict of interest would surely have appeared, since Puttnam had temporarily fallen out with Hugh Hudson and would hardly have endorsed the road to perdition on which *Revolution* seemed set, while Attenborough's cherished project, an epic about Tom Paine, the English-born father of the American Revolution, had been put on hold – i.e. abandoned – as soon as *Revolution* had been greenlighted.)

The board meeting that decided Goldcrest's fate and, even sooner, James Lee's was held on 18 July 1985. The account of it in *My Indecision Is Final* is the frankest ever published of a film company's death agonies, lasting most of the day as the board wrangled over Goldcrest's future and ending only when James Lee, sensing all his fellow executives were against him and some of them (Puttnam particularly) were in vehement opposition to allowing him to assume the powers of chief executive *and* production chief, yielded to the inevitable 'him or them', polled each executive one by one and, on hearing the predictable answer, retired. An announcement was made from the Wardour Street office that afternoon that Lee had offered his resignation and it had been accepted. Lee put on a brave face. 'I shall be taking a well-earned [*sic*] summer holiday,' he told the *Sunday Times*, 'and thinking hard. Read about it in my memoirs. They should be good.' (They have not appeared so far.)

On the same day, allowing for the time difference, Jake Eberts was working on the roof of the barn on his Ontario farm, when he received a call imploring him to return to the company he had founded and save Goldcrest from collapse. Not since Cincinnatus, the former Roman consul, had so revered a figure been called away from his plough so dramatically to resume control of his country's fortunes – or, in this case, his corporation's assets. He ordered a crash diet at Goldcrest: no more film-making for the moment; the closing down of the TV division; dismissal of about twenty staffers; a move back to offices in a low-rent district; and a hope against hope that *Revolution* might yet succeed in the US, and/or *Absolute Beginners* – which was now weeks behind schedule and looked to Eberts a depressing mess when he saw it assembled – would somehow click with the youth market. Not only had *Revolution* opened disastrously in the US on Christmas Day 1985, but *Absolute Beginners* eventually came in at a horrifying cost of £8.4 million, which was 30 per cent above what had been budgeted – even *Revolution* had come in at 'only' 20 per cent overage. Puttnam's production of *The Mission*, despite its award of the Palme d'or at Cannes in 1986, took rentals of only £8.3 million in the United States and, in Eberts's opinion, was the *coup de grâce* for Goldcrest. If there was no going back and raising fresh capital, there was certainly no going forward.

A financier, Frans Afman, whose name was to figure even more prominently in the misfortunes of the British film industry over the next few years, had been sounded out in August 1985, to see whether his Dutch-based bank, Credit Lyonnais, would open a new line of credit for Goldcrest. This may seem odd to people not acquainted with an industry whose production problems were then overwhelming it: but the fact is, the ability to pay the interest on future borrowing was always what mattered and Goldcrest, after all, represented a bare 1 per cent of the immensely wealthy Pearson Longman group. However, the latter, not being film-makers, saw no glamour in riding to its rescue; but sooner than lose face and see one of their subsidiaries go into administration, debts of £20 million were eventually absorbed by the parent company and the sale of what remained of Goldcrest, despite Eberts's heroic efforts, was next on the agenda.

Even in eclipse, at a standstill on the production front, it had the assets of its library of films and the less tangible, but still potent, attraction of its 'marque', its 'quality' seal. An American property developer named Earle Mack, who was looking for an entrée into show business, bid for it in 1987, promising an infusion of £5 million of his own capital in return for an 85 per cent shareholding; as soon as one guy shows an interest in dancing with the ugliest girl in the place, Eberts commented bitterly afterwards, all the other guys jump up and bid for her, too: he had fifteen enquiries about Goldcrest. The main rival bidders were Masterman, a company part-owned by Brent Walker, which Eberts did not favour. But a 75 per cent vote of shareholders was needed to deliver the company to Earle Mack: it failed by 0.6 per cent, largely because the Brent Walker group had promised to buy out the shareholders.

Goldcrest's name is still in the telephone directory, but largely for post-production work on other people's films. It had been brought down by its unwise choice of films to back from poor scripts with unreliable production supervision; by not having enough money to pay for those films as they ran away with their budgets; and by a board that allowed all these things to happen, almost simultaneously, without adequate regard for the changed conditions in the international market place or the escalating overheads at home.

After Goldcrest changed hands, James Lee worked as a management consultant, having failed to win a satellite TV franchise; he was to emerge in the late 1990s as chairman of Scottish Screen and then as a director of the Film Council and a £33.2 million National Lottery-funded franchise. Attenborough went to make *Cry Freedom*, in 1987, a movie aspiring to be about the black activist Steve Biko murdered by the South African police, which appeared to many to have more to do with the persecution of the white newspaper editor who championed Biko. And David Puttnam was soon to find his life and fortunes radically transformed, though possibly not in the way he would have chosen. Eberts returned to managing his own financial investment company, Allied Films, working out of a small room in Mayfair with a secretary-assistant. As he recorded, after Goldcrest collapsed virtually all funding for independent film productions from the City of London capital venturers dried up.

The high flyers of the film industry quitting their perches in 1985 was a phenomenon not confined to Goldcrest. Verity Lambert, the £100,000-a-year production chief at Thorn-EMI Screen Entertainment, resigned in July, saying 'the time had come to return to the actual work of producing my own shows [on television]': shows like *Rumpole* and *Minder*. Her stay at TESE had been short in duration and even shorter in profitability, though how much real autonomy she exercised is arguable. David Lean's *Passage to India*, which began shooting in the subcontinent in March 1983 with a £17 million budget and did not finish until June 1984, had been an inherited project. But under Lambert, TESE put into production a Scottish comedy, *Restless Natives* (budgeted at £1.2 million), a goonish farce, *Morons from Outer Space* (£5 million) and *Dreamchild*, a Dennis Potter-scripted fancy on the child who was the model for *Alice in Wonderland* (£4 million). The first took a bare £300,000 (it did well in Scotland, nowhere else); the second took less than £1.5 million from the home box office; the third had no cinema in Britain ready for it after its critically successful US opening.

After Lambert left, TESE closed down its in-house production, relying on 'satellite' multi-picture deals with independent producers such as Lord Brabourne and his partner Richard Goodwin (*Murder on the Orient Express*) and Jeremy Thomas, earmarking a rolling development fund of £1.5 million and a revolving credit facility of up to £150 million with twelve leading merchant banks – enough for whole or partial financing of twelve to fifteen movies a year. This looked lively enough. But the truth was, TESE's own life was in danger from mid

1985 onwards. It was to become, after Goldcrest, the second-biggest collapse in indigenous British film-making and a much nastier one in every way.

Thorn-Electric, TESE's parent company, did not look kindly on the film-making entity. Directors of other divisions, which manufactured unglamorous hardware, held an innate resentment against what they regarded as wasteful, extravagant film people who ate up the profits of their own hard, unglamorous work. Such resentment is not uncommon in a mixed conglomerate, though seldom articulated: no need to, really, since the bottom line did a good enough job. In spite of owning the chain of ABC cinemas in Britain, box-office profits were poor. TESE contributed a surplus of only £11.9 million on a turnover of £132 million and most of that came from international video distribution in the US. It invested more confidently in US-made films than in its own homegrown product: $300 million over the last three years. In short, its asset value – the largest theatrical cinema circuit in Britain, Elstree film studios, a library of 2,000 old movies and the Pathé newsreel collection – was worth far more than the business it currently did. It looked ripe for a takeover. Peter Laister, its managing director, a nice family man who enjoyed caravanning, and had been an exponent of the synergism theory – or cross-pollination of separate bits of a business to produce a beautiful hybrid – had been ousted in June 1985, after merely fifteen months during which profits had fallen by 30 per cent to £108 million. Sir Graham Wilkins, the chairman and chief executive at Thorn-EMI plc, was not a film man; neither was old Sir Joseph Lockwood, nickname 'The Quiet Millionaire', but he had had Lord Delfont, brother of Lord Grade, as his chief executive. And for a long time, until EMI almost ran out of money and had to be rescued by amalgamation with Thorn-Electric, Bernie Delfont had used EMI funds for British-financed, but US-made movies using Hollywood talents as his 'mercenaries'.

All was now suddenly changed. Sally Davis, director of the Association of Independent Producers, got wind of the change and expressed its alarm on 21 October 1985 in an open letter to Sir Graham Wilkins: '. . . we fear that within a short period of time, the company may become the victim of what amounts to an asset-stripping operation.' In other words, Thorn-EMI's value as a going concern could be less than the total worth of its properties, film rights and other material holdings.

Their fears were justified swiftly. Within the month the predators had begun to circle: among them Gerald Ronson's Heron Corporation;

Rupert Murdoch's newspaper group; the National Video Corporation; and Associated Communications Corporation, headed by Robert Holmes à Court who had ousted the once invincible Lew Grade summarily from his own company only a year or two earlier after the colossal failure of *Raise the Titanic!* drained away the last shred of Lew's credibility and credit.

One other contender, though included in the listings, was accounted very much an outsider in any takeover bid. 'Cannon Films is also said to be interested,' the AIP's November Newsletter added, almost as an afterthought. Within weeks, Cannon had become the centre of an epic sell-off battle and management buyout attempt. It was a contest without parallel in British film industry history. One that changed the pattern of film-making in Britain for ever and provoked the most shameful betrayal of indigenous film-makers by an uncaring and ignorant government.

3

Cannon a Go-Go

Let us now return to the politics – and the finances. The British film industry, as then constituted, did not want Cannon Films to acquire the assets of Thorn-EMI Screen Entertainment. Alarmed, most of the thirty-seven-member British Screen Advisory Council, chaired by Lord Wilson, met at the Department of Trade and Industry on 25 November and declared that selling TESE to Cannon would be 'catastrophic'. 'It would certainly lead to the elimination (in British Film Year) of anything which could be called the British film industry.' Members feared the consequences would be asset stripping and foreign domination of the industry – the two cousins who headed Cannon, Menahem Golan and Yoram Globus, were Israelis based in New York and registered in the Netherlands.

I was present at the BSAC meeting. The mood was tense, angry and apprehensive. David Puttnam suggested sending an immediate telex, expressing our alarm, to the Office of Fair Trading, which had to judge if such a sale was in the public interest or a monopolistic venture. Between them Rank and Cannon (and the Star cinema chain it had bought only weeks earlier) already controlled 80 per cent of the market; the merger of Cannon and TESE would create a chain two and a half times the size of its nearest rival, Rank. Cannon made no pretence of supporting an indigenous British film industry: it had promised only £2,000 to British Film Year and even that had not yet been paid. We immediately agreed to the Puttnam 'offensive'; then our Civil Service secretary reminded us: our 'host', the DTI, would not pay for even a telex. The minutes record: 'Mr Puttnam and Mr (Alan) Sapper, secretary of the cinematographic technicians, agreed to do so.' Lady Falkender, Lord Wilson's aide and confidante at Downing Street for many years, agreed to draft a letter to Geoffrey Pattie, the minister with responsibility for films – it, at least, would cost only a stamp. Puttnam also wrote to Sir Graham Wilkins, Thorn-EMI's chairman, expressing our 'unanimous' opposition to Cannon.

One left the meeting, not very confident that our artillery was heavy enough. But then it looked as if a white knight was galloping to the industry's rescue. He was Alan Bond, the Australian property and beer magnate, and winner of the yacht race that had at long last snatched the Americas Cup back from the US. When it was clear that TESE's bankers could not raise the necessary cash for a management buyout headed by Gary Dartnall – a BSAC member who absented himself from our discussions – Bond, at the eleventh hour, paid £15 million, including a non-refundable deposit of £10 million, trumping bids from Rank and Cannon (and their associate Gerald Ronson's Heron company). Bond later added another £10 million, for which he was to receive a remarkably generous 45 per cent stake in TESE. With this backing, Thorn-EMI agreed to sell TESE to Dartnall's management team on 10 December for £110 million.

Menahem Golan was furious at being trumped. Cannon's shares, which had been 20 cents each on Wall Street six years earlier, were now trading at $30: Golan was not used to such public rebuffs. BSAC leading members exchanged self-congratulations (not by telex). Sir Gordon Borrie, at the OFT, wrote on 11 December, 'My office ... confirmed to Mr Dartnell [*sic*] last night that the financial arrangements now concluded with Mr Alan Bond to preserve the integrity of Mr Dartnell's [*sic*] team have been concluded ... I do not propose to pursue the matter further.' Cannon did, though, with a rapaciousness and energy unknown among indigenous film tycoons.

The TESE–Bond deal was structured thus: £40 million of equity, £50 million of loans secured against TESE's 108-strong cinema chain and Elstree Studios, and $50 million of junk bonds to be sold in the US by brokers Bear Sterns. But the management buyout also had to assume trade and financial guarantees on commitments to co-finance a slate of US films over the next three years being put together by David Begelman, the disgraced Hollywood tycoon who had had to admit to cheque forgery while production chief at Columbia. In addition it would require new working capital. It thus needed to raise nearer £300 million than the £110 million it (and Bond) paid Thorn-EMI. The alternatives were grim: one was asset stripping TESE, which was the very event the buyout had been devised to frustrate; another was Bond renegotiating the deal and, if he failed, losing his £10 million deposit. The deadline was extended for three weeks from 28 February 1986, upon Bond giving a personal guarantee to cover any shortfall (and thus assume total ownership of TESE). Clearly Bond the Good Samaritan was working feverishly not to be 'lumbered' with an expensive company he had not wished to buy in its entirety; its main appeal to him was the 2,000-odd film library for use on his own Australian TV channel.

Michael Winner, the film-maker who had recently directed *Death Wish 3* for Cannon, wrote in the *Sunday Times*: 'Cannon Films ... are moving back to see if they can join the fun. ... The fact that various people who are not British' – opposition to Cannon was now being stigmatised by Cannon's allies as 'anti-Semitic': for Winner not to employ this term showed rare sensibility – 'are coming in worries me not at all. As for Gary Dartnall, one thing seems sure. He opened the champagne too soon. It may well turn out to be a farewell toast.'

On 21 March Gary Dartnall informed Thorn-EMI his management team could not complete the buyout. Bond had to act, or be £10 million poorer. For such a man the choice was clear. Denying he would asset strip the company, as an earnest of intent he went solo, putting up £110 million of his own money, plus a bank guarantee for the £168 million commitments to Begelman. Dartnall's gamble – or, as some had it, disastrous business judgement – played into Cannon's hands. TESE had gone to a buyer, in an enforced sale, who really did not want it; what would he accept to have it taken off his hands?

On the evening of 4–5 May 1986, lights burned all night at TESE's offices in Golden Square, just behind Piccadilly, as Gary Dartnall's team and the Cannon chiefs kept up almost continuous negotiations with Alan Bond's advisers in Australia. One junior TESE employee was ordered by Globus to get coffee. There's an all-night caff open round the corner, the Cannon chief was told, the invitation being to go get it yourself. At 5.45 a.m. on Friday morning, 5 May, Bond sold out to Cannon for £175 million – the first TESE man to be sacked was the one who'd failed the loyalty test as a coffee 'gofer'. Having owned TESE for precisely one week, Alan Bond made a cool £30 million on the sale-back, taking additionally a boardroom seat and distribution rights to the 2,000 films – which were all he had wanted in the first place. Golan exulted: 'I love England.' He had every reason to do so: his adversaries had let Cannon shoulder its way to victory, through financial mis-calculations and a pusillanimous unwillingness to muster forces in time or numbers to prevent these tenacious carpetbaggers capturing their assets.

British producers at the concurrent Cannes Film Festival were stunned; but self-interest quickly cleared their heads. BSAC met on 22 May, chastened and cowardly: eighteen members, or 17 per cent of the whole committee, were absentees, among them some most directly affected by Cannon's putsch – Gary Dartnall was holidaying in the Seychelles. The committee that had 'unanimously' opposed Cannon just six months earlier now resolved 'the takeover should be welcomed, if partly on grounds of pragmatism' – i.e. as it had happened, we can do nothing about it, so put on a brave face and smile. Golan and Globus were invited to meet BSAC. (Borrie's reply would merely say he would be 'interested to hear what happened' at such a meeting.) Puttnam cleverly proposed Cannon be invited to divest themselves of the cinema chain they had just bought ('There's no link between their purchase of cinemas and their production plans'), knowing, but not voicing, what we all knew: that ownership of cinemas was ownership of the money box and the cash flow Cannon would need to meet its obligations – not least to pay Alan Bond his money.

Puttnam and I were the only two members of BSAC to oppose the appeasement we sensed. Puttnam, writing privately to me a week later, said, 'It was a pretty sorry sight last Thursday, wasn't it?' He enclosed a copy of a letter addressed to Sir Gordon Borrie at the Office of Fair Trading ('You'll be pleased to hear that one or two other stouter-hearted chums have written similar notes in support'). His letter to Borrie said, in part, 'In May 1983 ... Rank and EMI controlled between them a little under 60 per cent of the theatrical revenues returned to film distributors in the UK. The impending merger [of Cannon-TESE] takes this figure to 72.6 per cent (January 1986). Surely there is no way of reconciling this increase with [your definition of monopoly].' Cannon also became Rank's biggest laboratory customer for making film prints, which would bring the competitive ethic into question. 'Many people in our industry find it difficult under the present circumstances to retain an independent voice in this debate.'

By this communication Puttnam hoped to open a 'second front' in the anti-Cannon battle, for the deal still awaited the approval of Paul Channon at the Department of Trade and Industry and he would be advised by the Office of Fair Trading. This regroupment, however, suffered a possibly fatal blow. Not only was it unsupported by an industry whose separate members were fearful of economic disarray if Cannon were thwarted, but Puttnam himself would soon not be around to lead the charge of this (very) light brigade. By opposing Cannon vociferously and publicly he had incurred the enmity of a group whose bosses had a lot of their own country's ruthless defence of perceived self-interest – even if, in this case, it set Jew against Jew.

The collapse of Goldcrest, Puttnam's power base, left him without corporate walls to protect him; he couldn't operate with peace of mind in an industry now dominated by a hostile Cannon: he simply had nowhere to go. 'The British film industry has nothing left to offer me right now. ... The [failure of] *Revolution* took away my capital base [in Goldcrest] and, without it, it was impossible to ask Warners to continue funding my projects in Britain. What was I do to ... make Cannon pictures? ... I feel like Shirley Williams [the Labour MP who crossed over to become a Social Democrat] when she said, quite rightly, she hadn't left the Labour Party, the Labour Party had left her.' He accepted an invitation to be president of the Council for the Protection of Rural England. In the circumstances, it had an ironic ring: 'Let us cultivate our garden,' was the philosopher's historic answer to the rude buffets of the world.

Menahem Golan and Yoram Globus enjoyed their summer of triumph. They were, in *Newsweek*'s headline, 'The Newest Moguls'. The Cannes Film Festival was their stage that year: they took a bow daily. Some felt it should be renamed the Cannon Film Festival. They had three films in various Cannes sections: Zeffirelli's *Otello* with Placido Domingo, Robert Altman's *Fool for Love* and Andrei Konchalovsky's action thriller *Runaway Train* – as it happened, none of them won anything. It did not matter: they came with the right names attached, inclusion was itself a prize. They staged a publicity coup every lunchtime, projects that cost nothing (yet) and commanded huge media coverage, suggesting boastful thinking was already immediate reality: a Fellini opus based on Kafka's *Amerika*; an Alain Resnais film; an Agatha Christie project scripted by Anthony Shaffer; Coppola to direct *La Brava* with Al Pacino ... None of these ever happened: perception was everything, chutzpah also. Golan did sign a deal with Jean-Luc Godard for a revisionist version of *King Lear* with Norman Mailer as the storm-tossed sovereign and Woody Allen as the Fool. 'Mailer is a natural for the part,' Golan announced, 'he has five daughters and a crazy life.' Unbelievably, this film happened a year or two later: it would have been better for everyone had it not.

Cannon's thirty-eight delegates to the festival, dressed in electric blue-and-white tracksuits, crowded lunch tables on the Carlton Hotel terrace to hear what their bosses had purchased that day. The festival, it was believed, would be crowned by Cannon's announcement that it had bought MGM: it already controlled 425 screens in the US and, being a 'small' company, was not banned by anti-trust laws affecting major studios from acquiring more power. As it happened, MGM eluded them: a bigger, more astute entrepreneur, Kirk Kerkorian, owned it. Golan, the front man, the promoter, the host with the most, ordering lunch for a hundred with a hand-wave, made the best of his disappointment: 'I have an important announcement to make . . . We have not bought anything today.'

Cannon had made its own space in America as it was now doing in Britain: by infiltration and the acquisition of assets that had valuable cash flow − cinemas, in other words. The Cannon cousins, known derogatively yet with sneaking admiration by their competitors as 'the Globs', or 'The Go-Go Boys', or 'The Nosh Bros', had been born with thick hides in the Israeli town of Tiberias. They had a genuine love of talent, at first, anyhow: Golan staged plays by Tennessee Williams and O'Neill in Hebrew in Tel Aviv; but film-making had the allure of power. Golan went to work for Roger Corman as an unpaid grip on a film called *The Young Racers* and became an assistant director. He had the nerve to request a loan of $300,000 to make a film of his own, offering Corman the rights outside Israel. Another Corman apprentice, one Francis Ford Coppola, gazumped him.

Undeterred, Golan returned to Israel and, with his cousin, set up Noah Films, named perhaps out of sympathy with the survival instinct of the commander of the Ark. The most important lesson of Golan's apprenticeship was 'Make 'em cheap'. Noah made them even cheaper than that. Between 1967 and 1978 it produced forty micro-budget movies, making it Israel's top producer. One of these, a cheeky youth comedy, *Lemon Popsicle*, an unapologetic Israeli version of *American Graffiti*, hit the jackpot. This allowed them in 1979 to buy a faltering US company, Cannon, whose shares were worth 25 cents. They followed this up by buying a string of cinemas in several European countries.

Personally, the two cousins lived frugally, keeping 'show' for their deals: salami sandwiches and a shared hotel room − 'We do it', said Golan, ever adept at attributing advantage to necessity, 'because we talk about our films until one of us falls asleep.' Their business strategy succeeded brilliantly because, as incomers, they could make their own rules in America: they made bargain-basement budgeted movies;

released them in the off-seasons; sold off the rights to other territories before they made them, thus covering their costs in advance – the sort of fail-safe equation that is the alchemist's stone in the film industry down the ages, but which wears out its magic and its welcome if the film flops for the buyers. A safer line of credit was the acquisition of 425 screens of a medium-size American cinema circuit which had ready cash available on Sunday nights.

As Cannon grew, so did a string of debts and the relatively small base for Cannon in America began to look as if it might not support such a leveraged operation. Then they met Frans Afman. Afman was vice-president of the Rotterdam branch of Credit Lyonnais, the world's top lender to film-makers, financing over 400 movies in the previous fifteen years. Afman has already been mentioned as the 'angel' to whom stricken Goldcrest had looked at one time, unavailingly. His bank had provided the $350,000 allowing the Cannon company to be bought – always borrow money seems to have been a Golan–Globus rule, never pay cash. Soon Afman's loan line to Cannon was $50 million, used for upfront money and completion guarantees. Low commissions and low corporation taxes in the Netherlands kept the producers happy. Many people thought Cannon was also being supported by the Israeli government; and so long as this impression persisted, lending confidence to, well, lenders, Golan–Globus did not dispel it. Cannon's acquisition of TESE, therefore, coinciding with Cannes, enabled Golan and Globus to say, with some truth, that they were now a credible and major part of the British film industry.

When Geoffrey Pattie, the Films Minister, paid a flying visit to Cannes, he felt compelled to open a dialogue with Cannon about the fears their expansionist policy was causing. Golan was unrepentant, even bullish. 'Our company is now worth $1.2 billion,' he told the Minister, 'all the government is giving British Screen for independent production is £300,000. I think it should be raised to £10 million.' Pattie, he said, 'looked at me as if I had come from the moon'. 'With £10 million', said Golan, 'you could fund twenty movies a year. Think, Minister, what benefits this would bring. Money just from the premières could go to old actors and retired technicians ... to people who are out of jobs.' Pattie had never heard such talk from a film producer. But then, nor had many film producers back home in Britain, where the Minister returned without promising to open the government's chequebook.

At Cannes, Cannon flexed its muscles and presented itself, with some success, as a class act, rather than a crass one, as was still the perception in America where the two were known as the makers of *Texas Chain Saw Massacre 2* and the would-be blockbuster *Delta Force*. 'Rug merchants' and 'maestros of schlock' were some of the kinder insults they had to endure, despite signing Sylvester Stallone with a $12 million fee for *Over the Top*, a movie about arm-wrestling. (It was certainly over the top for the usual Cannon budget of $4–6 million.) But quality costs, or, at least, stardom does. Yoram declared he was fanatically dedicated to what he called, using a term that was probably rare on his lips, 'cinema'. 'I wake up with cinema, I eat cinema, I sleep with cinema.' Lest this palled on the customers, Cannon's boss stated, 'We did $100 million of business' at Cannes, presumably in films pre-sold to territories. But even Golan added laconically, 'If only it were real money.'

Their quality credentials were underwritten by quotes from their beneficiaries. 'I have nicknamed them Gamma-Globulin. They represent new blood and the antibodies that cinema needs today' – Franco Zeffirelli, director of Cannon's opera release, *Otello*. Golan certainly knew how to sell himself and his plans to those film-makers one wouldn't have imagined to be sympathetic to his ethos. It boiled down to one brutally simple lure: 'Give 'em the money, and world-famous directors will love you.'

Having beefed up their image at Cannes, the cousins returned hotfoot to London in mid May to acquire credibility for their plan for British cinema. Their campaign was brilliant: a compound of zest, reassurance and the sort of boastful chutzpah that can sometimes be mistaken for commitment. They were speaking to an audience deeply worried about the future, who would cling to any promises that offered security.

Golan and Globus (now incorporated as Cannon UK) met with 'the industry' at the Café Royal on 22 May 1986, the very morning picked by BSAC for its emergency meeting on the Cannon takeover. Both cousins excelled themselves before a largely young, activist film-making crowd in the gilt and plush of the Regent Street conference room. Golan showed all his talent for persuading others of what they wished to hear, punctuated by wisecracks, interrupted by his own irrepressible chutzpah, and setting one nice little disabling time bomb under their former adversaries at TESE. 'The circuit will be developed. We will not sell cinemas' (loud applause) 'unless we have to or are forced to . . .' (a sudden hush). 'For every screen that will be sold, two will be opened' (resumed vote of confidence). 'The emphasis is on "make the movie" – to hell with development. We are rich. Our company is now valued at £1.2 billion. We can provide a lot of money for production' ('production': the word rang gold). Then Globus waved the smoking bomb discovered *that very day* among TESE's files: a confidential memo from TESE to its bankers, Standard Charter, committing the film company to sell within the next two years thirty-seven cinemas out of 105 – 'which is a third of their cinemas, and there is not one penny provided in the cash flow for the renovation of the [remaining] cinemas'. This was a stroke of near genius or, at any rate, ruthlessness.

Nat Cohen, the veteran producer who had backed international hits such as *Murder on the Orient Express* and, as head of EMI's wholly owned subsidiary Anglo-EMI, was responsible for the group's entire film production until younger, less cautious hands like Barry Spikings and Michael Deeley pushed him into the background, though not out of the company, knew too much to be laid off. Within hours of the Cannon takeover, Cohen stepped out of his chauffeured town car at the company HQ, where he found himself stopped by the doorman and security guards, who told him he was not to proceed to his office suite, but must hand over all his keys – including those of his now departed company limo – and leave the building. He was so dazed, he scarcely remembered where home was as he did the unusual thing of hailing a taxi.

His files were unlocked and rifled and, it is true, disclosed much embarrassing financial material. Among it was a 21 March 1986 report commissioned from accountants Peat Marwick revealing that TESE management did indeed plan to sell off Elstree and close thirty-eight cinemas (auctioning them for property development). The very plans it was believed Cannon had had in mind were now depicted as having been an impending act of industry betrayal by the anti-Cannon faction.

Alan Sapper, the union boss, raised the question of independent producers. Would Cannon finance them? Golan committed himself to a belief in the auteur system, attacked 'creative accountancy', revealed that the cheques he wrote for Cannon's first hit, *Breakin'*, were models of creative economy'. The producer should own half the movie, but the other half should be financed by others. No big upfront payments for the producer: a points system related to box-office success would replace this. A rather more subdued mood followed this lesson in production economics. Sensing it, Golan fell back on élan, which went down better than 'economy'. 'The way to make a project happen is to excite lovely Mr Otto Plaschkes, who will excite me.' (Relief and laughter.) Suddenly, Golan's nomination of the small, inoffensive, Austrian refugee, Otto Plaschkes, who had been called out of the blue during Cannes, elevated him to the post of Cannon's production *consigliere*.

Plaschkes had produced a small number of small films – *The Bofors Gun, Galileo, The Holcroft Covenant*, only one of which, Bill Forsyth's *Gregory's Girl*, would be familiar to the public (or his fellow producers). He did everything he could, within decency, to justify his new status, coming out with the sort of communiqué quote that has been so long in the cogitation that it has curdled a little: 'I had a fascinating thought the other day that in a way this parallels the 1945 General Election, when the electorate thought Churchill should win because of what he'd done for the country, but they voted Labour because they wanted a change. Screen Entertainment and Cannon was that kind of thing. If an election had been held here, Cannon would have been democratically elected.'

Golan wrenched the meeting back to less philosophical conjectures. 'The director should control the film, not the producer ... so long as he works within the budget. Cannon's share in British Screen is £300,000. I'm ready to increase it to a million.' (Loud applause: this man was a patriot, too, as well as a patron.) 'I'd like to see Rank putting in a million.' (Even louder applause: that company could do with a bit of the Cannon stuff.)

Then someone dropped a tiny fly in this soothing ointment. Would Cannon USA distribute Cannon UK's films? Golan snapped, 'That is a matter for negotiation. To open a film in the US costs $4 million. Last year in America we distributed *Company of Wolves*' – the Palace Pictures production – 'We lost money.' That was true: it was also true, as Angus Finney remarks in his excellent account of the Palace Group's rise and fall, Cannon made 'Neil Jordan's delicately constructed allegorical fantasy appear a Friday the 13th blood-and-guts offering'. It overbooked it, and sold it as a gorefest. The advertising bill was the most horrific part of a catastrophe that took a piddling $4.3 million in North America. 'But we are very happy,' Golan, the new Maecenas, continued, 'we are speaking about another deal with the same producers (Stephen Woolley, Nik Powell).' Nothing came of that, if it was true: the producers were already familiar with mutating creatures in homely garb whose bright-red tongues boded ill for the trusting folk who came to their bedside.

With this, the meeting dissolved into schmoozing, drinks and trying to get Otto Plaschkes excited. Golan and Globus seemed well pleased. With every reason: it had been a pushover. Maybe Cannon were the new Messiahs, not the new marauders.

As usual, a great part of this pep talk was devised to conceal the nemesis that was itself stealing up, like a wolf in the company of some very nasty US stock-market evaluations, on the Cannon Group itself. Great chutzpah attracts great scepticism. American analysts were already in that carping mood, believing the Cannon empire had been leveraged too fast and from too small a base by skilful self-promotion. How would it withstand setbacks that were seen as early and inevitable? 'We are outperforming Paramount, Fox, Disney, MGM, United Artists, Orion and TriStar,' Golan had bragged. But as a *Newsweek* commentator said, 'Cannon's profits for 1985 were $15 million compared with $78 million for Paramount.' The Securities and Exchange Commission was beginning an earnest and ultimately expensive study of Cannon's financial state in the US.

The truth was, Cannon needed all the cash stream it could divert from the cinema chains it owned – or near-owned. For the Office of Fair Trading was still sitting on whether the TESE takeover should be referred to the Monopolies and Mergers Commission – subject to the decision of Paul Channon at the Department of Trade and Industry. If this happened, the deal might be delayed for months, perhaps a year; anyhow any delay would be deleterious, perhaps disastrous, for Cannon's financial structure. Put bluntly, like its vastly more prestigious predecessor Goldcrest (deceased), it risked running out of money. Hence it was racing against time and was ready to give every assurance, call in any possible favour, to build up a picture of its own artistic validity and financial rectitude and, most of all, to quieten the clamour of the individuals or institutions that had opposed its plans for Cannon UK just a few months earlier. Those who knew where Golan and Globus came from, and wouldn't be placated – like David Puttnam – were sidelined, disabled if not quite disarmed, for their access to government was still a danger. (Others, like myself, with a different kind of weapon, they later attempted to ostracise by banning me from reviewing their films.)

It was in this mood of urgency that Cannon executives Barry Jenkins (managing director, Cannon UK), Michael Kagan (his deputy) and Maraca Pinto (financial director) met with BSAC on 26 June 1986, to put roughly the same case as their bosses had done the month before to the 'working' producers – i.e. likely soon to be out of work. The Cannon triumvirate assured BSAC, 'The studios would definitely be retained.' Cannon would finance three British films at £1 million each (total cost £1.7 million, allowing for distribution costs) employing first-time British talents. It would establish an all-industry fund to swell the finances available for home production. All of Cannon's British films would be shown in Cannon's US cinemas. It would close some cinemas that were too close to its rivals' successful theatres. It would build a seventeen-screen multiplex in Windmill Street, off Piccadilly Circus. Not one of these commitments was ever to be fulfilled. But the Cannon Three made a strong pitch. The result: BSAC resolved that 'Cannon's drive and energy should be welcomed and the council should recommend against referral to the Monopolies and Mergers Commission'. That is what the Cannon delegates had come to hear and it must have gratified them to hear it; what they thought was a lion's den had turned out to be a sheep pen.

The June issue of *AIP*, the independent producers' magazine, was the top note in this symphony of relief and promise that Cannon was orchestrating so well. 'Cannon and the Indies,' ran the leading article, 'Good to Go-Go.' AIP wrote to Golan and Globus to welcome the TESE purchase, 'and its prospective benefits for the British industry' and, of course, AIP members with satellite deals with TESE that Cannon had undertaken to honour.

Finally, on 13 August 1986, the Chinese butterfly fluttered its wings as Paul Channon made his determination over the matter of a Mono-polies and Mergers Commission referral, which Cannon's three execu-tives had reiterated 'would be extremely detrimental to the industry'. The Trade and Industry Secretary gave it the go-ahead. In doing so, he went totally against the advice given him by the Office of Fair Trading – only the second time in two years that OFT advice had been rejected. Worried at Cannon controlling 40 per cent of all cinema screens in the UK, it made a strong referral recommendation to Monopolies and Mergers. But Channon's department was obdurate. A merger reference, it said, would still not allow the Commission to consider the more general problem of alignment (or block booking of films with favoured distributors) 'which is a major anti-competitive force in the film indus-try'. Because one reform could not be effected by a referral, the pro-tection of the main asset should be neglected, or, to put it even more simply, because the family silver might tarnish, it is not worth locking the window against thieves. In a world of chaos, this had an attractive inverted logic. But what made it all the more bitter was the information accompanying the Channon ukase that the anti-Cannon case had carried more weight with Sir Gordon Borrie than most of us had suspected at the time. Had a referral been made, and due diligence done by M & M lawyers, as would certainly have been the sequel in the US, either the true state of Cannon's finances would have been disclosed, or else the crisis would have revealed it. Due diligence, though, is the weakest point in the procedures of British government departments: they are not equipped for the investigatory techniques, personal as well as formal, required to test veracity, character or motive.

Anyhow, it was too late. The stupidest act of folly in film industry–government relations had been done: virtually half the British film industry had been allowed to be sold to a pair of foreigners who, even as Channon nodded them through, were about to hit the economic crisis that led to their collapse less than three years later. By which time the film industry (as we knew it) had been irretrievably broken up, disseminated and debilitated – never again to stand a chance of being economically sustainable or independent of Hollywood domination.

Few had come out of it well. AIP had turned into a pussy-cat, eager for the cream (which was never to come). BSAC had proved a toothless tiger, fearing to attack. As if to underline BSAC's uselessness, Geoffrey Pattie, Minister for Industry and Information Technology, into whose brief films fell, gave BSAC notice to quit the Department of Trade and Industry premises after its last meeting there on 24 July 1986. We were being thrown out without a penny. Thereafter, we would have no meeting place, no secretariat, no office premises. Goodbye and good luck. 'Our future is obscure,' Lord Wilson noted lamely in reply. The ex-Prime Minister and Lady Falkender undertook to tramp the corridors of Westminster and beg for shelter, occasionally, in a committee room and if some nice girl down from Oxford or Cambridge could be found to take notes and look charming, too, maybe this assembly of leading film industry advisers wouldn't yet give up the ghost. No one, however, should expect coffee.

For one man, though, the future suddenly looked surprisingly bright. Almost as if kindly gods were listening, appalled at the wound suffered by the boy who had once been their darling, David Puttnam, now the 'outsider', mocked by Cannon and even shunned by those who hoped for Cannon's favour if they did so, was elevated out of this despair, so suddenly as to leave many observers blinking and wondering how the trick had been accomplished, and translated to another power of command, in another continent and another film industry. In mid June 1986 it was announced that Puttnam was to become chairman and chief executive officer of Columbia Pictures, the first Brit to run a Hollywood studio. His accidental destiny was thus settled by the Chinese butterfly's 'chaotic' influence on events. It came as a total surprise to him.

In the nine months since his election as president of the Society for the Protection of Rural England, he had, even more recently, been appointed Visiting Industrial Professor at Bristol University – both symptoms of his disillusionment with film-making. But now these posts would have to be combined with that of one of the five or six most powerful executives in Hollywood. Life indeed was 'chaotic', though a *Guardian* leading article of 30 July 1986 saw a certain divine unity: 'Columbia's view of him as a "prof" willing to shuttle across the Atlantic to stop bulldozers demolishing badger setts has ... still to emerge.' He departed for Hollywood, with Patsy his wife, at the end of June, elated, confused but grateful for a reason to leave the stage after the audience had walked out on his act. As Patsy Puttnam said she had put it to him, 'Do you want to look back at fifty-five, with another three or four movies behind you and wonder what it would have been like to head a studio?' No, he certainly didn't; and with Cannon in possession of half the industry and Goldcrest out of commission, it was 'Hail, Columbia'. His conviction was probably weaker than he was prepared to disclose, but Puttnam's talent has always been to convince others that what he sees is best for them. It required only a gentle push (from wife and friends) to convince him that what they saw as best for him was right – or could be made so.

My own telemessage to him, on hearing the news on 19 June, probably did nothing to resolve his thoughts or dissuade him from pursuing this escape route. 'Dear David,' I wrote. 'Are you stark staring raving mad or just out of your senses? Those who head the majors in Hollywood make deals not films. Finishing up in a dollar-lined dead end is not the fate for you. Our most exciting – and certainly fighting – times are just beginning. Stay here and say "Hell" to Columbia.'

With the industry in turmoil for most of 1986, the effect on independent producers was predictable: disorganised, yet not demoralised. It meant everyone had a more bitter fight to get their share of funding.

AIP's March Newsletter: 'Sectional interests are pitted with increasing ferocity against one another because the basic economics of the feature film business have broken down, and there just isn't enough of a live-lihood to go round any more,' wrote Simon Perry, adding in what became a famous phrase, 'It took only one big-league picture to go 20 per cent over budget to make [Goldcrest] broke beyond their wildest dreams.' He concluded, 'Almost any film that gets made is obliged to bear a disproportionate responsibility for all the others that might or might not.'

This was soon cruelly confirmed – yet again. *Revolution* had not been absolutely the last hope of Goldcrest: still to open in 1986 were *The Mission* and *Absolute Beginners*. Julien Temple's film was not quite so clearly a last-ditch Goldcrest hope: though Goldcrest invested in it, so did Virgin Films. Powell and Woolley, Palace Pictures co-chiefs, who had produced it, represented the Wardour Street culture clash, seeking to project a credible image of young iconoclasts going against the Establishment: commune film-makers as against corporate film-makers, innovators instead of traditionalists. Palace had taken the mickey out of Goldcrest (as its bosses would say) and hoped to outlast the swollen boardroom of banker film-makers. *Revolution* granted their wish sooner than they thought.

The irony was, their own 'event' film, *Absolute Beginners*, was begin-ning to look like Goldcrest's last, slender lifeline of confidence, if not ready cash. Palace had topped up its budget with £500,000 of its own money: at this stage, despite their success – at least in the UK – with *The Company of Wolves*, Palace still saw itself as mainly a video and film distribution basis. With Julien Temple's film, which exceeded its budget by £4.6 million, Palace were playing mainly with other people's stakes. As noted, the film went ruinously, irretrievably out of control and, accordingly, pre-release coverage upped the level of publicity necessary to validate it as a film and re-establish the makers' credibility as producers. 'It had to be over-large, over-indulgent to live up to its advance repu-tation,' wrote critic Kim Newman. Energy alone was not enough: it was absolutely all over the place, wasteful of its effects and huge sets, dazzling but confused, with the restlessness of an extended Pop video, not the rhythm of a movie musical. It distracted instead of concentrating. It did not look designed so much as cluttered. Too often one was simply aware of the endless movement, but had a hard time picking out the actual dancing. Maybe if it hadn't had to live down the absurd build-up, it would have seemed less of an anticlimax, but it could never have been a better film.

Even as a social record of youth coming of age in 1950s London, its various premisses were generationally at fault. It asserted for its phantasmagoria of youth that '1958 was the last year of the teenage dream'. In fact, teenage dreamers swiftly recovered from the Notting Hill race riots that climax it and were supposed to be an explosion in reality, and went on through the Sixties to participate in group fantasies of Swinging London far and away beyond anything their dreamy heads could have fantasised in 1958.

It was supposed to be about Soho's youthful 'spring awakening' in the immediate post-Suez period, but no relevant period resonance was caught by the Cinemascope cameras, no matter which side of a studio-built Wardour Street they were on. (One of the biggest extravagances, due to inexperience, had been to build *both* sides of that street, instead of simply re-dressing the one side. The teenage 'blitz babies' in the film were just reinterpreted the way 1980s punks like Woolley and Temple might imagine them. The 1959 musical, *Expresso Bongo*, was more authentic in every way.

In retrospect, it will probably have gained a museum value for the sight of Pop stars of the 1980s who played the roles: Eddie O'Connell, as the teenage paparazzo whose feet touch Soho like a fallen angel with a flash gun, certainly danced around, but he had little else going for him save ubiquitousness. Patsy Kensit, as his girlfriend Crepe Suzette; James Fox as a Mayfair fashion czar with smarmy charm in league with a Peter Rachmanite shark landlord (Johnny Shannon) to redevelop 'Little Napoli's' black ghetto for middle-class high-rises: today, they project the mustiness of certain neighbourhoods that appeals to social archaeologists. Likewise, the talent impresario Harry Charms (Lionel Blair), Vendice the 'First Mid-Atlantic Man' (David Bowie), the New Mosley Blackshirt (Stephen Berkoff). Mandy Rice-Davies, one of the call-girls in the political scandal of 1963 that toppled the Macmillan government, played the hero's mum. In view of her own history, she became the only character in the film with less speculative, better anchored connections; this tiny time-warp effect emitted a frisson of cynical pleasure. For a film climaxed by the first black rioting, there were extraordinarily few blacks in name roles: an exception, Tony Hippolyte as a jazzman called Cool was one of the few characters who breathed drama as naturally as he blew riffs.

The film had the LP and the Double Album preparing the way for its release. All it proved was that movie musicals have to be more than the sum of their tracks on the wax. It took a respectable 'curiosity' £1.8 million in Britain despite an almost totally hostile press; and did somewhat better than expected overseas. But too little to save Goldcrest who, as Woolley said sulkily, 'used us as whipping boys for their problems'. It has never been re-released in Britain – perhaps, with retinal phenomena like IMAX now available, it would find its outsize frame?

Woolley, reflecting after the event on the cost of his steep learning curve as producer on an out-of-control production, was already re-editing it in his mind: 'If we had made it the story of two American teenagers in London in the early 1950s and used bands like Culture Club and Bruce Springsteen, and not tried to cram in too much about Britain at that period but concentrated on the love interest, it would have been much more successful [in the US] because it would have been more accessible.' Its failure, according to Woolley, 'did threaten the credibility of the company'. Worse: it left its owners' self-esteem badly wounded.

Even before it opened, it was obviously not going to change the Establishment's view of them as cultural barrow boys. So *Mona Lisa*, when it was put into production in October 1985, backed by Denis O'Brien–George Harrison's HandMade Films, well before the final bills for *Absolute Beginners* arrived, had a straitjacket budget of £2 million tops. *Mona Lisa* was Palace's graduation piece: it brought acclaim and profit. It defined Neil Jordan's concern with the treacherous appearance of things: the flicker of hell when a door is opened into an unexpected room; the calvary of missable landmarks, until the traveller realises the unmistakable shape of a crucifixion awaiting him. *Angel*, *Mona Lisa* and films to come like *The Crying Game* and *The Butcher Boy* all possess this moment of epiphany: the judgement call has been fatally flawed.

Bob Hoskins (in a role once offered to Connery, whose agent asked too much), out of prison after a long stretch, finds all changed for the worst. He used to put the frighteners on folk, like the Krays: now the gang's payback job is couriering video porn, being paged by a pocket 'bleeper' – no job for an ordinary decent criminal. Then, ultimate humiliation, he's ordered to squire a tart (Cathy Tyson) about town, night and day: she, a call-girl; he, her minder – a bleedin' affront to self-esteem. Worst of all, she's *black*. Set in a London not to be found in any *A to Z* street directory but, like Jordan's fugitive in *Angel* travelling across country deeper and deeper into Northern Ireland's heart of darkness, the spiritual nature of the journey takes this very Irish (if lapsed) Catholic director to where his faith provides him with the comfort of a tortured conscience.

David Leland, shortly to make his own striking comic debut with *Wish You Were Here*, co-authored the screenplay and contributed some of its most brutal, hard-bitten elements; but when Hoskins's stubby hard man undertakes the rescue of a call-girl friend of Tyson's from the local vice baron (Michael Caine, rendering the story the same callous service as John Osborne did in *his* iconic gangster drama *Get Carter*), his knight errantry pursued down mean streets of carnal lust provide *Mona Lisa* with its deceptive romanticism. It turns into a fool's errand of mercy, because Hoskins reads the signs wrongly and, betrayed by the eponymous demon woman whose smile recalls the tricky one playing around the lips of her painted original, he discovers that he, yesterday's man, has been made the fall guy for today's corruption.

Few films of the 1980s seem extracted from the social fabric as tellingly as those of the 1960s. *Mona Lisa* was an exception: its contemporary amorality deepened with Roger Pratt's photography that shaded its events into a hellish London, where the whores lined up at King's Cross Station resembled fluorescent Furies.

Hoskins shared the 'Best Actor' prize at Cannes in 1986; and there, too, Puttnam enjoyed what was to be his 'going away' present when *The Mission* won the Palme d'or over Tarkovsky's *The Sacrifice*. As in *Chariots of Fire*, it was a film about conscience versus obedience. Set in eighteenth-century South America, where the Spanish and Portuguese traders who had followed the Jesuit missionaries were now finding their profits being dented by the latter's success in socialising the Indians, and converting them and setting up profit-sharing communes as well as congregations, the film opposes the mercenary sword (Robert De Niro) against the renegade cassock (Jeremy Irons), and pits Man against an impressively photographed, though uninvolving, Nature. It was didactic, without being particularly illuminating: the battle for minds and philosophies, crystallised with schoolmasterly pedanticism by Robert Bolt's dialogue, went largely by default in the film's strained efforts to win the battle for its own god, the box office. It needed Werner Herzog or, at least, David Lean: it got Roland Joffé.

The one character who escaped formulaic compression was Ray McAnally's cardinal who saw things with the pragmatism of a prelate committed first and always to his own church; but, bookending the film – a device added after preview audiences failed to understand the story – he remained a passive figure – though that was probably preferable to the Anglo-Saxon sensitivity of Irons's Jesuit pacifist-turned-warrior and the all-American sweatiness of De Niro's slave trader-turned-freedom fighter.

Curiously, this was the film that finally tipped Coca-Cola, owners of Columbia Pictures, to pick Puttnam as their studio's production chief. The soft-drinks company had deep-rooted South American connections. The Jesuit Order had left its mark, both spiritual and physical, on a couple of its influential executives in their impressionable schooldays. In *The Mission* (and Puttnam), their peripheral vision saw (or thought it saw) the means of reconciling a profitability without losing the messianic zeal for empire building.

By midsummer 1986, therefore, Puttnam was bound for his own mission in America; Cannon was, with some desperation, seeking to consolidate its holdings in what had been roughly half Britain's vertically integrated film industry; and ... oh yes, British Film Year drew to a close marked by three peculiarly cantankerous – but not inappropriate – Thames TV programmes on indigenous cinema directed by Richard Attenborough (amiable, complacent, actorish), Lindsay Anderson (chastising, sarcastic, dismissive) and Alan Parker (resentful, cartoonish, splenetic). Parker's programme, at ninety minutes a good half-hour longer than the others, was entitled *The Turnip Head's Guide to the Cinema* and, despite its humour, could not conceal its maker's fretful animosity against what he perceived to be a national cinema that practised aesthetic exclusion against the likes of him and his ad-market origins. His film still raises a smile, though a sour one. Less tolerantly, it memorialises one of the sharpest jibes by one film-maker at the expense of another: 'Happily, an Oscar is something Derek Jarman will never have to worry about.' The speaker was David Puttnam. It never occurred to him that Jarman would have displayed a fine contempt for those who *did* worry about such things as Oscars.

4

The Coca-Cola Kid

David Puttnam announced he was leaving the job as chairman and chief executive officer of Columbia Pictures almost as soon as he arrived in Los Angeles to take it up in September 1986. Why he limited his contract to three years only – and then announced the fact – remains a minor mystery. Later, on leaving the job, either of his own volition or because he was fired – another, somewhat larger, mystery – he explained, 'For the sake of my dignity, I had to time-cap it ... I was saying, "You can't fire me, I'm already leaving." ' Alan Parker surmised that his own partner hated himself for going back to a place which, on his first visit and brief stay as president of Casablanca Films, he had found the antithesis of everything he set a value on. 'He didn't like himself for the job he was doing. The only way he could live with it was to come at it in a combative way.'

That Puttnam would scarcely stay the term necessary to see any films he greenlighted into production and out on release was the first, most fatal, of the bad moves he made. 'David instantly made his private agenda his public agenda,' was how Francis (Fay) Vincent, the Coca-Cola executive who had headhunted him for the job, put it. Tina Brown, then the most influential journalist in America as editor of *Vanity Fair*, with access to all the principals who later opened up to her with their version of events, sought a deeper reason – in Puttnam's own psyche. He had two sides to his nature, she surmised in a lengthy investigative article, well researched and supported by (for once) attributed quotes from the Hollywood Establishment, that appeared in April 1985, about six months after Puttnam's first and only year's tenure at Columbia. The twin heroes of *Chariots of Fire*, Brown said, expressed the two sides of Puttnam's divided self. There was Abrahams, the Jewish outsider in the Cambridge Establishment, 'professional, a passionate meritocrat flawed by his fierce desire for glory ... very much a Puttnam figure', opposed to anti-Semitism and elitism of all kinds. And there was Liddell, his rival in the 1924 Olympics: 'the pure conscience-driven hero who believes his talent is God-given and cannot break his principles [in order] to run on the Sabbath. He is running for God.' Brown recalled the nine Oscars won by *Chariots of Fire*: 'The push of Abrahams gives [Puttnam] the rewards of Liddell.'

Fanciful though this sounds, I believe there is truth in it. Puttnam had arrived in Hollywood after the debacle at Goldcrest and a bruising (and losing) battle against Cannon. Defining himself and his goals was his priority; his mood made him self-righteously almost belligerent when Coca-Cola offered the job to him. He felt he could ask for anything and did so, bringing his wife Patsy with him when he flew to Atlanta, Georgia, Coca-Cola's headquarters, to see Roberto Goizueta, the corporation president, and Fay Vincent. Patsy was his accompanying 'conscience'. He did not want it to be said later, by her or anyone else, that he had deceived himself. He was unduly exacting, whereas anyone else offered the kingdom of Columbia would have been a humble supplicant or, at least, temporiser. He read the two executives his 'mission statement', the crucial part of which announced that 'the medium is too powerful and too important an influence on the way we live, the way we see ourselves, to be left solely to the tyranny of the box office or reduced to the sum of the lowest common denominator of public taste'.

It did not strike him that Coca-Cola functioned in just this way and, as Alan Parker said later, the trust and idealism Puttnam placed in the corporation that was about to hire him was odd, considering its product was popularly supposed to rot kids' teeth the world over. By coincidence, though, he found peculiarly receptive listeners. Goizueta, born in Cuba, was a devout Roman Catholic; so was Fay Vincent. At one time he had considered making the priesthood his vocation. Instead, Vincent went into business and came to Coca-Cola from the Securities and Exchange Commission to run Columbia when Herbert Allen, a Wall Street financier with a large stake in the studio, sold it to Coca-Cola for $750 million. Unknown to these two was Puttnam's own spiritual debt to the Jesuit Order when he had turned to a priest, Father Jack Mahonia, to seek comfort for the disagreeable and unexpected reaction of watching the torture scenes in *Midnight Express*, relishing the sadism and then making Puttnam feel guilty for not anticipating that his film could pander to the basest instincts of the very audiences he wanted to elevate by its story. The priest told him he could make contrition by using his skills to produce movies that engaged the moral sympathies of audiences.

Puttnam's last film, *The Mission*, with its pro-Jesuit subtext, appealed to the heads of a US corporation with roots in their Jesuit upbringing; and lest their business took priority over their faith, Puttnam's plans for Columbia were also reassuring. In brief, he proposed to 'internationalise' the studio, mixing its US-slanted output of films with movies whose stories, stars, directors and writers would reflect the humanist side of European picture entertainment. Coca-Cola was a global business, two thirds of its sales were overseas: a move to make movies that would tap the box office of countries where the liquid product circulated was welcomed. Puttnam had always hankered after 'the way it was' when films by Zinnemann, Capra, Kazan and others had a humanist reach, a moral core and a democratic impact. The Coke executives saw their own product in much the same light; they expressed faith in Puttnam's vision, particularly when he grounded it in his undertaking to run Columbia cost-effectively, bring down production costs, cut out studio waste and thus fortify Coca-Cola's stock-market rating, even then vulnerable to the poor run of box-office failures under Puttnam's predecessor at Columbia.

Patsy Puttnam later recounted how the meeting had ended. 'Coke told him, "We only understand excellence, we want this to be the best film company in the world." David ... said, "I know these are people who speak the same language as I do. I believe what they say." ' And he took the job. Patsy Puttnam later recalled his adding, ' "Of course, I may look ridiculous in two years for doing so." ' Actually, it took him only half that time.

His tenure, though short-lived, is valuable, for it illustrated what actually would be the effect of a European producer given plenipotentiary powers over a Hollywood studio. Yet this is not the heart of the matter. Puttnam's failure at Columbia wasn't simply a culture clash: it was more radical. It was a clash of the different aspects of Jewry. It showed what happened when the European Jew, restlessly intelligent and morally committed to bettering and improving the lot and aspirations of his fellow men, met head on the Hollywood Jew, pragmatic and entrenched in material success and the profits derived from exploiting human desires.

I went to see Puttnam in the early summer of 1987. He had turned down the usual appurtenances of the job. Not for him the BMW or Mercedes, a Beverly Hills home and a table at Spago, The Bistro or some other 'in' place. He wore corduroys and a cardigan; lived in a rented

house that Greta Garbo had maintained in an unfashionable area because
it was next door to her dietary guru and platonic companion Gaylord
Hauser; he drove an Audi; and we ate at some small place in the Valley.
On his office wall hung several conscience-pricking mementoes of the
past: a letter from Columbia turning down *Chariots of Fire* as having 'no
validity at all'; a framed quote by Darryl F. Zanuck: 'Renoir's got a lot
of talent. But he's not one of us'; and a framed letter from Harvard,
offering him a Kennedy Scholarship. All of which, while perfectly
sincere, announced his intention to travel his own austere road in a
community he saw as riddled with greed, vanity and false values. He
tried to shrink the power he possessed, at least in its outward mani-
festations, just as he succeeded in shrinking the size of some of the
5,000-odd scripts submitted to Columbia during his tenure, reducing
their bulk to the dimensions of a paperback book that he could stuff in
his pocket and take out any time to read. An economy that was to prove
very short-lived once he had gone. By then he had made his mistakes
and unfortunately they were not behind him but threatening to overtake
any success that looked on the way from the production roster he
assembled with exemplary speed.

Speed was vital, because he found Columbia with next to no films
ready to go, and some – like the extravagantly budgeted $40 million
Ishtar, with Dustin Hoffman and Warren Beatty, which was to turn out
a costly disaster, and *Leonard: Part Six*, starring Bill Cosby, a Coca-Cola
shareholder and spokesman, which was to play a crucial role in Puttnam's
loss of power – that he wished he could disown or cancel. He had a
$350 million a year budget to spend: $175 million on production; $100
million on marketing; $75 million on overheads. Finding he needed
total control over market and distribution, about which his contract was
alarmingly vague, Puttnam turned to Ray Stark, one of Hollywood's
most powerful producers with close links of money and influence to
Columbia; Stark, with one call to Coca-Cola, got Puttnam what he
wanted; but then one of the oldest Hollywood rules – 'a favour sought
is a favour owed' – came into play. Such trading was alien to Puttnam's
way of operating: he did not do business on the basis of personal
obligations, which he felt put him at a moral disadvantage. 'If you do
me a favour, I will go out of my way not ever to be doing you a
favour back,' Puttnam was quoted as saying, though one feels he couched
it less obdurately. 'If I do, I have to assume that what you did for me was
something other than a favour – it was a deal.' But Hollywood was –

and is – a town that lives by trade-offs among its powerful and privileged; Puttnam signalled he was not going to play that game. A bad start.

Within months, he was fulfilling his brief – cutting the cost of film-making from the 1995 average of $14.5 million to $10.7 million – and incurring contumely for such impertinence among his 'enemies', the top-ranking (and paid) stars and their agents. 'I want to make films for the rest of the world with people who are genuinely unknown,' he said – a text no Hollywood producer preached, at least from an open pulpit. And Puttnam's corner office in Columbia was very 'open', so that the so-called 'little people' in the studio gave him their loyalty (as well as mid-ranking independent producers who had everything to gain by his reductions in scale, cost and potential patronage).

It was the name-above-the-title stars who took offence. Puttnam referred to them collectively as 'thinking they're doing the studio a favour by allowing us to sign their cheques' and included in the constellation those directors 'who talk art while demanding national-debt salaries'. Such plain speaking was akin to undeclared war: the enemy did not need to be named, they knew who they were.

Knowing he could do nothing about *Ishtar*, Puttnam obeyed the instinct that had served him well throughout his career when calamities threatened – he kept well away from it. But one chance remark he made – uttered as an aside, some said, while others claimed diplomatically not to have heard it at all – caused him damage that no limitation exercise short of humblest apologies and a pilgrimage on his knees to Bill Murray's home could have settled. At a British Chamber of Commerce luncheon in Hollywood, early in 1997, he lauded Robert Redford as an example of a megastar who reinvested his talent and wealth in the industry, through his Sundance Institute; and he added, as some accounts had it, 'You don't see people – for example Bill Murray – putting back any dollars made from *Ghostbusters*.' A fatal quip. *Ghostbusters* was a Columbia hit (and the pre-Puttnam studio hoped it would spawn a sequel, maybe a franchise) while Murray himself was a heavy Coca-Cola stockholder, a buddy of Ray Stark and a golfing pal of Coca-Cola's chief executive, Donald Keough.

These people's well-based anger at the possibility of Murray 'walking', going over to Warner Bros and making *Ghostbusters II* for that studio, was increased by Puttnam's decision to treat his studio job as a three-year stopover. As a 'transient', they felt, he had no right to prejudice long-standing, hard-won personal relationships with the gold-card-carrying stars in the studio's roster. In short, he was burning bridges that his successors would have needed. But again it was Puttnam's morality, coupled with the frugality and sacrifice that had shaped his British career, at least in its early formative stages, which prevailed against the big spenders of Hollywood.

Ray Stark later went on record – an almost unheard-of act by this master of cloak-and-dagger diplomacy – as saying, 'Puttnam should have kept his mind open and his mouth shut.' This was tantamount to a death sentence, though even Stark and his powerful cronies were not yet able to line up the firing squad. It would not be long, however. On arrival at Columbia, Puttnam discovered the studio had 122 projects 'in development', the costliest and riskiest stage of film-making; these he quickly slashed to sixty-five and succeeded in reducing the 13,000 scrips submitted each month on average down to 150. But he desperately needed 'product' that was ready to go and, again following past form, he turned to friends whom he could trust not to exceed the film's cost and deliver on time: in many cases these were incoming British talents, with some of whom he had already worked.

He tapped David Picker, an American executive and long-time Londoner, who had succeeded George 'Bud' Ornstein at United Artists, where he enticed Sean Connery back into his Bond outfit for *Diamonds Are Forever* and later, at Paramount, greenlighted Puttnam's production of Ridley Scott's directorial debut, *The Duellists*. Picker knew the Hollywood–Pinewood nexus and, though American, Puttnam could say of him that he was 'one of us' and could protect his boss's back. Others he took aboard were Lynda Myles, as his European development and production chief, and Duncan Clarke, as his distribution and marketing supremo, and as financial adviser Steve Norris, who had been one of those closest to him at the old Goldcrest.

Other Brits with production deals set by Puttnam included Bill Forsyth (*Sylvie's Ark*, a 'warm and whimsical comedy'); Ridley Scott (the Tom Berenger thriller, *Someone to Watch Over Me*); Brian Gilbert (*Vice Versa*, based on F. Anstey's Edwardian comedy); Sandy Lieberson and Pat O'Connor (*Stars and Bars*, with Daniel Day-Lewis); Jeremy Thomas and Bernardo Bertolucci (*The Last Emperor*); John Boorman (*Hope and Glory*, a wartime episode of a London childhood). Jack Rosenthal was writing *Gabriela*, a romantic comedy, and Jon Amiel was submitting ideas. Rumour had it that Puttnam pleaded with Alan Parker to make a film at Columbia. Parker allegedly demurred: he may not have wished to jeopardise his own well-established Hollywood career and relationships. The subsequent coolness between the two former partners in *Midnight Express* and *Bugsy Malone* proved long lasting. Very soon, the sheer number of Puttnam's countrymen got the studio nicknamed 'British Columbia'. Which didn't help, by making it sound an alien outpost, in possession of gold that old Hollywood hands, wrongly or rightly, considered part of their national treasury.

Most of Puttnam's products were mainstream entertainment, eclectic and, if not exactly Eurocentric, then mid-Atlantic in appeal. In announcing them, he prudently omitted the news that he was developing films with European 'art-house' directors like Emir Kusturica, Istvan Szabo and Doris Durrie. Why invite trouble? But trouble was there and gathering quickly around him. Not all, but many of the films he was making were little different from small-scale British movies. As 'starters', they would do: but a year went by before any of them was ready for release – *Someone to Watch Over Me* was to be the first – and the time Puttnam had allowed himself 'to be a suit' before he returned (he hoped) to being a working producer, would scarcely allow him to order a second round of more ambitious projects.

His reference to Bill Murray – true or not – dogged him: so much so that he suspected one or two of the 'elder statesmen' his actions had affronted were deliberately pursuing a hate campaign against him, planting embarrassing stories in the papers, even employing a private investigator to find any 'dirt' on him. None, of course, existed; his twenty-five-year-old marriage to Patsy ensured that; his workaholic temperament, his six-and-a-half-days-a-week commitment to the job, left him no time to 'play around'. Puttnam's puritan clothes protected him as well as a flak jacket.

Rather than meet Bill Cosby, Coca-Cola's spokesman, head on over the film *Leonard: Part 6*, Puttnam assigned his own man, the British producer Alan Marshall, a rough, rebarbative character, to co-produce the movie. Cosby took this ill: an unfriendly act. As if digging in his heels, Cosby made demands that, calculated or not, asserted his own status and more: he insisted on blacks on the crew. Thus, as Tina Brown noted, 'racial nepotism' collided with Puttnam's 'colonial nepotism': Marshall's work was not made easier in this crossfire.

Puttnam's manner, though familiar to most of us in Britain, still grated on many in the Hollywood community. The conviction with which he spoke of his 'mission', indeed his tone of voice, quick-tongued, slow-pitched, earnest and self-convinced, sent out a message of moral right-eousness to people who felt more at ease receiving (and transmitting) standard Hollywood signals of duplicity and even rascality. A moral man in this town was like a preacher in a bar room. 'How naive I was!' he would later comment. 'Breathtakingly naive! ... When you are in love with making movies, you don't brush up against the realities of the job.'

Those realities were much more apparent to the board members and executives of Coca-Cola, no longer spellbound by Puttnam's messianic eloquence, but looking for bottom-line results and hearing far too many anti-Puttnam rumours and alarums about profitability being sounded by his enemies who were, in some cases, their own major shareholders. Puttnam had been promised complete autonomy, not needing to 'refer upwards' any project costing under £30 million – none such was on his production slate. Martin Ransohoff, a successful mainline producer whose films included *Topkapi*, *The Cincinnati Kid* and *Silver Streak*, had had his updated remake of *The Front Page*, relocated in the broadcasting industry, rejected by Puttnam, who favoured remakes even less than sequels. He took the project to a Coca-Cola executive, Richard Gallop, who obliged by greenlighting it for production by Tri-Star Motion Pictures, a company in which Coca-Cola owned a third of the stock. This was perilously close to second-guessing Puttnam. But if it registered with him, he ignored its warning – distant and unclear. He had Goizueta's promise of autonomy, hadn't he?

Puttnam had greenlighted sixteen movies when the blow fell – with awesome unexpectedness. So much so that David Puttnam first heard of it in a dawn call on 31 August 1987 from his lawyer in New York, who had read it in the *New York Times*, then turned to the *Los Angeles Times* which his paper boy delivered an hour or so later to read the (still small) print about the deal that Coca-Cola had done behind his back on 29 August, just two days earlier. Victor Kaufman, chairman and chief executive officer of Tri-Star, had been called to Atlanta and, in the same executive office where Puttnam had been offered the principality of Columbia, Kaufman was offered an even bigger share of the Coca-Cola movie kingdom. Tri-Star, he was told, would be taking over Columbia: the new entity would be called Columbia Pictures Entertainment. Would Kaufman accept the position of president and chief executive officer, with David Puttnam, head of Columbia, reporting to him?

The reason for this total volte face on Coca-Cola's part was plain to those who studied not movies but the movement of stock-market prices and company balance sheets. Coca-Cola had reported a loss for the second quarter of 1987 in its film-making sector after setting aside $25 million as a reserve to cover losses on *Ishtar*. 'Columbia Pictures' soft performance has been the albatross round Coca-Cola's share price,' Jim Robbins commented meaningfully in *Variety*.

The entertainment writer Aaron Latham later analysed Coca-Cola's strategy, and its technique and corporate policy. By such a wave of the wand, Coca-Cola could make all the share-depressing debts incurred by movie-making disappear off its soft-drinks balance sheet. It had worked the same trick a year or so earlier with its bottling companies, selling all of them to Coca-Cola Enterprises. The parent company, Coca-Cola, then sold 51 per cent of the stock to the public, retaining only 49 per cent, which carried no obligation to include its bottling plants on its books. In 1987, it now proposed to sell all its entertainment companies (Columbia Pictures, Embassy Communications and Merv Griffin Enterprises) to Tri-Star. It would be paid in Tri-Star stock, subsequently distributed to its stockholders, retaining (again) 49 per cent and being freed of the requirement to carry the entertainment companies' debts on Coca-Cola's balance sheet. Such fiscal restructuring would rid Coca-Cola of its debt – and also of Puttnam. It is unlikely that he was the reason for it: he was important but not *that* important. Maintaining Coca-Cola's share value and retaining its shareholders' confidence was vital – it had just suffered a severe and humiliating setback (for it) with the failure of its New Coke to claim any significant share of the soft-drinks market.

The collateral price to be paid for this manoeuvre was David Puttnam's job: he 'disappeared with the red ink'. Probably it was a human price Coca-Cola by now thought worth paying. As Fay Vincent later expressed it, with the resignation of a man who was shifted abruptly from overseeing a glamorous entertainment entity to overseeing bottling plants, 'When matters of faith conflict with matters of finance, finance always wins.' On 1 September Puttnam commented ruefully on being relegated to number two in the combined entity, 'The difficulty at present is not knowing whether [Victor Kaufman, now president and chief executive officer of Columbia Pictures Entertainment] is going to live with my contract guaranteeing me complete autonomy.' There really was no difficulty. Kaufman's Tri-Star had had a huge hit with *Rambo: First Blood, Part II*. Puttnam, before taking up his Columbia appointment, had been

asked which kind of films he would *not* be making. He had answered
'*Rambo*'. Kaufman believed in 'big' pictures; in stars and 'relationships';
and in the Hollywood 'community': in everything Puttnam had poured
scorn on or jeopardised. Richard Attenborough, one of those who
understood both Puttnam and studio power, said, 'Instead of having
only to deal with the people at Coke, David now had an in-house boss.
Not only does one need autonomy in Hollywood, but one has to be
seen to have it, too.'

At a meeting with Goizueta on 3 September Puttnam was apparently
given an assurance that he would remain in charge at the studios; a date,
12 October, was fixed for these assurances to be translated into money –
the budget for his second tranche of films. David Puttnam gamely clung
to office, as concerned for the fate of others – those people he had
brought from Britain – as his own. But one sensed lawyers at work on
the settlement.

His decision to go was made public, quite dramatically, on 16 September, in front of nearly 200 studio employees at one of the monthly
seminars, called 'The Reel Truth', which Puttnam had initiated as an
earnest of his 'open doors' policy. Ridley Scott's *Someone to Watch Over
Me* – in the event, an ironic title – had been screened, to general
enthusiasm; then Puttnam rose, standing to one side before a small
lectern, and announced he was leaving. There was an exhalation of
surprise, cries of 'Oh, no!' and, soon, even tears; for his short-lived reign
had won him plenty of adherents among the lower ranks who, over the
years, had seen the studio treated (as Puttnam himself had put it) 'a bit
like Poland: an awful lot of people over the years have felt they owned
it, and they get knocked backwards and forwards and sideways by
continuously invading forces'. Puttnam's envoi from the platform had
his characteristic style, picturesque and highly charged, in the manner
that very soon would be termed 'soundbites'. 'To some, I came to
whisper at dragons and tilt at windmills. But the truth is I am neither
Saint George nor Don Quixote. I am just a European motion-picture
producer who crossed the Atlantic to ask a few questions and possibly
seek a different way forward.'

If some detected a touch of vainglory in this humility, it was not
voiced there and then, that was to come. Did David Puttnam resign or
was he fired? He has always reacted fiercely to the latter interpretation.
But if you resign, at least one commentator asked, do you collect a
settlement of $5.4 million? (Puttnam has always disputed the accuracy

of this figure.) A *formal* resignation? Probably not: there was no need for that. A *form of words* was sufficient to signal the end of David Puttnam's thirteen-month rule at Columbia. In a mood of frankness, which often immediately follows such a démarche, Puttnam summed up his own fate pithily: 'It seems to me I've done one terrible thing. We reinvented the use of the word no.' This was somewhat understating it.

The new powers at Coca-Cola and Columbia moved swiftly into damage-limitation mode. 'PUTTNAM'S COLLEAGUES TO REMAIN AFTER HE'S GONE', said a *Variety* headline on 23 September 1987. But Hollywood insiders were not deceived. One by one, nearly all his appointees drifted away in the coming months. More ambiguous was to be the fate of the films produced under his aegis. The well-established practice of incoming studio heads had been to 'anticipate' that their predecessors' productions would not do well – why else had their begetters been replaced? – and release them quietly, or not at all. Puttnam watched the situation closely, though from afar, since he was back in England before Christmas 1987 and had set up his office at Shepperton Studios, his self-esteem as well as financial status boosted by activating his $50 million Warner Bros contract, with a production fund worth $50 million, which had been suspended when he went to Columbia. He planned to make two films a year for about $12 million each. Box-office hits for his slate of US-made films would be sweet vindication indeed. In his dreams, though.

The Hollywood Establishment had kept reasonably quiet in public about his departure, though rejoicing in private; but by May 1988, angered by what was called 'Puttnam's free-wheeling accessibility and eloquent soliloquies', they burst cover and the power-brokers who had always operated with 'deniability' through spokesmen unprecedentedly opened their minds and mouths to *Variety*, where Charles Kipps published, in two consecutive issues, the lengthiest and most damaging inquest on Puttnam's policies entitled 'The Rise and Fall of the Coca-Cola Kid'. The new men at Columbia authorised – or made available on request – figures for the thirty-three movies (nine inherited, twenty-four brought to the studio by Puttnam), of which fourteen had by then been released – and the bottom line did not look good. Production costs totalled $239 million; adding budgets for prints and publicity brought this to $432 million. Columbia to date had recouped $112 million; deducting exhibition rentals (40 per cent of this figure which cinema owners retained) came to $43 million. The company reported that it

contemplated an after-tax loss of $105 million 'primarily due to the
write-down of motion-picture product to the level of performance now
anticipated for these films'. In other words they were hypothecating
losses on even the unreleased films.

Puttnam called this 'a self-fulfilling prophecy'. He observed that the
Bertolucci–Jeremy Thomas epic *The Last Emperor* had won nine Oscars
and John Boorman's *Hope and Glory* had several Academy Award nominations, yet both films had been denied the extra push that was given
to kudos in order to convert it into cash. *The Last Emperor* was down-
played, in the opinion of media commentators, and *Hope and Glory* put
into neighbourhood cinemas whose regulars liked action movies. Fiona
Murphy echoed the general suspicion when she wrote in the *Guardian*
in June 1988, 'One cannot escape the impression that having got rid of
Puttnam and writing off the money, Columbia's present management
would be badly wrong-footed in the eyes of the Coca-Cola board if, a
year later, they were showing a profit after all.' Puttnam put it more
directly still: 'They're making absolutely sure [my slate of films] doesn't
make money.'

Probably, truth lay on both sides; bitterness certainly did. Puttnam
was bitter – time hadn't healed wounds that he kept scratching in
interviews. Columbia was bitter, trying to rebuild 'relationships' and
thinking enviously of the films that might have been theirs – a sleeper
hit like *Moonstruck* (made for another studio), sequels like *Ghostbusters
II*, *Jagged Edge II* – had their producers not been alienated by Puttnam,
as they alleged.

Figures apart and accusations on hold, the best explanation of why
David Puttnam's rule over one of the great Hollywood studios came to
such a mutually recriminating end was also one of the most succinct and
least emotional. Charles Kipps summed it up in the second of his two
collections of testimony published by *Variety*: 'He attempted to introduce
a personal philosophy into a broad-based industry while at the helm of
a public company.' Jack Matthews, in the *Los Angeles Times*, was just as
blunt, probably even more 'personal', too: Puttnam's terminology was
crucially flawed. 'When [he] spoke of quality he was referring to the
inherent goodness of particular films. When other studio executives
spoke of quality, they were referring to the commercial viability of
particular films. Hollywood is not Europe, and Puttnam should have
known the difference. Film is predominantly a business here, not a
creative art, and it is run by cautious businessmen who have nothing to

gain by revealing themselves in public debate.' The last reference was to Puttnam's evangelical zeal in missionary statements.

The damage to Puttnam probably went deeper than his ego. Already disillusioned by his experiences of a life devoted to a film industry that seemed unsustainable in Britain and untrustworthy in Hollywood, he set out again, almost a year to the day since he left Columbia, to be an independent producer. 'He could become a new Alexander Korda,' said the loyal Roland Joffé. Puttnam seemed to have taken to heart Jack Matthews's distinction between 'Europe' and 'Hollywood'; the slate of six films he announced for production, funded in part by his reactived $50 million deal with Warner Bros, echoed his 'inner voice', which he candidly admitted he should have listened to, 'but didn't. Hubris had taken over...'

Some of the six had a strong smell of mothballs: they appeared to be 'trunk films' put into storage after his hasty exit. They were: Jack Rosenthal's *Gabriela* (an off-beat romance set in a small Latin-American town); *Memphis Belle* (a bomber raid in an American Flying Fortress over wartime Germany); *The October Circle* (a thriller set in Bulgaria in 1968); *Opera Europa* (a multinational opera comedy to be directed by Istvan Szabo); *Shackleton* (the ill-fated Antarctic expedition of 1914); *Thumbs Up* (the inspirational recovery of Ronald Reagan's press secretary Jim Brady, wounded and paralysed in 1988 by the shots he took that were intended for the President, with Reagan playing himself, perhaps); and *Fade Out* (a Czech actress arrested by the Gestapo). 'I want these films to be international in the best sense,' he said unrepentantly. 'They will be made from a British base with British crews, but ... are not intended to be self-consciously British.' Some did get made; others still languish for various reasons, not least because of Puttnam's progressive disillusionment, hard to admit to himself, with the business of making films. The truth probably revealed itself to him gradually: he was richer in money terms than he had ever imagined, but poorer in achievement. Not burnt out, not extinguished, but thirsting for a new flame to carry.

Within a few years he would find fresh fuel in the revived fortunes of the Labour Party, renamed New Labour, and, for a short time at least, discover he had influence on the party's agenda. 'Education, education, education' – Tony Blair's mantra sounds precisely like Puttnam's predilection for drilling good thoughts into his listeners' hearts and minds, and giving solid expression to his own liberalism. That was where David Puttnam's new mission was to take him in the 1990s, not as 'the new

Korda', but, perhaps he thought so even then, as 'the new Kerensky' –
and take him further and higher in exerting his influence on society
than any programme of socially responsible films. He also had another,
more mundane, cause for retreating from film-making. Namely, the kind
of films he had once made – ambitious, entertaining and inspirational,
magnifying individuals' vision and amplifying their achievements or
sacrifices – were no longer the kind harvesting success and/or reaping
praise. The bare eighteen months that Puttnam had effectively been out
of Britain had seen a new generation of talented film-makers and
performers come of age and begin putting their view of contemporary
British life on screen – not always, in fact very seldom – in ways David
Puttnam or Richard Attenborough would have felt comfortable with.
Bryan Appleyard, in a survey of this radical kindergarten, called them
'The Children of Channel 4'.

Channel 4 had been founded in 1982, through a yearning by the
Conservative government to make it a deliberately separate entity from
the other Independent TV channels. Its core idea was to 'publish'
programmes created by authors 'originating' elsewhere – i.e. not 'in-
house' programmes. By 1987, 24 per cent of its output came from
independent producers and films accounted for a large part of this. By
then, some 140 films had been produced, representing nearly £40
million investment. The credit for this must go to David Rose, commissioning editor for drama since the early 1980s with a reputation for
successful series such as the police procedural *Z Cars* (BBC) and *Brookside*
(Channel 4), the gritty, issue-led soap opera that dealt with adultery,
murder and even incest. 'David Rose has taken over from Lord Grade
and David Puttnam as the face of British cinema,' *Screen International*
commented.

It started with a target of twenty films a year (highly ambitious, beyond
all British film companies' resources) and £6 million a year to spend on
fully or part-financing its programme, investing £250,000–300,000 in a
film by buying the TV rights, then doing co-production deals. In
addition, Channel 4 invested £750,000 a year in British Screen Finance
and another £500,000 in the British Film Institute's production board:
both developing and producing films that Channel 4 could buy into.
Such sums were matched by the government. Thus Channel 4 split the
risk of good TV drama with the film industry, gained kudos for its
patronage and saved cash.

Channel 4's example was followed swiftly by other independent companies, some of which had been hived off for tax advantages from their parent TV channels. One of the most notable was Zenith, headed by Charles Denton, who had begun in documentaries, become director of programmes for Lew Grade's ATV, then moved into Central TV (which produced such successful series as *Auf Wiedersehen, Pet*). Finally, in 1985, he (along with Margaret Matheson) moved into Central's wholly owned subsidiary, Zenith, which retained its independence despite being sold to Michael Green's Carlton Communications in 1987. Zenith was to produce *Prick Up Your Ears*, *Personal Services* and *Wish You Were Here*, three landmark films of this mini-New Wave. 'We've got to get closer to the enthusiasms of the public,' was Denton's maxim.

By 1988 Granada was planning to produce four films a year, though its purpose-built film unit functioned primarily as a development company and, throughout the next couple of decades, Granada's enthusiasm for feature film-making ebbed and flowed according to market conditions and its share price.

The world's stock markets, following 'Black Monday' (19 October 1987), were still jittery; yet periods of severe economic uncertainty had paradoxically proved energising for risk-taking entrepreneurs, and this was to be the case in independent film-making financed by packets of cash from private, public and government sources. The rising graph of cinema admissions lent plausible hope, even if more attractive exhibition conditions – the new multiplexes and the implanting of cinema-going as an 'experience' in British film-going – appealed to 'the enthusiasms of the public' rather than the films. From 70.2 million in 1985, admissions increased to 72.5 million in 1986; and now 75 million in 1987. This had its downside: to the Treasury, which derived its significant income from box-office taxes, all looked well and showed how right it had been to dispense with costly tax subsidies to film-makers. Still, bigger audiences infused independent film-makers with confidence.

David Rose's output at Channel 4 by the end of 1987 was sixteen to seventeen films a year, on a £9.5 million budget. It's true that very few of its films recovered their cost: it remained an 'art-house' producer until its breakthrough with *My Beautiful Laundrette*'s success followed by other films in which it was co-producer, *Letter to Brezhnev*, *Mona Lisa* and *A Room With a View*. Their critical and box-office reception in North America built up swift awareness there, just at the time independent distributors in the US were discovering how to tap into the tastes of discriminating audiences for 'something different' from Hollywood fare.

Success helped overcome the conservatism of video-store product. But an even more important perception was forced on Channel 4 at home. Initially, it had been intended to show their films first on TV and only afterwards give some of them a cinema release. This was because their write-off value only kicked in with TV exposure. This created considerable in-house controversy.

My Beautiful Laundrette resolved the dilemma by its success in British cinemas, but also by making Channel 4 aware that a cinema release delivered a ready-made audience for the film's première on TV. And as all such films were necessarily low-budget, they did not need to observe the agreement that still ruled the film trade – though beginning to break down – that British films should be subject to a three-year hold-back before being seen on TV. As Simon Perry said, 'The theatrical release takes away a negligible proportion of the television audience when compared with the awareness it creates in advance of the air-date.' Once this was established, the way was opened for many 'Film Four' productions – as they were known – to enter art-house and sometimes mainstream exhibition.

Over at the BBC, this development was watched by Mark Shivas, head of drama, with envy and resentment. The corporation's agreements with film unions covering additional wages and fees it would have to pay for converting a made-for-TV film into a cinema-released one prevented any films that the BBC financed for TV being premièred or subsequently screened in British cinemas. *The Little Sister*, an adaptation of a Philip Marlowe novel filmed in Florida, was one of the few BBC films to get a very limited cinema release in the United States in mid 1987; in its country of origin, cinema-goers could not see it. The BBC did not recognise the main film industry union, ACTT, and its own union members received lower rates of pay. Hence the resistance of the ACTT to BBC films reaching cinema screens. This savage restraint on trade, which Channel 4 avoided by working through independent companies, was characteristic of the corporation's weak-kneed genuflection to trade union protectivism: it effectively ruled the BBC out of film-making for several more years.

Only thirty-six films were produced in Britain in 1986, about 40 per cent with Channel 4 involvement; without it, production output would have been even lower. What gave David Rose's policy its distinctive character was his belief that the screenwriter was as important as the director. Film Four was soon seen as a 'writers' cinema'.

One writer in particular helped set the tone: Hanif Kureishi, whose success with *My Beautiful Laundrette* was matched by his own iconoclastic personality. Kureishi enjoyed offending against polite traditions and conventional values: he was an unapologetic provocateur in the Lindsay Anderson tradition, a rebel within the Anglo-Pakistani community and his own family; it's no accident that his talents found the perfect partner in Stephen Frears, who had served his apprenticeship with Anderson on *If . . .* and with Karel Reisz on *Morgan, A Suitable Case for Treatment.* These mentors helped define the two sides to Frears's nature, which Alan Bennett characterised in their first screen collaboration: 'one gentle and nostalgic, the other more energetic and violent'. Both Frears and Kureishi were subversives at heart, Kureishi being the wilder in manner and looks – Frears simply resembled someone who slept in his clothes. 'His idea of dressing up', Kureishi wrote in a Film Diary published in *Granta* magazine, 'is putting on a clean pair of plimsolls. The sartorial message is I can't think about all that stuff.' Nevertheless, Kureishi acknowledged, Frears freed him 'to include the vulgarity that is part of my character. It's made the films irreverent and cheeky, the way I am.'

My Beautiful Laundrette, to many, had the rough-and-ready look of 'found art', life picked up from the streets and, in some people's opinion, the gutter. But its author protested, 'Why make movies about standing about drinking tea while around the corner people are smashing windows?' This was very much Channel 4's viewpoint; and that of the production partnership, Working Title, consisting at this time of Tim Bevan and Sarah Radclyffe (not yet joined by Eric Fellner), who had identified an emerging cinema-going audience of young people who were educated, cheeky and irreverent.

The bleak economic outlook of Tory Britain at this time was altering the country's consciousness after the boom times of the early 1980s. The Docklands property market was tapering off; insecurity would quickly turn into fear for one's job, one's prospects, one's status. Quite suddenly, as the value of their homes went down, people were losing their sense of building on firm foundations for an emotional future as the unprecedented expansion of private credit led many now to be unable to meet their liabilities. They discovered that their dreams of emancipation from wage slavery lasted just as long as the reality of their wages. All of which put a new sheen on hopes for the recovery of the Labour Party and the new centre-Left in politics.

Such insecurity is good for creativity. Chances are taken and oppor-
tunities offered that good times would not have rendered necessary or
prudent. Much of this entered into the spirit, if not the narratives, of
the new films of the 1987–8 period. Sex was depicted in several of them
as a subversive force: but then, in the right hands, from D. H. Lawrence
to David Hare, it always had been. However, with the HIV infection
enforcing a new (if temporary) puritanism, several of the films depicted
a retro-view of a 1950s Britain where it was joyful to flout the constraints
of hypocritical morality codes and also safe to do so in a society as yet
unvisited by Aids.

David Leland scripted *Personal Services*, a biting social comedy set in
the 1950s world of a real-life suburban madam, Cynthia Payne, only
recently cleared of immorality charges and operating from a bay-win-
dowed semi-detached house where her alter ego, aka Christine Painter
(Julie Walters), provided a sort of National Health Service for the sexual
needs of ageing gents. As if working for king and country, the ex-
waitress who had reinvented herself as a queenly madam, dealt in the
way-out favours that men ask women to perform for (and often on)
them, and the tolerant views that women took of such requests (unless,
that is, they were specifically requested to take an intolerant view).
Comparing the bits and pieces of the men they've handled, like the
Three Witches in *Macbeth* swapping cooking ingredients, Christine and
co. created a vision of a British class system in which kinky sex and
family values coexisted; and by locating most of these outlandish fetishes
in an atmosphere of lower-middle-class gentility, Terry Jones's direction
tunnelled transgressively under the social order without bringing the
whole edifice down. It was definitely not a film that David Puttnam
would have publicly endorsed.

Prick Up Your Ears followed, based by Alan Bennett on John Lahr's
biography of the gay playwright Joe Orton (Gary Oldman), who had
been hammered to death by Kenneth Halliwell (Alfred Molina), his
jealous lover for sixteen years. Stephen Frears's film shifted the emphasis
from addictive cruising for boys in public toilets to the comedy of social
transgression and the tragedy of 'what happens when one partner goes
public, subsuming and discounting the other'. Joe Orton was a creepy
charmer whose grossness in the physical deeds of brazen pederasty
coexisted with a fastidious refinement in the written and spoken words
of his own black comedies. Bennett's prudent reworking of his life was
itself an Ortonesque pastiche, more about manners than the lack of

morals. The fatal liaison of Orton and Halliwell became a satirical reproduction of petit-bourgeois gentility, a very English 'marriage', with Oldman as the promiscuous hubby and Molina as the jealous wife.

Clipping the heels of the Orton biopic, precisely a week later, came *Wish You Were Here*, the directorial debut of David Leland, whose work in transforming Cynthia Payne's CV into *Personal Services* stimulated his own sentimental affinity for the world of 1940s and 1950s Britain; however, it was written as a reaction against those films which used the 1950s as a carefree romantic backdrop, such as Puttnam's *That'll Be the Day*, which poured a bucketful of rock'n'roll nostalgia over the youth cult of the time. Leland asked himself what had happened to knock the spark of rebelliousness out of young Cynthia. How did a Junior Miss grow up to become a Senior Madam? The film was Britain's most popular hit of that year, due largely to Emily Lloyd's heroine, sad, bad and just sixteen, who relieves the boredom of her generation by continually affronting convention in word and deed.

The suddenness with which Lloyd, at her very first appearance, with her 'flag-waving sexuality and foul mouth set on a collision course with propriety', filled the screen space and made it completely hers can be compared with the entry of Julie Christie swinging down a provincial main street as if she owned it in *Billy Liar* or Julie Walters in *Educating Rita* stomping independently across the college cobbles to 'better' herself under Michael Caine's tutelage. Just by inhabiting her role, not playing it; by using instinct, not training; by relying on natural looks, not make-up; by projecting an inner verve, not just dialogue – in short, simply by being there – Lloyd transfigured the film and proved herself, in one go, to have iconic status. Alas, she did not last. What happened next is typical of how British cinema to this day wastes its youngest and brightest in the limbo land of one-off movie-making. No second film was ready and waiting to confirm and enhance her overnight stardom: she left for America, where her ill-chosen roles got smaller and she with them.

With Lloyd's enormously naturalistic contribution, personifying someone who rebelled out of lack of affection, rather than because of any settled sinfulness, Leland's film was truthful to the people, places and age divide of the 1950s. While the adults in it look as if a demob suit has pressed them back into pre-war attitudes of subservient respectability, Lloyd and her adventurous lover experiment with an object not yet featured in a British (or, for that matter, American) film, though soon to do so shamelessly: a contraceptive. Her swagger boyfriend flashes the newly purchased Durex pack. Lloyd fingers it, like an amulet, then smirks. 'You've been done, it's empty.' Shyly, slyly, he manoeuvres closer ... and whispers, 'It's on me.' Richard Schickel was among the American commentators who recognised this primitive grass-roots stirring in British film-making in the latter half of the 1980s. He characterised Lloyd as 'a hormonal force of nature' and noted, 'The new radicalism is psychological, not political, and it is often expressed in a cheeky self-sufficiency.'

Writer-director Bruce Robinson's *Withnail and I* advanced the calendar slightly, into the 1960s, though self-sufficiency was not the keynote so much as self-pity. Following the misfortunes of two struggling young actors, living in domestic squalor of the slovenly male type in Camden Town, consuming prodigious quantities of drugs and alcohol as medication against the dole-queue blues, it showed the underbelly of the 'Swinging London' phenomenon that Hollywood had so successfully commercialised in the Sixties. The two characters, Withnail played by Richard E. Grant, a tragi-comic Wildean hero, posturing and dissolute, with a sharp tongue and cancerous temper, and his more innocent crony, the eponymous 'I', played by Paul McGann, his alter ego, constantly on an anxious simmer, beat a rattled retreat into what they hope will be the rest and recuperation of England's green and pleasant countryside. They find it occupied by a randily homosexual Uncle Monty (Richard Griffiths) full-bloodedly out to relieve 'I' of his virtue.

The savage accuracy of recall, in part autobiographical, by Robinson, who wrote the screenplay for the Puttnam–Joffé *Killing Fields*, made for an uncomfortable but hilarious trip down Memory Lane. The film quickly attached a cult following to itself – not all comprising 'resting' actors – and remains a cold-comfort judgement by a generation whose experience of that liberating era in British manners and morals ended in hangover.

The one Cannon-financed film of any social relevance that got made, despite the breaking of most of that group's promises to independent producers, was *Business As Usual*, writer-director Lezli-An Barrett's early feminist polemic. Glenda Jackson, soon to surrender her film career for the wasteland of Parliament and the hollowness of ministerial office, played a Liverpool fashion-store manageress sacked after protesting about indecent sexual advances to one of her staff by the area manager. Her ex-shop steward husband (John Thaw) and left-wing son (Paul McGann) quarrel over tactics for resisting this unfair dismissal. The theme here was certainly political: awakening the sleeping consciousness of Jackson's Thatcherite character so that her allegiance took a sharply radical U-turn. The lack of stridency makes the argument all the more powerful. The fallout from the film's opening was unexpectedly manifested in an editorial in *The Times*. It deserves quoting at some length, since so very few other branches of the media recognised the new militancy in young film industry people. Had they done, New Labour's comeback to government and power in the 1990s would not have been so surprising. These films tapped into the unrest and disillusionment of England. 'Britain's intelligentsia', thundered *The Times* on 20 September 1987,

> is a wandering tribe, hating Thatcherism. Its low view of Britain is most graphically illustrated by the more serious output of the British film industry. In *My Beautiful Laundrette* ... the plight of the white working class is even more desperate than that of the Asian community, while the implication in *A Letter to Brezhnev* is that the teenage heroine would be better off in the Soviet Union than unemployed in Liverpool. Most low-budget British films these days have an agit-prop purpose. The latest, *Business As Usual*, enthuses Mr Philip French, the film critic [of the liberal-Left Sunday paper, the *Observer*] 'unequivocally states that the best hope for the British working class, now as in the past, resides in organised labour and a united community'.

Dead accurate up to this point, *The Times*'s anonymous leader writer then rashly predicted that, 'Today's intelligentsia seems incapable of reinvigorating the Left of the political spectrum in the way that the Tories were brought to terms with the post-war world by a group of centre-Right thinkers in the late 1940s.'

Film-makers, possibly, were slightly ahead of leader writers in suggesting that the John Smith–Tony Blair resuscitation of Labour Party fortunes was inherent in the distempered state of England which the films depicted, even though using the time warp of earlier decades to do so. As the Docklands development was about to stall, leading to its biggest developer, the North American firm of Olympia and York, filing for protection from bankruptcy, another 'low-budget' film, though not one designed for 'agit-prop' purposes, opened: *Empire State*, directed by Ron Peck, whose previous film, *Nighthawks*, explored gay subculture and was described by the critic Mark Fincher as 'not so much a side-swipe at Thatcher's Britain as a last-gasp lunge at the throat ... an epitaph for Contemporary Britain'. It showed old working-class communities giving place to yuppie high-rises and clubland caverns like the nightclub of the title. Characters, capitalised and simplified (journalists, rent boys, pimps, financiers, entrepreneurs) criss-crossed and double-crossed one another in a swill of corruption until bare-knuckle fights evoked the primitivism of an even earlier East End. New Labour's ill-fated Millennium Dome was to be erected adjacent to some of this film's locations.

Prescience, however, demands context. It all but disappeared in a film that looked backwards to *The Long Good Friday* while hankering to be in the hard-edged big league of Hollywood thrillers. Producer Norma Heyman showed her resolution, or fixation, by attempting the same theme thirteen years later in *Gangster No. 1* (2000) whose anti-hero lopped off the limbs of his semi-conscious rival.

Sammy and Rosie Get Laid, the third collaboration between Frears and Kureishi, took place in a Britain where limbs had indeed been lopped off when a London police officer was fatally assaulted in race riots on the Broadwater Farm Estate. 'Take me to a part of Britain that isn't twinned with Beirut,' says Rafi, Sammy's dad (Shashi Kapoor), a crooked politician and torturer on the run from Pakistan, stepping out of his taxi into a radical battlefield for warring races: a police raid gone wrong; a black woman lying dead; arsonists firing the cars; drugs being openly traded; and everyone wanting an ethnic republic with themselves in charge and no interference from the police. Worse is in store for Rafi and his memories of the England he knew as a student, a place of 'tolerance, intelligence and hot buttered toast'. His accountant son Sammy (Ayub Khan Din) snorts coke, gobbles junk food, peruses porn mags and works on his mistress, an American artist with 'W' tattooed on each buttock, so that the whole says 'WOW' when she bends over. Rosie (Frances Barber), Rafi's daughter-in-law and a social worker, shows her concern for the suffering underclass by leaving her kisses indiscriminately on its lips, the way political leaflets are left under the door. Around the two of them is an extended 'family' of black squatters, Afro-Asian lesbians and various one-parent families and mentally subnormal derelicts. On the whole, Beirut seems preferable.

Sammy and Rosie Get Laid was, of course, overloaded: Kureishi was intent on pushing every distempered social misfit into his purpose-built purgatory of Thatcherite Britain. Characters became message bearers, voices became mouthpieces and the thesis that communal chaos is inherently more humane than social order is so over-indulged as to be self-negating. In the end, it was the sort of film that confirmed every prejudice held by the Right and risked alienating every sympathy retained by middle-ground liberals. *The Times* would find its leader column opinions amply corroborated. Sammy and Rosie do get laid in the end, along with another couple, and on a split-screen that turns copulation into a carnal layer cake. One critic suggested that if there were a sequel, it should be called 'Sammy and Rosie Get Aids'. Sex remained the subversive weapon of choice handled by the promiscuous young – in Richard Schickel's judgement 'with a minimum of romantic spirit and a maximum of haste'.

Rita, Sue and Bob, Too turned 'safe sex' in the age of Aids into titillating show-and-tell. 'Know what this is, girls?' asks Bob, the Jack-the-lad estate agent who's running Rita and Sue, two teenage babysitters, back home. Know it? Rita does, and Sue, too. So inside the sporty saloon, while one waits outside and the other takes her turn without much persuading, what was the first scene in a British film explicitly displaying a government-sponsored condom was played for mercifully rather less than its worth. 'A bit like cold sausage' is the girls' verdict.

In the spirit of Marie Antoinette, said to have ordered 'Let them eat cake' when told the people had no bread, Alan Clarke's film, based on Andrea Dunbar's stage comedy of manners on the cloth-cap estates of her native Bradford, proposed that the answer for those without work in Thatcher's Britain was 'Let them have sex'. It was the palliative for social sterility. 'Most of our people have never had it so good', Prime Minister Macmillan had said in his election-winning soundbite twenty-five years earlier. 'So often,' one could have added, on the evidence of Clarke's film. It was a revival of the old kitchen-sink milieux of the early 1960s now responsive to the new sexual forthrightness of the 1980s. Sexual energy was deemed to banish social hopelessness. No matter that the characters' own problems were left literally in mid-air, frozen in the final priapic leap into bed.

Rita, Sue and Bob, Too had been a personal project of Sandy Lieberson, when he was (nominally) in charge of production at Goldcrest; he took it with him when he left, no longer content to be second-guessed by Goldcrest's other executives. Terry Ilott, in *My Indecision Is Final*, co-authored with Jake Eberts, suggested that although its cost might have been modest, so might its box office. It would take it, and probably another two dozen films, to cover Goldcrest's annual overhead of £2.7 million in 1984. Goldcrest, Ilott reported, felt it needed 'a couple of films of the stature of *Gandhi* or *The Killing Fields*' to do that.

By the time *Rita, Sue and Bob, Too* had got produced, and opened to very brisk business, epic-sized projects had gone off the radar screen, out of sight, due to their huge costs, and also the new smaller-packaged socially observant and sexually audacious movies that the film companies which were spin-offs from television channels had made the anticipated norm of British production. Even as David Puttnam announced his new slate of six 'international' movies, his choices looked dated: the retro-nostalgia of film-goers reared in the era of public decency and private striving. Puttnam's and Attenborough's heroes, worthy, brave, compassionate and liberal though they were, could not compete for youthful (and sometimes not so youthful) fascination with the libidinous and promiscuous swingers, brothel keeping in suburbia, cohabiting homosexuals, brazen girlhood and a slew of gay relationship social comedies as contemporary as *Withnail and I* or as period as the Merchant Ivory production of *Maurice*, E. M. Forster's novel of suppressed Edwardian homophilia. Critics and discriminating film-goers reacted positively to the sheer exuberance of this tightly packed clutch of raunchy films, which deglamorised sex, yet made it look the only game in town. 'There is bravery and originality in the bluntness of these movies,' wrote Richard Schickel.

Puttnam was not well adapted to such change. His experience of films made for television had been disillusioning; he would probably have fared no better with films that felt they had television's immediacy coupled with cinema's intimacy. Above all, his own moral consciousness, while personally commendable, would probably have deterred him from putting himself body and soul behind many of these new movies that reflected a society at odds with itself and did so without moral condemnation. 'We're responsible for the degree of emotional and mental health of society,' he had told the critic Kenneth Turan in April 1987, when he was chairman and chief executive officer of Columbia Pictures. Attempting that noble experiment on his return to Britain would have recalled the painful precedent set by another, rather cannier, ruler of a small kingdom centuries before: King Canute. The tide had turned and was not running in David Puttnam's favour.

5

Cannon Self-destructs

It is doubtful if David Puttnam, ensconced at Columbia, had any time to follow events in Britain since leaving its shores at the end of summer 1986, but it should have been considerable consolation to him to see how swiftly the Cannon Group's 'luck' soured.

The bad news for Golan and Globus came from America first: the Securities and Exchange Commission was 'informally' investigating the company – principally the way it wrote off film costs. Most of the film industry gave a film five years to amortise what it had cost to make; Cannon was managing to do this in three. By June 1986, it revealed a working capital deficit of $105 million, yet, despite this black hole, reported profits up by 84 per cent, from $3.1 million in 1985 to $5.7 million. It was also alleged that its estimates of future profits – hypothecating, to use industry-speak – was unduly optimistic. Its share price began wilting: from $45.50 on the New York exchange in July to $30 at the end of August.

At the new $15 million Cannon offices in Beverly Hills, Menahem Golan denied any cash-flow crisis: 'Sooner or later we'll have a blockbuster that will send our earnings soaring 100 per cent.' What about Roman Polanski's disaster, *Pirates*, a reporter was indiscreet enough to ask. This pirate 'epic' had sunk with all hands immediately on launching at the Cannes Film Festival. 'We all make mistakes,' Golan replied with uncommon limpness. He himself was then directing Sylvester Stallone in a $30 million arm-wrestling action drama called *Over the Top*: arm-twisting was thought to be appropriate for the two freshly minted moguls.

As Cannon had grown, so had its debts; while its earnings were, well, disappointing. In the first half of 1986 it had achieved a return of just $19.3 million on an investment of $63.5 million, and the US–Canadian market for TV and video rights was softening. It had released six flops in a row. *Forbes* magazine commented, 'At $213 million, Cannon's total inventory is actually higher than Paramount's $199 million, even though

Paramount has something like eight times Cannon's revenues. The suspicion is that Cannon is booking revenues faster than it is recognising costs. Anyone who does this is a candidate for a fast write-down some-where down the line.' There was one obvious way to clear some of this debt: a sale of assets. Thus, within months of acquiring half the British film industry, Cannon began the staggered stripping of the assets of Thorn-EMI Screen Entertainment.

The spirits of British film-makers, which Golan's pep talk had tem-porarily raised, had relapsed to their more usual despondency by the end of 1986. Only fifteen films had been started that year, representing an investment of £42 million, compared with twenty-six (£109 million) in 1985. Norman Lamont, then Financial Secretary to the Treasury, was still unsympathetic to tax breaks. In 1982 there had been some thirty companies whom independent film-makers could approach for finan-cing; now only seven remained. Goldcrest had ceased production; Virgin was bowing out of film-making, since Richard Branson was taking his company to the stock market and film production figures, especially after the *Absolute Beginners* experience, did not look good when he was trying to raise £60 million. Cannon, therefore, was the best hope many independent producers had; and Cannon was failing them. 'There are worrying signs that many fears expressed at the time of the takeover [of TESE] are proving to be well founded,' said the AIP Newsletter for November–December.

To make good his boasts, Golan announced one of Cannon's biggest budgeted productions, to be made at Elstree: nothing less than *Spider-Man*, which he saw as the company's 'ticket to the big time' and, usefully, as a confidence builder for British investment. It was budgeted at $20 million. Cannon had acquired the rights as far back as 1983, at a bargain price of $225,000, and now dreamed of hiring Tom Cruise for the lead. It was doubtful, though, if Golan and Globus construed the comic-strip story accurately: the first script they commissioned is said to have featured the young Peter Parker metamorphosing into a giant eight-legged tar-antula. By the time a more 'conventional' screenplay was ready, Cannon's cash flow would have found it difficult to spin an appropriately expensive web. (Cannon disposed of its rights in 1990 to another ill-fated company, Carolco.)

A Cannon announcement in 1986 that *Superman IV would* get made was received coolly: it wasn't the sort of film likely to put British production on its feet again. By the end of the year, Cannon's only commitment to make British films amounted to two movies: Harry Hook's *The Kitchen Toto*, about a Kikuyu servant boy (a 'toto') sucked into Mau-Mau atrocities, which was based on its writer-director's own memories of his early life in Kenya; and *Business As Usual*, the afore-mentioned first feature by Lezli-An Barrett starring Glenda Jackson. Though reputable, even accomplished, such films (representing a meagre £1.8 million budget between them) were small beer compared with the feast Cannon had promised. Another film Cannon attempted to put into production, a Falklands War story provisionally entitled *One Hundred Days*, which promised controversial views of the British operation, was to finish up in court, rather than on location, when its makers were sued by Cannon for some £17,000-odd advance representing fees on a film Cannon did not make but claimed copyright in: Cannon lost, paying costs estimated at around £50,000.

The deals concluded by TESE with 'satellite' producers were in limbo: not one had been followed through. One by one, they were to be abandoned. The 'lucky' one that got away – set up by TESE well in advance of Cannon's takeover – was to be *Little Dorrit*, a two-part version of Dickens's novel, one of the most remarkable enterprises undertaken by independent producers John Brabourne and Richard Goodwin, and director Christine Edzard, which will be considered later. But it was as alien to Cannon's current plans as an earthbound meteor – and as accidental. The 'output' deal with David Begelman's Hollywood company, by which the British company paid to make American movies, was cancelled: perhaps Cannon's only welcome move, and one made by necessity not patriotism. Not a single site had been found in a new town for a Cannon multiplex. Otto Plaschkes had clearly failed to 'excite' Menahem Golan with any film proposals, for he declared, 'We clearly have to re-evaluate the whole basis of the deals. ... The company is not in the business to fund independent film companies.' Strange: that was what most of the credulous young film-makers convoked by Cannon in the aftermath of its TESE takeover had imagined it *was* in the business for.

Cinema admissions remained an ever-brightening patch of blue sky: they rose to 72 million in 1986, with Cannon cinemas showing a 6–7 per cent rise (against the Rank chain's 8 per cent): even so, a Cannon statement said, with uncommon prudence, 'It is crucial not to depend on the ticket buyer for recoupment of the cost of production.' Money troubles worsened. Cannon's bold gamble with big-budget movies – the $30 million *Over the Top*, with Stallone's $12 million fee and the $22 million *Superman* – caused the company to miss a £35 million repayment due to Alan Bond for his role in the TESE takeover (Cannon would stitch together another guarantee to the Australian entrepreneur). But servicing its borrowing was alone costing $30 million a year. And the ongoing SEC investigation, and other troubles, caused its share price to fall to $12 by December 1986.

A creditor owed $1 million obtained a court order to block Cannon's assets; and Warner Communications, seeing its chance, agreed to step in and bail Cannon out in return for a two-year option to take an equity stake in Cannon British and European chains (valued at $183 million, including existing debt) and video distribution rights to Cannon's films. If Warner exercised its option, maximising its seats on Cannon's board, said Julian Petley in the AIP Newsletter for May 1987, it would mean that effective control of 39 per cent of British cinemas would pass into American hands. But as a London property specialist, Conrad Ritblat, began putting thirty to forty Cannon cinemas on the auction block, one wondered how much would be left for Warner. In short, the legacy of British film-makers and film-making assets were being virtually 'pawned' within six months of Cannon being permitted to acquire them by the Department of Trade and Industry. The SEC findings were anticipated, with well-founded apprehension, in the new year. Meanwhile Cannon was contemplating the sale of the US Commonwealth chain of cinemas it had acquired in the same month as it took over TESE. In short, all was chaos: the Chinese butterfly's random curse was working its way through the system.

As well as cinemas, Cannon now put the TESE film library and historic Pathé News collection up for sale to Jerry Weintraub, best known then as producer of a minor hit, *The Karate Kid*, thus breaking the assurance given at the takeover that they would retain the 'integrity' of such assets 'as a predominantly British-owned and controlled entity'. On 20 April 1987 I wrote to Paul Channon at the Department of Trade and Industry, 'A sale to a foreign group would mean not only a loss of potential income to studios (and possibly financial contribution to the British Screen consortium), but would also constitute selling off a part of the cultural patrimony that our cinema has built up over many decades.' Mr Channon replied to me on 30 April 1987, '... my decision not to refer [Cannon's acquisition of TESE] to the Monopolies and Mergers Commission was in no way conditional on specific undertakings from Cannon ... The Weintraub sale may qualify for investigation by the MMC, under the provisions of the Fair Trading Act 1973, and is currently under preliminary consideration at the OFT.'

By May 1987 Cannon's stock had plunged to $5 on the US exchange. Appropriately, the cousins appeared at the Cannes Film Festival, not attired in their triumphalist electric-blue tracksuits of the previous year, but in dejected-looking black sweatshirts. About the same time, the root cause of their sudden descent into near-bankruptcy began to emerge on the financial markets: an American merchant bank had reneged on a verbal promise to pay for the TESE acquisitions, forcing Cannon to scrabble for $200 million to make good their undertakings to Bond and other creditors: $75 million of this had been promised in cash, which wasn't immediately there. Hype and chutzpah die hard: at Cannes, Cannon took out a fifty-seven-page spread in *Variety* – though this time in black and white, not colour.

British independent producers, lacking any resolute centre, made a poor showing in developing opposition to what amounted to a fire sale of British assets. The British Screen Advisory Council, turfed unceremoniously out of the Department of Trade and Industry building to fend for accommodation and secretarial help for itself, met on 7 May 1987, for the first time in the 'Moses Room' of the House of Lords, courtesy of Lady (Marcia) Falkender and Lord (Harold) Wilson – who was now honorary president, due to his ailing health. It decided it had no objection to Warner's option to acquire Cannon's cinemas 'provided existing Cannon cinemas would be retained, save where circumstances meant they would not be retained', a prime piece of sophistry. One BSAC member, Gunnar Rugheimer, who bought films for BBC TV, reported that he was also a consultant to Jerry Weintraub. It was revealed that Weintraub had taken, too, an option to acquire Elstree film studios by 31 May 1987 – a little over three weeks away. This should have been a spark in an even bigger powder barrel: it passed almost without discussion.

Alan Sapper reported his union had had a 'useful' meeting with the Weintraub Entertainment Group. Very properly, his first concern was for his members' jobs. My first concern lay otherwise and, on 23 May, I wrote to the Director-General of Fair Trading, Sir Gordon Borrie, dissociating myself from BSAC's pro-Cannon resolution. 'I am on record as believing that Mr Channon acted imprudently in declining to refer the Cannon takeover to the Monopolies and Mergers Commission, despite your own advice to do so, and I think that subsequent events indicate the unwisdom of [his] decision.' The same day I wrote to Paul Channon, 'To be blunt, your representatives do not seek the views of informed and independent people – too often they go to the messenger boys of Hollywood's entertainment industry. You seem to lack the broad background which, if it were available, would make your decisions less narrow. The advice you seem to take nearly always favours the extension of Hollywood's business and cultural domination of our screens: there is a "monopoly" in entertainment patterns as inimical to the public interest as that of baseless mergers . . .' Mr Channon 'took note' of what I had said; given the tone of my letter, perhaps, a temperate response.

No more useful was Sir Gordon Borrie's reply on 7 May to Sir John Terry, BSAC's deputy chairman, regarding the proposed Cannon–Warner merger: '. . . there are no powers whereby undertakings can be obtained in return for *not* referring a merger to the MMC. The question . . . can arise only if the proposed merger were to be referred to the MMC for investigation.' In short, catch-22.

In contrast to the previous year, when almost every day Cannon had announced some new acquisition at Cannes, each day of the 1987 festival was marked by dire rumours of the company's fate: a $60 million loss for the year ending 3 January 1987; accounts 'qualified' by their auditors 'as to the company's ability to continue operations as a going concern'. In addition, $32 million had been written down for 1985, tantamount to a write-off of profits for 1983–5, an operating loss of $92 million since 1985. Film costs still to be written off and carried on the books totalled $475 million. It was amazing what a SEC investigation could trigger. In addition, Cannon had sold their theatrical and video rights to Warner for a fraction of what they could have expected in the good times.

Cannon's financier, Frans Afman, of Credit Lyonnais, did his (considerable) best to counter chapter 11 (aka bankruptcy) rumours. 'Yoram and Menahem have no reason to panic. They have always liked to be very much in the limelight, which is fine when everything is going right. It is not so fine when things are going wrong, but they have to live with it.' And live with it they did at Cannes, their smiles as expansive as their stomachs and very much cool customers when taxed with their troubles. 'Personally,' Frans Afman said, with the frankness old friends can muster when occasion requires it, 'I think they will have to sell more. Fortunately, they have a lot to sell.' Michael Winner, Cannon's best friend among British film-makers, did not desert them either, declaring airily that 'the financial practices of film companies are known to be less than perfect . . .' Cannon, at that moment, had an equity value of $50 million and debts twelve times this sum.

At Cannes, Jerry Weintraub tempered his own little acquisition of British film history, acquired for $90 million, by promising to set up a UK company to manage it – 'and it will stay in Britain'. Subsequently, an office opened in Wardour Street whose front window displayed the great glories of Ealing Films and other national assets under the name 'Weintraub'. There was an even more bitter irony. Weintraub went to Cannes not to gloat, but to expand: he attended a meeting of Columbia Pictures international managers in Nice. The host was David Puttnam, still in the saddle at Columbia, though due for his great fall three months later. Weintraub's group had been launched in February 1987 with the help of a $14 million equity investment and a $156 million advance from Coca-Cola – who, even then, were finalising the plan that would force Puttnam out of his job. Thus he involuntarily played host to Jerry Weintraub, one of the beneficiaries of the TESE takeover that he had resisted so stubbornly the year before. The Weintraub bid for Elstree collapsed: $25 million was beyond his limit. 'Elstree is not for sale,' Golan said, then added runically, 'but everything has a price.' Meantime, the stressed company laid off 110 employees in the US and Europe.

Yet by July Menahem Golan, en route to the Moscow Film Festival, was surprisingly upbeat: 'I believe we will heal slowly.' He claimed the SEC investigation was what had adversely affected Cannon's standing. The cause of his optimism became known a few days later. A Luxembourg holding company, Intercorporation, hitherto not a player in the game, was lending Cannon $11.6 million. It already owned 11.2 per cent of Cannon, whose net worth had now dipped to $39.9 million at a time when it had to maintain a minimum equity level of $37.5 million to avoid debt repayments being triggered. The money would come from a purchase of 1,450,000 Cannon shares, which stood at $3.37 on 8 July. The purchaser would pay $8. And who was this white knight? Intercorporation, it turned out, was owned 25 per cent by Menahem Golan and 23 per cent by Yoram Globus: they were, in short, lending to themselves. Nothing, of course, wrong with that; but it showed how tight things were. They were to get tighter still. The rest of Intercorporation was owned by another mysterious Luxembourg entity, Interpart.

It was a situation made for the great nineteenth-century novelists, such as Dumas or Trollope, whose novels like *The Count of Monte Cristo* and *The Way We Live Now* incorporated sequences of financial folly and irresistible ruin. But the Cannon cousins were not at the point where Baron Danglars or Sebastian Morand gave up the fight. Even the publication of the SEC findings failed, like the animated characters constantly annihilated in cartoons and instantly regaining shape and truculence, to flatten the Go-Go Boys. The report, published in November 1987, found Cannon guilty of materially underestimating film costs in the first year of a movie's release, resulting in inflated earnings; it also alleged it violated other aspects of the security laws. The company refused to admit wrongdoing and received no punishment; it simply consented to SEC conditions, in order, it said, to assist restructuring. The SEC asserted that Frans Afman, of France's Credit Lyonnais, was a managing director of Cannon Production NV, a Netherlands Antilles-based unit – with a three-year contract valued at $75,000 a year through 1987 and consulting fees for 1986 of $100,000. In other words according to SEC, Cannon's chief banker had been on the company payroll. No longer, however: Frans Afman had ceased to be a Cannon director in December 1986.

Even as the report made *Wall Street Journal* headlines, control of Cannon was slipping away from its owners. To the already incredible cast of characters was added yet another new one: a Madrid-based real-estate company Renta Immobiliaria, controlled by an Italian entrepreneur who, or so the story went, had begun his career by being a waiter in the Savoy Hotel, London: Giancarlo Parretti. It emerged that Parretti was the principal investor in Interpart, which controlled Renta Immobiliaria, and had a half-interest in Intercorporation. On 29 September 1987, in a complicated deal, Cannon sold its theatres, Elstree film studios and its corporate headquarters in Los Angeles to Renta Immobiliaria for $338 million, before leasing them back again. Parretti thus became the biggest single force in a labyrinthine complex, now, it seemed, light years away in space and time from the takeover of the British film industry's former assets to which Paul Channon and the government had formally consented without the slightest informal inquiry into the nature of the purchasers.

Menahem Golan, with the springiness of someone who has fallen from a great height but bounced back again, called a news conference at Cannon's flagship cinema in Shaftesbury Avenue, London, to announce jubilantly that 'we want to expand into tourism, hotels, travel agency, banking and other investments'. Not films? Oh yes: 'We are planning twenty productions for the coming year.' Further celebrations, no doubt mixed with thanksgiving prayers, followed in mid November 1987, hosted by Cannon Cinemas UK but this time at Torremolinos, Spain – as was only proper, considering where power now lay – in one of the Melia group hotels controlled by Giancarlo Parretti. The guest speaker at the gala dinner was Michael Winner, escorting his then girlfriend the actress Jenny Seagrove. Winner, whose weekly restaurant column in the *Sunday Times* now took up more of his time than film-making, forbore to publish his evaluation of the menu and service – presumably it was satisfactory.

BSAC requested a meeting with Cannon to discuss the sale-and-leaseback of the prime studio assets: the company could not oblige. A BSAC meeting with an OFT official got us nowhere: the Minister's original decision not to refer the matter to the MMC 'could not be changed'. Why reopen that can of worms? In mid December Cannon informed my editor, John Leese, at the *Evening Standard* that the company was banning me from reviewing any films it produced, distributed or exhibited. The reason: 'carrying on what would appear to be a personal vendetta against the Cannon Group . . . [He] will not be permitted entry if he should attempt to attend a screening.' I did not make any rash attempt to do so: I received a large number of letters from other members of the film industry congratulating me on being relieved of this professional necessity.

For Cannon, the agony was considerably more painful. The company posted a huge 1987 third-quarter loss of over $19 million, making the setback for the year to date over $40 million. Its UK financial director quit early in the new year, 1989: the stated reason, without a shade of irony, was the need for 'a financial director with more experience of US accountancy laws'. Meantime, the Cannon–Renta Immobiliari deal hung fire and was eventually not to go through. The reason is still unclear, but Cannon, in 1988, began making noises suggesting it was moving its sphere of operations from the UK to Europe. With two partners like Parretti and Silvio Berlusconi, this was unsurprising. They had the money; Cannon had only the chutzpah, which was again in evidence at Cannes in May 1988, when a twenty-picture co-production deal with Berlusconi was announced: 'In two years' time, Cannon will be similar to today's Paramount and Columbia.'

Cannon was now part of Parretti's conglomerate company comprising insurance, travel agencies, real estate and banking. To this dog's breakfast of portfolio interests had come a considerable part of the one-time great British film industry. Parretti assumed the offices of president and CEO of the Cannon Group; Golan and Globus were shunted into the sidings as heads of a subsidiary, Cannon Entertainment, which was only 20 per cent of the new company that itself was said to be backed by $250 million by Parretti and his partner Florio Fiorini. Such a manoeuvre was calculated to steady nerves as rumours circulated the film festival that Cannon's loss for 1987 might be a whopping $100 million. Parretti would have 39 per cent of the Cannon Entertainment stock, Golan and Globus a mere 12 per cent; the rest, publicly owned. Parretti's aim in buying into what looked a terrifying loss was explained by the fact that the new company would be quoted on the New York Stock Exchange, not only as an entertainment stock but as one with diversified interests.

Parretti's juggling of assets, and even negative assets, was bewilderingly fast: he had, he said, control of twelve listed companies on the stock exchanges of Luxembourg, Spain, Italy and Switzerland. He acquired from Credit Lyonnais the languishing Rome film studios, built by Dino De Laurentiis and nicknamed Dinocitta, which he instantly handed over to Cinecitta for management. He sold Cannon's interest in their Italian cinema circuit to Berlusconi for $50 million. With Dinocitta, Parretti acquired the Villa Mignon and announced, benevolently, he was going to turn it into a rest home for retired actors: he got the Italian Deputy Prime Minister's *nihil obstat* to form a tax-free foundation for this charitable act. But lest investors felt him soft-hearted, he announced Cannon would make ten films in Europe, while Berlusconi would produce ten more.

The irrepressible Menahem Golan stated he would personally direct Brecht's *The Threepenny Opera* at Elstree: he couldn't wait, he said, for Steven Spielberg's *Indiana Jones and the Last Crusade* to finish shooting and relinquish the sound stages. Cannon also announced plans to build a ten-screen multiplex in London's Piccadilly. Neither of these projects ever came to anything, with Golan switching *The Threepenny Opera* to his native Israel.

Instead, post-Cannes, attention was concentrated on stripping the remaining one-time Thorn-EMI assets Cannon had bought. Principal among them was Elstree Studios, which was put up for sale on 29 June, even though it had just declared a small operating profit, undoubtedly due to the rental of its stages by the Hollywood blockbusters. It was deemed no longer a viable concern, which was probably true, since a percentage of the interest payable on money that Cannon used to buy TESE – £175 million, or $313 million – was attributable to Elstree and this pushed the studio into the red. AIP called this 'a flagrant evasion of film commitments', a phrase overworked in recent months. The AIP chairman, Roger Graef, said, 'The financial difficulties of this one company have been allowed to destabilise the whole industry.' It was estimated that closure of Elstree would cut the UK's feature-film capacity by one third. The Directors Guild of Great Britain spoke of its 'outrage'. Otto Plaschkes, once Cannon's 'artistic conscience', now head of the British Film and Television Producers Association, cried that the Elstree sale was 'another [*sic*] amputation' of the industry's assets.

My own notes made at BSAC's meeting on 14 July 1988 indicated the huge concern that Cannon's contractors might even now be stripping Elstree of its technical equipment, since the preservation order we had successfully persuaded Hertsmere Borough Council to slap on the property, once its sale was bruited, did not extend to the equipment, only the buildings. Barry Jenkins, Cannon's managing director, revealed the studio as worth £15 million on the books; BSAC's estimate was it was worth considerably more to a property developer. Attenborough and Puttnam dined with John Butcher, Under-Secretary of State for Industry and Consumer Affairs, aka the Films Minister, who had paid a visit to Cannes two months earlier and deplored the fact that Saab were providing the transport for the British pavilion: 'British participants at [the festival] should be driving around in British cars,' he said severely. Despite his patriotism, he was unable to do much for Attenborough and Puttnam, no doubt because he ceased to be Films Minister on 29 July. Another little-known name, Robert Atkins, got this 'poisoned chalice' job: he was the seventh appointee in as many years. Instead, the small borough council showed more proactive zeal, making it plain that the preservation order extended to movable and immovable assets, thus in small measure ensuring Elstree remained a film studio, not a parking lot and supermarket.

Elstree's Doomsday was officially declared as 28 October 1988, when it would be sold to one of several bidders, some anonymous. When the day came the winning bid, said to be for £34 million, revealed the new owner as Brent Walker, a company of mixed-interest portfolio, including what remained of Goldcrest, TV production interests, casinos, pubs and hotels, owned by a Stepney-born former boxer George Walker. Mr

Walker, himself estimated to be worth £50 million on paper with a company valued at £380 million, had told shareholders in his annual report for 1986, 'Unlike other film-makers we do not view film production as a high-risk business ... By careful planning, financing and strong management control, we can eliminate the risks that others may be prepared to accept.' This reminded some in the industry of Lord Grade's words of confidence before the *Titanic* iceberg hit him and sank his company. A faint, very faint, British cheer greeted the news that Elstree had been 'saved'.

To show the industry still had what it takes, BAFTA announced that a Great British Film Rally of cars built before January 1959 would take place just prior to next year's Cannes with the aim of 'promoting British films and television'. The route would pass by, perhaps halt at, notable vineyards and chateau hotels. The ex-Films Minister, John Butcher, may perhaps have been cheered to see that all eligible cars had to be British.

Parretti's fortunes, in the metaphorical sense anyhow, continued to wax. By January 1989 he had acquired control of Pathé, the prestigious French production, distribution and exhibition company, installed himself as vice-president and brought on to the board a Berlusconi representative – oh, and the Cannon Group. Actual ownership was reportedly vested in Max Theret, an entrepreneur with strong links to the Socialist government. He and Parretti had been assisted in the $160 million purchase with a $80 million loan from Credit Lyonnais. Parretti would soon be displaced from his Pathé stronghold – the French act more speedily and brutally than the British when what's considered a national asset is threatened by an alien takeover – but he would soon go on to make a bid for the one-time crown jewel of Hollywood, Metro-Goldwyn-Mayer and, briefly, acquire control. After that his story demands a larger canvas and a finer acquaintance with international finance than this book can offer.

Golan would form his own company, 21st Century Films, and continue film-making, much as he had done before the Cannon rollercoaster. I last saw him at the top of a stepladder at a Cannes Festival, nailing up the poster for a production he proposed making to the doorway of what had formerly been the barber's shop at the Carlton Hotel. The film's title was *Phantom of the Opera*, though any connection between Golan's production and the successful musical of Andrew Lloyd Webber would merely be in the eye of the beholder.

Another painful experience, in part caused by his association with

Cannon, befell Jerry Weintraub, who had bought TESE's film library, when his company revealed a net loss for 1988 of $40.9 million, compared with $18.3 million the year before. His domestic movies – *My Stepmother Is an Alien* among them, which grossed a poor $12.9 million instead of the hypothecated $50 million – had not performed strongly. Weintraub Entertainment Enterprises would have been hit even harder but for the rentals on the 2,000-odd films acquired from Cannon's asset stripping. Two years earlier Weintraub, with backing in excess of $461 million in bank loans, securities, Coca-Cola and the Cineplex Odeon group, had announced 'the biggest start-up in Hollywood history'. However, not all that money was in one single war chest, but doled out little by little, or not at all as confidence faded with his box-office returns. By the end of 1988 he had a severe cash-flow shortage. Weintraub was a well-connected film financier, a neighbour of George W. Bush Sr at Kennebunkport, with four other luxurious homes around the US, and an outsize personality to match his spending. A cash shortage was a new experience. In 1988 Weintraub had paid himself $1.53 million. Contributing to the financial squeeze was his purchase of the TESE library from Cannon in 1987. To help cover the $85 million price tag, his company had arranged a loan of $40 million from the Bank of America. This was separate from the line of credit he was then enjoying from several banks, including BoA. As Kim Master commented, 'Though the library's value has since increased, the additional loan [of $40 million] apparently spooked the other banks participating in the $145 million line of credit, and the Bank of America terminated its commitment to provide the latter loan. WEG has been scraping along on smaller loans ever since.'

All in all, the chaos caused by permitting a prime asset of British film-making to be sold to two incomers had caused a great deal of grief to many people, institutions, and public and private companies inside a mere few years: the Chinese butterfly's fluttering wings, initiating a chain reaction that transcended prediction and defied logic, had certainly done overtime work on the international film scene. Human folly was not yet exhausted, either.

6

Talents at Work

'O! for a Muse of fire . . .' implores the Chorus. But in Kenneth Branagh's version of *Henry V,* Derek Jacobi, who speaks the familiar line, fits it not to the illumination of a muse, but the flare-up of a safety match. As the gloom springs back, Chorus is disclosed in modern dress: a topcoat to keep out St Crispin's Day winds to come; a dark scarf to toss over his shoulder in place of a trumpet flourish. He is the conscience of the King, as well as the commentator. He leads us into a movie studio . . . the studio leads us into the play . . . and the play leads us into a film that was the dazzling screen debut of an actor-writer-director-impresario who, for a short time anyhow, looked the heir apparent to Laurence Olivier. Olivier himself was to die a month or two later, in July 1989, without seeing the film that was to challenge his own *Henry V* made forty-five years earlier as a rallying cry to a nation at war.

The British assembled again on French territory that May needed every kind of call to arms in order to lift their spirits. The light of a safety match would not have dissipated the pessimism. No British film had been judged worthy to compete. Branagh's *Henry V* was absent, too, from the main competition. Not as rumour had it, due to French *amour propre*, still wounded by the unforgettable cloud of Agincourt arrows, but simply because, when it was viewed by the Festival it was in an incomplete state. Its rough-cut ran to 165 minutes. Branagh and his executive producer, a young, well-connected City broker called Stephen Evans, got the money together: it cost £4.5 million, a lot at that time for such a project, of which the BBC contributed £400,000 for TV rights and the enterprising London cinema owner, Roger Wingate, did a £300,000 distribution deal.

The film was shown to potential buyers at Cannes in a side-street cinema: the King, in short, 'sneaked' in. (I sneaked in, too, and thus witnessed the power and glory of the film without having formed a single critical expectation.) Had *Henry V* gone into competition, and whether it won or not, it would have redeemed our national cinema's absence and answered the mystified foreign critics who had believed a renaissance in vigorous, radical film-making was well under way in the United Kingdom. The truth was that the film-making recovery, primed largely by television and the independent companies, had produced only a few short-lived spurts and then virtually dried up.

'There's a conviction that the quite brief, but rather sparky era of British cinema – which might have begun with *My Beautiful Laundrette* and ran through films like *Wish You Were Here* and *Personal Services* – has perhaps come to a natural close.' Thus Charles Denton, then chief executive of Zenith, the film production spin-off from Central TV. In the same breath he announced three new Zenith films, costing $5–8 million each, one about an Irish priest embroiled in war in El Salvador, another about a pair of black American musicians in the 1930s, a third about a disturbed child. All very different from the indigenous and exuberant British sex and social comedies Zenith had made its reputation with a year or so earlier. These were 'transitional' films, Denton explained, ones that would transcend 'purely British appeal' with something 'wider'. In other words fewer 'native sons', and for 'wider' understand 'American'. The modest hope was that by diluting their cultural identity they would appeal to wider audiences abroad: a continual delusion, but perhaps the hardest one to root out of the film-making consciousness of the industry. Anyhow, Denton was whistling to keep up his courage: none of the three got made. Even Channel 4's cornucopia spilled out fewer goodies that season. Anglia, Granada and Euston (the film-producing arm of Thames TV) had put their film plans on hold.

Such a climate change was characteristic of British film-making throughout this era and, indeed, of today's industry. Television companies were the engine that had been driving the revival over the two years from, say, 1986 to 1988; once they faltered the momentum died. One reason was the coming auction of Independent Television franchises in 1992, with no guarantee that the winning bids would be related to quality production or sponsorship – but simply to ability to pay more than the loser. For the moment, feature films appeared an extravagance: back to basics with all relevant economies was the order.

Channel 4 maintained it would continue to part-finance sixteen films a year, but would fund only one third of each. And David Rose, the godfather of its film-making division, was coming up to retirement age. His successor might swing a bigger axe. In 1988 commercial TV had invested £8.5 million in feature films; by mid 1989, only £3.5 million had been spent and the previous year's figure looked unlikely to be matched. The US market had shrunk alarmingly since the Wall Street crash in October 1987; its effects were now being felt in the world of independent production in the US. A surfeit of product led to stock-piling, to distributors ridding themselves of a film that didn't 'open big'.

The US independent film-makers, who had hit a gold seam in the video market in 1987, had predictably produced a product glut. 'We were lulled into thinking the Americans would take anything,' Working Title's Tim Bevan concluded gloomily. 'The fact is, they won't.' Debra Goldman, a shrewd industry analyst, wrote, 'By 1988, the indie party was over.' And British film-makers who had been welcomed for bringing a diversity of entertainment to audiences stultified by formulaic Hol-lywood product found themselves out in the cold – again. What made it all the sourer was the annual proof of how audiences in Britain were flocking back to refurbished old cinemas and brand-new cineplexes: 78 million in 1987, the highest in six years. Unfortunately, the films they went to were usually American. By mid 1989, for instance, *Rain Man* had grossed £8 million in twelve weeks; *Indiana Jones and the Last Crusade* took nearly £2 million in its opening five days. (Into the new century, perhaps, when *Bridget Jones's Diary* can gross £47 million in Britain, these sums don't look impressive: they did in 1989.)

American tastes for their own films had changed: a shift took place towards the end of the 1980s and just before the digital revolution, away from fantasy movies heavy on special effects to realistic stories rooted in contemporary American life. This left British studios, with all their technical crafts, short of the big US productions they had serviced regularly for years: *Batman* had been the last of its kind shot at Pinewood; *Indiana Jones and the Last Crusade* at Elstree: neither facility had a block-buster to fill its stages. The new James Bond adventure, instead of occupying its familiar berth at Pinewood, had been shot mainly in Mexico where labour was cheaper. 'If advertising commercials dropped, all studios would be in trouble,' said Andrew Mitchell, who ran Elstree for its new owners, the Brent Walker-Masterman purchasers from Cannon. The studio had turned its stages over to commercials (for Olympus cameras), Pop promotions and even live gigs and TV record-ings of comedy formats, such as *The Bruce Forsyth Show*. To this abysmal fate Cannon's debacle had condemned a once proud and even profitable British industry. In 1985 Britain had invested £67 million in film-making; another £154 million had come from the US; in 1988 the respective shares were £58.9 million and £66.7 million. In 1985, fifty-eight British films had been made; in 1988 the number had dropped to forty-three.

A few blue patches showed through the clouds. The BBC had at last ironed out a compromise with its film unions and was now prepared, cautiously, to invest in several small TV-type films for the big screen, the first of which, it was announced, would be *Stags and Hens*, based on Willy Russell's stage play, a comedy about randy males and lubricious housewives being victims of a double booking for their private cele-brations. (The potential for a sex comedy with a social edge was tan-talisingly latent in this idea, but unrealised in Mike Ockrent's *Dancin' Thru the Dark*; a decade would pass before *The Full Monty* exploited the male–female inversion of women shamelessly enjoying the spectacle of naked men.) British Screen Finance, under Simon Relph, had shown more resilience than most had believed possible: it had invested in thirty-six British films by the end of the 1980s and, even better, had painfully squeezed an additional £4 million from the still stingy government by emphasising that overseas earnings on British films in 1987 had been £254 million gross – largely due to the post-*Laundrette* bunch of sex comedies. Yet, for the first time, less money was being invested in films than in the making of TV commercials. And *Cultural Trends*, published in February 1989 by the Institute for Policy Studies, disclosed that government spending on the arts in general remained static throughout the decade. Once again, the start–stop economy of film-making seemed to have halted the new wave of talent, just when it needed the extra impetus to make an impression on the wider shores of world cinema.

Though Branagh's *Henry V* wasn't due to première in London until October, talk of it following its Cannes 'sneak' did a lot to lift film people's spirits or, at least, the media's professed patriotism. Branagh was perfect material. He had cut himself out of the pack of young-to–ageing actors all jostling for Olivier's crown which the memory of his still unequalled performances had kept out of their grasp in his lifetime. Now he was dead; all bets were on. Albert Finney, Derek Jacobi, Ian McKellen had already made names for themselves in non–classical roles, in other countries, even on other screens. But as Michael Billington, the *Guardian*'s influential theatre critic, wrote, 'If one actor has recently proved that the Olivier spirit is not dead, it is surely [Branagh].' He was only twenty-eight: Belfast-born, RADA-trained, acclaimed (like

Olivier) in both comedy (a Cockney Touchstone in *As You Like It*) and tragedy (*Hamlet*), modern drama (a more controversial Jimmy Porter in a *Look Back in Anger* revival) and television (*The Fortunes of War*). An all-rounder, multimedia man much as Olivier had become in his last decades and, like Olivier, possessing his own theatrical company which enjoyed Prince Charles's patronage and was aptly called Renaissance.

Branagh, a stocky figure not out of place as a rugby forward, gave little hint above the neckline of the matinée idol looks which traditionally went with mellifluous poetry speaking as well as the shrill squeals of female fans. Albert Finney, his nearest comparison, was better-looking; and though both he and Branagh became stars overnight, they owed it to different resources. Both were of the 'who dares, wins' mentality. But Branagh had energy and application as well as daring: the desire to surprise, the will to prevail. After his brilliant debut, Finney turned from striver to drifter: he let his best years pass preoccupying himself, on the money he made from *Tom Jones*, with other aspects of life than the actor's, in travel, particularly, and though his occasional film performances nearly always disclosed his talent for unpredictable choices and revelatory creations, Finney fitted too comfortably into 'the life between'.

Branagh, at first, seemed to have no life between his stage and screen ventures. Like many Ulster-born people – though his family moved to Reading when he was a child, driven by sectarian violence from Belfast – the Protestant work ethic was his fuel. The lack of inhibitions that often go with such a drive served his ambitions perfectly. In 1989 he published his autobiography, whereas Olivier had waited until he was seventy-five, borrowing its title, *Beginning*, from *As You Like It*: 'I will tell you the beginning/And if it please your ladyships you shall see the end/For the best is yet to do.' Some critics were not pleased: they felt it presumptuous to start writing your life when you had barely started making your name. But it fitted his cocky pride, an act of cheeky daring that compared favourably with Olivier's risk taking and compulsion to surprise. What critics missed was the implicit emphasis in his epigraph on the phrase 'The best is yet to do'. It is mostly misquoted as 'The best is yet to be'. Branagh did not make that mistake: rather than waiting for things to come about of their own accord, he took them in hand and *did* them. He said he wrote the book to top up the treasury of his Renaissance theatre troupe – perhaps so.

Branagh, however, was what Olivier was not – at least at first – a film fan. He was star-fixated in the respectable sense of the term. His ambitions were formed when he was given, no, not the collected works of William Shakespeare but a set of back numbers of the magazine *Plays and Players* and pored over every detail of the 'Golden Years' of Olivier, Gielgud, Scofield, Richardson, Guinness and co. Branagh had enjoyed a triumph with the Royal Shakespeare Company, playing Henry V, though he said immediately, 'I felt I was under-used, and had more to contribute: it was almost a physical sensation.' The need to be stretched – or as Lord Reith, founder of the BBC, used to put it in his own Scots vowels, 'straitched' – is a defining characteristic of Branagh. Films offer him the way.

It is worth pausing a moment to compare him with his nearest rival in stage and screen talent and, already, his superior in experience and celebrity: Daniel Day-Lewis. Aged thirty-two in 1989, with a lean face and rangy figure, Day-Lewis was a lightning conductor to Branagh's earthed status. Not to display himself in public, but to lose himself: this was his mode for work and after-work. His troubled childhood, a school runaway, a son who'd scarcely known his anyhow distant father before the latter's death: all his cinema roles, and some of his stage ones, were, he admitted, attempts to find a refuge from certain unspecified demons that once caused him to walk off stage during *Hamlet* and never resume the role. The Ghost in the play and his memory of Cecil Day-Lewis, the poet laureate, apparently coincided too specifically to be dealt with in public. 'Yes, that's there,' he told an interviewer in 1989, 'I never want to get into competition with my father in any way.' Losing all sense of 'self' in a role brought relief – the greatest. And so he developed a technique closer to American Method players than English actors in which the hidden or evident attributes of a role were developed so as to take over the actor. Already, as noted, his brush-cut Fascist punk in *My Beautiful Laundrette*, followed within weeks by E. M. Forster's prissy, pince-nez'd scholar in *A Room With a View*, had served notice that here was a star with a difference – a thrilling kinship with De Niro was the often repeated observation.

Day-Lewis was conscious of it, spoke revealingly, though frugally, about it. Yes, he had had the Dalai Lama in mind while preparing to play Richard II – Richard's dejection and determination during his imprisonment was the link that the actor found. Soon afterwards, a critic in *Time* magazine called Day-Lewis 'a one-man Tibet' – a state whose borders defied better knowledge of what was happening within. For

Macbeth the role model was John F. Kennedy, for Coriolanus John McEnroe – for his temper and inability to cope with praise or stress. For Philip Kaufman's film of the Milos Kundera novel, *The Unbearable Lightness of Being*, in 1987, Day-Lewis had immersed himself in the minutiae of surgery: the sexual licence his character allowed himself gave him rather more difficulty, but the final performance showed a man polarised by his twin natures, his vocational dedication and his personal indulgence, which had similarities to the actor's own duality. *Stars and Bars*, one of the films Puttnam had greenlighted at Columbia, directed by Pat O'Connor, deserved better – was its lacklustre performance influenced by the studio change of regime? – but again Day-Lewis showed his chameleon talent, this time playing a bumbling Bond Street art dealer sent to negotiate the sale of a Renoir from a dogpatch family in the Deep South. Though no Preston Sturges, O'Connor made a good stab at American Gothic, and Day-Lewis's tone of desperate displacement among the poor white trash, continually apologising though he's in the right and wearing his apprehensive face above his 'power' tie with rueful acceptance that the worst is always certain, put some people in mind of another rueful representative of status without competence – Prince Charles.

Branagh, possibly, could not have run Day-Lewis even close to some of these creations, but Day-Lewis could not have become Branagh's type of entrepreneur. '[Day-Lewis's] career has been marked by the self-effacing zeal of the craftsman rather than the triumphant zeal of the star,' wrote Fintan O'Toole in July 1989, after observing the actor on the set of *My Left Foot*, playing Christy Brown, a cerebral palsy victim, whose cussed refusal to be crushed by disability was the most extreme of Day-Lewis's astonishing assumptions of character. Significantly, he had been attracted to the role by the script's first direction – Christy Brown putting the needle on a record with his sole flexible limb, his left foot. Day-Lewis made this single part of his body speak for the inarticulate rest, the way he opened the film, snaking out a bare and scrawny foot, tweaking a record from the shelf, shaking the disc out of the sleeve and putting it on the turntable, lifting the needle arm *and even locating the desired track*. He endowed the film with instantaneous wonder even before his tongue subverts the disease that has kept it stuck like a key in a lock that can't be turned and his grunts and gibbering begin to make intelligible sense.

The precise craftsmanship such a minor miracle of dexterity involved spoke directly to a man who had set out to be a cabinet maker, not a star, and who was to show the master craftsman's zeal for *making* things, solid, useful objects of daily life, shoes and house fittings, as an objective co-relative to the construction of characters. Such challenges gave him access to the serenity of the master craftsman. The danger, which was to become real in a few years' time, lay in the seductive pull of such off-screen handicrafts, given a film career crowned by an Oscar (for *My Left Foot*) and the financial independence to pick and choose, and even retire from acting for several years, seeking the 'serenity' of the workbench in place of the public limelight of the sound stage.

A young British star like Day-Lewis, in international demand, was not common in the 1980s where the ageing presences of Caine, Connery and Bates remained the reminder of the prodigal 1960s. Timothy Dalton had already been subsumed into the James Bond role, after which the mantle of greatness that had been prematurely run up for him after his stage successes fitted a little more loosely. In fairness, the new Bond film, *Licence to Kill*, called for a star who didn't bring along a classical tradition. Beefed up to compete with Hollywood's new brutalism and continuous nastiness, Dalton's Bond had also abandoned the celibacy so recently adopted for *The Living Daylights* in the age of Aids and reverted to sexism – he checks his blonde Bond girl into his South American banana republic hotel as 'my executive secretary' and answers her bristling query 'Why can't you be mine?' with the smirking put-down, 'Because it's a man's country down here.'

Loyalty to Her Majesty's secret service did not swing the plot this time: it was personal vengeance, Latino style. The series' special British quality of impudent make-believe had been sacrificed to the 'diehard' ethic of cold-blooded violence. 'Sadism for the family' was how I had described the first Bond, *Dr No*. *Licence to Kill* was now suitable for only *part* of the family. Dalton's relish for sending villains to their doom with a wisecrack attached had looked strained in his Bond debut, *The Living Daylights*; now the terminal gags were transferred to the villain, leaving Bond with precious little to show for all the athletic activity. 'For every plausible reason, he looks as bored in his second Bond film as Sean Connery did in his sixth,' wrote Richard Schickel in *Time*. The search for a new Bond got under way – to Dalton's relief, one suspects.

This poverty of heroes on and off the British screen, stars with the power to get things done, helped prepare the way for Branagh. 'Enter the King' was the script's instruction for him as well as for Henry. His film opened in Britain in October; a few weeks later, on 13 November 1989, its star-producer-director – prudent reticence made him forfeit a screenplay credit – was on the cover of *Time* magazine with the legend 'Branagh the Conqueror: The man who would be Olivier', and six inside pages. Richard Corliss, who wrote the cover story (with Anne Constable reporting from London), made an acute assessment of his claim to the title: 'In seven whirlwind years, he has become the most accomplished, acclaimed and ambitious performer of his generation.' He called Branagh 'an icon of Thatcherite initiative', whose entrepreneurial skills were only equalled by Andrew Lloyd Webber – whose *Starlight Express* opened that year – and who did not share in what David Hare called 'the bitterness in British politics . . . that has spilled into the arts'. Branagh was comfortable with his royal patronage; he was a cultural conservationist: 'He prizes restoration over strident relevance.'

All true and significantly so, given the long interregnum since any British star could command *Time*'s cover for his or her face. Up to then, Branagh had been hardly known outside American play-acting milieux: after this he was famous, though already there were faint-sounded warnings of that old sin in the eyes of the gods, even the success-worshipping American deities: the sin of hubris . . . of too-clever-by-half Ken. If there was such a risk, it wasn't a clear or even a present one to those who laid eyes on *Henry V,* a vividly visceral, populist experience, endowed with less chilly aristocracy than Olivier's and much more physicality. It was steeped in blood, battle mud and a reminder of how Henry's reconciliation with his Continental cousins – Paul Scofield was the King of France – was soon lost in the vendettas of the English civil wars. (This at least excluded Branagh from Thatcher's 'one of us' club, since it was interpreted as a warning against the supporters of British opposition seeking to retard Europe's drive towards greater unity.)

Branagh reclaimed the play from Olivier's legitimate infusion of World War Two jingoism. He emphasised the treachery of English nobles ready to sell their country to the enemy – unthinkable in 1944. Bardolph is hanged as a looter, again a bad advertisement for triumphant allied armies in 1944. The great test was, of course, Agincourt. How could the new film match, never mind surpass, Olivier's epic, the poetic sweep of excitement, the accelerando of galloping horsemen, the sudden silence followed by the avenging hiss of arrows through the air, orchestrated and amplified by William Walton's music? Very simply, Branagh made do with less and made as much of it. The cavalry charge is largely unseen in the mists, but amplified to the volume of twenty Grand National horse races. The English arrows have an angrier hiss. Where Olivier opened out the scene to battlefield dimensions with the order 'Charge', Branagh kept his big effects in check until the word 'Surrender'. Then the screen opened up into a panorama of still steaming death, ravaged earth and bloodstained pools through which Branagh's King, mud-bespattered like a rugby player, staggers with the body of the young potboy from the Boar's Head in his arms. In contrast to Olivier's tableau of patriotism, this new contender dedicates the day to heartbreak, not glory.

Branagh could not have foreseen his film opening in the immediate aftermath of Olivier's death; there was some mildly malicious criticism of the 'opportunistic' timing, but in a real sense, it was perfect timing. 'Let us scotch the myth', wrote Michael Billington, 'that Olivier was a glorious, starring anachronism in an age of ensemble acting and recognise both that audiences are hungry for the inklings of a strong personality and rejoice that his rage lives on in others unchecked.' Branagh was proof of both – for the time being. Not many industry figures saw *Henry V* when it was 'sneaked' at Cannes: in general, film-makers don't see each other's films, which is why so many of them delude themselves with a belief in their own uniqueness, unaware that it's long become formulaic. But they were sufficiently concerned by the prospect of unemployment on returning from Cannes to set up a meeting with Lord Young, now Secretary of State for Trade and Industry.

His predecessor, Paul Channon, had been moved to head the Department of Transport. As if this politician, who had let half the British film industry be sold to Cannon, was born to preside over misfortune, his tenure there was balefully distinguished by an unnervingly high incidence in the latter half of the decade of fatal disasters on river, rail, the London Underground and at sea. Though Channon could not be held personally responsible for these, they had happened on his 'watch'. And all significantly altered public awareness and revealed how the frequency and ferocity of loss of life were contingent upon political and economic policies. Before he left office, *Private Eye* gave the Minister the nickname Paul ('Crash') Channon. He certainly bore more responsibility for the national cinema's disaster than any other single politician. Film people already knew that, of course.

They found Lord Young just as obdurate when they gathered on his

doorstep on 18 July 1989, all but carrying a placard saying 'Have Soup
Bowl, Will Beg'. Caravaggio could scarcely have equalled the chiaroscuro
applied to the picture they painted of industry penury. In 1948, when a
similar plea had gone up, a Board of Trade memorandum penned by an
anonymous civil servant had shown a marked lack of charity. 'The film
industry is not one which normal financial channels look upon with
favour,' he began, mildly enough; then he really opened fire: 'Its habits
are peculiar, most of the people engaged in it are rogues of one kind or
another, and a good deal of money has been lost by unwise investment
in it or by the uncontrolled behaviour of producers.'

Doing the begging this time round were not rogues of one kind or
even the other – most of them, anyhow – but a posse of the most
respected film-makers who could be mustered. What they wanted now
was money to join forces in co-productions with European movie-
makers, so that at least they would have that market sewn up if America
proved too hard to crack. (The fact that the American market *always* proved
too hard to crack was discreetly omitted.) No deal. They were sent away
and told to consider themselves lucky that the government might [*sic*]
continue the £1.5 million of annual subsidy it gave to Simon Relph's
investment bank, British Screen. This funding's shelf life expired in
1990. Lord Young hinted, out of residual shame perhaps, that he was of
a mind to extend it. Whether, of course, Lord Young would still be
there by that expiry date was politely not mentioned; the headlines
already suggested he was for the chop in another government reshuffle.
It was ever thus with those who had responsibility for films. 'What! will
the line stretch out to the crack of doom?' Macbeth's shocked enquiry
seems particularly apposite to film ministers. Being told that a delegation
from the British film industry was waiting upon them with demands for
cash must by now have come to seem like the news that Birnam Wood
was starting to walk to Dunsinane. After turning away the little band of
hope, Lord Young might well find himself out of a job. But the film
industry's thoughts were on its own fate: it thought it would soon be
out of a future.

Working quietly at the end of the 1980s, causing no fuss between
films, fixed intently on their own vision and performing minor miracles
of economy and hope in order to realise it, were three film-makers:
Mike Leigh, Peter Greenaway, Derek Jarman. Two of them proved long-
distance runners, still active in the new century. One of them, Jarman,
lost the race in pathetic circumstances, dying of Aids and thus depriving

film-making of its always cheerful, often jeering outsider's voice. They became – along with Ken Loach, who was mostly working in television at the end of the 1980s – the best-known British film-makers on the European continent. Not, though, in their conservative or philistine homeland.

It shows what may have been lost to British cinema that Mike Leigh's *High Hopes* was only his second feature film in seventeen years (after *Bleak Moments*, to whose title it offered an ironic echo). Stage work and television had kept Leigh busy in between. *High Hopes* showed an advance into social politics, not simply private anguish. It was a look at life, and lifestyles, in 1980s London, with seven characters and four principal dwelling places exemplifying, hilariously or sadly but always with punctilious precision of decor and dialogue, the way life has opened up or closed in for the people under Leigh's roofs.

First, a King's Cross flat tenanted by a bearded, ageing ex-Commie, sharp-tongued but no longer biting, and his live-in girlfriend, ex-CND, now park gardener, both radicals without a cause turning into stoic recluses, with a large cactus in the living room, a metaphor for the poor under Thatcherism ('cos it pricks your arse every time you pass it'). Next a detached home in status-ridden suburbia inviting horror at the kitsch explosion in the lounge, dinette and Jacuzzi, owned by a fly boy who expects his daily profit to fall off the back of a lorry and a wife who sees the world through colour-supplement spectacles. Third, a London terrace house not yet gentrified, home to a grumpy, lonely, forgetful old lady and a single-bar electric fire that's an invitation to hypothermia. Next door is the gentrified version – paint line indicating clear class division – the compassion-proofed residence of a pair of yuppies.

Leigh's film was a condensed version of 'how we live now'. He opened up the seams of everyday British life and mined them for comedy and pathos, using his by now well-established practice of making his cast investigate and eventually 'become' the people they played: his yuppies, for instance, lunched at Harrods for self-indoctrination. There was already a slight criticism of his treatment of the poor and deprived – 'patronising' it was muttered, a view that was to swell with the years, though more a reflex caused by Leigh's proven dedication to social anthropology rather than any real lack of empathy with the have-nots. Somewhat more worrying was his cruelly funny burlesque of the have-it-alls. He was never to get the two quite in balance, partly because the privileged classes were expert deceivers, resisting being cracked open for inspection. But the truth of each creation in *High Hopes* crossed the style change as well as the class divide: it was as if Age Concern had met up, in unlikely circumstances, with *Spitting Image*, the comedy show featuring well-known caricatures, and somehow managed to get a dialogue going. The result was a movie that was politically caustic, socially acute and hugely entertaining. In Ken Loach's gap years, Leigh reminded us of a contemporary Britain in which we all lived.

Peter Greenaway had already followed the unexpected success of his feature debut, *The Draughtsman's Contract*, with *A Zed and Two Noughts*; in *The Belly of an Architect* he had drawn even closer to the mental geography and arcane hideouts of Continental Europe – thus distancing himself with deliberateness from Anglo-Saxon tolerance and under- standing. That he was travelling alone obviously did not worry him in the slightest: he probably found himself more at home, in his own sensibility, when not having to deal with his countrymen's aesthetic blindness and parochial deafness. Set in Rome, the new film recorded with precise prognosis the steps to calamity and then extinction of an eminent architect, whose belly is the first image in the film, mimicking the rotundity of St Peter's, a fleshly landmark amid the religious fantasies of Roman Catholicism – and, in Greenaway's diagnosis, just as infected. With what, though, it was hard to say: perhaps the view of life as a self- fulfilling conspiracy that claims body and soul eventually.

In *The Draughtsman's Contract*, his hero painted himself into a corner where his murderers were waiting, alarmed by the clues to their guilt that his sketches disclosed; in *The Belly of an Architect* his hero is also illuminated by a foredoomed mortality as his days of grace expire and he loses his health (to a malignant tumour), his wife (to a philandering colleague), his self-respect (to the city's *dolce vita*), his work (to a bur- eaucratic cabal) and his life (to all of the aforementioned inflictions). Once the autopsy was over, *The Belly of an Architect* was seen – by some – to have the macabre beauty of a tomb with a view. Greenaway's imagery deployed architecture in a Kubrickian fashion, relishing symmetry that shed beauty but also engendered apprehension; while his photographer, Sacha Vierny, deployed his own art in such sympathy with the master's eye that it was hard not to think of him and Greenaway in terms of the twin couple in *A Zed and Two Noughts*.

Offering no explanations to populist feelings (predictably in a temper over Greenaway's perceived 'elitism', probably to his satisfaction), *The Belly of an Architect* was all but dubbed, in a phrase the Prince of Wales used derisively about the New Architecture, 'a carbuncle' in the British cinema. I found it heartening: I was in a very small minority.

A year later Greenaway was in Paris, ever nearer to his spiritual matrix in Continental Europe, shooting for French television, as a contribution to the 200th anniversary of the Republic, what he described as 'a poetic documentary' on the corpses retrieved from the Seine during the French revolutionary terror. All the characters, bar a couple, were cadavers. Intestinal fascination made itself apparent in this work, too, in that he regarded the human body as nothing more than the alimentary canal wrapped around muscle. Mortality was close to his heart (as well as belly): he had once made a four-minute film entirely about thirty-seven people who had fallen out of upper-storey windows. His films had become more and more directly allusive, teeming with details and metaphors taken from painters that he combined with this Jacobean fascination with violent death, with whole heaps of it, despatched with a swagger and chronicled with an actuary's pedantry.

As a taxonomist – a list maker – he has no rival, though his inventories have usually a baleful character and his attraction to numbers has assumed the outline of a compulsive-behaviour syndrome. One number that is usually small – around £2 million in 1989 – was the budget of each cinema film he made, collected in advance of shooting from a loose syndicate of state and private financiers by his customary Dutch producer and partner, Kees Kasander, a man with an eye for the small print on tax breaks and subsidies. Thus Greenaway operates in relatively relaxed financial parameters – like Woody Allen at the other end of the human comedy – and can afford himself the luxury of critical hostility. At least for the generation to whom he still appears subversive.

The Cook, the Thief, His Wife and Her Lover, with its emphasis on the connection between sex, greed, power and sumptuary violence, was premièred in the very month that the British boom in property went into reverse and many over-indulgent entrepreneurs lost their lunch. The film's metaphorical power wasn't loot, not even on the tabloids, though its excesses fed their own appetite for the sins that Greenaway's gaudy morality incited. 'It's about how everything passes from the mouth to the anus,' its maker observed in an understatement. The connection between food and faeces was complemented by a recurrent emphasis on fornication during the eight-day duration of the action, set in a flamboyantly baroque restaurant owned by the thief (Michael Gambon) who bullies all in sight, especially his long-suffering wife (Helen Mirren).

The cook (Richard Bohringer) accepts any humiliation, so long as he can practise his culinary art. The lover (Alan Howard) is an unlikely figure, a bookish client with whom the wife starts an affair. It begins in the restaurant lavatory, climaxes in the pantry and ends detumescently in a cold-storage van among dead fish. In Greenaway's cookbook, revenge was a dish that people of taste no longer preferred to eat cold, but piping hot.

The film was unlike anything ever cooked in a British kitchen. Greenaway explained it was an update of Jacobean tragedy. However, it also works – better, perhaps – as an allegory for the film industry itself. The cook is the director turning out masterpieces with the financial backing of the thief, aka the producer, only to have his vulgarian employer spit upon them. In revenge, he gets to stuff the lover, a man whose trade is in words, like a screenwriter, down the scoundrel's throat at the prompting of the wife – his naked muse. However one takes it, with a pinch of salt, or a dose of Alka-Seltzer, Greenaway's film was a work of undeniable eccentricity, savagery and visual nausea. It radiated its maker's subversive relish.

Greenaway and Derek Jarman had that in common, as well as a talent for painting: Greenaway showed (and sold) in commercial art galleries, Jarman gave his collages and assemblages away to friends. Jarman used his painter's eye when he made films: he required no script and, though he was a good writer, his words alive with thought, he preferred intuition to commentary when he held a camera. 'Imagine if Henry Moore had to explain what he was going to do with a sculpture and then make it fit with the words.' The British Film Institute, which had part-financed Greenaway's first feature, had put up £475,000 for Jarman's *Caravaggio*, a film about the homosexual romance between the artist and his male-model lover in which the artist killed the thing he loved, then, according to Jarman, tipped posterity off to the crime in a 'confessional' painting of St John's beheading. Jarman had two strokes of luck with the timing of his film. One was the death of Jean Genet the week before it opened, which reminded one how totally an artist could fuse his own sexuality with his commitment to criminality; the other was the attempt by Winston Churchill MP, son of the late prime minister, to extend the Obscene Publications Act to television which had recently shown Jarman's *Sebastiane* with its homoerotic impudence and nudity, and *Jubilee*, his apocalyptic snook cocked at Elizabeth II's anniversary. In *Caravaggio* the Pope observed, 'Revolutionary gestures in art are a great help –

keeps the "quo" in the "status".' Jarman saw the Establishment's move against him as an attempt to do just that.

Caravaggio was, and remained, the film closest to his heart, and other parts: like the painter, Jarman raided the stock of sacred images and converted them with impunity into celebrations of human carnality. His public work was fully merged with his own sexual predilection, while the deliberate anachronisms introduced into seventeenth-century Italy – Vespa motor scooters, cigarettes, typewriters – symbolised for him the continuity of history, liberation and oppression.

'If I didn't exist, then Mary Whitehouse and Winston Churchill would have had to invent me,' he told an interviewer, Michael O'Pray, in 1986. *Caravaggio* was a portrait of the film-maker, as much as the artist. It was sad that Jarman's life was to be as foreshortened as Caravaggio's. He discovered around Christmas 1986 that he was infected with the HIV virus and cheerfully celebrated that, too: 'Sexual encounters lead to knowledge. . . . Straight men have all the responsibility, and responsibility is not liberating.' He confessed he would have to make his next film in a hurry. 'No metropolitan gay man can be sure he will be alive in six years' time.'

The Last of England felt like a communiqué from a war artist who knew his days were numbered. Shot in Super8, with a crew of seven instead of the union minimum of twenty-one, it cost a mere £130,000, a third of it put up by a German company – like Greenaway, Jarman found it easier to unlock foreign funds. It borrowed its title from Holman Hunt's Pre-Raphaelite painting of shipboard emigrants bound for the New World but making forlorn eyes at the Old as it receded. Jarman's own voyage of self-discovery was more a commuter's trip than an epic voyage of embarkations: flights of fancy, childhood memories, home movies, figments of contemporary consciousness (terrorism, armed repression, urban degeneration) and bits and pieces of homoerotic flashiness (masturbation on a Union Jack) intended, perhaps, to be a red rag to Mrs Whitehouse and her ilk. It worked on the level of nostalgia; as a state of the nation address only fitfully. The promo clichés of every Pop-group video had vitiated its power to shock, though Jarman's by now well-known condition gave it an elegiac emphasis that softened its formulaic content.

Posterity had now a problematic appeal to him: he spoke more and more frequently of growing things – 'I always wanted to be a gardener' – and on the balcony of his flat in a block in Charing Cross Road he had a sprig of green in a tub: a chestnut sapling grown from a conker he had found on Chekhov's grave on a visit to Russia when he took his film *The Tempest* to Moscow. It was both comfort and conundrum. 'Whom is one to bequeath a garden to?' He was shortly to retire to his reclusive tar-paper shack at Dungeness, where the wild flowers of the sea coast gathered around him in the shingle while the nuclear power station loomed in the distance like one of his own apocalyptic symbols. 'Perhaps all gardens now are potentially remembrance poppy fields,' he said. Jarman's films were to be like markings on a grave head, compared with the poster display that Greenaway represented. As 'outsiders', both of them incurred the ignorant mockery of a conservative film industry.

The biggest 'British' film of 1988 was *A Fish Called Wanda*, written by and starring John Cleese, and directed by the Ealing veteran Charles Crichton. Cleese, however, wanted an American studio to finance it. David Puttnam turned it down at Columbia – something of a mistake since MGM's investment of £7.5 million eventually yielded £20 million worldwide. It topped the American video charts in 1990.

The decade's most eccentric film, *Little Dorrit*, was produced, appropriately, in the area of London whose economic difficulties simultaneously foreshadowed the recession of the early 1990s. *Little Dorrit*, a six-hour-long, two-part version of Charles Dickens's novel, was made in studios at Rotherhithe, on the very same swath of the Thames, known as Docklands, where developers were holding their corporate breath to see if the strapped-for-cash yuppies could fork out the cash to pay for their new riverside homes as the property boom reached an unheard-of peak, 27 per cent higher than in 1986, while the stock market went into free fall in October 1987. Apart from Abel Gance's *Napoleon*, few filmmakers attempted what Christine Edzard did – or with so few resources except abundant human talent. Her film was compared at the time with the populous stage production of *Nicholas Nickleby*. A poor comparison.

With her producer husband Richard Goodwin, and his partner John Brabourne, she made Victorian London arise in all its greatness and meanness under the ships' timbers that still held up her warehouse studios' roof. The other miracle was one of imagination, not construction: she did not let the movie sink under the logistical weight of its own populous authenticity. She made it live. Such numbers, such faces and figures, and such performances! After Lean – and some said better than Lean – it is the best Dickens film. Or 'films', since, aping the Victorian stereopticon toy, Edzard filmed the story in double vision. By aligning two separate viewpoints on its characters and events – the first entitled 'Nobody's Fault', being that of a good-hearted but weak young man, while the second, called 'Little Dorrit', being seen through the eyes of a resilient and strong-willed girl – Edzard produced a single stand-out view of era, place and people. The Thatcherite values were implicitly under attack in the first 177 minutes: corruption, heartlessness, get-rich-quick fever of the speculative classes were contrasted with the inner-city desolation of the poor caught in the debt trap. The cast was contemporary, in attitude if not apparel: slum landlords, crook financiers, uncaring bureaucrats, ruined speculators and front-page suicides. In its edifice in which the indolent and incompetent served their time and filled their places, the Circumlocution Office had its parallel in present-day Whitehall. But just as one is lying back, drained but exhilarated by people's misfortunes and miracles – like the Dorrit family released from the crumbling hive of the Marshalsea Prison, a boarding house with bars for bad-debtors – Edzard proceeded to tell the same story over again, from a fresh angle, filling in the gaps, fleshing out the characters, all in ways that shaped the political focus and altered the perspective on the social scene.

With 211 named players, the cast list was like a National Gallery of all the talents: too many to name or even to apologise to for not naming. Pre-eminent, though, was Alec Guinness as William Dorrit, the haughty gentleman-sponge. Among Guinness's six best screen performances, it is at the very top. He has never held us so breathless as during Dorrit's dementia at his elder daughter's sumptuous wedding feast, when the old lag in him, shifty but without shame, his mind wandering back to his prison cell and genteel knavery, bids the throng of titled grandees, 'Welcome to the Marshalsea.' Edzard released in Guinness what other directors, including Lean, never managed to reach: his instinct for self-dissimulation as a cover-up of himself from himself. 'In the part of William Dorrit', Guinness later said, 'I probably explored unpleasant things in myself.' As his biographer, Garry O'Connor, wrote: 'His sensibility nourished the role, feeding it with everything from the past he could muster' – and more, too, from his own hidden sense of shame at the semi-Dickensian past that came to light, his illegitimacy in particular, during Guinness's later years. He found a lifetime in the part. An anonymous critic in *Newsweek* called the film '... the first post-modern Dickens film ... for the uncertain end of a chaotic century'.

The film arrived in a London where headlines were intimating the home-grown chaos of the years of Tory rule: 'Private Affluence and Public Guilt' ... 'The Politics of Disaster' ... 'Thatchervision: the Blindness of Greed'. The ravages of Aids and the emollient charity of the Live Aids concert; violence on the streets as pickets clashed with police over Rupert Murdoch's successful attempt to drag the newspaper industry from the dark ages of composing-room rule into the electronic age of proprietorial print shops; the biggest storm ever to hit Britain in October 1987; and one fatal transport disaster after another of the kinds already noted that took away people's sense of personal security and public responsibility. Dickens, the great reporter, would have been in his element. The country felt it had been pitched out into the cold and the dark. The film industry, of course, as the 1990s arrived, had already got used to those disconcerting elements.

7

From the Depths

Some time in early spring 1990, Richard Attenborough lunched with Peter Palumbo, the millionaire patron of the arts ('music, travel, gardening, reading' ran his *Who's Who* recreational entry, firm in the English tradition of pleasure and patronage). Palumbo had recently been appointed chairman of the Arts Council: he would be knighted the following year by *his* patron, Mrs Thatcher. Attenborough was then trying to set up his film about Charlie Chaplin. 'Filming is the easy part, financing is horrendous,' he told Palumbo. The money would be American, he added.

'What, for an Englishman like Chaplin?'

'I'm afraid so. We simply couldn't set up a film like that here. We've hardly any film industry left.'

Barely two dozen British films were scheduled for production in 1990, compared with thirty-eight the previous year and fifty-six in 1988. Unfavourable dollar–sterling exchange rates were deepening the gloom. There was talk at Pinewood Studios that the elaborate set built for *Batman* would be crated up and re-erected in the Mexican film studios where the last James Bond adventure had been shot: a British studio film costing £5 million could be made for as little as £1 million in Mexico. 'In Nicholas Ridley,' David Puttnam said – and Puttnam was a man more frequently given to nuzzling the hand that fed him than savaging it – 'we've got a Secretary of State [for Trade and Industry] who gives the impression that he would regard it as his greatest success . . . if he could close the British film industry down.' Simon Relph had announced he was resigning as head of British Screen Finance at the end of 1990 to go back to independent production. At least that sector offered the company of fellow *misérables*: running a film bank, in contrast, was simply looking after stagnant accounts.

As Palumbo listened to Attenborough's gloomy tidings, he said, 'Does the boss know all this?' The 'boss' was the Prime Minister, to whom

Palumbo was very close. He declared that she must be told and in turn
told Lord McAlpine, a Tory grandee who was Tory party treasurer and
bag carrier, and he, in turn, told the 'boss'. When Attenborough met
Mrs Thatcher, 'Why do we not have the leading film industry in
Europe?' she is said to have enquired in her blunt way that expected not
only an answer but action to make the answer good.

Thus did Charlie Chaplin, an expatriate Brit who had spent his most
creative span of life as a resident of Hollywood, inspire Mrs Thatcher to
set in motion a salvage operation for the British film industry and keep
its most favoured, if financially strapped, talents from emigrating to
Hollywood. Picking up his cue from Attenborough, though failing
perhaps to appreciate the irony of it in the aftermath of his own aborted
American adventure, David Puttnam added, 'Our talent will always go
to Hollywood because it isn't nurtured here. You go where you are
allowed to feel significant' – or at least boss – for a bit. The outcome:
'THATCHER CALLS SUMMIT TO HELP AILING FILM INDUSTRY' as the
Independent headlined it at the end of May 1990, just a few weeks after
those on the invitation list to meet the Prime Minister in Downing
Street had returned from Cannes and were perhaps aware that a healthy
suntan was not the complexion of woe that would count in their favour.
The date was set for 15 June – time for the tan to fade – and holidays
were put on hold and a buzz of hopefulness, not loud enough to be
called avarice, ran through the restaurants that film-makers in search of
comfort food as well as finance still patronised.

Early acceptances came from producers Lord Brabourne, David
Puttnam, Nik Powell and Simon Relph; directors were thinner on the
invitation list, John Boorman (who lived in Ireland) being the most
notable. Bryan Forbes, who had headed Elstree Studios when Lord
Delfont ran its parent company, Thorn-EMI, did not attend the summit
but, in a letter to the *Independent*, recalled that for the £5 million he'd
been given to work with, twenty films had resulted and a group profit
of 300 per cent on the investment. Presumably this timely reminder of
what small amounts of money could do was intended to *encourager les
autres*.

The Downing Street agenda was fine-tuned – perhaps more finely
than some of those attending would have wished. Joining in European
ventures was to be the goal, rather than the old dream of 'cracking
Hollywood'. Even Downing Street was not *that* visionary, despite Mrs
Thatcher's old friend and Hollywood power-broker, Lew Wasserman,

being included in the gathering of VIPs. They were to explore ways of co-production in the single European market that was scheduled to open up in 1992. European companies were eager to have partners who spoke English. One of the hardiest, if most fanciful, shibboleths of such co-production deals was that films made in the English language held the key to successful American distribution. It was never proved to be so – and enough dashed hopes littered the release schedules to disprove it – but this peculiarly chauvinist fiction was still, in 1991, the straw at which many of the summiteers clutched.

'Films can project a culture,' said Puttnam, reading the clues in the tea leaves even before the Downing Street teapot had filled the cup. 'I distinguish between a language and a culture. I think they coexist and it is perfectly possible for an entirely French film to be made in English.' He was right, of course: in a few years' time, 'entirely French' films like *Vatel*, which opened the Cannes Film Festival in 2000, would be made 'in English', even though it was set in the time and at the court of Louis XIV; but it, and some others like it, were among the worst French films ever made. English didn't commend them: it damned them. In fact, the European co-production deals generally failed to get off the ground for financial rather than linguistic reasons: Britain simply didn't have the subsidies that the French, Italian, Spanish, German co-producers were expecting as an equity pledge for their own countries' usually well-subsidised investment.

Even before the summit, some expressed scepticism about the Tory leader's eagerness to hear the pleadings of hard-up movie makers or, indeed, prospective pro-European partners. 'Movies' and 'Europe' were not words that Mrs Thatcher held in reverence. More likely, the encouraging sounds made by the party that was even then pulling itself into shape for the next general election, the one that would be called New Labour, had more to do with Downing Street's tea and sympathy. Attenborough and Puttnam had both been to see Neil Kinnock, then Labour Leader of the Opposition. His party had shown the kind of pragmatism that could be converted into money for film-makers: it had tabled an amendment to Norman Lamont's Finance Bill (aka 'the Budget') seeking to transfer tax relief from property deals to film-making via the Business Expansion Scheme. The property market had now reached the point of overheating and was shortly to suffer meltdown. The Labour leadership probably didn't believe more votes would come its way if it embraced film-makers; but reviling property dealers and

embarrassing the nervous Tory government that was soon to deal with
the cries and heartbreaks of home owners left with negative equity on
their doorsteps as the value of their dwelling places slumped was good
enough reason to greet Attenborough and Puttnam with welcoming
(though still empty) hands.

As recently as July 1989 Lord Young, then Secretary of State for Trade
and Industry, had given the same film-makers short shrift when they
had pleaded their poverty before him. But Young was out of office by
mid 1990 and the buck passed to Eric Forth, the new Films Minister at
the DTI, the tenth to hold that portfolio in as many years. Mr Forth
knew nothing about films: but that wasn't necessarily a disqualification.
Some film people judged it an asset. Only a few voiced a deeper concern.
One was Nik Powell. 'I don't believe it's the number of films made that
counts,' he said, referring to tax breaks, 'it's the number of hits that's
important. We don't want a major deterioration in quality, as happened
in Australia.' He was referring to the rush of government generosity that
followed the Australian New Wave of film-making which, in a couple
of years from 1975 on, had produced *Picnic at Hanging Rock*, *The Last
Wave*, *Newsfront*, *My Brilliant Career*, and launched the careers of Peter
Weir, Philip Noyce, Gillian Armstrong and others. Overgenerous tax
subsidies from Canberra, delighted at finding moving pictures put Australia on the world map more influentially than even canned pears,
resulted in doctors, dentists, accountants and anyone with cash looking
for a tax break financing films, generating oversupply, debasing quality
and driving the makers off to Hollywood. Powell's words would apply
even more strongly to the later years of the 1990s – and be equally
ignored.

The summit agenda was set by three papers supplied by Nicholas
Ridley, Simon Relph and Richard Attenborough. It would last four to
five hours and Mrs Thatcher's office put the word around that she did
not want people saying 'their party piece'. She did want 'real discussion'.
(That she also wanted them to have agreed in advance what *they* wanted,
and how they'd go about it, seems not to have struck anyone as con-
tradictory to the spirit of the exercise. When they assembled in No. 10's
conference room, they of course all said 'their party pieces'.)

It was unfortunate that the summit precisely coincided with the
publication, in June 1990, of *My Indecision Is Final*, the searing account
by Jake Eberts and Terry Ilott of the internal wrangling, financial confusion and managerial incompetence that caused Goldcrest's collapse

just four years earlier. Thus the participants would have been able to read the (generally excellent) reviews of the book before they proceeded to ignore its caveats. No one mentioned it in No. 10, though; they were all on their best behaviour. Very little information actually emerged from the Downing Street summit, possibly because much of what was said had already been said so many times before that none of it was news.

Bryan Appleyard, a sceptical commentator, probably guessed correctly when, five days in advance, he predicted what would be said from 9 a.m. until a break for a light lunchtime collation: 'David Puttnam will talk rapidly about the need for a British-based film academy that will make English the language of a new Europe-wide industry. Attenborough will launch into impassioned rhetoric about the moral necessity of British movies to be made. He will probably cry.' Attenborough was indeed impassioned, though not lachrymose. But his cleverest move, some judged, was to bring in Lew Wasserman, whose persuasive voice was said to have so moved Mrs Thatcher five years earlier that her government had abolished the Eady Levy tax on the box office, thus freeing more coin for American-controlled distributors to take home. The 'elder statesman' of Hollywood told the PM that Britain had the potential to become the Hollywood of Europe. As a harbinger of this good news he – or, rather, Universal Studios – planned to build a theme park at Rainham, Essex. Even Wasserman must have felt this was a somewhat flimsy foundation for the 'Hollywood of Europe'. His more solid motive, along with his Hollywood peers, was to make sure that the American film industry would not be increasingly isolated and possibly taxed by European governments bent on protecting their own film industries from Hollywood's global capitalism. It would suit the Americans to see the British form closer links with European producers and institutions, thus furnishing American film-making-in-Britain with a friendly conduit, or a convenient cover, for their own operations on the Continent.

Even before Downing Street put out the welcome mat for British film-makers, American film-makers were so eager to return to Europe they scarcely paused to wipe their feet before opening production offices. This was the irony: Mrs Thatcher was being persuaded to see Europe as an 'opportunity'; Hollywood saw the new trading community as a threat to its quasi-monopoly of European movie entertainment. It was good policy to be part of it (if only to thwart it).

In January 1990 a man from Paramount announced his studio was opening a London production office. I was present and saw the faces of the Brits invited to hear the news brighten. Yes, Paramount's honcho continued, his studio 'intended to originate and develop pictures with European talent'. His listeners' faces fell slightly. 'European ...?' Oh, you mean the money will go abroad and not into honest British wallets? Erm, well ... yes, perhaps. In 1990 Paramount had bought 49 per cent of Zenith, the British production outfit which made *Personal Services*, *Prick Up Your Ears* and other successes. That helped explain Charles Denton's hint that Zenith would have fewer 'native sons' on its production slate, more movies with 'wider' appeal – i.e. American-style movies shot in Europe with an all-American cast, or the adaptation of John le Carré's spy thriller *The Russia House*, that Pathé, the French conglomerate, was shooting in Europe with Sean Connery and a load of American dollars. Paramount's move, the first of several by Hollywood majors, was a pre-emptive strike against any nasty fiscal or quota ideas the European community might have when a one-market trading area came about in 1992 which might leave Hollywood on the outside looking in. Join ... join ... join before they close the door, or at least make it a tighter squeeze.

Universal announced it was considering building a studio, in partnership maybe with the BBC, on the bit of estuary ground whose disused gasworks had been turned into a plausible 'double' for bombed Saigon when Kubrick shot *Full Metal Jacket* there. Warner Bros were expected to follow – after all, they were in partnership with David Puttnam already. Richard Attenborough and Universal had a 'sweetheart deal' for his Charlie Chaplin movie.

It was reassuring to the new wave of potential American film-makers-in-Europe to know that although the Community's rules allowed it to take protective measures (i.e. quotas) to protect their native film and TV industries against American dominance, the rules added '... where practicable'. A classic let-out. It meant that European governments were not going to risk populist uprisings on a Romanian scale by banning the ever-popular Hollywood blockbusters that dominate every 'Top Ten' list in every country on the Continent. But there was no harm in making sure, was there? And keeping an eye on your Hollywood rivals at the same time. This would have seemed good news to the Brits, had their spirits not sunk so low. There was an added suspicion that any new American production spree might mean indigenously British subjects being given a Hollywood make-over, the way Fay Weldon's *Life and Loves of a She-Devil*, a quintessentially British-made piece of TV entertainment, had been denatured and turned into an American vehicle for Meryl Streep and Roseanne Barr. The purists – yes, some still survived – felt the advantage wouldn't be to the Brits if all the Americans-in-Britain wanted was that vivisected entity known as an 'international' film. Perhaps we should look to Continental Europe for our production deal? That certainly was appealing to British producers, but the truth was it was extremely difficult to do co-production deals with well-subsidised European partners, as long as our stingy government refused to put a like amount of cash in the pot.

Such self-interested considerations helped create the momentum that got the Downing Street summit scheduled. Now they were in the State Drawing Room – yes, actually hobnobbing with the Prime Minister, and Dickie and Lew had her ear. Mrs Thatcher expressed her gratification at the example Lew Wasserman set of 'enterprise culture' by proposing his new improved version of Universal's theme park on English soil. She turned to Attenborough and said, 'Why didn't you come years ago?'

'Because I wasn't asked,' he replied. (Legend later attributed to Attenborough's answer the customary luvvie embellishment of 'darling'.) But it was clear that the film summiteers left Downing Street in higher spirits than when they entered it. Perhaps Nicholas Ridley's rather grudging promise to look at the situation and see what he could come up with spelled money in the wind. It would certainly not have been made if a figure of some kind hadn't been struck in advance. Mrs Thatcher didn't want a repetition of the argy-bargy that ensued when a similar meeting with TV executives had taken place in 1989. The outcome was: two working parties were set up to examine structural modifications to the industry and investment incentives. Lew Wasserman had stressed how valuable tax breaks had been to US film investment throughout the 1980s. One working party would be chaired by the Department of Trade and Industry and one attended by Treasury officials. Mrs Thatcher's newly kindled enthusiasm was not going to be let get out of hand by those who held the actual money purses. Summing up the seminar, Iain Johnstone wrote in the *Sunday Times* that the true achievement lay in having achieved a meeting with the Prime Minister in the first place. Once civil servants took over . . .

Opinions were canvassed among film people *not* present. They were pessimistic. 'The government could help the film industry by resigning,' said *Withnail and I*'s screenwriter, Bruce Robinson. Hanif Kureishi did not go this far, but was pretty disgruntled: 'I don't think the government should do anything. They're ignorant, suburban people who wouldn't know a work of art if it bit them.' The truth, which became evident almost before the Downing Street tea party did the washing up, was that such a meeting hadn't really been intended to satisfy so much as show willing and help feed the hungry, provided they adopted Tory shibboleths and helped themselves. It was intended to be just enough (and no more) to demonstrate that cultural commitment could haul the government up to the impending election. Just enough (and no more) to be able to say to Labour, with a smirk, 'Who needs your lump of sugar?'

A financial mouse crept timorously out of this mountain of misplaced faith. Tax incentives were judged the quickest way of changing the weather. The report of the Fiscal Incentive Working Group recommended attracting risk capital back into the industry. Well and good; but the prospect was considerably dimmed by the requirement that risk capitalists should keep their investment in a film for at least five years if they didn't want to lose their tax relief. Sensible, yes; but taking far too noble a view of tax avoidance. The other result was slightly more solid: a promise of £5 million, spread over three years, to encourage European co-productions. It, too, got nowhere, however: by mid 1991 the first instalment hadn't even been paid over by the DTI. And even earlier, the *patronne*, Mrs Thatcher herself, had ceased to be Prime Minister, deposed by the internal revolt in the Tories' parliamentary party. Perhaps the two people who saw most clearly where their future lay were Attenborough and Puttnam. Shortly after the Downing Street seminar, it was announced that they had joined the Labour Party.

Where television investment in film-making was concerned, 1990 was a watershed year. Small was no longer beautiful. The best years of Channel 4 were behind them: the company that had spent £500,000 on *My Beautiful Laundrette*, a screenplay that other potential backers had found 'too British, too dirty, or both', and been rewarded with a critical and commercial hit, was running low in its appetite for what had become known as 'a Channel 4-type production': a sharp, contemporary, youthful-feeling work that said, or implied, how destructive Thatcherism was to the bone and marrow of the nation. The writers of the Fifties and Sixties were now approaching middle age and their fires had cooled. David Rose, the true begetter of many such films was due to retire after spending some £50 million on around 160 films.

The coming auction of TV franchises now made the companies leery of the 'luxury' of film-making. Don Boyd's view was that 'Channel 4 has not been a launch pad for British cinema'. He pointed out, justly, that the initial TV investment still meant a struggle to raise the rest of the budget. 'It has too often thrived at the expense of those who wanted to make films, relying on them to raise the money.' Roger Wingate, one of the most alert distributor-producers, concurred and added that many Channel 4 films were too limited: 'it would seem as if the vogue for the small British film is past.'

David Puttnam, perhaps happily aware that his new film, the first of the few he would make in his post-Columbia Indian summer, *Memphis Belle*, was a film with epic pretensions, chimed in, 'Three decades of television culture have scaled down our ambitions.' People were afraid to write 'real movies', he said. 'It's simply impossible to imagine a British screenwriter coming up with something like *Ghostbusters*.' But hey, wasn't *Ghostbusters* the sort of star vehicle (for Bill Murray) that Puttnam had spoken unkindly of in his 'mission to reform' Hollywood's selfish extravagance? Film people need to have short memories. Adrian Hodges, in charge of the National Film Development Fund, recalled how depressing it was to get one submission after another written by 'people who work in cramped, low-budget environments [and who] try to cater to that market'.

Tim Bevan, whose Working Title company was now profitably linked to the nascent PolyGram Filmed Entertainment, blamed British literary culture: 'Scriptwriting in the US is a service industry.' In the UK, apparently, it was too often still the author's medium, not the people's one. He was on less arguable ground, though, when he accused young writers of having to work in 'language-led areas', like television, and forfeit their visual literacy. And Colin Young, director of the National Film and Television School, housed in ramshackle premises resembling an abandoned kibbutz, well outside town, spoke with the cynicism of depletion: 'The only difference between Britain and the States is that, over there, writers are paid handsomely to get screwed.'

What all this boiled down to was that the excitement of the new wasn't there any longer. Its very success had bred indifference as well as imitations. BBC TV, having overcome (by the usual means: licence payers' money) the antagonism between the cinema unions and its own unionised workforce, had spawned Channel 4 lookalikes by 1990 – the unimaginatively named Screen One and Screen Two, both of them afflicted with that sense of 'shrinkage', of films too small in scope and appeal. Had even one of these 'telly films' been as successful as the small

American film, *Sex, Lies and Videotapes*, that had taken the Palme d'or at Cannes and broken box-office records in European cinema then all would have been easy to forgive. But none was. The town seemed eerily silent, perhaps because those who had once made a big noise with British films, small and large, had left it by the beginning of the Nineties.

All headed for the same destination: the United States. Ridley Scott was filming *Thelma and Louise* (1991); Alan Parker had made *Mississippi Burning* (1988) and was currently working on *The Commitments* (1991), an American-financed film shot in the Irish Republic; Adrian Lyne was preparing *Indecent Proposal* (1992); Stephen Frears had shot *The Grifters* (1990), one of his finest, if not most financially successful, films. He was now better known as the director of *Dangerous Liaisons* (1988), which he had made in France with an all-American cast and Hollywood financing, than as the young blood who had pumped social vitality into *My Beautiful Laundrette* just three years earlier. All these British talents were now well integrated into the Hollywood studio mode – big stars, big budgets, big stories. Their native screen seemed American. Only Frears showed a creditable volition not to pull up his roots entirely. In future years, he would skilfully commute between American and British subjects, cinema films and small-budget ones for TV.

As the Eighties ended, the British film industry was settling into the formulaic mould of entertainment scaled down to fit available budgets and the expectations of the TV audience, but with, sometimes, an ironic bonus. Ken Loach's *Riff-Raff* (1990) had been a Channel 4 commission ... after intensive lobbying, misgivings about releasing it theatrically were overcome. The British Film Institute arranged limited screenings; then it was taken on by Palace Pictures and secured distribution in those cinemas – fewer than 200 screens out of 3,000-odd in the UK – which showed foreign-language or art-house movies. In Europe, where a culture of cinema *exhibition* existed and was valued, Loach's film was a popular success, achieved full-scale releases in several countries and won the new European Film Award in 1992. The multicultural building site, the scene of Loach's mixed bunch of workers, a tragi-comedy of urban survival through resilience, radical will and bawdy humour, could be transferred to the industrialised heartlands of Continental Europe without diluting its authenticity. Subtitled or dubbed, sometimes into the argot and accents of the country, its chameleon quality assumed the national identity of the Spanish, French, German or Italian proletariat – and their appreciative young audiences. There were reports that some foreign film-goers actually thought Loach had shot his movie on their turf. It hit the main vein of militant satire that pulsed more strongly through the history of some of these nations than through the body politic of Britain: the metaphor of the rat hunt on the site of a former hospital being converted into luxury flats was a message *sans frontières*.

Where he confronted the power of capital full on, as in his later *Bread and Roses* (2000), about organising immigrant labour in Los Angeles, Loach could be didactic and boring. No such risk with Hogarthian characters such as Ricky Tomlinson's militant labourer hitting out at the capitalist system in an act of arson as desperate as it was doomed. Tomlinson, who had once been under surveillance by the British security services because of alleged left-wing extremism, projected a bawdy reality that compensated for the dispassionate refusal of Loach's style to adapt itself to the action as a participant rather than a spectator. Loach's most successful films usually have central characters who are more demonstrative than their director.

Riff-Raff was rightly called Loach's comeback film, after the conspiratorial strains of *Fatherland* (1986) or the reductive politics of his Northern Ireland melodrama, *Hidden Agenda* (1990). *Riff-Raff*'s running comedy of defiant acts, growing ever more violent and impotent, had a humanity that was to provide the template for some of the British films of the mid-to-late Nineties, like the same director's *Raining Stones* (1993), Mike Leigh's *Naked* (1993), Mark Herman's *Brassed Off* (1996) and, of course, *The Full Monty* (1997), all films about individual regeneration amid urban decay achieved through defiance of Thatcherite economics.

Mrs Thatcher herself had been the victim of the Tory putsch by the time *Riff-Raff* was released; but it is doubtful whether any of the film industry VIPs in Downing Street would have felt it prudent to push its credentials in front of the then Prime Minister as the sort of European film they had in mind when they begged for co-production money.

Genre is one of the first refuges for film-makers in an industrial recession. The British gangster film re-emerged in the first year of the new decade. In part, it was the product of the same hankering nostalgia for the Fifties (or even earlier) which had provided the short-lived stimulation for the early C4-financed films. It may also have owed a little to the widening popularity of media studies, a genre-led discipline: in 1990, 166 media studies courses were listed in the British Film Institute handbook; they had doubled by the end of the decade. *The Modern Review*, a publication wilfully and often eccentrically championing the importance of populist art, cinema, TV and literature, appeared in 1991, lending legitimacy to the cult of genre and sometimes veneration of trash. The glossy American monthly about movies, *Empire*, which had begun publishing in Britain in 1989 and soon became the best-selling magazine of its kind, pushed the all-important fifteen- to twenty-five-year-olds towards Hollywood genre movies; while the British Film Institute's rejigged monthly, *Sight and Sound*, declared in its first editorial, published in May 1991, that it had 'no interest in nostalgia for the good old things; it wants to start from the bad old things'.

More and more, popular culture was being pushed towards American fashions and formulae. Much of this was inimical to culture in the wider sense, not just in its British department. As the critic Geoff Brown wrote ten years later, 'People's awareness of cinema has contracted, not expanded. As each year's releases pile up, cinema accumulates more past, and more gets forgotten, never known about, even in academic circles' (*British Cinema in the Nineties*, p. 30). But what was known about, studied and turned into cults were some of the British hits of earlier decades: *Get Carter* or *The Long Good Friday*, 'the bad old things' that had 'done good' and were emulated in films like *Chicago Joe and the Showgirl* (1990) and *The Krays* (1990).

The first was purportedly based on the so-called Cleft Chin Murder, which happened in wartime Britain – 1944, to be precise – when an American GI, Karl Hulten, and his British moll, Betty Jones, killed a cab driver. The film, directed by Bernard Rose from a David Yallop screenplay, represented the event as a Hollywood-type fiction, both characters (played by Kiefer Sutherland and Emily Lloyd) being hooked on mimetic behaviour of the Bogart–Cagney–Robinson movies of the Thirties. No sooner has Lloyd met Sutherland than she is seeing him in gangster pinstripes and a slouch hat; to him, she appears the ensemble of a moll who is ripe for a grapefruit to be pushed in her face. They are presented in such flash fantasies as the Bonnie and Clyde of wartime England. The money and artifice are lacking in the film to pull this off, make it convincing or, indeed, consistent. All that was left was the framing device of Emily Lloyd imagining herself to be the star of a Hollywood première, walking out of 'our' film into 'hers'. But it is a 'frame' without a picture. The period look was sketchy, where discernible at all in the helpful blackout, though the sex was bang up to date and Messrs Durex – as was now commonplace in 'safe sex' days of the early Aids alarm – got what looked like product placement. One would not have seen condoms in a Hollywood movie *de ces jours*: the American cinema might show murder, but knew where to draw the line.

Chicago Joe and the Showgirl, costing £3.2 million, was the biggest gamble to date taken by Working Title, the outfit then run by Tim Bevan and Sarah Radclyffe, in which PolyGram Filmed Entertainment had bought a 49 per cent interest in 1989. PFE was itself owned by the Dutch electrical goods conglomerate Philips. Michael Kuhn, head of PFE, was seeking 'cornerstone companies' that PFE could use to build an entertainment entity in production and distribution that would eventually challenge Hollywood's dominance in Europe. He saw Working Title as an essential component of his grand plan, as well as 'turning good ideas into good films – but at acceptable risk'. Kuhn wrote later, 'Tim [Bevan] and I both agreed that until UK producers could spend more time on making a script and a movie work, than they did on trying to get a movie made, there was little hope of moving forward.' *Chicago Joe and the Showgirl* was much less successful than had been hoped; but it got things 'moving forward'. The partnership between Working Title and PFE, little noticed outside the industry at the time, was soon to acquire artistic muscle and turn into the most significant in British production of the late Nineties. Kuhn was not invited to the Downing Street summit, but it was with such a man that the future turned out to lie.

The Krays, directed by Peter Medak and written by Philip Ridley, was a more successful capitalisation on East End nostalgia for the pair of twins, Reggie and Ronald, whose community spirit still endeared them to any contemporaries that were alive by the 1990s, and deepened the well of folklore whose mythic properties were exploited in the film by the casting of a pair of contemporary icons, Gary and Martin Kemp, stars of the Spandau Ballet Pop group. They might be the wrong dietary type, Pop-skinny where the Krays were ox-like bulky, but the authentic twinship of their own fraternal looks fed into the film's sense of sinister synergy – of evil breeding greater evil out of its own likeness. To many people's surprise, the film dwelt more seriously and at length on the role of women, as grievers and cosseters in the extended family of the Kray twins: the first bloodstain to appear on screen belonged to a birth, not a killing. And the mother love of the Bethnal Green matriarch (played by Billie Whitelaw) was blind to what her fledglings did after they turned into birds of prey. The two territories of empire – the urban crime kingdom where gangsters treat their own kind like pigs for the slaughter and the front-parlour world where they are rebuked by their mum for bringing dirt in on their shoes – seldom meet. But their existence lifts the film out of the exploitation category, puts it into a Brechtian world of heroic deflation. The bulk of the production money for *The Krays* came from a video company: but hopes that this might be where new finance lay were not built on.

David Puttnam's first post-Columbia production, *Memphis Belle* (1990), directed by Michael Caton-Jones, was also a retrospective work; a hands-on aerial-warfare film whose re-creation of the eponymous B17 Flying Fortress on a bombing mission over Bremen in 1943 showed the same sort of fascinated nostalgia for the old and the vintage that had once been a trademark of Ealing Films: the plane was more a flying factory in which the crew of ten, all of them American boys – for Puttnam had to kowtow to the chauvinism of the US market – slaved away like pieceworkers with the death-dispensing machinery of fifty years ago. A fascinating lesson in industrial archaeology, it conscripted Puttnam's favourite theme of teamwork, character splitting open under pressure, played-down heroics and the moral drama of sacrifice. But because of the historically accurate youth of the cast, hardly out of boyhood, the film lacked a frame of reference to larger questions of life and death outside their immediate concern for survival. It was an honourable reproduction piece. It gladdened a viewer's eye, but without the stimulus of fresh vision.

Out of the tail of his eye, the same viewer might have observed the continuing effects of the chaos theory that had begun with the sale of half the British film industry's assets to Cannon, and their subsequent dispersal, takeover and buyout. Cannon's erstwhile 'saviour', Giancarlo ('The Waiter') Parretti, was seemingly as indestructible as any comic-strip villain. After acquiring the Cannon Group in 1987, which he and his partner, Florio Fiorini, had first seen as a property investment, Parretti had succumbed to the baleful infatuation of movie moguldom and had persuaded Time Warner to guarantee a $650 million loan to his Los Angeles company, Pathé Communications, formed after he believed he had bought control of Pathé Cinema, to pay Kirk Kerkorian $1.3 billion for MGM–UA film and TV studios. The loan had come through just ten days after a Naples court had convicted Parretti, so it was alleged, for fraudulently declaring the bankruptcy of a chain of newspapers nearly ten years earlier. He was freed on appeal. By this deal Time Warner would gain access to the 3,000-odd MGM–UA film library, while Parretti's ownership of Pathé gave him control of over 1,500 cinemas in Europe. 'You pay with what you buy' was the man's business credo. However, the French government, thoroughly alarmed by this development in a company regarded as of patrimonial as well as profitable importance to France, blocked the Pathé sale to Parretti in June 1990. 'After examining the case,' Pierre Beregovoy, French Finance Minister, announced, 'it was decided the planned deal would have threatened public order.' This arcane reference was never clarified. It did not need to be. Information had been sought on Parretti from the French Departments of Justice, Defence and the Interior, as well as the Stock Exchange watchdog. The MGM–UA deal went through, thanks to Credit Lyonnais, with the steadier hand of Alan Ladd Jr in overall control.

The Italian's business film empire building, which had begun when he had bailed Cannon out of near bankruptcy, was further cramped at the end of 1991 when Parretti was arrested at Rome's Ciampino Airport as he was about to board an aircraft for Tunisia and taken to Sicily to answer charges of tax evasion and criminal association. By this time the names of Golan and Globus, his erstwhile partners, were hard to find mentioned anywhere in the film-trade papers.

Certainly, all of this was more exotic than events in the sad little British film industry, now near total despondency, as it entered the 1990s. A few whose memories were longer than the usual attention span of film people, who think it prudent to forget the wrongs done them, or at least not to allude too openly to them, may have speculated how differently things would have turned out had the British government, in 1986–7, been as obdurate in blocking Cannon's bid for power as the French government had been in denying Parretti's.

8

Contemporary *and* Traditional

Nineteen ninety-one surely represented the nadir of the film industry's hopes that the Tory government would 'do something' for it. By the time the Downing Street working parties came to report to their *patronne*, Mrs Thatcher herself had been turned out of office by a party putsch; and two Films Ministers had come and gone. Even Norman Lamont, Chancellor of the Exchequer from whom all gifts flowed, threw them not even a smile of comfort. 'The film industry makes an important contribution to entertainment and culture in this country,' he began patronisingly, in his Budget Day speech on 19 March 1991. (Yes, yes, man; we know that, man; *go on!*). 'Having studied these proposals [for tax breaks] carefully, I am afraid I cannot accept them.' So that was it, was it? No, listen . . . 'But I remain sympathetic, and if they [the working parties] have any alternative proposals to put to me over the coming year, I shall happily consider them.'

Like most oracles' utterances, this needed decoding. Wilf Stevenson, director of the British Film Institute, who had headed a working party, unlocked the subtext of Treasury-speak. 'The clearest thing the Chancellor is saying is that the door is not closed,' he interpreted. Yes, yes, but what in heaven's name would coax it to open? May came and went, but not even the first tranche of Mrs Thatcher's bounty, the £5 million for European co-productions, was paid over. Nicholas Ridley hadn't liked this Downing Street *douceur*: with Her Inside gone, and Ridley himself out of office in the government reshuffle, his department was in no hurry. Lamont, likewise, resisting the collective shoulder that Attenborough, Puttnam and Stevenson tried applying to the post-Budget door of the Treasury, rejected the proposal to make business expansion schemes (aka tax breaks) attractive to film investors. British Screen Finance had been promised £6 million in tranches in January 1991: by midsummer, the first £2 million hadn't arrived. British Screen had temporarily to stop co-funding new films.

A British Film Commission (BFC), with the aim of encouraging foreign film-makers to shoot their movies in Britain, was indeed called into being in May. Funded with £3.5 million (for four years, anyhow) and headed by Sydney Samuelson, an industry 'elder statesman' and one-time head of a film equipment rental firm with a useful Hollywood address book, it undertook to hack a path through the lantana of (usually restrictive) regulations, governmental and local, lying in wait to trap film-makers. Lord Hesketh announced the new initiative in Parliament on 10 May, then jetted off to the Cannes Film Festival to repeat it to a depressed group of film-makers who generally felt it was too little, too late.

Lord Hesketh and his grim-faced Civil Service 'minders' did not take kindly to a British journalist (it may have been me) reminding him that setting up yet another body to woo foreign film-makers to come to our shores ignored the reality of the many native film talents who were leaving these shores just as soon as they could get a green card to work in America. 'Will BAFTA set up a "Read My Lips Award", for British stars obliged to talk American to earn a living?' I asked, quoting the fact (unknown to his Lordship) of Kenneth Branagh and Emma Thompson, Albert Finney, Timothy Dalton, Bob Hoskins and Greta Scacchi all currently playing American characters in Hollywood films. Lord Hesketh departed in some dudgeon. He was not the dimmest Film Minister, though certainly the fattest to date, and one of the shortest-lived: he was already on his way to another job as Government Chief Whip in the Lords. He bore the burdens of office and corpulence, and inquisitors like myself, as well as he could in an overheated plastic pavilion where the Brits on the Croisette came to drink and watch the Cup Final; then, thankfully, flew back home to his clubs (White's, the Turf) and more congenial responsibilities – racing cars and horses. As far as the British government was concerned, the film industry could be on another planet.

The Cannes Festival in 1991 was dominated by the newly brunette-dyed figure of Madonna, there to support her film *Truth or Dare*. Her full-length, wraparound, in-depth egoism, a phenomenon of push-button provocation, distracted attention from any art that was on show – precious little that year – in a festival that looked more like a huge house party for one Pop superstar. Britain's entries were painfully few: an ambitiously conceived, but irretrievably muddled British Film Institute production, Isaac Julien's *Young Soul Rebels*, shown in the Semaine de la

Critique section of the festival. Made by a black London co-operative, it involved an incoherent story of punk rock and homosexual murder in the Queen's jubilee year, but gained applause from the French press and went on to win the Critics' Prize.

A Rage in Harlem was a $9 million production which not one of the 10,000 of those passing by its posters on the Croisette would have supposed was nominally British since it was shot entirely in Cincinatti, starred Forrest Whitaker and Gregory Hines, exploited slapstick and gore, and portrayed its all-black cast as stereotypes of con men, pimps, whores, killers and simpletons. The production company, however, was Palace Pictures. 'It seemed that to ensure our future, the American box office would have to be our ultimate goal,' its producer, Stephen Woolley, later wrote in an act of contrition. In spite of having Miramax, the most skilful company in movie marketing, as their US partner in the film, which was part of a key three-picture deal, *A Rage in Harlem* did not create much of a stir anywhere else.

Another Cannes entry, *Assassin of the Tsar*, re-creating the shooting of the royal family during the Russian Revolution, was also part-British. Its co-production credentials rested in part on the unlikely presence of Malcolm McDowell as the assassin. As so often at festivals, it was Ken Loach who 'spoke' for Britain. Loach's already mentioned *Riff-Raff*, his celebration of working-class solidarity, proved popular with critics and audiences: so popular in fact, that Channel 4 changed its mind and instead of scheduling an early British TV screening, planned an extended theatrical release. 'And who else, apart from Mike Leigh,' asked Ian Christie in his *Sight and Sound* report (July), 'is trying to show a recognisable image of life on the cusp of Thatcher's Britain?'

Leigh's new film, *Life Is Sweet*, had opened in London a few months earlier (1991) and was not selected for Cannes. It mixed the sad, serious and farcical with more densely detailed observation of the inner and outer lives of a working-class family on a suburban housing estate than a year's run of *Coronation Street* or *EastEnders* episodes. The film's 'impacted' character was reportedly what discouraged the Cannes selection committee. Literally, everything in it counted. Leigh himself, quizzed as to what his film was 'about', sardonically listed its contents in alphabetical order, from 'accordions, affection, alcohol, alienation, anorexia, baby-wear, ballet, baths, birdcages ...' through a hundred more items down to '... X-chromosomes, youth, zeal and zest'. Even allowing for such hype, a stratagem which mollified his customary impatience with such questions, Leigh's film resists categorising. 'Farcical psychodrama' was the nearest shot.

Ernest Bevin, the Old Labour statesman, used to say that what he deplored most in the British working class was its low threshold of aspiration. The family in *Life Is Sweet* have their daydreams, even their sexual fantasies: 'Workers' Dreamtime' would have made a good alternative title, recalling the morale-boosting World War Two radio show, *Workers' Playtime*, whose aural conveyor belt of popular music stimulated the production hormones in the munitions factory workforce.

The trouble is, *Life Is Sweet*'s characters spend all their time coping with life, without ever taking charge of it. Focusing hilariously on the misbegotten opening of a 'gourmet' restaurant by Timothy Spall's self-punishing loser, representing the 'enterprise culture' of Thatcher's Britain, it contrasts the social aspiration that collapses into knockabout comedy with the efforts of another chef (Jim Broadbent) to get rich quick from a beat-up mobile snack bar that his clearer-eyed wife (Alison Steadman) considers to be less a gold mine than a rust heap. Her daughters, one a professional plumber (Claire Skinner) who's got it all together and wants to unblock her life by emigrating to the US, and the other a screwed-up feminist (Jane Horrocks), ex-anorexic and closet bulimic who can't keep it down, represent twin poles of a generation distanced from their parents. All Mike Leigh's identity traits are visible: in particular the wife with brains who became a motherhood drop-out and now strives to make a home fit for a family who take her for granted. A speech from Alison Steadman's heart opens a real marital wound, only to close it again with a healing sincerity that gives the story unexpectedly heroic dimensions.

Leigh was to employ precisely the same emotional 'closure' ten years later, in another ensemble study of council-estate life, *All or Nothing*, by which time his unfriendly critics – there were some – were accusing him of practising a patronising mockery of the working classes. (Mocking the middle classes was OK, naturally.) Less overtly political than *High Hopes*, his savage cartoon of social losers and winners in Tory Britain, *Life Is Sweet* proved a crowd pleaser with a cutting edge. Its laughter hurt.

Ken Loach, so often Leigh's running mate in social concern, was cruelly exposed for its naivety when politics overtly shaped it. He attempted a Costa Gavras-type theme in *Hidden Agenda* (1991), a conspiracy-theory thriller set on both sides of the Irish border inspired by the Stalker inquiry into Ulster's policing and justice system. The political line on offer was embarrassingly simplistic, not much more than a 'Troops Out' piece of propaganda. The script, by the Marxist writer Jim Allen, dealt in stereotypes even a Trotskyite would have thought outmoded: silky-voiced English politicians waiting to take coffee in the library before dishing up their blackmail threats to the Stalker-type policeman (Brian Cox) so dumb that he lets himself be decoyed into a Republican club on guest night when hidden paparazzi are present; and an American civil rights worker (Brad Dourif) who is appalled by an Orange parade – no wonder: as Loach presents it, it is like the march of the zombies. The Brits are shown as bogeymen who scare the children, manhandle their mothers and ransack Republican households. The Republicans are portrayed as life-enhancing humanists, passing the collecting plate round for prisoners in the Maze and listening to folk songs that brand the English as terrorists down the ages. So weak was Loach's direction and so poor the argument that his indictment of political corruption was done a visible disservice by the strength of Jim Norton's performance as an RUC supremo defending his 'reactionary' policies with a vigour that was fatal to Jim Allen's knee-jerk sympathies. Stripped of all pretensions to be about Ulster politics as seen from the sympathetic ranks of Sinn Fein, *Hidden Agenda* was revealed as simply one more paranoia-fed melodrama of a kind that television documentaries like *Stalker, Death on the Rock* and *Who Bombed Birmingham?* did with far more authority and likelihood. Much of it was made in the safety of King's Cross, London, rather than in parts of Northern Ireland, which British film crews were reluctant to reach – at least it hid that security issue effectively.

An impassioned press conference followed the film's presentation at Cannes, which reached such a volume of charge and counter-charge on issues of accuracy between Loach, Allen and myself – all three of us, admittedly, with our own unhidden agendas to pursue – that the media, who were drifting off to lunch, actually came running back in to hear the argy-bargy: something almost unheard of at Cannes' usually anodyne autopsies on the competition films. The public's response was so muted as scarcely to be detected. Loach and Allen had learned a valuable lesson from this experience when they made *Land and Freedom*, set in the Spanish Civil War, four years later: they celebrated a lost cause more skilfully than they had pushed a contemporary agenda.

Of the more or less overtly political films made on the British main-

land – very, very few, save for TV – Hanif Kureishi's *London Kills Me*
honourably attempted to get to grips with the realities of Notting
Hill race riots. It was his directorial debut. Stephen Frears had been
approached to direct Kureishi's screenplay but demurred, feeling perhaps
its savage comedy was too close to *Sammy and Rosie Get Laid* (or else
feeling unequal to the creative struggles with Kureishi whom he had
called, part-jestingly, 'a provocative little sod'). The film might have
better represented British cinema at Cannes, in place of Loach's effort;
but it was not ready in time.

Produced for Working Title and Channel 4 by Judy Hunt, on a
starvation-level £1.5 million budget, its setting was the coexisting worlds
of rich and poor in Notting Hill, a drug-culture hot spot but also a fast
rising 'fashionable' housing location for the gentrifying classes. Its ethnic
mix was politically bizarre, yet the screen had scarcely utilised it. *Absolute
Beginners* had simply exploited its showbiz exoticism. Kureishi's film
complemented Isaac Julien's *Young Soul Rebels*, but ethnicity was not its
dominant theme and it had more political 'savvy'. Both films dealt with
'lost kids', a street 'posse', predatory but communal, rootless though not
soulless, a deliberate snook cocked at Thatcher's notion of the family
unit. 'They were living out the Thatcherite dream – they were on the
street dealing really hard,' Kureishi told Philip Dodd. 'It was like a parody
of what the yuppies were doing at the same time in the City.' It gave
Kureishi an especially satisfying kick to be filming part of the story in a
house formerly owned by the Tory grandee and Cabinet Minister
Michael Heseltine. Jon Gregory, Mike Leigh's customary editor, gave
the film qualities that concealed Kureishi's inexperience. Its contemporaneity was its strength.

If Leigh and Loach and Kureishi could 'do' contemporary better than
any other directors at this period, what remained of the British film
industry leaped at any chance to show it could still 'do' traditional. Even
before the Cannes Festival ended, a sizeable part of it had taken off for
Washington DC, at the invitation of the Library of Congress, to stage a
week-long event entitled 'The Great British Picture Show'. Over a
hundred feature films – the usual suspects from Korda to *Chariots of
Fire* – were screened beneath the restored Union Station, which was
draped in Stars and Stripes and the Union flag. Stars and directors
attending included Richard Attenborough, John Mills, Michael York,
James Fox, Stephanie Beacham, Ben Kingsley and – yes – even Michael
Winner, whose scorn of his native film industry was the standby of every

journalist assigned to write its obituary and seeking a quote. Bowler hats were worn, furled umbrellas were carried and the band of the Royal Marines blared out rousing marches the length of Pennsylvania Avenue.

It is safe to say that Peter Greenaway sought no place in the parade – or, as it happened, at Cannes. He opted to enter his new work, *Prospero's Books*, at the Venice Film Festival a few months later and just a week after its London première (30 August 1991). Based on *The Tempest*, the film is perhaps the closest to self-portraiture that Greenaway had come. John Gielgud plays an elegiac yet elemental Prospero, as well as his creator, Shakespeare. He manipulates people, even invents them when necessary – except for the final scene, his is the only speaking part – and the cold, analytic, superior potentate, impatient with mortals of lesser intelligence, struck some as a self-congratulatory refraction of Greenaway's own personality. 'How can they call it "pretentious"?' he exclaimed in an interview before the première. 'What do they think I'm pretending to?'

That had by now become the conundrum which Greenaway's films set the critics. *Prospero's Books* did not make the riddle easier. He deconstructs the play completely, then re-creates it through his own encyclopaedic erudition. The conceit is to suppose that Gonzalo threw some books into the vessel in which Prospero sailed into exile – twenty-four books, according to Greenaway the numerologist. A bestiary, a natural history, a cosmology, a herbal, a manual of architectural forms, a Utopian treatise, pornography and so on. The books assume an enchanted life whenever Prospero makes mention of one of them. It is picture-making by a master polymath. As Prospero recalls events prior to the opening of *The Tempest* in flashback and plots vengeance with the aid of his counter-coup allies, Ariel and Caliban, Greenaway annotates his words by embodying them in a flux of imagery. As well as having the photographer Sacha Vierny as his own court magician, Greenaway was now able to wave the electronic wand of Japanese technology – including Hi-Vision TV and a Quantel Paintbox – over the stunning sets of magician's cell, sea coast, bathhouse, library, temple, cornfield and cesspit. With such collaging tools, and their shape-shifting possibilities, this particular director seemed to have indeed become Master of the Universe. Well, *his* Universe, anyhow. It was one of his most culturally fertile works. He used his own vast referential knowledge of world architecture and European art – expounded brilliantly in an invaluable but little-known interview with John Wyvern in *The Art* newspaper that June – to expand the four walls of Prospero's cellular imagination and turn Gielgud's fantasies into the autobiography of a Renaissance nobleman.

It is more than high-tech: it is high patrician stuff: pan-European cinema which bypasses the proletarian requirements of populist cinema. It was the moment when Greenaway disdainfully taxed even his art-house audience's loyalties by passing beyond their ready understanding. Those who had felt reasonably cosy with the Agatha Christie-like clues of *The Draughtsman's Contract* nine years before, now felt incompetent to sit the examination. Such a director could never be happy in any national cinema; but then, since Greenaway creates his own world, he shall never know remorse.

A rather touching coincidence occurred on the Venice Lido that September. Greenaway's film shared the festival screen with Derek Jarman's new work, *Edward II*. Jarman, of course, created his own absurdist, gay version of *The Tempest* in 1980, more a camp concert than a court masque but confirming his fluency in being able to transmute a stately play into hippy idiom without loss of timelessness. Both directors have a common fixation with books of magic, obscure lore, perverse historical events, architectural follies, phantasmagorical costumes, colours and names, as well as the metaphorical and metaphysical processes of their trade. Each may have wondered which of them was figuring in the other's dream. A second coincidence: both had published books only weeks apart: slim volumes, but ones that tax a reader to keep his head above the overflow of their authors' bursting cistern of imagination and cerebration.

Greenaway's publication was the screenplay of *Prospero's Books*, a 'crib' that acknowledges none of the limits that form the normal boundaries of film scripts, but calls for additional reading lists. Jarman's book was, by contrast, relaxed. Entitled *Modern Nature*, it took the form of a diary of daily events, from January 1989 to September 1990, in the life of a man dying of Aids, though living a surprisingly active existence in a pitch-black shack with yellow window frames on the shingle beach at Dungeness, surrounded by a surrealist garden he has made out of the salty vegetation and odd flotsam and jetsam. Prospect Cottage is filled with objects possibly on loan from Greenaway's grey cells: ancient books, histories, herbals, atlases. The owner clearly considered himself a magus-like figure, an ex-urban Prospero, self-exiled by his illness in this lonely but lovely place in the Calibanesque shadow of a sinisterly temperamental nuclear power station. The occasional pretty-boy Ariel in psychedelic swimbriefs flits by. Tilda Swinton, Jarman's muse, makes a plausible Miranda. Life now apes art precisely and touchingly.

The reviews of his book were like premature obituaries of its author. 'Being HIV positive prompts an appetite for life and curiosity,' wrote Jonathan Meades. 'Jarman has remained in the ghetto of his own making because of his uncompromising nature and peculiarity as an artist – which is indissociable from his sexuality.' And J. Hoberman, the American critic, calling Jarman 'the last English romantic' in a programme note for a Jarman retrospective at Cinemathèque Ontario in October, 1991, added an opinion that concisely represented his status and importance in the last year or so of his life. 'As much as his recent work is fuelled by what England has become under Thatcher – its greed, consumerism, intolerance, insularity, militarism – Jarman has not been warmly regarded by the British left, whose conception of a counter-cinema stresses political analysis and the denial of pleasure.'

This view of him is probably what cost Jarman's film *The Garden* (1991) any official recognition when it was shown at the Moscow Film Festival in July 1991, in a society still cautious about acknowledging perestroika's cultural relaxations. Among the last jokes that Jarman lived to enjoy was hearing that his film, set in his own Dungeness dogpatch masquerading as Gethsemane's more exalted location, had caused a muted scandal by his confrontational declarations of his own homosexuality – still a matter of disrepute and, worse, potential imprisonment in the USSR. It was ignored in the name of what the Russian critic Aleksandr Timofeevsky dismissed as 'elevated provincialism'. The pleasure principle was anathema to Soviet orthodoxy as the exaltation of gayness was to British homophobia.

Against this background, Jarman's modern-dress version of Christopher Marlowe's *Edward II* (1991) attempted to reclaim the play for Gay Rights. It was not one of his revisionist successes. Where Marlowe's play offended was because the king's transgression in falling in love with an upstart commoner was a threat to the class hierarchy of the times, even more than to its morality. One could lose one's head in Edward's day because one didn't keep one's place. The new emphasis on Outrage's agenda unbalanced the play, turning its own social morality into anti-Clause 28 propaganda – the local by-law banning teaching institutions etc. from homosexual proselytising – and forcing a reductive narrowness on to a passionately flamboyant work. Nothing in it, no once-mighty line of Marlowe's, was as moving as Jarman's own, wistful remark to a journalist who interviewed him in *the* garden: 'My last wish is that someone looks after it when I'm gone.'

This, then, was the working scene in Britain's film industry midway through 1991: a near-disaster area. The promise brought over by the American studios, which had opened production offices in Britain over the previous couple of years, had not materialised – partly because the potential threat to Hollywood's dominance posed by the single European market had receded. After two years the oldest such 'overseas' unit, Paramount UK, had managed to get only one film into production – and that a version of *Wuthering Heights* starring Ralph Fiennes as Heathcliff and the French actress Juliette Binoche as Cathy. Its executive producer, Ileen Meisel, had decided Emily Brontë needed more youth appeal. Even better, Pop appeal. Thus the Irish recording star Sinead O'Connor was cast as Emily, scribbling away at the MS of the novel while a storm raged inspirationally outside the casements. 'Brontë's story operates at the same level as *Pretty Woman*,' Ms Meisel was quoted as saying, hopefully. 'What is important is that the movie manages to express the feelings – the fears – that young people have inside about first love.' It was also important that Paramount found new stars in Europe, so as not to have to go on paying Mel Gibson millions. Neither the feelings of youth, nor the finances of Paramount, were greatly helped by the resulting film. Paramount UK put up the shutters.

Much of the British film industry felt that day was coming for it, too. The Tory government's recent economic assistance to the film industry looked like small change thrown to importunate beggars to make them go away. The sums of money involved, the initiative in setting up the British Film Commission, were welcome, of course, but petty placebos. They did not signal any resolution to alter the structure of British film-making. Much more influential were proposals concurrently being hatched in secret by a New Labour think-tank. One of the party's most formidable figures, the forty-five-year-old Labour MP for Dunfermline East, revealed them a few months later, on 18 September, at a seminar in the context of New Labour's 'Industry 2000' conference. Gordon Brown was then Shadow Trade and Industry Secretary. He spoke on 'regenerating the British film industry'. It was immediately apparent to everyone present that he was better briefed and more keenly aware of the industry's problems than any Tory minister. Mark Fisher MP, himself a one-time documentary film producer and scriptwriter, now Opposition spokesman on the arts, was a co-author of the paper.

What Brown said was not widely reported outside the trade press: Labour's election chances still did not look bright. But almost everything New Labour was to do for film-makers, once it gained power, was spelled out, or latent, in his proposals. Brown began by reminding his film industry audience why they were here. Film investment was at its lowest in years. In 1985 it had been worth £272 million: by 1989 it was under £79 million. Everyone was the poorer (noises of assent). What the British film industry lacked was a coherent policy framework encouraging *consistent* investment. The Tories' recent £5 million for European co-production, spread thinly over three years, was quite 'inadequate'. The indigenous output was 'too small'. Making fewer than fifty films a year didn't yield 'enough throughput for an industry with a low hit ratio and high unit costs'. Unscrambled, this meant that more films needed to be made in order to increase the odds on one of them being the box-office hit that would pay for all the rest and be profitable. What was required was 'a critical mass' of film: this needed money (louder sounds of assent). Let expenditure on a film be written off more quickly (applause). Write-offs were currently limited to 25 per cent a year on a diminishing basis: to write off 90 per cent of a film's costs could take eight years. Totally unsatisfactory (renewed applause). Relief should be given as and when expenditure was incurred. Throw in the cost of prints and advertising, too.

New Labour would also encourage exhibitors and distributors to invest in production. It would give private investors tax incentives: let them put their money into movies, instead of buying houses to rent. Abolish the Business Expansion Scheme, which with its 'capping' was no use to those on higher rates of tax. Labour would replace it with a 'Growing Business Scheme', which had the right sound, even if details were vague. We were ideally placed to do all this. 'Our culture, our values and our philosophy are close to our European partners ... while our common language and cross-fertilisation of talent with the USA makes us infinitely better placed to export our products to the biggest market in the Western world.' Gordon Brown sat down to thunderous applause.

Now, in what he said there was a lot of delusional philosophising. When some of the fruits of it began to ripen, during Labour's coming years in power, they turned out not to be the sweetest ones on the bough. And others never matured. The notion that by increasing the number of films, you thereby increased the chances of box-office success was particularly treacherous: you simply risked multiplying the number of badly and quickly made films. The notion of a common language facilitating US sales was also based on wishful thinking rather than practical experience: films with poor commercial prospects in the US would not find ready buyers just because they were English-speaking (and even this was fanciful, as any Hollywood soundtrack proves). Gordon Brown promised, 'Under Labour, Britain will play a much fuller part with our European partners.' This, too, sounded good; until a questioner narrowed it down. Then it seemed to mean not partnership, but leadership: we would do the talking for Europe – after all we spoke Hollywood's language, didn't we? Perhaps; but what they talked about in Hollywood didn't have much to do with Anglophone kinship. Or even, perhaps, with making movies. It was about making money. And we weren't terribly fluent in that. But shibboleths and chauvinism could be tolerated if more solid substances were on offer by Labour – like tax breaks.

Brown's reference to investments by other sectors of the industry, not simply production, was also shrewd. The film industry – any film industry – is distribution led. Distribution is the locomotive that pulls the gravy train; production is simply the fuel tender. Encouraging the exhibition arm to put its hand in its box office and invest in 'the product' was also on the ball. The exhibitors owned the 'money box'. Historically, in Britain, they kept the biggest share of a film's gross – usually 35–40 per cent – and yet they put nothing back into anything save bricks and mortar (and, until recent years, too little into that).

It is a pity that what Gordon Brown and co. saw so clearly in 1991, when New Labour was in opposition, failed to shape the party's film policy when in government with the same shrewdness and realism – then it was production, the most 'glamorous' sector of the industry, but traditionally the money-losing one, which seduced the new architects of the new British film industry. Such expensive lessons, though, were compensated by power; and both were still somewhat in the future. In 1991, what Gordon Brown proposed made sense and spelled survival. He ended with a rallying cry: 'The aim is to establish the UK as the Hollywood of Europe.' Not the best trumpet voluntary, perhaps. It simply echoed the hollow self-hype of a half-dozen British film moguls who had 'taken on' Hollywood over the years – and gone bust. But his listeners, pretty desperate people, felt they could accept such a vision of heaven tomorrow if it delivered on earthly promises a little sooner.

The one company that seemed to be flourishing in the recession was Palace Pictures. By 1989, Nik Powell and Stephen Woolley, its joint heads, had found a money-rich partner in Miramax, a New York corporation run by the Weinstein brothers, Harvey and Bob, whose own aggressive marketing of so-called 'arty' films and even rumpled personal apparel mirrored the raffish look as natural to the British outfit as a trademark of no-bullshitting integrity. The Palace group of companies – video shops, editing suite, the Scala cinema (where Woolley had started as a film-fixated usher) and a Dutch records company called Boudisque – had a sales turnover in 1989 of £20.54 million, compared with £14.8 million in 1988 and £11 million in 1987. It had a staff of over ninety and the group's net loss of £100,000 in 1987 had been converted into a new pre-tax profit of £500,000. Small beer, possibly, compared with the empire-building plans that Michael Kuhn was laying for PolyGram Filmed Entertainment; but then PolyGram had backing from the huge Philips electrical and hardware conglomerate. Palace was a corner shop to PolyGram's department store. But it had the 'buzz' for risk taking.

Angus Finney, in his chronicle of the company's fortunes, *The Egos Have Landed*, quoted a European producer as saying, 'Palace was a legend you just couldn't help hearing about, even though you weren't quite sure what it was all for.' Perception, as Finney subsequently remarked, was everything. But cash counted, too. Palace seemed to have that: the merchant bank Guinness Mahon's entertainment division advanced a revolving fund of £2 million, not profligate, perhaps not even sufficient to remove cash-flow worries. But British Screen's investment in Palace Pictures – five since 1987, two of which had already earned this finance house its money back – as well as a Dutch bank, money raised from investors before the 1990 recession and now Miramax's partnership in producing and distributing Palace films . . . it appeared a minor miracle of survival and thriving. Palace and Miramax had luck on their side with their first joint venture, *Scandal* (1989). It looked an unlikely subject to whet the Americans' appetite. It was the story, as Lord Denning's subsequent report on the whole affair put it, 'of rich men in high places and coloured men in lower', of the society osteopath Stephen Ward who killed himself on the day of his sentencing for living on immoral earnings, of the call-girls Christine Keeler and Mandy Rice-Davies, of their West Indian lover Johnny Edgecombe, of the Soviet Naval attaché Eugene Ivanov and of John Profumo, War Minister in the Macmillan government in 1963, who was ruined by his unpardonable indiscretion in lying about the affair to the House of Commons and in sharing Keeler's endearments with the Soviet attaché Ivanov. A rich mix.

By the late 1980s much blame was being laid for the decline in moral standards on the permissiveness pioneered by 'young people' in the 1960s; *Scandal* was to point the finger of shame at the immorality of the older generation. Palace had been expensively nursing the project as a TV series since the early 1980s, spending nearly £200,000 on it. BBC TV had rejected it for fear of offending the governing Establishment almost twenty years later. Yorkshire TV put it into turnaround; Palace retrieved it, budgeted it at £3.2 million, did a $2.35 million deal for North American rights with Miramax who scented the marketing potential in the sexual hypocrisy of British high society. Michael Caton-Jones, a miner's son, ex-punk from a squat and a graduate of the National Film and Television School (where Stephen Frears taught) was signed to direct it as his first feature. Such a man, Woolley reckoned, had every incentive to 'stick it' to the Establishment.

The subsequent film called for the caustic ironies of Bertolt Brecht, but sometimes got the pants-down talents of a Brian Rix stage farce. Yet both were bizarrely appropriate to the indiscretions of classes of people who should never have met, or at least been exposed in times when the class divisions were less porous. The movie re-called the past into the witness box in order to give evidence about the strangely similar present. In both 1963 and 1989, a Tory government was fast losing popularity and showing the strain of lengthy office. The 1960s enjoyed the 'never had it so good' slogan of political complacency; the 1980s responded to the 'you can have it all' incitement to material success.

John Profumo's fall from grace then was echoed by the fateful indiscretion and loss of office of Cecil Parkinson, one of Mrs Thatcher's favourite ministers. The film had an ominous contemporaneity. Indeed, it directly preceded Margaret Thatcher's fall, just as the Profumo scandal heralded Harold Macmillan's. It would have profited from having more space to fit all the facts. Some of the key figures were sidelined, others used as exotic colour; but John Hurt caught Ward's spongy charm, a social pimp, not a mercenary one, and the stand-out performance was that of Bridget Fonda, who played Mandy Rice-Davies, perfect in accent and pert with everything else, who alone appeared to catch the whiff of celebrity – that defining odour of the 1960s – and relish it with the knowledge that it would protect her from infamy. Ian McKellen, cast as

Profumo, suffered from the film-makers' legal caution, which made the man seem simply wimpish rather than unvirtuous, as well as a balding wig so crassly made that from certain angles his central ridge of hair gave him the appearance of a Huron Indian. The sexual content suffered, as it generally does on screen, from looking tacky rather than corrosive – glass phalluses for table decorations! – and the orgies were so amateurishly enthusiastic that the churning drawing-room scene resembled a repertory company's green room rather than a secret clique of society reprobates. But as Angus Finney says, 'Palace's handling of the film's UK release was exemplary.'

Miramax benefited from a wrangle over the film's rating in the US, eventually reduced from a threatened 'X', which would have restricted the advertising in many 'family' newspapers and on TV, to a come-hither 'R', which allowed in the all-important seventeen-year-olds or more. After ten days the British box-office receipts totalled £2.25 million, more than *Dangerous Liaisons* had taken in several weeks; in North America, it grossed over $15 million. It sealed the bond between Palace and Miramax. For the first time, a British independent film-maker had a sponsor in the US that loved it and indulged it – for the time being, anyhow.

Riding on the success of *Scandal*, Stephen Woolley, who held the creative reins of the yoked chairmanship with Nik Powell, the latter providing the management horsepower, immediately planned four new films to go into production in 1990 and began shooting two others simultaneously in London and Glasgow. One was *Hardware*, a robotic SF horror flick directed by Richard Stanley and co-produced by a Dutchman, Paul Trijbits, who had been a Pop promoter. The other was *The Big Man*, directed by David Leland and starring Liam Neeson and Ian Bannen, a 'confrontation' drama on American macho lines about an unemployed miner that culminated in a savage bare-knuckle fight. Here, too, Woolley tried to stress the continuity with an earlier era of what he saw as Tory misrule. The contemporary story was given a backdrop of the 1984–5 miners' strike, so as to indict what the makers perceived to be the injustices of the Thatcher years. Woolley invested a great deal of hope in it, along with £3.1 million spread over Miramax, Palace Video (which bought TV rights), British Screen and pre-sales to European distributors. It failed miserably. Its intended heroic dimension simply did not materialise; instead, it appeared depressing, downbeat and monotonous. Even the climactic fight, which had been intended to challenge the macho ethic, appeared to endorse it and turned off women film-goers. In London it was premièred against social unrest arising from the unpopular universal poll tax: people didn't want to see more of the same in a film about an aggressively divided community. Its box office did not take enough to cover the prints and advertising. Audiences in the US defied Miramax's efforts to find an angle. Miramax, as has been remarked, will not tolerate two things: losing an audience and losing money.

Its failure also prompted British Screen to revise its relationship with Palace. Simon Relph had retired in 1990 and his successor, Simon Perry, was having second thoughts about committing the film-finance bank to invest automatically in a Palace production. It was owed over £351,000 by Palace on previous British Screen investments; this would double in a few months' time if repayments due could not be honoured. For the moment, though, Perry held off. As he told Angus Finney, he admired Palace's marketing skills and their ability to pull the rabbit out of the hat just when everyone thought the trick had failed.

Undaunted, too, Woolley and Powell, still backed by the Weinsteins, pushed ahead with other films from the middle of 1991: Neil Jordan's *The Miracle*, US director Bill Duke's *A Rage in Harlem*, Peter Richardson's *The Pope Must Die* (a comedy that had to have its title changed to appease Catholic sensibilities in the US, where it became *The Pope Must Diet*) and *Dust Devil*, Richard Stanley's dreamlike story of ritual magic and slaughter shot in the Namibia desert. Stephen Gyllenhaal's *Waterland* was made in association with the US company Fine Line. It was an unwise time to expand. Britain was heading for a deepening recession. The projects were iffy ones, depending on a finesse of taste or drama. Supervising them, too, stretched resources, Woolley being thousands of miles away from Palace headquarters at a time when Powell was being told by his bankers that the company needed additional equity investment.

The years of inattentiveness to streamlining Palace's financial operations were catching up with it: as Angus Finney reports, its administration had been so weak at times that it neglected to invoice clients who owed it box-office receipts. Its understandable quest for quality sometimes made it necessary to spend large sums of money on post-production re-editing and occasional reshooting. 'Enhancement fees', according to Finney's breakdown, came to over £100,000 for each sizeable Palace production, thus reducing profit potential. When its actuaries advised retrenchment, selling off its editing suite, video stores and Boudisque business, and concentrating on core activities of making film, it was too late. The retail stores had long leases and likely buyers had other uses for their money – like supporting their own businesses.

All these growing worries, of course, were not widely known to the film community, one that bases its own business on the confidence lent by the image it disseminates, rather than on any shakier reality. Powell and Woolley, one reluctant to delegate responsibility, the other reluctant to stay home when film-making demanded his presence, kept their concerns confined within the plywood walls of Palace's ramshackle headquarters in Wardour Mews, a grungy alleyway whose downmarket appearance was actually a point of pride in a company that scorned the pretentiousness of the 'suits' in Wardour Street, Soho Square, Golden Square, or in the marble-and-glass offices, cinema and executive suites that PolyGram had carved out of the interior of a Grade 2 listed building in St James's Square.

Palace told itself that it put its style where it mattered: on the screen. Its pre-credits logo was literally a palace. But as one watched it, a shooting star arched over its turrets, then fell to earth. Perhaps this was not such a good omen. It signalled the transience of even the brightest entities. Palace's stellar performance showed up with magnified intensity in the gloom that enveloped the film industry in 1991. Few imagined its own star was so soon, and so abruptly, about to suffer a humiliating extinction.

9

Independent Struggles

An interview with Nik Powell, co-chairman of Palace Pictures, published in *Variety* in May 1991 as the Cannes Film Festival opened, described his maverick company admiringly as a 'studio in miniature'. To be fair, this accolade owed more to the interviewer's zeal than Powell's optimism. The truth was, Palace was collapsing. The film community in London is small and gossip is usually rife; but few knew, or guessed, the extent of Palace's predicament. As Angus Finney remarked in *The Egos Have Landed*, 'perception is everything.'

Powell was certainly aware of the company's overstretched commitments, swollen payroll – it had over a hundred employees, no longer 'family', so to speak, many not even knowing each other's names – and the accelerating seepage of resources through money-losing subsidiaries that should have been sold off months earlier and now were increasingly difficult to dispose of as the British recession deepened. An unexpected blow had come in October 1990, when the two satellite channels, BSB TV and Rupert Murdoch's Sky, merged to form BSkyB. Palace could no longer count on healthy bidding between two channels for its feature film library. The ill-fated BSB had, to Hollywood's delight, forced film prices up to £900,000 for an individual movie – a ludicrous sum for an unsung and unseen satellite channel.

October continued to be a cruel month. Palace and PolyGram Filmed Entertainment, the newish start-up corporation under Michael Kuhn, had put in a joint bid (with other interests) for the London Weekend TV franchise. In October 1991 it was unexpectedly rejected: they were told it didn't meet 'quality standards'. Stephen Woolley wasn't that concerned by this setback: a dedicated cinema man, television seemed to him a diversion. Probably he was right. But to Powell, the man with management know-how, the situation was clearly perilous.

What seemed a stroke of good fortune in 1990 turned out to be a serious misstep. Roger Wingate, an energetic property developer and cinema owner, used to come to Cannes in his yacht every year, keeping a low profile while looking for films to buy. He had the money, but sometimes missed the movie because he didn't pick up the 'buzz' about it early enough. He made a deal with the two Palace partners who had proven they had ears and eyes for the quality product they and Wingate wanted: a £400,000 revolving fund to pick up 'product' on which Wingate's cinemas, which included two first-run Curzon theatres in Mayfair and the West End, would have first option. The deal was launched in November 1991. The downside was that it put the marketing of the films they acquired in the hands of Wingate's nominee: Palace were thus stripped of the very skills that had made it most envied and successful. Daniel Battsek, a man of youthful flair and boundless imagination, who handled marketing, left the company at the start of 1992. He was snapped up immediately by the wholly owned Walt Disney subsidiary, Buena Vista. It was a body-blow to a groggy Palace. Battsek was one of the few capable of grappling realistically with day-to-day management.

Powell was distracted by the greater priority of simply saving the company. Obviously, what Palace needed was a partner with financial muscle. That seemed to be only Kuhn. The PolyGram chief was encouraging, indeed eager. PolyGram's film arm resembled the conglomerate's records company where Kuhn had started post-Cambridge University life as a lawyer. His basic plan for the $200 million film operation was to acquire small 'label' companies that could supply a variety of product – much like the diversity of creative and performance artists contracted to a major recording company. His association with Working Title, already noted, was still requiring him to 'carry' this mini-studio until its filmmakers, Tim Bevan and Sarah Radclyffe, had a profitable track record.

Kuhn saw attractive possibilities in Woolley and Powell – though about Palace he was rightly hesitant. Yet if new management practices could be put in, it looked right for a friendly bid from PolyGram. Then Kuhn found out about the deal with Wingate: it would conflict with any distribution deal PolyGram worked out with Palace for films that Woolley and Powell made or acquired. However, not wishing to lose a potential PolyGram acquisition, Kuhn offered to buy, for £4.6 million, the Palace library, about 450 films to which they owned rights, including golden franchises like the *Nightmare on Elm Street* series, and megahits like *When Harry Met Sally*. He also offered about £2 million for Palace's interests in sixteen completed films whose total production investment value was £65 million. And knowing cash-in-the-hand was even more desirable than offers-on-the-table, he provided a safety loan of £1.275 million to Palace's beleaguered bosses. The proviso was, of course, that PolyGram's accountants did due diligence on Palace's financial situation: in short, a very aggressive audit.

Kuhn is an individual who does not tolerate sloppiness. The narrow but valuable sidelight he was later to cast on his own corporate ambitions, in the book *100 Films and a Funeral*, included, as an appendix, a one-page 'Control Sheet Master', detailing the control and assessment of all PolyGram projects. This sheet struck terror into those it did not bedazzle and bewilder. It was the visible sign of a tough taskmaster not at all in thrall to a film's creative aura or its makers' imaginative aspirations. 'I further distilled the results of each greenlit film [i.e. one approved for production] on to a small card which I kept in my briefcase,' Kuhn wrote, 'so that anywhere, any time, I could remind myself of our intentions when we approved the film and compare it to the actuality.' Kuhn's intentions for Palace appeared providential to the latter's owners: it was the 'actuality' that was to doom the company.

While all this was happening behind the screen of Cannes in 1991, Woolley was desperately getting together the finance to keep his production programme going. He didn't therefore have much time to attend to day-to-day distractions, like putting off creditors and stemming financial leaks. By the middle of 1991 Palace was preparing to produce *Waterland* and *Dust Devil*; but the one that really excited Woolley had been in development since 1982: it was the film that became known as *The Crying Game*. That year Woolley had seen a feature entitled *Angel*, the debut of a young Irish writer-turned-director, Neil Jordan, and had shared critics' excitement over a story that went into the dark heart of Ulster terrorism by taking an uncommonly indirect and imaginative route – not through blood and guts, but via a Kafkaesque moral maze. Woolley and Jordan, both film buffs, became a creative item almost on the spot. Now, eight years later, after a series of hits (*Company of Wolves*, *Mona Lisa*), failures (*High Spirits*) and succès d'estime (*The Miracle*), a treatment Jordan had written called 'The Soldier's Story' was proposed as their next film.

For much of the intervening years, Jordan had found his inspiration blocked: what began as the kidnapping of a British soldier in Northern Ireland by IRA terrorists was getting nowhere. Some inimical pressure – perhaps the then real danger of retribution if IRA men were depicted in all their true brutality – kept Jordan from working it out. No one knows – if it hasn't yet been revealed – how the breakthrough occurred. Put it down, perhaps, to 'inspiration' – or to some collateral event or suggestion. But according to Woolley, Jordan said to him at the Berlin Film Festival 1991, where *The Miracle* had been well received, 'What if the IRA man who's been partly responsible for the death of the kidnapped soldier looks up the man's black girlfriend in London – and finds out eventually that she's a man?' It was like the carbon arcs fizzing into a light beam: both film-makers could see it already on the screen.

There had been films of a similar nature, or that came close to it in theme. One was David Puttnam's 1984 production of *Cal*, directed by Pat O'Connor and scripted by the Irish writer Bernard MacLaverty from his own story. In it, a reluctant IRA recruit falls for the widow of an RUC policeman whom he's helped to murder. 'The Soldier's Wife', as Jordan's original script was now called, must have been getting awkwardly close in feeling to the constable's widow at this point. But *Cal*, and the others, all lacked the single transgressive element, the sexual duplicity, that took Jordan's film off the paper and gave emotional suspense the gasp of erotic surprise. The revelation of the true sexuality of Dil, the dead soldier's fiancée, would require the still rare exposure of the male penis in a mainline commercial movie; but this was a plot that spelled c-a-s-h in an industry that progressed by challenging, sometimes honourably, more often sensationally, the conventions of the times and the permissions of the censors. At least, this is what Woolley hoped: the reality was that 'The Soldier's Wife' or *The Crying Game* – as it was eventually retitled – was a difficult 'sell'.

Jordan completed the screenplay's 'third act'. Then Powell, with the script in hand, approached a new French company, Ciby 2000, hoping to make a co-production deal. Ciby 2000, based in Paris in 1992, eventually established a London office (behind the British Film Institute's Stephen Street premises). Its title was literally a pun on the American epic-maker, Cecil B. DeMille whose name rendered Anglophonically became 'ci by deux mille'. That should have been a warning. Its founder, Francis Bouygues, a construction magnate and owner of TFI, the television channel, was a chauvinistic film buff eager to challenge Hollywood's dominance, give European film-makers confidence and make profitable films – he had already had a hand in Bertolucci's *Little Buddha*, Lynch's *Twin Peaks* and Almodóvar's *High Heels*. But his enthusiasm did not extend to a film in which one of the main characters was a transsexual in drag, Powell was told.

Woolley was no luckier when he approached Miramax: they were eager, but only if a woman were cast as, well, the woman. Jordan thought this made the whole thing as dishonest as if a black-up white actress had played the part of the mulatto Dil.

Ultimately, no upfront US coin was in the production and Palace had an exhausting time – and made severe financial pledges of their own – before British Screen and Channel 4, plus various territory sales to European distributors, made it possible to begin production very late in 1991 with an anorexic-looking budget of £2.3 million, brought down from over £3 million by self-denying fee deferments. 'If any film were to encapsulate Palace's commitment to film production and British cinema, it would be *The Crying Game*,' Stephen Woolley wrote in the aftermath of what was to be Palace's last movie. *The Crying Game* took Jordan back to the ambiguous perception of sexual identity that had contributed to *Mona Lisa*'s fascination. It, too, had a dusky beauty (played by Cathy Tyson, whom Woolley and Jordan, despairing prematurely of casting *The Crying Game*'s lead with a feminised male actor, had actually auditioned for Dil's role). It, too, had a man who let himself be duped by a woman whose true gender he doesn't recognise until it's too late. Jordan took the correct signpost in rejigging 'The Soldier's Wife' – away from political motivation and towards sexual politics.

The film was tinder for the times. It created a blaze of comment and the need to 'keep the secret' presented those already in it with a smug sense of superiority. Yet the revelation of Dil's true sex, which changes the nature of the film in a flash, so to speak, also tempts one to re-examine the original relationship of the black army hostage (Forrest Whitaker, who had just starred in Woolley's US production of *A Rage in Harlem*) over in Ulster and Dil, his mulatto lover in London. It is implausible. Either the hostage, too, is unaware of it; or else he conceals it from the IRA recruit (Jordan's favourite, hangdog-looking, but emotionally magnetising, interpreter) with whom he bonds during his captivity. If the latter, then it raises questions about his sexual predilection the screenplay can't acknowledge – and never does. *The Crying Game*'s narrative construction is broken-backed: unsurprising, considering its genesis in twisting a story of sentimental politics like *Cal* to fit the subsequent and much more interesting exploration of sexual identity. But largely through the finesse of Jaye Davidson's performance as Dil, the beautiful mulatto who works as hairdresser by day and as a *chanteuse* in the pub scene by night, Jordan keeps the contemporary story exerting an ever tightening grip. In short, he strikes the strain of murderous Irish nihilism – represented in the film by Miranda Richardson as an IRA assassin – which *Angel* first sounded so chillingly – and then eases into the mood of romantic melancholia that has become his own signature.

The *Crying Game* opened in London midway through the autumn. It did very good business, despite an IRA bombing campaign launched on the capital that very month and what Woolley considered a 'tepid showing' in the arts (not the critical) sections of the national press due to its sympathetic treatment of a terrorist character. Much of the good 'word of mouth', the most influential part of a film's publicity, was due to the responsive exhilaration of being so ingeniously deceived as to Jaye Davidson's sex. In turn, this ignited intriguing questions about which Oscar category he might fit, if nominated: 'Best Actor' or 'Best Actress'? Though nominated ('Best Actor'), he did not win an Oscar: Jordan did, for 'Best Original Screenplay', and *The Crying Game* received four additional nominations including 'Best Picture'.

By Oscar night, 29 March 1993, Palace Pictures was already history. It had gone into liquidation the previous August. Recognising how fragile its affairs were, though still awaiting his accountants' report on the company's viability, Michael Kuhn's PolyGram had made a £2 million bridging loan to Palace in January 1992: it was too little and too late. The cash drain prevented Palace buying distribution rights to films like *Reservoir Dogs*, *Delicatessen*, *The Player* and *Twin Peaks: Fire Walk With Me*: 'natural' Palace product that, if acquired, would have kept ready money coming into the stricken company whose creditors were making daily visits. It was also victim of the success it had pioneered: other smaller, no less active but financially more prudent companies were snapping up such goods and using the aggressive marketing techniques Palace had evolved.

When accountants Ernst and Young delivered their report to Kuhn at the end of March 1992, the PolyGram chief was livid. The situation was far, far worse than he had anticipated. Angus Finney records his outraged response: 'We said, [to Palace] "This is outrageous. Give us our money back." ' By early April it became clear that any PolyGram deal was 'off'. Did PolyGram 'pull the rug' out from under Palace, as the latter's wounded executives felt in the immediate aftermath? The answer is it did not need to. The company was about to collapse from a confluence of bad luck, lack of capital, poor management that never really escaped from the 'haphazard hippie idealism' that had been its foundation, an absence of ready-to-hand box-office hits and personal hubris. Much the same mix, in fact, that had caused Goldcrest's collapse six years earlier. But Goldcrest's directors were personally shielded by their status in the community of film-makers and bankers: Palace's raffish crew were visible street targets for all the contumely and insults from desperate creditors, large and small.

It was a very unpleasant time. On 16 April 1992 Palace applied to go into administration, a halfway house between bankruptcy and voluntary settlements that permitted trading to continue. Who would trade with it, though? Finney's analysis of the crisis disclosed that producers immediately began reclaiming the rights to their films: Palace's video library, valued at £9 million, dropped to virtually nothing. It was formally put into administration on 7 May 1992. On that day, Michael Winner commented, Palace put out a press release which said they maintained 'a high level of commercial success and remained consistently profitable. That was when the bailiffs were taking the desks out, and my technicians' – Winner had just finished a gross-out comedy, *Dirty Weekend* – 'had bounced Palace cheques in their pockets. Profit in the British film industry obviously has a different meaning to the rest of the world.' Palace finally entered liquidation in August.

'Who's Crying Now?' was the logo on custom-made T-shirts that quite a few of the smaller fry in the industry sported in the presence of Woolley and Powell at the following year's Cannes Festival. Bitter, spiteful perhaps, but understandable: many companies that traded with Palace were hurt, a few of the bigger creditors had to fire staff. How much did Palace owe? No precise figures have ever been publicly disclosed but estimates range 'somewhere' between £6 million and £15 million. It included a claim of almost £100,000 by HandMade Films on distribution rights for *Nuns on the Run*, a farcical comedy secured by Palace without upfront money, which had been a runaway success. 'Their business side was never as good as their flair for releasing films,' a HandMade executive was quoted as saying, which put it in a nutshell.

The Crying Game's box-office success came too late in the day to snatch a reprieve out of a death sentence. Miramax, which had refused to back the film upfront, bought the North American distribution rights when they saw it for $2.5 million. Their skilful marketing made it what *New York Magazine* called, 'the obsessional entertainment *du jour*'. Jaye

Davidson was photographed by Annie Liebowitz for a Gap ad: for
Americans, the film's IRA terrorist aspect was simply an exotic backdrop. '*The Crying Game* is the movie everyone is talking about,' wrote
Richard David Story. 'But no one is giving away its secret.' The com-
plicity of film-goers was a crucial element in its success. It grossed $63
million, though the expense of Miramax's publicity campaigns, prints,
etc, substantially reduced this: the Weinsteins would have made their
profit on ancillary TV and video rentals. In Britain it took well over £2
million. Such sums or, rather, the *perception* of their success might well
have given Palace breathing space; it's unlikely that they would have
spurred PolyGram's white knight to ride to the rescue. What Kuhn had
seen in Palace's accounts was a monstrous abyss; he drew back in horror.
The deal done prematurely by Palace with Roger Wingate was also a
discouraging factor. PolyGram, which was its own distributor, had no
need to share profits with a third party. But Kuhn knew the value of
'personal services', as distinct from corporate management. Woolley and
Powell had the production experience, the kind of track record that
PolyGram wished to buy into. As individuals they had not been declared
bankrupt; they were assisting the banks, as well as they could, in long-
term repayment prospects. There was nothing to stop them picking
themselves up, dusting themselves down and starting all over again.
Which is precisely what they did.

   To the astonishment of many in London's film community, and the fury
of some, inside a very short time they incorporated themselves as Scala
Productions – named after Woolley's old alma mater, the Scala Cinema.
They were backed by a deal that funded their overheads and gave PolyGram
a 'first look' at any projects they developed and an option to produce
them. 'Hopefully,' a chastened but far from despondent Woolley added in
postscript, 'the Palace experience of overstretching and over-diver-
sification will prevent us from repeating our mistakes.' On others, Palace's
collapse left many scars; it compounded the British film industry's embattled sense of systemic failure. But even in the short term it did not inhibit
the careers of Palace's two chiefs (or indeed of employees who, as will be
seen, climbed out of the mess into future positions of influence in the
industry). And in the slightly longer term, Woolley and Powell were to
become partners in a state-subsidised film consortium backed by even
more millions in public money than Palace had lost. Whatever else it might
be, 'crying' was not the name of the game in the film industry.

★

Under thirty films were produced in Britain in 1992. One reason: the British film industry had spent some of its best months the previous year across the sea in Ireland. *My Left Foot* had kick-started Anglo-Irish film-making by proving that a film made there could turn a worldwide profit and garner Oscars; *The Commitments* continued the seductive music. Stories about people who let their passions show and gave no trouble with class accents travelled well in the US. 'British films tend to hold back on the emotions,' said Romaine Hart, a prominent London distributor, 'you could never accuse an Irish film of doing that.'

Each of the films, roughly two thirds of them American-financed but usually directed by and starring Brits, capitalised on this cultural equivalence of Hollywood-made movies, grounded in generous tax breaks. Each had distinction, freshness and performance. Albert Finney's rural police sergeant, alienated from the folk comedy of *The Playboys* by the law he must enforce and the love he can't possess, gave Gillies MacKinnon's film, co-authored by *My Left Foot*'s Shane Connaughton, its heart of Celtic darkness. Finney's bull-necked, bowed and ultimately broken man was the cruel stroke that every Irish comedy needs to complete it. Mike Newell imaginatively blended grungy gypsy tenement life in Dublin's outer slums with the bracing outdoor freedoms of Irish myth in *Into the West*. He plucked the trouble and strife of an even wilder West out of the remote landscape. In *Hear My Song* the quirky talent of Peter Chelsom, a less whimsical Bill Forsyth, spun an amusing and melodic shaggy dog story out of the search for Josef Locke, a buccaneering Irish tenor of yesteryear whose tax returns (like the Inland Revenue men) had trouble catching up with him. A large and exuberant cast, gathered from both sides of the Irish Sea, behaved like the bouncing ball that ushered audiences along on the old-time singalong cinema shorts: they hit each note of character comedy with unerring emphasis. The fiscal popularity of Ireland made the stinginess of Britain seem almost punitive, even though going to Ireland didn't always guarantee art or box office. This fact became gratifyingly evident – to *les misérables* over in Britain, anyhow – when $44 million was blown to little effect, save the Irish pocket, on making the immigrant melodrama *Far and Away*, with Tom Cruise as the boy from the bogs and Nicole Kidman as his Galway lass.

Throughout the decade the Irish film industry was quoted to British legislators as a kind of emerald Camelot where artists could burnish culture and have their taxes reduced, too. Not exactly reality; but again, perception is everything. In Britain, by contrast, the Palace crash cast a shadow over an already gloomy economy. The Canadian company developing the potential of Canary Wharf as a media-cum-City centre had gone into administration. The great tower itself stood forlornly on the Thames embankment, bereft of all but the most rudimentary infrastructure of roads, restaurants and light railways, like some monument to a latter-day Ozymandias. 'The end of a dream,' the journalist Ivan Fallon called it. Palace's crash was just a faint echo of the Docklands' collapse; but the latter showed that even the most generous government tax breaks could not work miracles.

The film industry was wearily reconciled to five more years of Tory rule after John Major's unexpected electoral victory. David Mellor, Minister for National Heritage, had assumed responsibility for films. But the industry was almost too tired of undelivered promises to hope for better things. Even the British Film Commission, a high-sounding initiative which, however, had only money enough to pay a staff of four, eventually came alive in April 1992, some eighteen months after the Downing Street summit: it looked stillborn. 'At best quaint, at worst useless,' said Michael Winner, who had himself turned his attention increasingly away from films to eating dinners and reporting on them for the *Sunday Times*: a wise move in an age of scarcity and doing credit to Winner as consumer, if no longer producer.

'People forget that the three *Star Wars* films were British-made, three *Supermans*, sixteen Bond films, and *Batman*. All British-made,' said the Commission's head, Sydney Samuelson. And now? Three episodes of the American soap, *Married With Children*, were all that could be looked forward to at the half-year mark: Pinewood was making commercials; Elstree stages were being rented out to Pop bands practising for their gigs. Terry Ilott had not been exaggerating when he wrote, at the start of 1992, 'The downturn now has been so long and so deep that many people are worried that the entire infrastructure has unravelled.' It was amazing, but no national production statistics were documented in the UK for the film industry: a sign of how content the government was to keep its distance.

Channel 4, now under David Aukin, head of drama, had increased its 40 per cent average contribution to a film's budget: but only because costs had risen, not due to optimism. The cost of a typical Channel 4 film in 1982 was £400,000: now it was £1.8 million. Nevertheless the TV channel had to date part-funded nearly 250 films. BBC TV, producing about twelve films a year now, had an average investment of £700,000 in each. The discrepancy between the two TV companies was due to the BBC films being made to fill a small-screen time slot and having a very short-term theatrical release, though one of them, *Truly, Madly Deeply* (1990), a sweetly elegiac story of a widow (Juliet Stevenson) the love of whose life (Alan Rickman) is brought back from the grave to bring her comfort (and invite his spectral mates in for a night of watching old Woody Allen films on the box), did well in cinemas and launched the directorial career of Anthony Minghella. The dearth of ambitious productions was a boon to such self-consciously 'small' films, though in retrospect the attention it won them was exaggerated.

Cannes turned down *The Crying Game* for competition in 1992: the slot was filled by the final part of Terence Davies's *Distant Voices, Still Lives*; his trilogy of wretched Liverpool family life as one of ten children with an abusive father, a timid mother and Dickensian extremes of abuse and deprivation. He marked the beginning of his happiness by his father's death freeing him to go and see his first film, the aptly titled *Singin' in the Rain. The Long Day Closes* was his homage to these blissful days. Its emphasis was on small joys and the passive pleasures of looking and listening; but the presentation was tableauesque, the style impressionistic and Proustian in its allusive drift from one event to the next before settling almost psychedelically on some single vivid image like the sunlit corner of a carpet until the part comes to stand for the entire texture of domestic security.

Few film-makers had been so scarred by life as Davies and his film enshrined a touching Truffaut-like belief in the power of cinema to anoint an abused soul. Inside Davies was a harder centre than he had any right to hope for, but he had resisted transforming it into yet one more rebel's manifesto. He took the 'less travell'd path' of inward joy and turned a hard life into an aesthetic experience. For which he deserves honour. Davies accepts what Ken Loach would refuse, though there is a certain ironical congruence between the two. Asked what he would change, if he could, Davies shied away from Loach's customary political agenda, yet showed he wasn't taken in by the world: 'If I could change anything, I would be very good-looking, with a very good body, and be really, really stupid – because then the world is your oyster. I know it.'

Where were the golden boys and girls of yesteryear? As mentioned, some like Finney were in Ireland; others were seeking the gold dust of

Hollywood. Daniel Day-Lewis, the only international heir to Caine and Connery, was starring in Michael Mann's *The Last of the Mohicans* as Hawkeye, the white boy of Irish parentage raised by Mohican Indians. The part showed off his natural glory: physicality bursting from him in the American manner, but retaining his sensibility and a reserve of mystery, running as if preparing for take-off, taking to land and water with amphibian grace. One grieved not to have a British landscape to fit this player's assumption of its epic proportions.

Kenneth Branagh and Emma Thompson were in Hollywood, too, surprising everyone by playing four roles – two each – in *Dead Again*, a pastiche thriller directed by Branagh who claimed he needed his wife of three years co-starring with him 'to contribute a more trustful, collaborative atmosphere … in a Hollywood that's merciless to its proven talents, never mind absolute beginners'. They had not 'gone Hollywood', though, simply recognised that Renaissance Films needed an international dimension (plus American players) to make its ambitious film agenda, containing several Shakespeare adaptations, popular and bankable.

Was he juggling too many projects, even for an Ulster Protestant who thrived on the Protestant work ethic? In April he played Hamlet on BBC Radio 4; in May, it was Coriolanus at the Chichester Festival. He was editing his new British social comedy, *Peter's Friends*, and playing a Gestapo man in the Disney film *Swing Kids*. 'Well, I feel on top of my game,' he told concerned well-wishers. 'My definition of success is control.' It was now apparent that for Renaissance Branagh was resurrecting the old Victorian-Edwardian tradition of actor-manager with business control.

Yet the aura of invincibility was a fragile crown and, in a country like Britain, the polymath wore it at his peril. Branagh quite possibly did not appreciate how the tide of media wonderment at his Orson Welles-like energies in every department could easily turn into a choppier sea of comment. Ironically, his marriage afforded opportunity to the envious, or simply bitchy. His success in the 1980s had owed much to media friendliness and the sense of a lone hand daring to turn itself to what its owner's will drove him to achieve. Commentators praised a company like Renaissance sustained by private finance, not supported by public subsidy. But once they became 'Ken and Em', as they were ominously paired in the prints, the theatrical coupling that had worked magic for 'the Oliviers' never manifested itself as 'the Branaghs'. On the contrary, it became part of the media game to assess how the career of one was drawing ahead of the other (or being retarded by too fulsome allegiance to the other). And then the dread word 'luvvies' cropped up, signifying a self-regarding and uncritical coterie of mutually admiring talents. Perhaps there was no truth in this, or not much, but when the media decide by instinct, or simply tedium with their own recycling of the same praises and phrases that, really, it is time for a change, opportune to sharpen the wind a little and not temper it for patriotic pride or easy access to celebrities, then the signals are set at danger. By the time Branagh and Thompson recognised this it was too late: they had crossed over from the review columns, where in general they still enjoyed respectful and rewarding notices, to the gossip columns and the less friendly features.

The teeth were sometimes sharpest in the least expected pages. 'Kenneth Branagh is, like Jesus, the son of a carpenter. He has even less trouble attracting apostles.' Thus the *Sunday Telegraph* in November 1992. The same article unearthed a particularly damning judgement by Branagh's peer, Richard Eyre, which had appeared in the *Guardian* (and was often to be quoted): 'Branagh lacks that sense of danger, that recklessness, savagery and lurking melancholia that, with Olivier, made for something dark. Ken ... he's nice. He's decent.'

The occasion for this assault by direct and indirect thrust was Branagh's new British film, *Peter's Friends*, a movie that, fairly or not, attracted a sniffy accusation of the 'old pals' act' even before it opened, since so many of its cast were also Branagh's friends – one of them his wife, another his mother-in-law, the rest ex-Cambridge University chums who had performed together in the *Footlights Revue* and now, older, richer, but no wiser, converged on an ancestral pile of ivy and stonework in the Home Counties belonging to the eponymous Lord Peter so as to see the New Year in. Comparisons were made with *The Big Chill*. False ones. In that American elegy to lost illusions, the group of friends took themselves and the world seriously; in *Peter's Friends* the outside world doesn't exist and all of them are totally self-absorbed. In short, 'luvvies'.

It was now remembered that in his premature autobiography, *Beginning*, one of the less good-natured things Branagh had done was to criticise Terry Hands and Trevor Nunn of the Royal Shakespeare Company, where he had been singularly unhappy, as constituting an inaccessible Cambridge University elite. Yet here he was, casting another Cambridge coterie in his film! The synergy often worked well, wittily, effectively when the dynamics of a disturbed weekend were illustrated in the way that language was used to expose virtue and vice, folly and fantasy, and the ego trips of the characters collided with each other at unexpected bends in the road. But its humour was largely interpreted as hubris.

Branagh had still a loyal personal following, but he no longer seemed a regenerative force. Indeed, Emma Thompson's triumph in one of the few British films of distinction that year, the Merchant Ivory production of *Howards End*, put her on a solo pinnacle that she scaled by her own sure-footed nerve. As E. M. Forster's radiant Edwardian bluestocking, a woman of intelligence thrown on to her own resources by the exigencies of life, she emerged as the leading actress of her generation. Vanessa Redgrave, in a smaller role in the film, looked more than ever like someone passing on the torch to her successor.

Like Branagh, Thompson is an overachiever in the best sense: restless when not working. Work had the edge on marriage. Marriage was 'making room for another person's soul in your life', she said, 'a Herculean labour.' For the moment, anyhow, the 'room' had to be 'one's own'. Marriage, for both, simply looked the signal that each gave the other to say he or she was comfortable with each other, where work was concerned as well as love. But Thompson at this time referred to her generation as 'molten', and it became clear that she didn't want to risk cooling off until she had tasted experience separately. The lukewarm notices she and Branagh had got when they acted in the revival of *Look Back in Anger* were a warning to her that too much success, too soon, too publicly enjoyed, too mutually achieved, could generate a backlash.

Of the two, Branagh has the masculine energy, Thompson the feminine intuition. On the whole, the latter proved the better protection – this and the sense of humour that her husband's commitment too often lacked. What was the difference between being directed by James Ivory and Kenneth Branagh, she was asked, and answered pertly, 'The difference is, I didn't have to make James Ivory's supper when I got home from work.'

The lifebelt one might have hoped would be thrown to the sinking film industry had on it the name 'Rank Organisation'. It remained firmly tethered to dry land. The almost total absence of Rank from the production scene for two decades is one of the least investigated but most shameful episodes in the industry. Here was a corporation that had been one of the great engines of the film economy in post-war years and right up to the end of the 1970s; a 'vertically integrated' structure possessing studios, cinemas, a distribution arm, half a theme park in Orlando, Florida, a library of old films from the 1930s and the biggest film laboratories and video duplication facility in Europe, widely known (if no longer renowned) for its name and products, with an American partner (Universal) and ties to European distributors.

After the collapse of Cannon, Goldcrest and now Palace Pictures, Rank was left as the last hope of British film finance. Small hope! The Gong Man, that oiled and muscled athlete who had introduced each Rank production before the credit titles, had let his constitution go flabby from inactivity. Rank simply did not wish to be a 'player' in the film game. It had pursued deliberately and shamelessly the profit to be found in nearly anything that hadn't got to do with the risky business of film-making: bowling alleys, hotels, copying machines, bingo halls, motorway service areas, betting shops. Rank was (or had been) in all of these. But where film-making was concerned, Rank was almost nowhere to be seen.

The new men who now ran Rank had succeeded the late, and greatly feared, John Davis, an accountant whose film-mogul ambitions had taken an expensive loss on trying to 'crack Hollywood' with super-productions. These ultra-cautious men had resolved that you couldn't lose money on films – at least not much – if you didn't make any yourself. Better (or at least much, much safer) to invest in the calculable benefits of other film-makers' work by distributing it (for a fee) and exhibiting it (for an even bigger fee). Its cinemas were filled 90 per cent of the year with Hollywood product; its studios were rented out to Hollywood film-makers; its deals with Hollywood made mouth-watering sums available to American movie-makers whose product was formulaic but reassuringly familiar. The corporate philosophy was 'Safety First'.

Around this time, October 1993, a retired employee of Peat Marwick Mitchell, an accountancy firm employed post-war by Rank, drew the attention of Rank's chief executive, Michael Gifford, to the startling conclusion of a report he alleged had been commissioned from his old firm in 1948: namely that it would be 'commercially advisable' for Rank to cease film production. Should the report not be released to the media? Jim Daly, managing director of Rank Film and TV Services, replying on his chairman's behalf, claimed that neither he, nor other 'long-standing colleagues' – Daly had been thirty years with Rank – had heard of this report. Company policy was to destroy documents after they have ceased to be relevant. In any case, he considered journalists spent too much time on 'nostalgia' and didn't need another excuse for dipping into the past. Forty-five years later, the alleged report's conclusion had become extremely relevant; and to call the attention that the media were giving to Rank's past 'nostalgic' was a polite understatement. It was being severely indicted for not letting its enormous production potential lie idle.

Rank, it is true, supported British Screen Finance, with a very small annual tithe: nothing to compare with the £60 million it announced, in 1987, that it was ploughing into other people's movies to co-produce or acquire them – which meant, in most cases, American-made ones – distribute them abroad and add to its own library of 'rights'. 'Most of the high-profile companies in our end of the business have gone bust,' said Jim Daly. 'I think we are happy keeping a low profile and staying in business. We're not film-makers,' he added, 'we don't believe we have creative talent.' But by the early 1990s, people were starting to ask, did Rank have any *business* talent?

Only the arrival of American Multi-Cinema, in the mid 1980s, prodded Rank to enter the multiplex business. Its £60 million co-investment strategy for acquisition and co-production with US partners, which was entrusted to Fred Turner, managing director of Rank Film Distributors, remained timidly underused: Rank preferred entrench-ment to investment. It might as well have put the money in a building society account. The Rank executives had pre-eminently that kind of mindset. Despite cast assets, they felt more comfortable being small savers. Michael Gifford, Rank's chief executive officer, was particularly risk-averse. As a younger finance executive he had served the great Quaker interests of Rowntree, the confectionary manufacturers; then he had come to Rank, an organisation originally founded by the Methodist tycoon J. Arthur (later Lord) Rank to make films for religious pros-elytising.

Nothing altruistic or spiritual seemed to have adhered to Michael Gifford. Giving evidence some time later to the House of Commons Select Committee on the National Heritage, he did not turn a hair when reproached by its chairman, Gerald Kaufman, one of the few MPs conversant with the film industry. No, he assured them, Rank did not see film-making in its future, particularly British film-making. Rank preferred to increase its revenues by acquiring leisure entertainments, like the Mecca hotel chain in 1990, or simply sit back and let its lucky Xerox investments bring in half of the 1991 pre-tax profits. The downside of this, however, was that indebtedness to the banks increased as well; interest charges kept rising; the Xerox investments had an end date on them; despite cinema attendance in Britain rising to 98 million in 1992, Rank's multiplex competitors drew more and more of the bulk of it and caused the profits of its film and TV division to dwindle. Gifford might say, 'We are in the business of making money, not movies,' but by 1992 some had begun to wonder if even making money was a long-term option. Profits dipped from £37 million in 1990 to £22 million in 1991. Investors began to worry about the effect on shares of Rank's debt, £989 million according to Michael Gifford. Rank's operating profits covered interest charges just three times. Rank started to sell off some Mecca hotels, but the property boom had burst by late 1992 – Britain, in November, was forced into an ignominious departure from the Exchange Rate Mechanism, which left the pound sterling in disarray on the international exchanges and forced chairmen of companies like Rank to face up to the banks' demands and their shareholders' jitters.

As not infrequently happens, a company is stimulated by bad news into making feeble gestures of a kind it had forsworn in less boisterous times. Thus Rank, to some amusement, announced in October 1992 that it was going to co-invest in ten films over the next two years. The first was to be *Come Again*, a 'high-concept' comedy set in New York, written by Nick Evans, who had written and produced *Just Like a Woman*, a transvestite comedy produced for Zenith, in which Rank had invested: it figured on some of the 'Ten Worst Films' lists of its year. *Come Again* was originally slated to be a Paramount UK production before that initiative was wound up. Not good omens, not good at all. The other nine films are lost to history, since Rank's existence as a film industry entity took priority with quite alarming suddenness over its rekindled interest in sex comedies.

Reports began circulating in the City around the end of 1992 that Rank, nervous of waiting for an upturn in the economy, was considering selling off its film interests – Pinewood Studios, distribution company, Odeon cinemas, library – in order to reduce its debt. A price of £300 million was whispered, though some put it as high as £500 million. (The operating assets were valued on Rank's books at £365 million.) Michael Gifford issued the customary denial. But under pressure he qualified it: 'If someone offered good money for Rank Film and

Television, I'd be fired if I didn't take the opportunity to sell it.' A quote attributed to him in the *Evening Standard* put it more colourfully: 'I would sell my grandmother at the right price.' Disregarding the kith-and-kin valuation, a sentimental one, perhaps, what would be 'the right price' for an asset like the Rank Organisation's film business?

Michael Grade, head of Channel 4, son of Leslie Grade and nephew of Lew Grade and Bernard Delfont, former tycoons whose film empires had collapsed in the 1980s, felt he should find out ... perhaps make an offer. Grade by the end of 1992 was head of a consortium of investors, swiftly co-ordinated by Chemical Bank in order to buy out, after fifty years, the one-time powerful and now abjectly passive part of the country's cultural heritage. Grade seemed aware of history being made or, rather, remade: 'I want to help revive the British film industry,' adding, 'Rank is a sleeping giant.' At least part of the giant stirred usefully in its slumber at this announcement: Rank's shares rose 12p.

10

Talking Film Finance

In the spring of 1993, first one or two individuals, then a few more, finally it seemed the collective British film industry raised its nose in the air – and sniffed. It smelled money. Despite the length of time it had been since that fragrance reached their nostrils, film-makers recognised it at once. Far off, maybe; still downwind; but if they could smell it, something must be cooking. It was the National Lottery. In Hollywood, when they want to make films, they go to the banks. In Britain they were to go to the bureaucrats. Which explains, in large part, why Hollywood has a film industry and we have not – simply film-makers. Screwing money out of the banks is hard enough, but coaxing cash or tax breaks out of the bureaucrats had so far defeated the best and the brightest – indeed, the most devious and sly – minds in the film community. The Lottery changed the odds.

In May, and for the next month or so, the carpet in the Horse Guards Road offices of Peter Brooke, Secretary of State at the Department of National Heritage (DNH), felt the weekly tread of the film industry's leading players. Nine meetings in all were scheduled with producers, directors, distributors, exhibitors, TV chiefs, video renters and, yes, even arts supremos – though no film critics. Were Brooke's intentions honourable? Did the Tory government – at last! – intend to throw pennies or pounds into the old beggar's hat? Or was it simply a snide move, as cynics said, to refute the charge that those initials 'DNH' stood for 'Department of Nothing Happening'? The trouble was that those invited to give their views were still not united in what they wanted done; some were going along simply to stop others doing what they didn't want done.

In April 1993, British producers had come out with a demand for a levy on US-owned multiplexes in the UK; they made their profit from Hollywood films that occupied the screens 90 per cent of the year. Plough some of it back into British films, came the demand to the

DNH. The exhibitors turned out in force at the Café Royal on 28 April 1993 to put that one to sleep. Ian Riches, the hearteningly named president of the Cinematograph Exhibitors Association (CEA), asked, is this fair, is it honest? Over £500 million had been spent since 1985 on building new cinema complexes (seventy to date) or refurbishing old theatres. It had taken one corporation – United Cinemas International (UCI), a joint initiative of Paramount and Universal Studios – a good six years to turn even a modest profit, an act of faith in an industry on which British investors had given up. Were they now to be robbed of the fruits of their labours? He spoke from the heart. Mr Riches was also a director of UCI. 'At the end of the day, the public are the final judges and you cannot force [British] culture upon them when they'd really rather see *Lethal Weapon III*.' (Only one truly British film had made it into the top fifty films shown in the UK in 1992: *Carry On, Columbus*. It reached fiftieth position.) In other words what we have we hold.

David Puttnam jousted with Peter Brooke on the BBC's *Today* programme on 19 April 1993. Puttnam demanded a levy on blank or recorded video tapes. In other words what the public bought to use in Camcorders, or play on TV screens, would yield a good few pence to finance films. Neat and fair, maybe, but a non-starter. Not just because the British Videogram Association opposed it, pointing to the recession's downturn in the sales or rentals of home video, but also because Treasury gospel rejected the levying of taxes earmarked for specific good causes. It would affront orthodoxy and imperil autonomy.

The British Film Institute (BFI) had made its pitch early, before the DNH even opened for business. Jeremy Thomas, the film producer recently appointed BFI chairman in succession to Richard Attenborough, and its director, Wilf Stevenson, had met Robert Kee, Under-Secretary of State at the DNH, on 23 March 1993, to promote the BFI's case for distributing Lottery funding to the film-makers rather than the Arts Council of Great Britain under its chairman Lord Palumbo. It got a brisk turndown and went into a sulk.

As soon as he got back to the BFI's Stephen Street offices Thomas wrote Kee the sort of 'surprised and pained' letter that passes for polite chiding and earnest plea for second (and more generous) thoughts. 'In effect, the British film industry is being told that the DNH does not think the BFI is doing a good job, and that the Arts Councils are the best bodies to allocate funds for film: a decision which is in my view at best perverse, and at worst highly damaging to the BFI board, and to myself as its new chairman.' He asked for the BFI to be named 'on the face of the National Lottery Bill as a distribution agency, with 15 per cent of the Arts slice [of Lottery moneys]'. The Arts Council, he argued, only had a narrow remit in relation to film, video and broadcasting – basically, the funding of avant-garde work and of documentaries about artists. The BFI had sixty years' experience in funding film-makers. A somewhat inflated claim, though the BFI production board had more recently given directors such as Peter Greenaway, Terence Davies and Sally Potter their head start.

The BFI had a UK remit, Thomas continued, whereas the Arts Council of Great Britain covered only, well, Great Britain. (This was a sly move: the BFI's charter had only covered 'Great Britain' until it was extended in 1992 to take in Northern Ireland, the fourth part of the UK – and only after I, as a BFI governor, had spent many months overcoming the Northern Ireland Office's reluctance to extend the British remit any further into that troubled province.) Still, Thomas thought the argument worth a try; Kee's reply proved it wasn't. Apart from this undoubted snub to the BFI's claim to speak for 'the industry', never mind 'the institute', Thomas and Stevenson feared that losing out in the Lottery stakes would cost them J. Paul Getty's substantial private funding of its work if the Arts Council began duplicating its patronage. The American multimillionaire, a long-time UK resident and a film buff with an obsession for Will Hay comedies to which the BFI's archives catered, might pull out.

After this inconclusive meeting, the BFI joined forces with the Producers Alliance of Cinema and Television (PACT) and both sent a dossier to Peter Brooke calling for him to refer the film industry to the Monopolies and Mergers Commission. PACT also called for a 'blockbuster tax' on all films grossing more than £4 million in the UK. There was no response. Nik Powell, the former head of the now insolvent Palace Pictures, had been appointed chairman of the Film Strategy Group, a 'think-tank' of producers convened in the autumn of 1992, after the Downing Street summit, to advise the Department of National Heritage. It produced six papers – on production, exhibition, distribution, video, TV and revenues – all arguing for government intervention. The most inflammatory one called for a tax on distributors once revenues reached an agreed threshold: this would provide £80 million a year for feature-film-making. Five distribution companies would have been affected, all but one of them American owned or controlled. This plan, too, got nowhere. The American film companies in the UK were, as usual, too busy fighting their own cause – safeguarding every pound sterling that could be sent back to the US as dollars earned by British talent – to rush to the aid of the indigenous talents that contributed to this one-way trade. A *Financial Times* report estimated that American films shown in the UK in 1992 earned £240 million, or ten times more than native British films did. The Americans could well have afforded a tip for the Brits; but they preferred to tell Peter Brooke to dig into his own pocket, not theirs.

Feelings had been made rawer by the 40 per cent withholding tax being levied on foreign film talents who came to work in Britain. Even though the tax eventually came back to the film companies, which obliged their Hollywood stars by paying it for them, and there was no 'double taxation', it rankled to have to pay 40 per cent of salaries just to bring them to Britain. In short, among these overtures being made to Peter Brooke no one was playing off the same concert sheet. Contradiction and confusion was everywhere; vested interests lay behind each seemingly positive proposal; 'art for art's sake' was translated into 'money for God's sake'. The same old grind.

One man, however, came up with a proposal that was to bear seed – though not for several years yet and then was to produce blooms that were nearer the overweening style of the triffids, those monstrous growths that overran Britain in John Wyndham's science-fiction story, than the fructifying hopes its proponent foresaw. He was Michael Deeley, the former EMI production chief, now an independent producer and member of the British Screen Advisory Council (BSAC), the self-financing, all-industry body whose fifty-odd members – including myself – met, as stated, every other month in the faded grandeur of the Moses Room in the House of Lords, so called because of its mural depicting the Infant Christ among the bulrushes: it was the cheapest accommodation we could find as the Department of Trade and Industry refused to find a penny to fund us. The biblical reminder was not an inspiration. The members generally valued it for enabling them to keep a close eye on their own interests as well as a sharp one on each other's.

Deeley, on 25 February 1993, presented his 'solution' based on funds from the 'arts' allocation of Lottery income going to found a National Film Corporation (NFC). Deeley recalled that his own former group, Associated Film Distributors (AFD: a partnership between EMI and Lord Grade) had failed because it hadn't sold its films in the US in advance of starting to make them – and because it had to bear production and distribution costs there. When it presumed to second-guess the world market, AFD went bust. Goldcrest had failed because the US advances it did secure were too small a proportion of their major pictures – recoupment was impossible, short of a runaway hit.

The NFC, said Deeley, could be established with a one-time funding of £75 million of Lottery money – '£25 million for three years would be sufficient to create an ongoing production programme with the critical mass necessary to make the NFC a world player.' No film would be financed without a prior commitment from a US distributor of *at least* 40 per cent of its budget in return for US rights. Assurances from major non-US territorial distributors of *at least* 20 per cent must also be secured. Negative rights and copyright were to remain with the NFC: very important in building a film library. A fund to develop scripts would be set up. Best news of all, whoever bossed the outfit would be remunerated on a performance-related basis. It wouldn't be 'jobs for the boys'.

Wouldn't it cut across British Screen Finance (BSC), someone asked? It was currently doing nicely under its new boss, Simon Perry. 'No,' said Deeley firmly. 'BSC does an excellent job with limited funds and its financial return [which was to reach 50 per cent] is impressive ... The artistic level of its films is irreproachable. [But] the NFC is a different creature with a different mindset – treating films more as a business of international scope with widespread popular appeal.' It should be self-sufficient after three years. It would fund or part-fund twenty-four films a year. It would attract 'runaway' British film-makers back to work in the UK. It would stimulate employment. It would tap into tax subsidies abroad and, we hoped, at home.

We all looked at each other on BSAC much as stout Cortés gazed on the infinite prospects of the Pacific, with wild surmise. Hearts were lighter – wallets already heavier in expectation – as we traipsed through the dismal stone corridors of the House of Lords out into the bright new world of a reinvigorated British film industry. Only one snag occurred to some of us. Unless Peter Brooke changed his mind, the Deeley plan would not happen. The DNH was already committed to the idea that one fifth of the National Lottery should be set aside for 'the arts', including films; but it should fund capital projects, not revenue-producing investment. In other words the cash could be used to build a cinema, but not to finance the films to show in it. One was called 'patronage' and was very proper to the British mindset; the other was more dubiously known as 'business', and anything could happen there and usually did.

There was only one gleam of hope, one tiny sunbeam in Parliament Square as we emerged, dazzled by the Deeley plan. The 1991 Budget, which had given film-makers a modest tax concession to write off part of the cost of a movie the moment work began on the script, had tended to regard the film as a 'capital project'. Could Peter Brooke be persuaded to be as enlightened as his senior colleague Norman Lamont, Chancellor of the Exchequer? The 'elder statesmen' of the industry – or, as they had become known by now, even before the arrival of that cult film, 'the usual suspects', namely Attenborough and Puttnam – were now looked upon to use all their considerable persuasion to concentrate Mr Brooke's mind on the semantic problem of regarding 'revenue earning' and 'capital funding' as, really and honestly, distinctions without a difference ... or not much of a difference. 'It's our last hope,' said Lord Brabourne, a film producer (of *Murder on the Orient Express* and other 'quality' films), a BFI governor and perhaps the man with the best connections of all, as the son-in-law of Earl Mountbatten. Between the front door of the DNH and the back door of Buckingham Palace, surely there was some way in for the film industry, some persuasive access to the powers that be and the Grail cup of the National Lottery that would refresh so many thirsty talents.

What Simon Perry, who had taken over at British Screen Finance in 1991, thought of a secondary Lottery-funded body such as Deeley suggested opening for business across the street, so to speak, is something that this subtle and prudent operator never spelled out at the time. Perry was then forty-nine and that rare figure in the British film industry, an Old Etonian. In 1975 he raised £25,000 and made a teasing little film entitled *Knots*, based on the then fashionable theories of the iconoclastic psychologist R. D. Laing. This gruelling experience generated the active sympathy he showed for first-time producer-directors.

Perry had co-founded the Association of Independent Producers (AIP) in 1976; two years later he joined the London bureau of *Variety* to 'learn the business'. He learned, principally, that 'there's a madness needed to be a film producer; what's generally missing from your average television producer is the survival spirit'. He joined the National Film Finance Corporation, under Sir John Terry, and supervised script financing. In 1982 he formed Umbrella Films and, with director Michael

Above: Ewan McGregor, in *Trainspotting,* 'the performance that defined his talents, but also set him an unmatchable standard.'

Right: The explosive nature of Robert Carlyle, in *The Full Monty,* 'lights the fuse that gives the film its indignation, its sense of people living at the extremes of their society, yet tempered by the affectionate bond between the divorced dad and his small son.'

THE POLITICIANS

Clockwise from top left: 'One shouldn't blame Paul Channon for precipitating the downfall of the British film industry by one tiny decision in the summer of 1985.' ✦ Nigel Lawson 'proposed in his Budget speech to withdraw the one hundred per cent capital allowances from film-makers in March 1985. It brought home to everyone how much the industry had existed on the Treasury subsidising them with lost tax revenues.' ✦ Virginia Bottomley 'succeeded in coming up with £4.3m in lottery reserve cash to pass on to the Arts Council.' ✦ Chris Smith's 'immediate aim was to double British films' share of the UK market to twenty per cent.' ✦ Mark Fisher: as Labour's Shadow Arts Minister, he 'promised his party would do even more to help the industry.' ✦ Peter Brooke, National Heritage Secretary: his office carpet 'felt the weekly tread of the film industry's leading players.' ✦ Norman Lamont, as Chancellor of the Exchequer: 'his November 1993 financial summary brought no relief to the industry.'

Right: Daniel Day-Lewis: 'different in temper as well as talent, unpredictable in a part, or the pitch he brought himself to, until you saw him on the screen – and then, maybe, may not immediately have recognised him. A Method actor by instinct, rather than training.'

Below: Hugh Grant (second left) in *Four Weddings and a Funeral*: 'the template for his screen persona had been described by the author of one of the novels in whose screen adaptation Grant had appeared. E.M. Forster, in 1936, said in *Notes on an Englishman*, "It is not that an Englishman can't feel – it is that he is afraid to feel. He has been taught at his public school that it is bad form. He must not express great joy or sorrow or even open his mouth too wide when he talks – his pipe might fall out if he did." Minus the pipe, this is ur-Hugh Grant.'

THE PRODUCERS

Clockwise from top left: Tim Bevan and Sarah Radclyffe: 'identified an emerging cinema-going audience of young people who were educated, cheeky and irreverent.'

✦ George Harrison: HandMade Films, 'an eccentric outfit run by the Beatle George Harrison and an American "hyphenate" – a lawyer-accountant-producer, Denis O'Brien.' ✦ Lew Grade (right), with his brother Bernard Delfont, 'before the Titanic iceberg hit him and sank his company.' ✦ Stephen Woolley 'looks like the one who understands the bluff that is movie-making, the one best able to execute the three-card trick.' ✦ Simon Perry: 'the basic economics of the feature film business have broken down, and there just isn't enough of a livelihood to go round any more.' ✦ David Puttnam: 'always the boy who did his homework.' ✦ Jeremy Thomas 'bounced on the knee of his godfather Dirk Bogarde.'

Above: Kenneth Branagh: 'a stocky figure not out of place as a Rugby forward, gave little hint above the neckline of the matinee idol looks which traditionally went with mellifluous poetry-speaking as well as the shrill squeals of female fans.'

Left: Emma Thompson, for much of the period of this book, was married to Kenneth Branagh and seemed to work exclusively with him. But Thompson 'at this time referred to her generation as "molten", and it became clear that she didn't want to risk cooling off until she had tasted experience separately.'

THE DIRECTORS

This page clockwise from top left: Alan Parker on film-making and politics: 'You keep patting us on the back, telling us how clever we are, how many Oscars we win. But you've never helped us at all. I've spoken to so many ministers in the past, I finally gave up and went to the USA.' ✦ Peter Greenaway 'would probably have been the first to admit this was scarcely in the English tradition of film-making - and been proud to deny it. "My cinema has more to do with the sense of metaphor ... I'm not a film-maker ... I'm a painter in cinema."' ✦ Ken Loach's 'most successful films usually have central characters who are more demonstrative than their director ... Loach is at his best when the causes he adopts are lost ones.' ✦ Mike Leigh: 'a proven dedication to social anthropology.' ✦ *The Madness of King George* 'marked Nicholas Hytner's apparently effortless transfer of Alan Bennett's stage play at the Royal National Theatre to the screen.'✦ Michael Winterbottom: 'preferred the American model of the "road" movie with his calling-card work, *Butterfly Kiss*'.

This page clockwise from top left: Terence Davies in *The Long Day Closes* 'took the "less travell'd path" of inward joy and turned a hard life into an aesthetic experience. For which he deserves honour.' ✦ Neil Jordan: 'a confident, highly original talent, with a painterly eye and a novelist's sensibilities.' ✦ John Madden (seen here with Judi Dench): *Mrs Brown* 'instantly established Madden as a favoured Miramax director, a privilege he justified by delivering *Shakespeare in Love* to that American patron the following year.' ✦ Stephen Frears (directing *Prick Up Your Ears*): 'a director with something of his mentor Lindsay Anderson's eye for the realities of the social scene, though without Lindsay's rage to change.' ✦ David Leland: his *Personal Services* was 'a biting social comedy set in the 1950s world of a real-life suburban madam.'

Clockwise from top left: Julien Temple: from a background of 'pop-disc promotional films.' ✦ In *Into the West* Mike Newell 'imaginatively blended grungy gypsy tenement life in Dublin's outer slums with the bracing outdoor freedoms of Irish myth.' ✦ James Ivory (seen here with Anthony Hopkins): *The Remains of the Day*, 'Merchant Ivory's most successful production, had everything except a heart.' ✦ Guy Ritchie was 'without formal film-school training: it is doubtful if it would have done much for a talent already well annealed in the cut-and-thrust of the Pop industry.' ✦ Bill Forsyth: *Sylvie's Ark*, a 'warm and whimsical comedy.' ✦ Richard Attenborough, one of those who understood both David Puttnam (in his period running Columbia in Hollywood) and studio power, said, 'Instead of having only to deal with the people at Coke, David now had an in-house boss. Not only does one need autonomy in Hollywood, but one has to be seen to have it, too.'

Radford, produced *1984* from the Orwell novel, and *White Mischief*, about the dissolute colony of upper-class English expats living a sybaritic life in wartime Kenya. His cultural ties, linguistic fluency and marriage to a Frenchwoman may have persuaded him that British film-makers should look to European partners, not to US projects. 'If the UK provides an alternative to what Hollywood offers, we'll have a reasonably healthy climate,' he said in an interview at the Cannes Festival in May 1993. His production record at BSF reflected this. Later on, his bias was to prove fatal in his struggle to retain independent life and liberty when New Labour, in 2000, set up the Film Council, which spoke the language of Hollywood and hardly any of those of Europe. But for the moment Perry was doing nicely, free to make all decisions involving sums of less than £500,000 and, although still acknowledging a desire to be a producer, wryly admitting that 'I must be the most disadvantaged producer in Britain, because I can't apply to [my own banker] British Screen.'

Perry operated a rolling £4 million financing fund at BSF and claimed, 'If you were to ask me if I wanted more money, I would say yes, but not gigantic sums. I'd like twice as much: not to invest in more films necessarily, but to take a bigger stake in those that we do.' An optimist, a frugal spender, a pan-European, Simon Perry was a rare species in 1993 and, like rare species, extinction was a more likely event than survival. But not just yet . . . Two other men are worth noting at this time, principally for the roles they emerged to play a few years hence.

One was Charles Denton, who had founded Zenith with his partner Margaret Matheson in 1984, having been programme controller at the independent television companies ATV and Central. Zenith had nurtured film hits such as *Prick Up Your Ears*, *Wish You Were Here* and the TV detective series *Inspector Morse*. In July 1993 he was appointed head of drama at BBC TV, where Mark Shivas ran BBC Films. He made no bones about how he saw the job. 'Theatre?' he said. 'I never go to it. I can't stand the idea of all those actors on stage miles away.' His function was not to impose a creative vision, but to be 'a creator of the right circumstances'. In other words a facilitator. He had a buccaneering energy and was described by a colleague as 'clever at jumping on to a ship worth boarding'. He was to play a significant role in the distribution of National Lottery money to film-makers through the Arts Council after 1995. Time, then, to examine the 'circumstances' that he and his panel of fellow patrons created.

Curiously enough, film industry crises and (less frequently) achievements often coincided with Cannes, just when the major players were deep into deals, premières or simply long lunches at beach restaurants. So while Peter Brooke talked the future of film financing in London, the money got spent on the Croisette. This year, 1993, however, it wasn't simply the consumption that was conspicuous: British films were too. 'CANNES PICKS BRIT PIX' was the front-page headline in the British trade weekly *Screen International*, mimicking the telegraphese style of *Variety* the better to celebrate the fact that only one Hollywood movie (*Falling Down*) was in competition, whereas Britain had a record five. Altman's *Short Cuts*, Scorsese's *The Age of Innocence*, Spielberg's *Jurassic Park* had all given Cannes the go-by: not unworthiness, it was said, simply unreadiness, though for such movies, with budgets the size of a national deficit and publicity campaigns of presidential-election complexity, as well as the presence of 2,800 media people ravenous to feed instant praise or condemnation into fax and laptop, the risks of 'opening cold' at Cannes were perhaps just too dangerous to take in May 1993. Anyhow, the Brits filled the vacuum.

The paradox of having an industry that couldn't get its act together while its film-makers were pushing their best wares in front of the world at Cannes was present in the minds of many. Stephen Frears's *The Snapper*, adapted from Roddy Doyle's story of a Dublin floozie's illegitimate baby, had already been aired on British TV. But Cannes gave it what the BBC denied it: a big-screen première. It instantly became the most popular film in town, despite the subtitling panting behind its viciously funny Dublin vernacular. Peter Greenaway's Anglo-Dutch co-production, *The Baby of Macon*, an agnostic's version of the Nativity, confirmed this director's ever increasing compulsion to shock, assault and ultimately thwart his audience. Its story, of a miraculous birth of a baby to a wizened old crone used by the Church and the Virgin (Julia Ormond) who passes it off as her own in order to exploit the devoutly gullible and enrich the greedy kinsfolk, was based on a thirteenth-century Mystery Play that is performed in a cathedral before a seventeenth-century audience. But even this device scarcely cooled down its attack on Catholic iconography and superstition. Gasps of revulsion and bewilderment from a vocally divided audience greeted the infant saint's tears, urine, faeces and spittle being sold as holy relics before his tiny body is dismembered piecemeal for auction.

Greenaway would probably have been the first to admit this was scarcely in the English tradition of film-making — and been proud to deny it. 'My cinema has more to do with the sense of metaphor,' he said. He could have cited a couple of recent advertisements — one for the Benetton clothing firm which featured a new-born baby slathered in blood and mucus, the other of a fashion model holding a child in the pose of the Virgin Mary — as evidence that his metaphors were contemporary commentary. But, like the brilliant designer of Benetton's poster campaigns, Greenaway's shock value flaunted his own virtuosity at the expense of his theme that children have been exploited down the ages for propaganda and publicity. There was a feeling that Greenaway should now place his extraordinary talents for the baroque and the esoteric on hold for a bit, and find his way back, if he could, to the world that other people inhabited. He had gained artistic recognition of a kind few English film-makers ever achieve abroad. But even Prospero knew when to give up his conjuring tricks.

Actually, Greenaway was already showing withdrawal symptoms, though for quite a different reason. 'I'm not a film-maker ... I'm a painter in cinema,' he declared and, after one or two more ventures in film-making, he was to become more active in his second career, that of peripatetic curatorship, staging exhibitions in Rotterdam, Paris, Geneva, Vienna and other cultural capitals that combined the imperiousness of the autodidact with the oppressiveness of the taxonomist. Within a few years, British cineastes would be saying of Greenaway, 'He was never really one of us ...' Again, this would hardly have disturbed him. He never truly had been: that was one of the things that made him strong and unique — too strong and too unique to 'fit in'. Derek Jarman, his exact contemporary, on the other hand, fitted more comfortably into the role of a public disturber, using his homosexuality as the mainspring of his revisionist view of things English.

At the time of Cannes, however, Jarman, aged fifty-one, was literally on his last legs, stricken since 1986 by Aids and now suffering its most venomous ravages. His body was closing down little by little. A 'walking lab', one friend reported he called himself, 'pills sloshing against portions of his insides'. Another friend, Nicholas de Jong, the theatre critic, wrote of him 'facing up to death without a flicker of self-pity or sadness' as his body fell apart.

Wittgenstein was Jarman's last feature film. Written by the Marxist professor Terry Eagleton and produced by the ex-Trotskyite Tariq Ali, a co-production of the BFI and Channel 4, it was a series of campy tableaux and pontificating aphorisms drawn from the life and works of the possibly demented eponymous Cambridge philosopher. The game of intellectual footsie between dons and the boys forming the rough trade who catered to the bodies and souls up at Cambridge was played against jet-black backgrounds that emphasised the posturing of famous figures of literary salon and lecture theatre: Tilda Swinton's Day-Glo attired Lady Ottoline Morrell, John Quentin's bisexual dandy John Maynard Keynes and Michael Gough's sulky Bertrand Russell. For anyone to make such a movie would have seemed eccentricity enough. For a dying man like Jarman it had an absurd heroism.

With his sight failing, Jarman relied on virtually the only sense remaining true and kindly to him – his hearing – to make one of his last films, *Blue*, seventy-six minutes in which nothing at all was seen save a blank blue screen. It was structured round his illness: its soundtrack constituted an aural hospital diary in which the voices of his friends and frequent 'stars', Nigel Terry, Tilda Swinton, John Quentin and Jarman himself, narrated the highlights of a life passing: the night sweats, the drug trials, the hit-and-miss of finding a vein to inject ... Costing £90,000, it was screened on Channel 4 with a simulcast on BBC Radio 4. Friends running errands found a message he had scrawled on the wall of his London flat before quitting it for his Dungeness cottage. 'Dear God,' it read, 'please send me to Hell. Yours, Derek Jarman.' He could never have been happy in heaven was the thought.

If Greenaway's film caused scandal and concern at Cannes, two of the other British films in competition did much the same for the audience at home: Mike Leigh's *Naked* and Ken Loach's *Raining Stones*. Together, they formed an extraordinary pair of social documents about life on the edge in the Britain of Margaret Thatcher and now John Major. These two film-makers go to the parts of society that Members of Parliament couldn't reach. Many an MP would have been wise to take an early look at them when they opened in London (Loach's film on 8 October, Leigh's on 4 November).

Naked laid bare the angsts on the mean streets of London. It froze the blood. It was unlike every earlier Mike Leigh film in which there had been at least one character, using a working-class loser, whose social temperature was normal, set at blood heat and who deserved sympathy. Not here. *High Hopes* and *Life Is Sweet* had tempered economic hardship with comic resilience or family togetherness. Not here. *Naked* was a howl of moral anarchy. Its rakish, thin anti-hero played to the grungy life by David Thewlis is a homeless urban nomad who latches on to people by the biting eloquence of his tongue and the priapic randiness of his body. To him, humanity's 'just a cracked egg, and the omelette stinks'. He was Leigh's updated version of Colin Wilson's *The Outsider*, or John Osborne's angry young man: fluent, insulting, destructive, misanthropically funny and misogynistically brutal. Girls were taken in by his mongrel looks, submitted to his taunts, but came back for more. To Mike Leigh's fans, it looked an astonishing breakaway from the current correctness of feminist empowerment: female masochism, it suggested, needed its male tormentor. The girls in the film (Katrin Cartlidge, Lesley Sharp) are not gutless. They look like mascots who have fallen off the back of a Hell's Angel's motorbike. Their humour is hard-bitten. 'Now you've failed to make the stairs,' quips Cartlidge to Thewlis as he's fumbling with the laces of her Madonna-like corselet, 'try the lift' and she directs him to the zipper. But even such females appear to have only two functions in the film: to be picked up and to be laid flat.

From its opening scene of rape in a back alley to its closing shot of Thewlis limping determinedly towards us like a vampire looking to replenish his tank with human bile, *Naked* defined the social void of British life and its streetwise denizens in the Nineties. No wonder it aroused indignation in some quarters for denying John Major's vision of a society at ease with itself. No one listens, no one answers. In Thewlis's brilliant sociopathic performance, which won him the 'Best Actor' prize at Cannes – Mike Leigh won 'Best Director' – the film projected the dark monomania that economic recession was breeding in Britain. It was still being shot on that ruinous day in November 1992, when the Chancellor of the Exchequer temporarily lost control of the nation's economy and, after additionally losing £16 billion in attempting to prop it up again, Britain humiliatingly quit the stability of the Exchange Rate Mechanism. *Naked* prophetically suggested a country living in the aftermath of that financial apocalypse.

To those who saw it first at Cannes, the film looked like a metaphor for all that was going wrong in Britain – not least the destitution on the streets that was matched by an absence of compassion or even charity. There, through the sunshine and the Mediterranean blue of sky and sea, its very accents sounded like a displaced threat. Homeless drop-outs were joining beggars in our own capital city's streets and the mantra, 'Giz your loose change' was becoming the predominant interruption of pedestrian life. *Naked* put such sounds, such sights, on the screen. It came out of the relative poverty of a stricken film industry and reproduced the harsher poverty of national life.

If Leigh's film was driven by a working-class outsider, anarchic and predatory, Ken Loach's *Raining Stones*, which took the Critics Prize at Cannes, showed its maker still had faith in working-class solidarity whose eternal optimism occasionally requires pragmatic opportunism to survive. It was about the daily scams and petty thieveries that supplement income support for the unemployed on a sprawling Northern housing estate. The largely unprofessional cast had soaked up social reality from their own daily hardship. One felt they could find their way blindfold about this bit of blighted England where the house-proud look across the road at the vandalised. In style, it recalled *Kes*, that affecting tale of a sturdy little weed who refuses to lie down when the world tramples on him.

It begins with two mates stealing a sheep, making a bollocks of slaughtering it in the backyard, taking it to the local butcher who, in the best middle-man tradition, takes his own cut and leaves the working-class heroes with only the skin. That won't put food on the table. It's the capitalist system in miniature.

In its plain, punchy, proletarian language, *Raining Stones* resembled *Riff-Raff*. Thankfully, it had none of the didactic politics of *Fatherland*, Loach's 1986 lecture on East and West in divided Germany; and despite its significantly Roman Catholic characters, it had none of the Republican bias of his 1990 propaganda film, *Hidden Agenda*, a 'Troops Out' polemic that fizzled risibly into oblivion. It was Loach punching at his right weight: witty, humane, intimate, disrespectful ... Human need licenses crime. Slapstick clumsiness exonerates petty criminals. But the simple plot, scripted by Loach's frequent Marxist collaborator, Jim Allen, threw hints of awful comeuppance ahead. The movie's picaresque tone darkens like a shadow under the waters on which the lads have cast their bread when a loan shark snaps up their debt to him. The man's death, with the parish priest's apparent blessing on his killer, falls on the humble heroes like the divine curses afflicting mortals in Greek theatre. It was epic in feeling, if not size.

A film showing small souls beset by great forces was horribly in tune with what many in recession-hit Britain were feeling in 1993. Social justice, it said, needed to follow logic, not law. By refusing to declaim their message through the loud hailer of Marxism, relying instead on a desperate ribaldry, Loach and Allen won themselves an immeasurably larger audience, even among the Thatcher doubters of the Right, who usually turned a deaf ear to their brand of left-wing dialectic. The temperature of the work was blood-heat, compared with the social hypothermia of Leigh's *Naked*. Together, the two films cast the shadow of an everyday British nightmare over Cannes' sunnyside event. Not coincidentally, perhaps, the Heritage Secretary found it inconvenient to pay his customary visit to the Croisette that year.

Kenneth Branagh's *Much Ado About Nothing*, ineligible for jury consideration because it had earlier opened in the US, but shown *hors de concours* at Cannes, restored the smile to England's face, though the suntan was American – part-financed by the Goldwyn studios. It turned the 'luvvies' accusation, now a daily staple of anti-Branagh comment in the British media, into the virtue of 'family togetherness' by presenting a version of Shakespeare's play that reflected its star-director's own ecumenical and ensemble talents. Branagh was more and more being seen as a solvent, a man who could melt projects down and remould them to a democratic shape and with popular appeal. The sociologist Stuart Hall referred to this tendency of the Nineties as 'the low-powered motor of Majorism', and this is what drives *Much Ado About Nothing*. The Prime Minister's favourite land of village green and warm beer found its corollary in Branagh's revisionist view of the play, replacing Messina and the indoors with Tuscany and the outdoors. It was the Bard's Chiantishire – a landscape of seductive looks, high colour and bland pleasures.

Granted all that, however, the film's aversion to Shakespeare as a national icon in favour of his translation into a consumer's playground had much to commend it. 'It brings sunny vitality to an old canvas,' said Richard Corliss in *Time*. The very real heat of the locations in Tuscany, at the Villa Viognamaggio, home of Lisa Gherhardini Gioconda, the 'Mona Lisa', promoted the play's intoxicating mixture of idleness, lassitude, intrigue, eavesdropping and spying upon one another. Summer madness turned everyone's head in the play. An upper-class masquerade, where the people played mischievous, ultimately tragic practical jokes on each other, fitted into Branagh's predilection for assembling friends around one – though it was perilously close to the charge of 'luvvyness' that was now standard in almost every interview or profile of him in the British media. He saw the potential – 'This is a play about star quality, so we'll do it in movie-star close-up,' he declared – without realising how it could provide circumstantial evidence of theatrical cronyism.

Branagh (as Benedict) was perfectly partnered by his wife Emma Thompson (as Beatrice), lovers who are at each other's throat before they are in each other's arms, stropping the razor edge of their tongues on their sexual enmity and shaving Shakespeare's text, with its insulting puns and innuendoes, with spectacular precision. While these two twisted their tongues round some of the playwright's most tortuous phrasing and parsing, the Americans in the cast (Denzel Washington, Keanu Reeves, Robert Sean Leonard and Michael Keaton) flaunted their physicality. It was Branagh's best trick, letting Hollywood in on the joke. The Hollywood quartet worked a treat. They injected a full-blooded vitality into what could easily have been a precious exercise in the classical idiom. Riding in line straight into the camera, these gallants from Don Pedro's army have a *Magnificent Seven* brio. 'I always liked the ballsiness of American film acting, the full-blooded abandon,' Branagh said. Jubilantly stripping to wallow naked in the open-air baths, they seem at first to endow the text with a little too much ado. But their charge of transatlantic vitality soon marries itself to the poetry.

To some at Cannes, their presence echoed Colin Welland's war cry when *Chariots of Fire* scooped an armful of Oscars: 'The British are coming.' That boast proved hollow. But *Much Ado About Nothing* revived it, only now one could holler, 'The Americans are coming.' Yet Branagh's perceived fondness for pleasing the audience, unpicking a play filled with tight knots of tricky language and giving it a linear simplicity, went against the grain of much critical comment – in Britain, anyhow.

In America, in mid 1993, he was still hailed as 'the new Orson Welles', treated 'like a rock star' as he went around promoting the film and declared in *New York Magazine* to be 'something of a boy genius ... who can fuse Pop melodrama with high art'. British opinion was much less fulsome, much less.

The danger of being married to an actress whose own fame ran in tandem with his for a while, then drew ahead, now emerged more openly and painfully. To set husband and wife 'against' each other, by constant reference to their supposed rivalry, was one of the most distasteful things about the ordeal in print that 'Ken and Em' were now having to suffer at home. Even as a unit they were, as an unsigned profile in *The Times* put it, 'disliked for their success, considered insufficiently self-deprecating' and felt to be conning Americans about highbrow culture. Emma Thompson's brand of feminist politics did not go down well in Britain. During the press conference for *Much Ado About Nothing* she had talked about women's menstrual periods. 'She wants it both ways – to do the American scene and to preserve her English reserve.' It appears she had agreed to pose in the nude and be covered in gold shellac for a cover of *Esquire* magazine, in order to parody-publicise her winning the 'Best Actress' Oscar for her role in *Howards End.* At the last moment, she changed her mind: it was too vulgar. Perhaps she was right. '[But] in politics,' the profile writer continued, 'she also wants it both ways – to be a Left winger, but the *respectable* Left. Labour Party, pro-CND, anti-apartheid, pro-choice.' Her 'sin', in some people's eyes, was premature political correctness. Others welcomed her Oscar win, however, seeing her emerging from 'the resplendent shadow of her husband, all-everything British showbiz phenomenon Kenneth Branagh', as Richard Corliss put it in *Time*, the magazine that barely a year before had made Branagh its cover boy.

What had created for the Oliviers their public sense of inviolability – whatever the truth of their married life – went into reverse for Branagh and Thompson around this time, a more spiteful era less in awe of fortune's darlings. Commentators in Britain began pitting their careers against each other, handicapping them like thoroughbred racehorses, allowing each new venture by one or the other to alter the odds for or against them. From this moment, at the peak of their joint success, their careers began, imperceptibly at first, to draw apart. Branagh had decided to direct a new, revisionist version of Mary Shelley's *Frankenstein* – without Thompson. With her new film, *The Remains of the Day,* she seemed to be drawing ahead of him. *Time* magazine had switched allegiance. 'Emma's a gem,' was now its cover line under a portrait that caught Thompson's classical looks, 'the luck of the genetic draw', as the inside story said.

A Merchant Ivory production, *The Remains of the Day* co-starred her with Anthony Hopkins whose role as Stevens, the morally compromised butler who subordinates himself to his Fascist master's class and political ideology, was the last truly great acting that this exceptionally fortunate actor rendered the British screen. After honours (a knighthood, no less, for playing a human cannibal in *The Silence of the Lambs*), he would step on to Hollywood's escalator of fame and be carried to heights of public adulation before he succumbed to fame and taxes, and became an American citizen. What human feelings he was permitted to show in a film based on the novel by Kazuo Ishiguro transfer the Japanese ideal of submission to one's superiors to the English country house. There Hopkins's butler, Stevens, is in thrall to his master. This contradicts virtually every representation of a butler in English fiction, comic or serious. There he is considered superior to his lord and master. Thus *The Remains of the Day* has a unique claim to be a Japanese theme in an Anglo-Saxon setting.

Hopkins's performance took the 'stand and wait' definition of butling as its key to character – stillness became him, the Noh-like stillness of Japanese theatrical tradition, though one must set against this the advice passed on to Hopkins by Julian Fellowes: 'When Stevens is in the room, the room is emptier.' Butlers go unremarked and unnoticed – the silent service. Nearly ten years later, Fellowes would write a brilliant screenplay, *Gosford Park*, for Robert Altman, this time viewing the upper classes between the wars from the viewpoint of a very different set of below-stairs servants. Thompson's housekeeper, on the edge of middle-age and hanging on with fingertips and hope, is the character who engages understanding and commands pity – feelings that Hopkins's Stevens excludes himself from exposing. She attacks his bachelor sanctity with little sorties of premeditated kindness and, when that isn't appreciated, uses impertinence, mockery, sarcasm and finally (and desperately) disdain: anything to breach his defence. Her unreciprocated gesture when she tries to pry away from him the romantic novel he's been shamed to be caught reading has a creepy tension – as if she were stealthily opening the man's trouser flies. Thompson revealed the loneliness of someone who once had been independent. Longing for love, she settled for security. The actress's strength lies in the character's defeat: before one's eyes, she changes into commonplaceness, shrinks in interest and exits from the story into the waiting death trap of a dead-end existence. The film, Merchant Ivory's most successful production, had everything except a heart.

The quietest man of all at this time, barely noticed by analysts of the film industry's past, present and possible future, was Michael Kuhn, the Cambridge lawyer and ex-records executive, who was stealthily 'growing' PolyGram Filmed Entertainment. In the first year of operation, PFE had made a 'moderate after-tax loss', but, according to Alain Levy, president of PolyGram, the parent company, 'was financially on track'.

Levy confirmed that PFE's $200 million capital financing and long-term objectives were moving 'slowly and carefully' towards studio status, with 25 per cent of PolyGram's overall income to come from film by the year 2000.

Kuhn himself had moved over to Los Angeles in January 1992, renting a few rooms from PolyGram's lawyers on a quiet Beverly Hills drive, and setting about ensuring PFE would have a regular supply of US-made movies so as to set up his own distribution network in the US – big movies through joint projects with a major studio, eventually Universal, and small ones through his own distribution company, Grammercy Pictures. He left the international side of things in the capable hands of an Englishman, Stewart Till, a former executive at Rupert Murdoch's Sky Television.

Kuhn was cautious to the point of timorousness, definitely not the customary style of budding moguls. But he was well aware that Philips, the Dutch conglomerate that owned PolyGram (and thus PFE) was an ultra-conservative outfit with its roots in Dutch Calvinism. Jewish chutzpah would not have been the right mode, he decided. 'If we had movies that did not work,' he wrote later, 'our quarterly results were smoothed out [by the few that did in the first two years] and losses did not hit the bottom line in as big a way.' And thus the Philips board was kept happy, or at least quiescent.

Such small manoeuvres, 6,000 miles from London, may seem remote from the problems consuming the British film industry in 1993. But the wisdom of it would soon be seen, when PFE unexpectedly struck gold with a film called, unpromisingly, *Four Weddings and a Funeral*. That lay ahead . . .

11

Just One Film

Christmas 1992 was a frugal festivity for Michael Kuhn and his small staff of thirty in Los Angeles. They had squeezed into a 'tiny room in a cheap Third Street restaurant' for a party and dinner that must have cost the company's parsimonious Scots accountant $200 tops.

By Christmas 1993 all had changed. Kuhn and PFE were 'in the money', or had good reason to think they might be. A few months earlier, in September, they had sneak-tested a little British-made comedy called *Four Weddings and a Funeral*. Nobody much liked the title: the word 'death' was thought to be a turn-off. Alternatives were culled from Grammercy, the US distribution company that PFE had bought. 'The Pleasures of Merely Circulating' was one. 'Loitering in a Sacred Place'; 'Skulking Around'; 'Tales of True Love' and 'Near Misses'; and, finally, 'Strays', were other uninspired ones. 'Of this last,' Kuhn later wrote, 'they rightly remarked, "This one needs some good copy to set up."' Kuhn had little faith in title changes, but then what did he know? Anyhow, the film went on the screen on 22 September 1993 at a Santa Monica theatre. The audience liked it, kind of – but asked what happened afterwards to the characters in it.

George Lucas's *American Graffiti*, twenty years earlier, had started this fashion in 'reality' fiction, with end-credit captions and stills, continuing the CV of the group of buddies into later life. *Four Weddings* (as it still was and shall be known here) gained this addendum; then, after an even more encouraging 'sneak' in New Jersey, had the honour of opening the Sundance Film Festival in January 1994. Sundance took it to its heart. And so, soon, did America. This was the 'break' PFE had striven for and, indeed, without which it might have been closed down by Philips, the electronic giant and its conglomerate owner, which was impatient to see bottom-line results.

Four Weddings became a phenomenon: for several years, until *The Full Monty*, the biggest-earning British film ever made, a one-off event, a so-called 'sleeper' that crossed over into a global box-office hit. Opening in America had been the most crucial decision in its marketing fortunes. Before its British première (13 May 1994) it had been officially stamped a winner in the land that most mattered to British profit and pride. Kuhn's exploitation of a movie with no names known to most Americans – save Andie MacDowell – was masterly. Having no big budget for prints and advertising, he used stealth and subterfuge, opening the film on a couple of screens in New York, then gradually expanding this 'platform release' and adding prints and advertising if box office justified the expense.

The first figures in from New York were dismaying: very 'soft'. But a very nervous Kuhn quickly found out why: the movie had been screened in the cinema's smallest auditorium, people queuing hadn't managed to get in. A sly deal was done: the cinema was 'persuaded' to swap the little British comedy over to the big screen for the evening show, displacing the American movie, but garnering the all-important week-end 'averages' for *Four Weddings* that would be the carrot for other movie houses to book it. The movie went on to gross over $50 million on 1,000 US screens. Yet what it tells us about the British film industry it came from is precisely nothing. Few 'one-offs' do. That is their perplexing charm; the reason their spell can seldom, if ever, be repeated with the full potency of the original.

In retrospect we may think we know: the answer, surely, was Hugh Grant, then thirty-two, with thirteen film roles behind him, mostly (and gratefully) forgotten save for a cameo in *The Remains of the Day*, a cuckolded husband in Polanski's *Bitter Moon* and an Edwardian under-graduate unsure of his sexual predilections in Merchant Ivory's *Maurice*. *Four Weddings* changed the perception of him – for life, possibly. It was, of course, a good time to be a British actor in America: Branagh, Irons, Day-Lewis, Hopkins, Fiennes, Neeson were the pathfinders to stardom over there. But Grant's role in *Four Weddings* was the catalyst for some-thing more than stardom: namely, America's love affair with him on screen and off. 'He combines the elegant appearance of Cary Grant with the sheepish, fumbling Everyman appeal of Jimmy Stewart,' said the *New York Post*. Near, but no cigar. The senior Grant had used charm as a stalking horse, handling women smoothly but surely, with a hint that if he weren't such a gentleman, he could easily and willingly mishandle them.

Hugh Grant wasn't that sort at all, even if he insisted, in his initial bewilderment, that he was much nastier than he seemed. In fact, the template for his screen persona had been described over fifty years earlier by the author of one of the novels in whose screen adaptation Grant had appeared. E. M. Forster, in 1936, said in *Notes on an Englishman*, 'It is not that an Englishman can't feel – it is that he is afraid to feel. He has been taught at his public school that it is bad form. He must not express great joy or sorrow or even open his mouth too wide when he talks – his pipe might fall out if he did.' Minus the pipe, this is ur-Hugh Grant.

In the comedy scripted by Richard Curtis and directed by Mike Newell, he is a continuous victim, not at all a predator. Off screen, too, for his public image, he quickly assumed the vulnerable role: he stammered and dithered and used charm as an escape route to dodge commitment to all the girlfriends past, present and future who stalked him in the film at his friends' weddings. True, he cohabits with a tiny firecracker of a girlfriend called Scarlet – 'Like Scarlett O'Hara, but much less trouble'. But this is simply to show the character isn't gay, or a virgin. Grant at the time had *his* steady girlfriend, Elizabeth Hurley, but she was based in Los Angeles while he lived in Fulham. He turned their seven-year liaison to the profit of the character – usefully also deflecting more probing enquiries – by confessing he shopped for clothes for her in London: 'I've become rather worryingly interested in women's clothes. I find myself buying *Vogue* for pleasure. In a year's time, I think I'll be wearing them.' 'Hugh Grant is a romantic hero for a feminist age,' said David Denby in *New York Magazine*.

A man so appealing could not possibly be threatening: they think they can handle him and they can in the film. Even when he wakes up beside Andie MacDowell, the American beauty who's finally bedded him, one can practically see the steam rising from Grant's tousled brow as he imagines himself in a 'fatal attraction' fix – not for nothing did screen-writer Richard Curtis hone his comic craft on parody and satire – and becoming enslaved by a one-night stand with the pick-up from hell who'll pop his pet rabbit in the stewpot if he spurns her. This was a novel kind of romantic hero, a self-deprecating ditherer who is awakened in the film from his emotional trance by the kiss of MacDowell's American princess.

The producers, Working Title's Tim Bevan and Eric Fellner (executive producers) and Duncan Kenworthy (producer) kept pushing MacDowell forward for interviews – she was the only one in the cast who had negotiated a points deal and, as it turned out, made more money than anyone else from it – but were met by requests for Grant.

'You don't understand, he's not the star of the movie, she is,' they insisted. Wrong: he was.

Grant's interviews as the film's grosses mounted – more than £17 million in the UK after just two months – suggest a mimetic interchange occurring between himself and his role. 'I'm so pathetically passive' is his apologetic refrain. Yet now and then, he comes out with a remark like a well-polished Curtis line of the script. Asked what he does with himself when not maintaining telephonic connections with the long-distance Hurley, instead of more intimate commitments, he owns up to playing football, but with a team from the Victoria and Albert Museum. 'It's not the hardest team in the world. Our left back is keeper of seventeenth-century sculpture.' Pure Richard Curtis. *Four Weddings* defined Hugh Grant, quite as much as he embodied the character, and he gratefully standardised his future career on it.

Actually, the chemistry between him and MacDowell in the film doesn't work all that well. Who would lay a bet that MacDowell's adventuress out of the pages of *Vogue* (US edition), having already chucked her first husband (Corin Redgrave) for being 'three times my age', would hook herself permanently on to Grant's callow chump? Perhaps the makers foresaw a sequel in which 'Divorce' would take the place of 'Funeral' in the title. No matter the unlikelihood: the US and then the UK went for it and him. Hollywood no longer bred that gulp-and-golly sincerity which James Stewart used to oxygenate the romantic comedies that had since been replaced by airless sitcoms.

The timing was perfect. British commentators, however, had a more complex reaction to the film. Curtis's screenplay brazenly advertised its artificial construction: engraved invitation cards preface each nuptial event. The same people are featured: friends and hangers-on who go wedding-hopping, much as people go table-hopping. It is a networking culture, more show business in some ways than social, society swells, footloose college graduates, rich folk, poor folk, colourful and good-natured gays, in short a tranche of British 'magazine society' designed for export to America as much as Tiptree jam or Crawford's shortbread, yet less precisely labelled than those dollar-earning comestibles. The Grant character's job, income bracket, professional status, even post-code – all things that matter to the class-ridden English – are left vague. His familiarity with morning coat and wedding cravats is worryingly out of sync with the nerdish gaucheness of the black boots, ankle socks, pale legs and shirt-outside-the-shorts kit he wears in town in summer on his day off (when not attending weddings or a funeral). The huge cast of society swells, debby girlfriends, old school chums, county oafs, City tycoons and grandes dames, all guzzling, sluicing, chattering and bonking, resemble Condé Nast's magazine empire joining the Groucho Club on a day's outing. They tumble haughtily and rowdily through the film, registering types rather than individuals, giving shorthand performances with a look or a line, not directed so much as edited together. This is Britain class-consciously packaged for the Yanks – clever to open Stateside first. To American audiences it was Pop sociology; to Brits, telly satire.

Ironically, it took the scene of a gay character's funeral – an Aids element, but not standard in similar American social comedies – to root the film in recognisable reality. This single episode of mourning, backed by a W. H. Auden verse, makes a far more memorable show than the comedy of multiple marriages. Richard Curtis, with this film, established not only his own fortunes, but his lightly satirical, comically neighbourly style in subsequent films like *Notting Hill* and *Bridget Jones's Diary*. It became the bifocal house style, too, of Working Title when a film of theirs was set in a recognisable England, but needed to fit a transatlantic vision. Curtis succeeded Branagh as the populist interpreter of national heritage; Richard's Folk replaced *Peter's Friends*. In Kenneth Branagh's new film, *In the Bleak Midwinter*, a comedy about fractious thespians rehearsing *Hamlet* in an unheated rural chapel, its bilious luvvies looked wan and worn compared with Curtis's smart young things.

Though it appeared to be about the English upper-middle class, with a few proles and plutocrats thrown in for fair measure, its core message was that everyone was pretty equal, or thought themselves to be so. One commentator whose overview of the film seemed dead right – significantly not a film critic but a media analyst – was Stephen Glover. 'Welcome to Utopia: I like it here' his article in the *Evening Standard* on 25 August 1994, was headed. 'This is not the grim, pinched England represented in the media,' he wrote.

> It is our glorious birthright, for us to rediscover as Englishmen, and no part of it is inaccessible for reasons of class. Nor are any of us inaccessible to one another. John Major has spoken of a classless society in which there are no class differentiations. Such an outcome is, of course, inconceivable. *Four Weddings* represents a more convincing alternative. In this world, class differences are still evident. But the

film's point is they do not matter. They should not form barricades between people. They are not relevant to the relationships we have ... It presents a Utopian view of our country, but one not altogether removed from changed realities in which we have a Labour leader [Tony Blair] who went to public school and a Tory Prime Minister who attended a comprehensive.

For Working Title, the PFE-owned production company behind *Four Weddings*, its success secured firmly their stake in the British film industry. They had made it. 'For the first time in history,' said Tim Bevan, 'we have got a British company – us – which has the resources to make big pictures.' Well, not quite: this begs the question. *Four Weddings* was a 'little picture', made for under £3 million, which had done phenomenally well. And Rank still had the resources, though the ultra-cautious people who ran Rank were stubbornly opposed to using them for film-making in Britain. But Working Title, from this time on, grew into a major player.

Bevan was thirty-six, a doctor's son, who had started work at John Cleese's Video Arts in the 1980s; Eric Fellner, now his partner after running his own Initial Pictures and producing *Sid and Nancy* in 1986, was thirty-four. Son of a City financier, he had begun as a runner for a video company. Bevan, a handsome figure with a rugby player's build, was regarded as the brink man, risk-taking, robust and, if necessary, a bit of a bully; Fellner, tall, gangling and balding, was thought to be the nuts-and-bolts man, more diplomatic and prudent. Those who asked if they operated a 'bad cop, good cop' technique in their deals would sometimes get the reply, 'That's supposing one of them could be a good cop.' Both hankered 'to bring a piece of Hollywood to London'. As they understood it, this meant bolting a European sensibility on to solid American construction, producing stylish films with good commercial prospects aimed at a youngish, yuppie-bracket audience, which could cross the Atlantic and meet with success in that peer group there, too. They were also, in due course, to produce American films such as *Bob Roberts*, *The Hudsucker Proxy*, *The Hi Lo Country*, involving independent talents, or a British director like Stephen Frears.

To the fanatically neat-minded Kuhn, Working Title had been an unpleasant shock when he went into its corporate structure; but, true to his 'hands off' attitude to companies swallowed up by his voracious acquisitions appetite, Kuhn left Bevan and Fellner alone to pursue their own instincts while keeping a close eye on the results. His hands off operation (so long as they delivered) had repaid him beyond imagining. Peter Bart, editor of *Variety*, wrote that PFE 'had the slightly glazed look of a Las Vegas tourist who put a few dollars in the slot machines and suddenly sees thousands spewing out'. The only drawback, little noted by commentators at the time, was that PFE had done a video deal on the film with Columbia Pictures before the box-office figures came in: so the American major would enjoy that bonanza.

Otherwise, the success of *Four Weddings* gave PFE a powerhouse presence internationally. All the sweeter since, unlike the French Canal Plus, or the independent and rather freakish operation Ciby 2000, PFE had not tried to elbow a place for itself at the Hollywood big shots' poker table and been beaten out of the game. It had simply set up its own 'school' of players in the US and UK. Up to 1994 results had been mixed, though defensible where keeping the frugal Dutch Calvinists in Philips's boardroom calm was concerned: *Posse*, a black Western pro-duced by Working Title, had done quite well others like Peter Medak's *Romeo Is Bleeding* (1992), or Vincent Ward's *Map of the Human Heart* (1992) had proved, in Kuhn's opinion, 'pretty dreadful'. Working Title was the breakthrough. By January 1995 it had grossed $250 million worldwide. It had had one benefit other PFE films had not enjoyed: its own distribution and marketing people in charge in the US. It did not depend on a major (more usually minor) American distributor: its enormous success seemed to be bearing out Kuhn's belief that marketing one's own product was the key to riches. At least riches one could count, if and when they rolled in, and keep. In a systemically dishonest industry in which, as has been noted, revenues were more often diverted than payable, being a producer-distributor was the sole way of riding shotgun and making sure the money got to the bank.

Four Weddings raised spirits in the rest of the domestic industry. But they were unnaturally high, anyhow, in 1994. Newcomers were popping up all over the place, their youth or inexperience protecting them from the endemic depression of those who had been around long enough to grow embittered. One senses a new generation coming into view, if not quite of age, few in number but impatient to make waves. The way most thought they could do it was follow the American genre model with 'crime' films, 'relationship' films, 'road' films, etc. Films like *Alien*, *Blade Runner*, *The Blues Brothers*, *Salvador* were their culture models.

In *Time Out* magazine, Trevor Ray Hart defined them as the kids who had come of age under Mrs Thatcher in the 1970s: 'They want a mass audience, they do not want to be ghettoised.' Their eyes looked westwards. 'In order to change the way [Hollywood] looks at Britain,' said Jeremy Bolton, a twenty-something and already producer of *Shopping*, a gangland melodrama (1994) about ram-raiding to order in an English Midlands city, 'you have to make a movie that has impact in America. ... There is no useful British film tradition for young filmmakers.' Bolton had a confidently ironic take on his youth. 'Isn't it one of the most important sociological effects of Thatcher that you become old quicker, in terms of your ability to make money? She compressed the gap between twenty and forty extraordinarily. That is something we've inherited. It means I can sit here at twenty-eight and think of producing a movie of $15–20 million without getting a cold sweat. It seems to me totally achievable.' *Shopping* proclaimed, in almost every frame of his partner, twenty-eight-year-old Paul Anderson's direction, its urge to kick ass, the ass in this case being the polite conventions of the period productions of Merchant Ivory and the British art-house film as he and his producer perceived it.

In spite of being determinedly in the mould of Hollywood's guns'n'-crack movies, it was aggressively promoted as an almost patriotic act, a British-made movie catering to the impulse of deprived kids who have had no teenage criminal heroes of their own, but only the blacks of south-central LA to identify with and emulate in the screen orgies of looting and riot, in which 'the enemy is the consumer world'. It introduced two names soon to be synonymous with New British cinema, Jude Law and Sadie Frost, the Bonnie and Clyde of this grimy British metropolis, who embark on a short-lived career of outlaw vandalism.

Bolton and Anderson, graduates of Bristol and Warwick Universities, pitched the movie by throwing together clips of the aftermath of actual ram-raids, as police cameras had filmed them, and backed them thematically with a music track 'borrowed' from *Alien*. Robert Jones, formerly of Palace Pictures but now an acquisitions executive representing PolyGram in France, as well as German distributors, saw their potential; David Aukin, now at Channel 4, gave them development money. They raised the budget by selling it on a promise of 'Luc Besson stylishness'. Like *Four Weddings*, it was shown at Sundance, now 'the Glastonbury of film festivals'. The magic worked: world sales followed. The film is almost entirely taken up with dissing authority by day, joyriding by night and targeting department stores for ram-raiding – or 'shopping', as it's flippantly tagged. It's an euphoric expedition, directed with all the glib skill of a video-promo background, that doesn't halt until the hijacked car has screeched to rest amid the wreckage of the consumer society.

Channel 4 and its chief executive, Michael Grade, helped finance such a morale booster. Unfortunately, while Bolton and Anderson were skilled in presenting an over-the-top celebration of 'aft' martyrdom, their ability to deliver goods of substance, or fill the space inside their heroes' heads with anything but the dimmest of wits – 'Come on, let's go' ... 'Don't fuck with us' ... 'I'll take your face off' – created a total vacuum. They had nothing to say that Loach's *Riff-Raff* or Mike Leigh's *Naked*, two films of comparable budgets and social settings, hadn't said more successfully and integrated more thoughtfully with the tough, resilient and nihilist underclass of 1990s Britain. It was creditable to deliver an action thriller – that sold well around the world – but looked like a hyped-up Anglo-American clone of many a US film that ran on speed and destructiveness. It was not exactly an apprentice piece: Tony Imi (lighting photographer on *Enemy Mine*), Mike Proudfoot (camera operator, *Batman*) and David Stiven (editor, *Mad Max 2*, *Crocodile Dundee*), all experienced old masters in the film business, worked on it; their excellent contribution conferred on the film the impression of a sale of eye-catching goods that had been specially 'bought in' for the occasion.

As visually confident, but as empty, was Danny Cannon's *The Young Americans*, set in a British city, based on models like *Get Carter* and *The Long Good Friday*, and pitching its credentials to an American box office with slaughter, drugs and Harvey Keitel as an American cop seconded to advise the drugs squad. It was produced by Paul Trijbits, a Dutchman from the Pop industry who was to become an important cog in the Film Council a few years later. Though it fell short of its commercial potential, its calling-card strength got Cannon instant employment directing a British-made US-financed (at $26 million) comic-strip spectacular, *Judge Dredd*, starring Sylvester Stallone. It was a box-office failure. *Time Out* ran a significant feature itemising such new and promising acting talents. It is worth naming some of them, if only as an index to their future success, or lack of: Jude Law (debut in *Shopping*); Sadie Frost (*Bram Stoker's Dracula*); Sean Pertwee (*Shopping*); Alan Cumming; Elizabeth Hurley (*Beyond Bedlam*); Naveen Andrews (*London Kills Me*); Ian Hart (as John Lennon in Ian Softley's *Backbeat*); Kate Beckinsale (*Much Ado*

About Nothing); Katrin Cartlidge, Gina McKee, Lesley Sharp (all in
Naked); Linus Roach (in Antonia Bird's *Priest*) and Toby Stevens. Such
a crowded kindergarten suggests the sheer numbers of talent in 1994
competing for a chance to graduate; and how much sheer luck was
involved in the careers of those who did.

Significantly, the talent north of the border, in Scotland, seemed to
have found the high road to England with surer feet than some of those
in the stamping grounds of London's Soho. The Celtic fringe of British
film-makers were more assertive, self-confident and original: also more
physically passionate in a way that made their films travel more easily in
young markets abroad, particularly the US. Like it or not, such films
also had a moral edge to them, or at least a concern for society in the
1990s. *Shallow Grave*, like Neil Jordan's *Angel*, owed its 'discovery' to the
Cannes film market in May 1994, where it created more excitement
than official British entries such as Mike Figgis's stuffed remake of *The
Browning Version*, updated by Ronald Harwood with four-letter words,
nudity in the boys' showers and Matthew Modine as the new young
brash Yank science master.

Shallow Grave was scripted by John Hodge (a Glaswegian doctor, soon
to surrender stethoscope for full-time writing), produced by Andrew
Macdonald (Emeric Pressburger's grandson and a National Film and
TV School graduate), directed by Danny Boyle (fresh from a BBC TV
success with *Mr Wroe's Virgins*) and had three fresh stars: New Zealand's
Kerry Fox (an ex-Jane Campion graduate), Ewan McGregor and Christopher Ecclestone: three lively but smug yuppies inhabiting a cosy
Glasgow flat as if each were a privileged tycoon, who discover their
fourth, new and mysterious flatmate dead in bed with a cache of cash in
a suitcase under it. Although the money smells as ominously as the
decomposing body, the trio decide to bury the latter in the eponymous
shallow grave and keep the loot. Thus begins the downhill start of a
minutely observed and disconcerting spiral into greed, betrayal and
terminal Grand Guignol. It was soon perceived as a metaphor for the
inbuilt vices of the Tory government's enterprise boom; a plausible
subtext, anyhow, that coexisted with the much more gripping presentation by Boyle of the moral dilemma. One felt the film-makers' joy
and confidence in their material and its manipulation: a film of quality
that also made commercial sense.

All the talents in it were soon to go from 'hopefuls' to 'achievers'. All
this was heartening and solid evidence that the shape of the artistic

landscape was rapidly changing. Unfortunately, the financial one, with the exception of initiatives like Michael Kuhn's PFE, funded from abroad, remained as barren as ever. Kenneth Clarke had now succeeded the hapless Norman Lamont as Chancellor of the Exchequer and his November 1993 financial summary brought no relief to the industry. The last and still the only concession to film finance had been the accelerated write-off, inside three years, of a movie's budget: no matter how many candles the film people lit at the Treasury altar, the Chancellor still refused to grant an immediate 100 per cent write-off. Ironically, the much trumpeted success of films such as *Shallow Grave* and *Four Weddings* made things harder at home: government praise for them and their makers was very like someone eulogising a swimmer for unexpectedly winning an Olympics medal while simultaneously holding his head underwater.

The poor state of the pound sterling, after the Fixed Exchange Rate debacle in November 1992, had brought American movie-makers back to Britain to take advantage of cheap money and working practices that were more flexible than Hollywood's now more militant film unions were ready to concede. Thus British studios were booked solid with US-financed movies: the same old story, boom or bust. Robert De Niro was in Mary Shelley's *Frankenstein*, which Branagh was directing; Stallone, as mentioned, in *Judge Dredd*; Julia Roberts and John Malkovich in *Mary Reilly*, directed by Christopher Hampton; Mel Gibson was here, too, filming *Braveheart* in Scotland. There was method as well as money in American studios' decision to return to Europe. Hard-pressed American diplomats were still haggling over the revision of the General Agreement on Tariff and Trade, which regulated taxes and quotas on European imports. The Motion Picture Association of America, under the machiavellian figure Jack Valenti, was always swift to scent danger on the European trade winds for his members' products. It may not have been the crucial factor in shifting production of some of these blockbusters to Europe, and language-friendly Britain, but it played a part. It also enabled British government ministers to look their own film-makers in the eye, usually across a well-laden dinner table, and hope that their hosts didn't have to face a choice between dying or paying the bill.

This helps explain why tempers were lost when three film-makers of renown answered an invitation, in December 1994, to appear before the House of Commons Select Committee on the National Heritage. Alan Parker, Ken Loach and Mike Leigh had agreed to give evidence, knowing

Gerald Kaufman's committee was being lobbied by that redoubtable duo, now known as 'Dickie'n'Davie' (the newly ennobled Lord Attenborough and the newly knighted Sir David Puttnam) to persuade it to make films eligible for funding from the forthcoming National Lottery.

Loach asserted that his industry had been 'betrayed' by successive governments; one screen in every American-owned multiplex in Britain, he said, should be reserved for British films; a levy on tickets should be ploughed back into the native product.

Alan Parker said bluntly, 'You keep patting us on the back, telling us how clever we are, how many Oscars we win. But you've never helped us at all. I've spoken to so many ministers in the past, I finally gave up and went to the USA.' Does this mean you're no longer a true British film-maker? asked Sir John Gorst MP. Parker bristled audibly: 'There are many great artists [*sic!*] who have worked in other countries.'

Michael Fabricant, a Tory MP, referred to Ken Loach's *Ladybird, Ladybird*, a film about an irresponsible mother who kept giving birth to children who were instant welfare charges. If it were available to be seen on more screens, he asked, would many people wish to see it? Loach, keeping his cool with difficulty, replied there had to be a wide range of choice on offer – there wasn't at present. Parker, whose anger management was notoriously spasmodic, burst out with, 'I'm getting bored, to be honest. You're saying to me, "You make rotten uncommercial films, which no one goes to see" – but which just happen to be of different politics from you.'

Joe Ashton, Labour, said that art versus entertainment was the perennial problem: a philosophical statement not inviting dissent. Then he unwisely defined the problem in personal terms: the 'art people' were always moaning and groaning, making films no one wanted to see, holding their hands out for subsidy.

Loach exploded: 'I've heard some confused philistines in my life ... in the week that we see your party trying to ditch Clause IV' (Clause IV in Labour's manifesto tied the party spiritually to the trade unions).

Gerald Kaufman intervened. Like President Merkin Muffley in Stanley Kubrick's *Dr Strangelove*, rebuking custard-pie-throwing top brass and VIPs with 'Gentlemen, you can't fight here: this is the War Room', he reprimanded Loach, 'We can't discuss Socialism here. We will discuss Socialism later.'

'If only ...' Loach rejoined.

Ashton cited the success of the *Carry On* comedies.

'Oh God, is that what you want!' Parker bellowed.

'You people are elitist,' Ashton snapped.

'I'm not,' cried Parker, 'my last film was *The Commitments*' (about the Dublin working-class rock band).

Ashton was unapologetic. 'Ninety-nine per cent of my constituents are philistines,' he put on record. 'Maybe I represent them. You are making films for each other.'

At this point Mike Leigh leaped into the heaving waters of dissent. 'I resent that! Most of us are committed to entertainment.'

Patrick McLoughlin MP retorted, 'You might not like it, but it's true. There hasn't been any [demand] from the public. We're not here to be hoodwinked by people who do very well out of the film industry anyway.' That did it.

Struggling to hold his temper, Ken Loach replied, 'I think you treat yourself with great pretension if you think you are here to receive lobbyists and supplicants. You are here to have a view of the world as it should be. People come to this place because they have a working-class view of culture.'

It was doubtful if people came to Parliament with that in mind, but by now the two sides were not so much listening to each other as asserting pride and prejudice.

'You make a film about Clause IV,' was Ashton's last shot at Loach, 'and see how many will turn up to see it.'

Loach retorted, 'That shows how low your party has fallen.' He left the committee room abruptly.

The Select Committee then resolved to send a fact-finding team to Hollywood to look for ways of 'putting the British film industry back on top'. That they decided to do so showed how little they had learned in their interrogation of film-makers. As to so many before and after them, Hollywood with all its treacherous glamour beckoned like a mirage. The timing was ironic, anyhow. British studios were in the middle of one of their fully booked periods in mid 1994, due to the favourable dollar exchange rate, the vogue for period subjects and historical dramas, and the energising effect of *Four Weddings*.

The Scott brothers, Ridley and Tony, bought Shepperton Studios for £12 million in March 1994, promising to upgrade it for American-financed productions: *Four Weddings* and Branagh's forthcoming version of *Frankenstein* had been made there. The Scotts were hard-headed technician-directors, not at all in love with 'heritage culture', who had made most of their hits – notably Ridley's *Blade Runner* and Tony's *Top Gun* – for American studios. Some questioned whether they were ever really part of British culture. At the start of their careers, perhaps, yes: certainly Ridley had put the quintessence of what was English into his TV commercial for Hovis bread loaves when working (along with Puttnam, Adrian Lynne, Alan Parker and Hugh Hudson) in an advertising agency before beginning his feature film career with *The Duellists*. Tony Scott, like his brother, had trained at the Royal College of Art, where both of them found their talents lay in visual imagery – some critics of their later films said that 'appearance' was all that mattered to them – and manifested an early obsession with controlling every aspect of their work. Now this non-luvvie, non-U pair had returned to Britain. 'FROM HOVIS TO HOLLYWOOD AND BACK HOME AGAIN' was how a *Sunday Times* headline welcomed the return of the natives and their acquisition of Shepperton; it seemed like an omen of change on the way, though what it might be or where it might lie it was too soon to say.

Hollywood-made films had had a bumper year in 1993, creaming profits off the British box office – £170 million gross on the top fifteen films shown in the UK, all of them American – and then remitting most of the profit back to the US studios assisted by treaty arrangements that restricted British taxation simply to the amount retained in the UK. It was calculated that the major Hollywood-owned distributors in Britain paid little or no tax on the £1 billion transferred since 1990 to their parent companies in the US. They cut down their tax liabilities to a mere £14 million by declaring, perfectly legally under the double-taxation safeguard, profits of only £42 million, the amount retained in the UK. Like Willie Nelson, the American entrepreneur who robbed banks because 'that's where the money is', everyone knew where the cash was in the UK: the Americans had it. The problem was getting more of it into British hands. True, Disney had paid for the 1993 Christmas lights in Regent Street, but with *Aladdin* making £17 million gross in British cinema circuits this was a mere snip. British films had taken a poor £15 million in the UK in 1993, a third of what they had made in the previous two years.

Film folk banded together in the form of the Producers Action for Cinema and Television (PACT) and summoned the media to the Savoy Hotel in March 1994 to hear their proposals. They boiled down to persuading the US distribution companies in Britain to divvy up a percentage of their profit and plough it back into British-made movies. Was it practical? Yes, and politically advisable, was the answer. The ongoing GATT talks, ever more rancorous, had spared the loophole that permitted countries to protect their patrimony by discriminating against foreign – i.e. American – film-makers. The French were already doing so (wouldn't you know). Was Britain likely to follow their lead? Well, maybe, but not directly, not in so many threatening words. Hollywood movies counted as America's third most important export; the battle to protect their free movement would be a savage one, fought with the overwhelming forces of Jack Valenti's Motion Picture Association of America.

Those assembled at the Savoy Hotel grew perceptibly quieter as Valenti's name, then similar to Darth Vader or, even later, Lord Voldemort, was mentioned. Imposing a British box-office levy on Hollywood films was tempting – a sweet £30 million for sure – but politically explosive. And no one could be sure the British Treasury would back it: the Treasury hated taxes that were specifically ring-fenced for 'good works'. The Savoy meeting was really a rally, rather than a revolutionary programme, designed to strengthen the hand of the Culture Secretary, Peter Brooke, in his negotiations with the Treasury's Minister of State, Michael Portillo.

More welcome than a compulsory levy, it was believed, would be a 'proposal' made to American companies in the UK that they put part of their pre-tax profits into so-called Film Deposit Receipts. These FDRs, which would attract a tax break, could then be used for investment in British-made films, traded between distributors like negotiable bonds and thereby give an air of cultural philanthropy to commercial self-interest. This was a clever plan. Its timing was good. Though the US would contest any GATT tax or quota on US product to the limits of its power, it would be politically prudent to show the colour of its money before the natives with whom you were trading showed the sharpness of their teeth. Why this plan got nowhere is hard to understand, but possibly it was due to the increasing hope that films would be eligible for funding from the National Lottery due to be set up in 1995. If so, it would solve all the problems, wouldn't it? No more begging for money; it would be on everlasting tap, from the pockets of the public, too, and not the whingeing taxpayer. So the tax-credit FDR scheme languished, though, like many another, it was to be revived years later when the

National Lottery's free spenders had done their worst and nearly wrecked the film industry.

One other flag of opinion was fluttered like an SOS at the Savoy Hotel. For a plea for salvation, its message was distinctly sour. It was the reiterated insistence among those present that what was needed from our film-makers was more 'popular' films: 'ones the public really want to see,' as someone put it, disparaging the 'elitist art-house' productions of Loach, Greenaway, Leigh and Jarman. The last-named was a particularly inopportune target of such abuse. Derek Jarman had died on 19 February 1994, sustaining to the last the bravado and mischievous braggadocio that had made him the Prospero of his film-making generation. Romantic, dandyish, endlessly experimental, provocative and propagandist, he had created an unequalled series of films cut to the bias of his sexual preference, but all bearing more or less successfully the feverish stamp of the maker and his times. Surely one of those at the Savoy rally could have said so: none did. Not that they were ignoble; many were simply ignorant of Jarman and his kind.

Yet some of those who now advocated 'crowd-pleasing' movies – a cry that was to go up, just as insolently and as fruitlessly, in the next decade of National Lottery plenty – had come terrible croppers attempting to please and finding no crowds queuing in response. Michael Winner's *Dirty Weekend*, a sleazy and unsuccessful farce, would have been glad of the box office of a Mike Leigh film, for instance; and Danny Cannon, who touted *The Young Americans* as an example of a 'popular' British movie, simply produced a second-rate Hollywood clone about macho gangsters on the mean streets of London Town.

I left the Savoy with the feeling that while making any movie was hard enough, to proclaim that what was needed were more movies that made 'commercial common sense', implying that one's efforts had been misdirected into the art-house ghetto, seemed like the sour grapes of the unsuccessful. With a perpetual war of independence going on between British film-makers and the Hollywood monopoly of their cinema screens, one could ill afford a quarrel in the bosom of one's own family. If all one was going to do was encourage American-made movies in Britain, with Hollywood looks, values and construction built into them more or less subtly, then we should have an industry of no more cultural identity than a service station on the M25. The old habits overwhelmed the talk of new initiatives.

For one film-maker, however, 1994 was an unhappy year. Kenneth

Branagh was not the first artist to find that setting up his own company to make films was the easiest part of it. Keeping it going was harder. Keeping it profitable was harder still. Renaissance Films had been established in 1988 by Branagh and his stockbroker partner, Stephen Evans, to raise £4.5 million for *Henry V* – £2.9 million of that from eighty-nine private investors. It grossed nearly £7 million in the US and £560,000 in the UK, but even with global returns, the film had not yet broken even. *Much Ado About Nothing* had so far been Renaissance's sole moneymaker. Now the company was being sold. It was in the black, said Evans, but investors deserved their money back after five and a half years. Allowing for a tax break, all eighty-nine would make a modest profit. But Renaissance had found it impossible, given the distribution system that required 'rights' in return for footing the bill for prints and advertising, to build up a 'library' of its productions that would serve as collateral for future film budgets.

To keep Renaissance going was a drain on Branagh's energy and when he was now being offered very large fees by American producers to direct and star in their films, the investment value of his own company had to take second place. But even the uncertainty of this secondary market was about to be brought home to him in the most severe setback of his career.

The catastrophe was the $35 million film, Mary Shelley's *Frankenstein* (4 November 1994), which he was directing and starring in, with Robert De Niro, for Francis Ford Coppola's company. In retrospect, the savagery of the critical attack on the film, and its maker, seems a reaction to the over-praise Branagh had enjoyed and exploited. The talent scene in Britain was suddenly much more crowded than it had been, even five years earlier; and Branagh's achievements looked less exciting to the movers and shapers of opinion. The bursting out into sudden blaze with *Henry*, the patronage of Prince Charles, the premature autobiography, the conquest of America, even his marriage to Emma Thompson and the nexus of 'luvvie culture' that united new impresarios like 'Ken and Em', and their talented friends and performers – his new film had a lot to 'justify' and a sense of the media lying in wait for it is inseparable from the woundingly personal tone some of the reviews took.

His mistake had been to be too faithful to Mary Shelley's novel. People went expecting a horror movie, even more frightening than James Whale's 1930 classic with Boris Karloff. But for Branagh, part of the exhilaration of directing was reinterpreting a classic work. Thus

Henry V had been a populist view of kingship in the form of a tousled boy in spirit and attack like a rugby forward, rather than Olivier's imperious commander; *Much Ado About Nothing*, a formal exchange of wordplay and lovers in the shadows of a ducal court, became a sunbathed game of mental hide-and-seek in Chiantishire. *Frankenstein* was similarly transfigured, becoming much less a shock-horror film than a serious dramatisation of contemporary fear that science was rushing ahead of humanity's ability to control it.

Branagh, playing Victor Frankenstein, was no longer a mad scientist but a serious nineteenth-century philanthropist ahead of his time in his belief that, by replacing the parts, one could re-create a new form of life. The monster, played by Robert De Niro, reflected the moral confusion of our own times over artificial life, in vitro fertilisation and so on. In a time when the women's movement was forging ahead, the film portrayed Victor Frankenstein's sin as that of usurping the female role and giving birth to a child-man. The compulsion to create life is part of Frankenstein's memory of a mother who dies in gory childbirth: it drives him to cross the frontier of science and arrogantly assume the woman's role, as well as that of his own heavenly maker. The monster was not a terrifying golem-figure, but an overgrown man who acts like a lost child, deprived of parentage, raging against the world because he does not know where he fits into it. Whale's film, too, had had its social message. His monster was a Depression-era manifestation, roving vainly and wildly around the country like tens of thousands of homeless American hobos, though the Gothic style of the film, and Karloff's terrifying automaton, ensured that fright was the foreground emotion, not social breakdown.

Branagh consciously intended his creature, coming once more to the screen in another period of recession, to be a symbol of social dispossession and powerlessness. But these ideas of Branagh were betrayed by a screenplay – by two Americans – that vulgarised the story, had dialogue ('Don't bother to scream' is typical monster-talk) that must have been agony for someone like Branagh whose own tongue was more used to having the world's greatest poetry resting on it. The birth of the creature carries a frisson of wonderment as it tumbles out of a vat that looks like a cradle but has undertones of a coffin and threshes on the laboratory floor, manic yet still mute, while its maker attempts to subdue its panic at being pulled alive into an alien world.

The descent from speculative intelligence into the Hollywood basics of bloodletting and horror demanded by the dollar paymasters who financed the movie was swift, brutal and derided in Britain and America. Branagh would continue to act in other people's films, and direct and produce at least two more revisionist versions of Shakespeare, *Hamlet* and *Love's Labour's Lost*, but this experience and the feeling that its critical reception, however justified by the film's failings, had been made the occasion of a personal vendetta caused his confident momentum to falter and dwindle.

He had, as we have seen, published a jaunty autobiography entitled *Beginning* before he was thirty. A darker and bitter tone, though no doubt one bolstered by Ulster pride and resilience, will likely characterise any sequel he may publish, perhaps under the title 'Continuing'.

12

Lottery Promise

Nineteen ninety-five was a decisive date for the film industry. It was the best of years; it became, in retrospect, the worst of years. It was the year when the National Lottery started to fund film-making in Britain, the result of which confirmed the view that cynics take of 'answered prayers'. Never before had film-makers had it so good – or made so many films that were so bad. A policy that was conceived in haste, under pressure of vested interests, and applied at random, with the pretence of competence, only produced a film industry that lacked the survival vigour of natural selection and never came near to achieving the announced goal of sustainable independence.

The euphoria had been gathering perceptibly ever since the National Lottery had come on stream in the middle of 1994. For the film industry to benefit, however, it was essential to have films regarded as 'capital expenditure', not simply 'revenue generating'. Unless this essential distinction were conceded by John Major's Tory government – or, rather, the Treasury – not a penny of the millions of public money – not taxpayers' revenues, note, but gamblers' outlay and hence disbursed with a more flexible conscience – would come the way of the industry. It was make or break.

The industry's 'elder statesmen', Lord Attenborough, Sir David Puttnam, Lord Brabourne, lobbied MPs, top civil servants, even, it was rumoured, Downing Street. Meantime, the very same National Heritage Select Committee, which had recorded a notable argy-bargy with Parker, Loach and Leigh in late 1994, continued its public hearings on 'The British Film Industry'. Considering how short tempers had been a few months earlier, it showed remarkable patience – even, was it possible to hope, sympathy.

I gave evidence before it on 20 January 1995. It did not take long before one realised that, with the exception of Gerald Kaufman, a film buff (and, as I must admit an interest, one-time rival for my own film critic's job at the *Evening Standard*), many committee members' experience of the film industry was limited to film-going – and that, rarely. Anthony Coombs (Tory) said he enjoyed Sylvester Stallone movies; Joe Ashton (Labour) picked *On the Waterfront* as his favourite film; John Maxton (Labour) loved the *Indiana Jones* saga. This wasn't all that reassuring for British films. But the committee appreciated plain speaking, which, as old parliamentary hands, they could easily sort out from lobbying, and appeared almost refreshed to be told that 'hardly any measure that was introduced over the last fifty years to assist the British film industry has not been abused in some way ...' Most witnesses did not take this line, but then they came from the industry.

Have we not, in fact, got a rather thriving British film industry in TV? I was asked. A shrewd question (one of few) whose answer bears repeating: 'It is the difference between a magnifying glass and a microscope that the magnifying glass enlarges one's perception of things, the microscope concentrates it. Both are very useful and both have their place; but I would like to see the television programme, for instance, that could achieve a box office of £220 million, the way that *Four Weddings and a Funeral* has done. I think that the way a country can magnify the perception of it, where those overseas are concerned and indeed where its own inhabitants are concerned, is immensely powerful for reasons that are not financial sometimes so much as emotional when [the view of it] is shown in cinemas and not simply confined to television.'

Much else that I said is already part of this story and need not be repeated. In any case, my evidence probably counted for very little in making up the committee's collective mind about backing the industry's pleas for tax breaks and/or Lottery cash. Had it counted, the outcome would have been very different. I wondered, though, how the committee had received the relatively new Secretary of State for the National Heritage who had preceded me.

Stephen Dorrell was the latest holder of that office and, if not the worst, was to prove the most embarrassing. He had been at the Health Ministry until July 1994, when David Mellor, the then Heritage Secretary in succession to Peter Brooke, had been disgraced in a tabloid scandal and resigned. Dorrell told the committee in January 1995 that he could not remember when he'd last seen a film, or what it was. While having a bath he had tried and failed. He could remember going to see *An Inspector Calls*, the old Priestley play, imaginatively revamped by

Stephen Daldry to underline contemporary class guilt, and was due to go to *A Christmas Carol*, which had been given a politically correct make-over by one of the Labour Party's veteran supporters, John Mortimer. He admitted to listening to Classic FM, the radio station. The word 'philistine' hung around Dorrell; but his civil servant minders were withering in response to that accusation. 'The Minister is not playing the media game of saying what books he has read or likes. It is no more relevant than to ask him what is his favourite tea. He is not Minister for Tea.'

David Mellor had been much more brazen: in his short reign as Heritage Secretary, he often dubbed his department 'Ministry of Fun'. Dorrell's more dour approach was perhaps explained by his referring to Oliver Cromwell as his 'hero'. It was Cromwell who had closed theatres, banned musical entertainments and destroyed paintings in churches. Dorrell was still regarded as very much a Treasury gamekeeper, despite his departmental brief as a heritage poacher: 'A Marks and Spencer man in a Soho full of designer clothes' was how a writer described him. But if the film industry, listening to him give evidence, wasn't all that encouraged to think he'd dole out the Lottery dosh, at least its members felt comfortable knowing he did not put much trust in art. (Not like some film critics.)

The committee then upped sticks in Parliament and went on a fact-finding tour – to Hollywood. This jaunt drew some scepticism. But, in fact, it was a timely move, given the muscle that European culture ministers were attempting to flex at the increasingly acrimonious GATT talks taking place at the same time in Brussels. US films accounted for 75–90 per cent of the European box office and TV rentals; quotas for US cultural imports were being demanded. Hollywood had good reason to be nervous: the US audio-visual industry was the country's second biggest, worth nearly $9 billion in 1994, and 60 per cent of its returns came from Europe. The spectre of European protectionism haunted Hollywood's establishment. As things turned out, the G7 members of GATT agreed to disagree over cultural quotas; Hollywood exhaled again. But a British parliamentary committee, touring the studios in a rented minivan, was probably received more courteously because Britain, it was known, was opposed to quotas on US entertainment.

The committee members were trailed by a BBC TV team, which they agreed to, provided no interviews took place round swimming pools. Ordinary US film-goers, whom they quizzed in movie-house queues, didn't exactly raise their spirits: Anthony Hopkins was one British star everyone named, but because he had recently played Hannibal Lecter, the home-grown American cannibal. 'Kevin Branagh' was a brave shot, though 'no cigar'. The committee soon quit the vox pop and went to the studio honchos for opinions. Sam Goldwyn Jr, a faithful investor in British films including the new *Madness of King George*, praised 'niche productions', which the committee considered a vote of confidence.

Bill Mechanic received them at Universal Studios and, more vaguely, commended 'ideas that travel'. Gerald Kaufman, a defender of unalloyed Britishness, wasn't so sure: it was all right for films to travel, but ideas must not lose their national passport. He had recently attacked *Four Weddings and a Funeral* on grounds of traducing the national identity by an ingrained bias to flatter Americans to whom it had to be sold. 'The celluloid never-never land we were shown for 117 minutes bore no resemblance to what goes on in this island of ours.' He added, 'An Oscar? Let's hope not.' Did his Hollywood hosts take offence? Even if they knew his views it's unlikely. *Forrest Gump* won the 'Best Picture' Oscar at the 1995 awards; and that's how Hollywood would have wished it.

Michael Kuhn, who was making Hollywood his base while he expanded PFE into a global production and distribution studio, put the committee's chauvinism in realistic perspective. He said PFE would make films wherever it wanted and owed no particular loyalty to the UK. Kuhn was still riding high on *Four Weddings'* huge box office. Yet film-making still accounted for only 11 per cent of parent company PolyGram's sales in 1994 and PFE had incurred a loss of £17 million on sales of £398 million due to five or six films failing to live up to the success of *Four Weddings*.

Kaufman and his caravan returned to the UK by economy-class flight, but were soon off again, though this time simply a hop across the Irish Sea to see how Ireland did things. Their visit coincided with the Dublin première of *Interview with the Vampire*, produced by Stephen Woolley, late of the bankrupt Palace Pictures. Privately, most of them loathed this excessively gory US production. But better cheer was available. Michael D. Higgins, both a poet and Irish Arts Minister, was quizzed about how his country's film economy was doing: it was booming, he replied. The reason: 'Tax breaks,' said the beaming Irishman. Under Section 35 of the Irish Finance Act, which allowed film-makers to write off costs against tax, investment had grown from £1 million in 1990 to £100 million in 1994.

When they issued their report, tax changes of this kind were the committee's prime recommendations and warmly welcomed by the industry where, at the time, film production expenses were treated as capital expenditure, depreciating over a number of years and therefore not immediately deductible against tax. (In television, on the other hand, production expenses could be written off in the year they were incurred: the perceived inequality had long been a gripe of film-makers.) 'With such incentive,' said John Woodward, then chief executive of PACT, representing some 1,300 producers, 'Britain would become the centre of film-making in Europe.' Euphoric, maybe: certainly so in view of what was to happen: but very, very cheering. It was all an early and significant sign of a more relaxed attitude to making one industry, film-making, into a 'special case'.

It appeared that Irish hospitality and the success story a generous host like Michael Higgins had to tell was a crucial influence in the new, more friendly view of the immediate needs of British films and their makers. *Four Weddings* had lifted everyone's spirits; it had also ironically distorted the UK box-office figures for 1994, in which British films took an unprecedented 11 per cent of the market – marvellous, until one appreciated that this one film alone accounted for 7 per cent of that. It's unlikely that the Heritage Committee recommendations alone would have pried cash out of the Treasury. It still abhorred a 'special treatment' policy. What did that, was the huge and instant success of the National Lottery. This was gamblers' money and therefore particularly appropriate to be recycled into a gambling industry like film-making: it wouldn't cost the Treasury a cent in revenues, that was the political beauty of it.

As 1995 progressed, so hopes rose and rumours circulated that the National Heritage Department now saw films as being eligible for a Lottery subsidy, provided the Treasury agreed. On 6 June 1995 Stephen Dorrell announced an £80 million Lottery money boost for the film industry: the biggest windfall in its history. The key decisions were that the Arts Council, then chaired by Lord Gowrie, should invest £70 million of Lottery cash in film-making over the next five years, with £10 million earmarked for promoting British films. An immediate beneficiary was to be Ealing Studios, which had been bought in 1994 by a company, BBRK, that at once announced grandiose plans for new comedies 'in the Ealing style' and promised at least ten films a year – within six months it had gone into receivership, leaving the BBC, which had taken a lease on part of the lot for film-making, with a £3.5 million loss.

Now the Lottery bailed out the iconic old site of Michael Balcon's enterprise, which had, as the gateway plaque still said, 'made films that showed Britain and the British' to the world. The immediate injection of £3 million of Lottery money, plus an agreement to make it the 'campus' of the National Film and Television School – a deal cut by Puttnam, who was the school's chairman – seemed good value. Yet already objections were heard. Dennis Vaughan, who had helped persuade the government to set up the Lottery, said, 'I think this is a very bad precedent and not the ideal use of Lottery money. Once the Lottery is patching up debt, it's not going to be the new constructive thing we were aiming for. The main purposes of the Lottery are not being respected.'

Though these strictures applied to the Ealing rescue operation, they were to become very much the refrain of those who perceived the inherent perils of using Lottery money for purposes other than the 'calculable assets' and 'identifiable public good' that had been named as Lottery imperatives in Dorrell's announcement. It was a symptom of how huge amounts of money, placed in hands that had shaken the tin cup for years, were going to destabilise and finally subvert the original intentions of the donation. Criticism was made on much the same grounds about earmarking £180,000 for Lottery cash for 'Cinema 100', the celebration of the industry's centenary scheduled for 1996. One hundred and fifty thousand pounds (part Lottery, part City of London subsidy) would 'prime the pumps' for the London Film Commission, a quango designed to help film-makers exploit the capital's scenic resources and unscramble local prohibitions on location shooting. (This would be a mini-catastrophe: by 1998 its shortfall had to be covered by £98,000 of government cash; nor was that the only occasion. In 2003 it was reconstituted as Film London.) A feasibility study would be undertaken, said Dorrell, to provide a West End showcase cinema for British films. (This came to nothing.)

Other discontents with Lottery funding for film-making were voiced on different, if familiar, grounds: £80 million wasn't enough. 'The promise of more money is enough to keep us hopping along for a few months,' said David Puttnam. 'It is one shoe of a pair. The other is tax breaks.' Besides being insufficient, the proposals were tainted. They were

Tory ones. 'Deeply disappointing,' said Chris Smith, the Labour MP, then Shadow Secretary of State for the National Heritage. 'None of this amounts to very much ... Sixteen years of Tory government ...' and so on. Within a year or so, Smith would exchange 'shadow' for 'substance' and become Labour's first – rebranded – Secretary of State for Culture, Media and Sport, and would sing from a different hymn sheet. For the moment, though, he practised disappointment and disdain.

The grounds for doubt were actually beginning to be clearly apparent, but few voiced them in ways that made sense – and certainly none among the beneficiaries of Lottery millions. The danger was that films would now be made primarily because the money to make them was there – and being dispensed by a bureaucratic agency, the Arts Council, that had absolutely no experience in dealing with an entrepreneurial industry. The 'arts' tranche of the Lottery had originally been dedicated to 'capital projects' and this had already been substantially perverted by the successful lobbying of the 'usual suspects' in the industry so that film-making was eligible for the subsidy.

I queried this early on, in September 1995, in a letter to Stephen Dorrell. Back came a reply from Hayden Phillips, then Permanent Secretary at the Heritage Department, asserting that film-making had every right to be considered not just a process, but a product. It resulted in 'a capital asset' – i.e. a film – that had a long life and could be 'exploited to produce income over a number of years'. It was plain then that the deal had been done: it had been 'sold' to the politicians by the film producers on grounds that appeared reasonable by business standards – except that film-making was by every standard an unreasonable business and a systematically dishonest one, too. Such a view would not be welcomed, I knew: politicians, and their civil servants in particular, never go back on their policies until circumstances enforce some discreet deviation. Nothing of that kind would be accomplished by a film critic.

However, I answered Phillips's letter and, for the record, wrote to him in fairly blunt terms on 6 October 1995:

Stephen Dorrell saw a way of getting funding to the film industry without needing Treasury approval (which he wouldn't have got) and the policy was then adjusted to opportunism by re-defining what a 'capital project' was. It is not just a matter of semantics, though: it is contrary to what Parliament had in mind when it created the National Lottery ... A film is a wager, a bet, a gamble, and to refer, as you do, to 'the generally supportive views of a wide range of very different people in the industry' is akin to saying that a convention of croupiers thought it a good thing to build more casinos.

The reply simply reiterated – as such Civil Service replies do – the government's new and improved view of film-making as an 'asset'. I felt it time to go public. 'More often than not,' I wrote in the *Evening Standard* on 24 November 1995,

> when the 'asset', the reel of film, is taken out of its tin can to start earning its living on the cinema screen, it results in a whopping loss on the balance sheet. Film investment represents the funding of hope over experience, the same motive as makes a punter buy a Lottery ticket. It is radically different from the projects that Lottery cash was meant to facilitate ... Unlike a film, the worth of such solid, if not always glamorous, projects is calculable in advance. Their social utility is evident; their artistic worth, estimated. Their enjoyment by individuals and the community in general can usually be relied on.

(One of the guidelines for seeking Lottery cash had been a need to 'demonstrate that the proposed object will promote the public good'.) 'In short, they are a safe bet. Film-making, by contrast, is an irrational, unsafe and often wildly wasteful gamble with only a slim chance of winning.'

Without naming him, I queried Phillips's shibboleth about the incremental charms of film exploitation.

> Even supposing that a film so funded is lucky enough, as my DNH mandarin maintains, 'to produce income over a number of years', whom will this income benefit? The nation and the community? I do not think so. My belief is that most of it will go straight into the bank accounts of privately owned production companies and the pockets of individual film people ... it is not what Parliament intended should be done with public money. In the urgency to get the scheme up and running, the consequences haven't been thought through. ...

The DNH, I concluded, 'has started to stake film people's creative bets and finance their dreams'. The headline I suggested appeared over this broadside: its seven words turned out to be the truest I ever composed: 'LOTTERY MILLIONS WILL BE WASTED ON FILMS.'

If anything tempered the industry's enthusiasm it was this: the Lottery funding was in the hands of an arts body. Perhaps apprehensive that staking films to the extent of £80 million would generate envy and resentment among those not sharing in the windfall, as well as covetousness and jubilation among those who did, the DNH declared that such films as were funded had to be ones with cultural overtones, or at least films that, for one reason or another, would have found it hard to gather together the prime finance. In other words, they were not necessarily 'commercial' in the broadest sense (though if they made money that was fine). Consequently, the Arts Council was the designated dispenser of public money for film-making. This was a crucial mistake. It was rash enough to try to impose a bureaucratic pattern on an entrepreneurial industry, with all the form-filling and step-mounting this entailed, but to ask a body associated with 'elitist' culture to pronounce on the merits of proposals from an industry associated with populist entertainment should have set the alarm bells ringing.

The Arts Council declared that a 'pilot' scheme would be mounted for the first year, until April 1996. This had less to do with prudence than ignorance. Hardly anyone at the Council knew how commercial film-making operated, or was eager to distinguish between 'art' and 'box office'. The only method that occurred to them was to dip their hand in the till, fund a few films – and then watch. Peter Gummer, chairman of the Council's Lottery board, said, 'Funding will increase the quality, number and range of films produced in this country and secure a future for our industry.' David Puttnam added, 'We are confident that a flow of secure funding from the Lottery ... will have the effect of attracting new investors and encouraging the production of high-quality films *which might otherwise be too risky* for the commercial marketplace.' (Italics mine.)

The first statement here is a mere piety; the second is wishful thinking and was soon quietly abandoned. New investors did come into the industry in the years ahead; but they came because of what Puttnam had called 'the other shoe' – i.e. tax breaks – and not principally because of Lottery funding. And the film projects that were deemed 'too risky' for the 'commercial market' had to contend with a fact that was already blindingly obvious, except to those who didn't wish to see it – namely, the fact that, once made, they might still be either 'too risky', or, as was increasingly to happen, too bad to be exploited successfully in the 'commercial market' or even in the 'art-house' one. All depended on taking a gamble; and, as things turned out, the Lottery millions would have been more wisely placed with a bookmaker like William Hill, who at least gave better odds than the industry shibboleth of seven films out of ten being dead losses, two just about covering their costs and one being a hit – a long-shot 'maybe'.

'It was unlikely', said Mr Gummer, 'that Lottery contribution to any single film would exceed £1 million.' At least this was prudent: the average budget for a British film, according to the Policy Studies Institute on Film, Cinema and Video, had been falling over the last few years. In 1983 it was £8.4 million; in 1993 £3.2 million. This reflected falling investment. The Arts Council perceived films that might benefit from Lottery funding to have budgets 'likely to be between £5–10 million', according to Mr Gummer. This didn't recognise the market reality that hardly any independent British film – i.e. one not financed, or co-financed by a Hollywood company – could risk a budget of even this 'size', especially if they were considered 'risky' projects.

By September, the first tranche of Lottery-funded films was announced. The very first one broke the £1 million limit: an adaptation of Thomas Hardy's *The Woodlanders* (total budget £4.3 million), directed by former documentary film-maker Phil Agland and scripted by David Rudkin, received £1.3 million. Among the others were: *Love and Death on Long Island* (£2,300,874), an ironic comedy adapted from Gilbert Adair's novel by first-time feature director Richard Kwietniowski and set partly in the US, which got £750,000; *Galivant* (£334,366), a BFI production of an extremely idiosyncratic 'road' comedy documentary by Andrew Kotting got £170,000; *Glastonbury* (£125,000), about the Pop festival, got £36,061; and *Crimetime* (£3,817,755), a serial killer story starring Pete Postlethwaite, got its £302,421 Lottery funding largely on the strength of its Dutch director George Sluizer's success eight years earlier with *The Vanishing*, a genuinely chilling psychodrama (but more on this later). On the whole most of these looked safe enough, even conservative projects, with a strong 'heritage' flavour, especially when a film of the Royal Shakespeare Company's stage production of *A Midsummer Night's Dream* (£2,300,000, including £750,000 Lottery grant) was added in October 1995, followed by a film about the Oxford and Cambridge Boat Race, *True Blue* (£3.5 million and £1 million from the Lottery) within weeks.

On closer inspection, though, most of them had co-funders able to put up the total budgets themselves. All had access to other sources of venture capital; they did not need public money to 'make it happen'.

Among them were Channel 4, British Screen, BSkyB, BBC Films, Telefilm Canada, Nova Scotia Film Development Corp (Nova Scotia 'stood in' for Long Island in Gilbert Adair's film), the British Film Institute (then receiving a £17.5 million grant-in-aid) and various European funding groups.

The award of £35,000 to *Glastonbury: The Movie* was particularly questionable; it gave its co-funder, MTV, the TV and video music channel, exactly what they wished: a Pop promo for the event. Other voices questioned the grant of £84,000 for Frantz Fanon, *Black Skin* (total budget, £320,000), co-funded by BBC TV. It was a study of the French intellectual propagandist whose writings highlighted Algerian and Tunisian colonial development. It did not appear to be within the spirit, or indeed the letter, of the Lottery guidelines, though quite politically correct. All co-funders were the kind of investors that the Lottery wished to bring into the industry; but for most of them public-assisted investment was more attractive than risking more of their own or other investors' venture capital.

To British Screen Finance the advent of Lottery funding must have seemed a mixed blessing; it was supposed to supplement, not compete with, established film financiers – but the huge subsidy from the Lottery was likely, at the very least, to distort the market, attracting some projects directly to the Art Council's moneybags that BSF might reasonably have expected to partner, or, simply, putting up the cost of movie-making because 'the money was there', which in turn would compromise BSF's more slender resources or even price it out of the market. And none of these hopeful forecasts was willing to face the reality that, unless the fresh finance released a sudden outpouring of new talents, particularly in the form of scripts, bankable projects would not be available in any greater numbers than they were at the moment. Nothing was as simple as it had seemed.

By October, voices from the 'market place' were being heard and their tones were not friendly. Perhaps, by then, some producers had been turned down by the Arts Council's advisory board (which in turn was supplied with opinions on the scripts submitted by a very scratch lot of underpaid readers). Adam Dawtrey, in *Variety* on 23 October 1995, amplified the criticism of what was already being dubbed 'a ramshackle system'. 'The whole thing is evolving into a classic British shambles of the highest order,' he reported, quoting an unidentified 'senior film adviser' to the Arts Council. The council's Lottery Director was Jeremy

Newton. Dawtrey wrote, 'He [Newton] argues that it's better to start spending on as many films as possible than to sit around for two years trying to design a perfect system.' Though an oversimplification of what was going on, this emphasised how the patrons of the Arts Council had developed, with dismaying speed, a system that differed very little from the hit-and-miss modes of commercial film companies – except that the Council didn't need to worry overmuch about a return on its money: it was public subsidy that might, or might not, come back like bread on the waters.

Part of the industry's bitterness, it became clear, was that not enough of 'the bread' was going to the commercial members of it, who considered themselves every bit as much entitled to be supported by it as the cultural aspirants, absolute beginners and public benefactors who got grants for their films. 'Britain's hard-nosed film producers, who learned to survive under the harsh disciplines of the free market, have no experience dealing with the Arts Council's peculiarly English brand of woolly paternalism,' Dawtrey wrote. Particular criticism was made of the composition of the panel that rubber stamped, or rejected, the script readers' recommendations: it included (at this date) an architect, a jazz singer, a museum curator and two directors of provincial theatres. 'Only David Puttnam provides a dose of film expertise.' It was already adversely affecting the commercial market place. Buyers of international rights had begun making lower offers of co-production capital because they now expected Lottery funding to make up the difference to the seller – if the seller could get it. Clearly a lot of experienced sellers couldn't.

It didn't mollify many when the Arts Council, in October, devolved some £5 million of Lottery money to British Screen Finance, earmarked for films by 'established directors'. This was thought simply to concentrate 'more power and money in familiar hands'. Truly, there was no pleasing these film people. 'The Lottery is just amateur hour,' Dawtrey's damning report concluded. It was awful to be shown the kingdom of heaven and then to be told to stand aside and let the folk who hadn't earned it enter: that, anyhow, was how commercial film-makers saw it. That hadn't been in their prayers.

The Arts Council, in its ignorance, failed to take account of another, more sinister, trend. Over the last few years a growing number of completed films was failing to get released. In 1983 only 2.3 per cent of British films were still unreleased theatrically within a year of completion. By 1988 it was 9.3 per cent. In 1989 it jumped alarmingly to 27.6 per cent; in 1991 to 30.5 per cent; in 1992 to 31.9 per cent; and by mid 1995, when Lottery funding came on stream, some thirty-five films finished two years earlier were still awaiting release. To the Arts Council the output of feature films in 1994 appeared gratifyingly high, and indeed it was: eighty-four films were made in the UK, representing an investment of £455 million, a new high, even though thirty-five of these were regarded as predominantly British (i.e. non-American-financed) and represented investment of only £53.36 million. To accomplish this, when just one major player, PolyGram, was left showed that even before the Lottery funding arrived investment capital was not exactly scarce and just needed 'encouragement'.

The downside of this, however, was that at the very moment Lottery funding 'primed the pump', increasing the inducement to make more films, many that had been made were sitting on the shelf, eventually to be sold direct to video, TV or abandoned and written off as a tax loss. This the Arts Council, and the Heritage Department, totally failed to see coming and, naturally, were not alerted to by those who hoped to benefit from Lottery handouts. As always, films were made to generate income, mostly with little hope of profit; and getting the cash to get them started was more than half the battle for producers who promptly paid themselves their own fees upfront. Sometimes it was the whole battle.

Getting the money back was another matter that the Arts Council failed to understand. 'In most transactions', Sue Rose, press officer at the Arts Council, wrote to me on 5 January 1996, 'the Arts Council seeks to recoup its investment on an equal footing basis with the other equity investors (so no one investor is paid out first) and proportionately according to the amount invested in relation to the total invested by others.' This might work in an industry more open and honest about such matters, but not to stand 'in the first position of recovery', the one that banks like occupying, was a huge disadvantage in seeing any money come back. As long as it was accounted for, 'remoteness of profits due', the phrase recurring on thousands of film investors' statements, was not likely to worry a public body unduly. Losses were defendable, if not exactly explicable; they had been incurred for 'the public benefit', hadn't they? The phrase became more and more vague as time passed, until it embraced such things as expenditure by film crews in local cafés, tourism to film locations and so on. Tracing it in detail was made difficult by the arcane nature of the film business, long accustomed to not leaving even the scent of the money for the public watchdogs to follow.

A pattern quickly emerged, that never changed throughout the first phase of public subsidy for film-making in the UK. Money invested in a film is at first transparent; once spent, it becomes opaque; generally thereafter, as far as profitability goes, it turns invisible. With all the non-public money sloshing around the industry pool, the only need for Lottery money to top it up was the political need to subvert the cost-cutting Treasury's refusal to cross the palms of those vexatious beggars, British film-makers, with silver pieces from tax breaks. An unexpected irony occurred before the end of the year.

At the very moment it was handing out public money to the film industry, the Arts Council itself received the unkindest cut of all: its budget was reduced by 5 per cent (7.5 per cent, if inflation was taken into account). The cause of this was brutally simple: with the Lottery's success – over £1 billion raised inside the first year – the Treasury had an irresistible excuse to replace funding from taxation with this new source of revenue. Accordingly, it cut £66 million from the Lottery's Heritage Fund, which went to the National Heritage Department, and it was obliged to pass the cut on to Lord Gowrie's Arts Council. At the very same moment the Treasury gave an almost matching sum, £65 million, in duty reductions to the betting organisations which had been whingeing about the reduction in their profits caused by the creation of the Lottery. A classic case of robbing Peter to pay Paul. When his arts budget was cut, Gowrie went on what he called 'dignified strike', refusing to distribute arts largesse for the month of December 1995. 'Throughout the holiday period, we were in beer-and-sandwiches mode with our Ministry; so we have been able to retrieve £4.9 million from the Lottery . . . we have passed this money on to the arts.'

A new National Heritage Secretary had been appointed – yet another – in succession to the luckless Stephen Dorrell. She was Virginia Bottomley, formerly the Health Secretary and a speaker at the Tory party conference at Blackpool in 1994, when she declared, 'A civilisation is judged by its culture.' Over Christmas 1995, she met Gowrie and was persuaded to be more 'civilised', at least in the matter of Arts Council cuts: between them, they had managed to claw back most of the £5 million that the Treasury Secretary, William Waldegrave, had called for. The cut stood, but Bottomley had succeeded in coming up with £4.3 million in Lottery reserve cash to pass on to the Arts Council. She said she accepted the Arts Council's argument that it needed to charge more for the extra time now required to sort out the Lottery awards. 'Flexibility' this was called. It was clear that the Lottery rules were being rendered more and more flexible regarding the distinction to be made between capital funding and revenue funding, already erased in the case of the film industry. The months ahead would bend the rules to breaking point.

A few months later, in July 1996, over lunch, I explained my concerns about the over-funding of film-making to Grey Gowrie. He listened attentively, wished to know more, but was clearly a prisoner of circumstances. What would you do? he challenged. I told him that, given a free hand with Lottery money, I should ignore producers' demands for money and, instead, invest it in buying the cinema chain formerly owned by Cannon, then sold to MGM and recently up for sale. 'Then', I said, 'you would own the money box. You could show Hollywood movies and make money out of them, and also have the guarantee of a showcase for British movies.'

'It's an attractive vision,' Lord Gowrie replied. 'Unfortunately, the Arts Council may not run a business.' The question of why, therefore, it was doing business with the film industry was sensed by both of us but remained unspoken. Events would soon show that it was not a business for any public body to have dealings with.

13

No Rank Revival

Michael Gifford, Rank's group managing director, presented the aspect of an implacable object when he appeared before the Commons Heritage Committee on 26 January 1995. With all its still considerable resources for film production idling away through the risk-avoidance policy of his board, this impassive man was not going to yield an inch to MPs' questioning. He sat hunched, inflexible ... Film-making? Forget it, was his attitude, put less bluntly, but with a sort of passive arrogance.

Joe Ashton (Labour) said to him, 'Even last week Richard Attenborough mentioned Rank, that you, with your resources, ought to be like the BBC and Channel 4, and one or two other people, doing something to help the industry.'

A pause, then: 'I did not hear a question in that,' Mr Gifford replied. Well, *respond*, man! one could almost hear the MPs willing him. Everything Rank did, or didn't do, was judged by the balance sheet, he at last said firmly. It had invested £25 million in 1994 in film productions.... The committee men perked up. But it was other people's productions, mainly Hollywood's, in return for international distribution rights. Rights, rather than risky film-making, made Rank open its moneybag.

Well, how much would it take to establish a 'sustainable and internationally competitive English-language film production business'?

Mr Gifford, face expressionless, said crisply, '£500 million.'

And Rank would not contemplate that? No; no way. Then why was Rank still 'in' movies?

'Most of the money we make by engagement in the industry is in making copies of video cassettes for the major studios of North America and Europe, and in providing services in our film laboratories.' That told it all.

Once the most powerful film production company in Britain, Rank, under the control of men who exercised the cautious approach of a small-town bowling-green club and indeed, in their company uniform of blue blazers, grey flannels and panama hats at their annual Cannes luncheon, looked like the bowling club on a day excursion, had finished up being simply a service industry for other film empires.

Gerald Kaufman, the committee chairman, was scathing: 'I am somewhat at a loss as to why an organisation founded by a man [the Methodist evangelist-businessman J. Arthur Rank] who had very, very great ideals indeed, who was in it for money, but was not only in it for money, but who had personal religious and social ideals, that you feel it perfectly acceptable that you should operate simply on the basis of how much money you can get in and not in any way feel an obligation to put back some of that money.'

Not perhaps the most elegantly structured rebuke, but if it stung Michael Gifford he did not show it. Attendance done, he left the committee room flanked by his lieutenants. The 'vision thing', as it was later dubbed, was not for him; his sight stopped at the balance sheet. However, this was looking somewhat unhealthy at the start of 1995. In many City people's view, Rank was getting a poor return on its investment, even if it avoided stepping into the Great Grimpen Mire of filmmaking. Operating profit for 1994 was £227 million, up £88.3 million on 1993; but net capital expenditure at that time was believed to be £1.2 billion. Rank had paid £900 million for the Mecca leisure business in 1990, when the country was dipping into a deepening depression. Gifford had cut Rank's stake in the profitable Xerox copier business from 49 to 29 per cent, raising £620 million; but some thought this imprudent. Xerox had once been Rank's salvation; now it was simply short rations. Such figures, more perhaps than his performance in front of the Heritage Committee, started the rumours in late January that Michael Gifford (£488,000 in salary and bonus in the year ending October 1994) was considering quitting before the expiry of his contract in January 1998, when he would be sixty-four. By March 1995 the rumours hardened: Rank, it was reported, was headhunting a new chief executive. In August 1995 he was still there; but the Macmillan Dictum was now coming into play. 'Events, dear boy, events,' Harold Macmillan had replied when the Tory Prime Minister was asked what the decisive factor was in politics.

In big business, too, as Rank now discovered. It had failed to win the contract to operate the National Lottery – which had gone to the Camelot consortium. Now it suffered a fresh public setback, one that came out of the past in the shape of the cinema chain that had once belonged to Rank's rival, Associated British Picture Corporation, and had then been bought by the Cannon Group which, in turn, had had to dispose of them to Giancarlo Parretti who, in his turn, had had to make them over to the Credit Lyonnais as collateral for loans. The bank had to dispose of them by the end of 1995, so they came on the market once again, a kind of movable asset, as ceaseless in their passage from one owner to another as the cursed vessel of the Flying Dutchman was from one ocean to the next. (If only they had been anchored and begun to make money for a British owner who made movies.) They came on the market early in 1995. There was again a fear that a foreign buyer would acquire them, as those 'bad news' Israeli cousins, Golan and Globus had done.

David Puttnam organised a letter-writing campaign to Michael Heseltine, then President of the Board of Trade, a title he had resurrected from Harold Wilson's days, more fitting to his imperial aura, he felt, than Secretary for Trade and Industry. Puttnam complained of Rank's poor investment record in British film-making, which argued against the sale to Rank. I wrote independently to Heseltine. My letter was really a reiteration of the one written to Paul Channon twelve years earlier, pleading with him not to let Cannon acquire the cinema chain and the other former ABPC assets, then representing roughly half the indigenous British film industry. The reply, communicated by Heseltine's assistant private secretary on 21 February 1995, was much the same. Heseltine would await advice from the Office of Fair Trading and take a decision whether to refer any sale to the Monopolies and Mergers Commission, 'in the light of that advice'. In other words, nothing had been learned from the past, when Channon had ignored the OFT advice and nodded the sale through to Cannon – thus starting the chain reaction of film industry catastrophe.

By May 1995 the bidders for the 120 cinemas were a piranha pack: they included Time Warner, Sony, Michael Green's Carlton Communications, Electra Capital, Rank, Richard Branson's Virgin Group and two consortia led by previous MGM management. Even Alan Bond, the Australian who had made millions by simply holding ownership of the cinemas for a week or so in 1986 before passing control of them on to Cannon, came briefly into the auction room. Rank was lead bidder with a £200 million bid; but adding so many cinemas to its own 316 screen Odeon circuit would inevitably have meant a reference to the

MMC; to pre-empt this, Rank quickly said it would sell off some cinemas of its own where the box office was ailing.

Virgin offered an unconditional cash bid: juicy bait. Despite an attempt to injunct the sale by Parretti, whose recent troubles with the Italian legal system proved no deterrent to pursuing his extraordinary career, Virgin won the auction on 6 June 1995 by increasing its bid to over £200 million with the help of Reading-Craig, a US-based specialist in leveraged buyouts and turning drive-in cinemas into shopping malls: scarcely a good omen. In one go, therefore, the Virgin Group became the biggest cinema operator in Britain. A victorious Robert Devereux, Branson's brother-in-law, a one-time producer (*Absolute Beginners*), cele-brated the acquisition. He announced, 'We intend to shake up the industry.' Investing in British films, perhaps? Not at all. There were more pressing priorities, well, more glamorous: games arcades and a Planet Hollywood restaurant in the flagship cinemas. Coca-Cola would be immediately replaced by Virgin Cola. That had top priority. 'Youth is at the heart of the Virgin experience,' Devereux said. Certainly movies weren't. The excitement lay in turning cinema-going into 'an American-style experience'. Virgin's glow of enthusiasm was all the brighter because it had only recently lost a deal with Luke Johnson and Hugh Osmond, the young entrepreneurs who brought Pizza Express to market.

For Rank, however, not possessing the bounce of youth, failure to acquire the cinema chain was a setback at just the wrong time. It added to the impression that Rank could no longer cut a deal. Those who felt they could do better began edging nearer. Among them was Michael Grade, chief executive at the time of Channel 4, but a man who had inherited his uncle Lew Grade's passion for moguldom: an emotion more readily satisfied in film empires than TV suites. He and a consortium had already, twice, made an offer of £400 million for Rank's Pinewood Studios and been rebuffed by Gifford. At the Heritage Committee's hearings, Grade had gone on the attack, bitterly indicting Rank for refusing to put money into production. 'Their investment record in British film is lamentable for a company which is the biggest, the largest single and only integrated equivalent of a Hollywood studio.' How long Gifford would continue to say no to Grade's shopping expedition to buy the studio, or even be there to say it, was now in question. Once again, the physical assets of film-making in Britain looked about to be put in pawn, while the artistic assets – for there still were some – continued to fend desperately for themselves, at least until their Lottery ship came into port.

Having sold the MGM cinemas in the UK, Credit Lyonnais then decided to put the MGM studios up for auction. One of the bidders, in early 1996, was PolyGram's Michael Kuhn. Kuhn had been snapping up cinema chains, distributions and TV companies all over Europe, Asia and America; MGM would have been the prize exhibit of his policy to create, 'in one leap', the first truly pan-European studio to rival any in Hollywood. His boss, however, Cor Boonstra, had other ideas. Kirk Kerkorian, the previous owner of MGM, stepped in first with his bid and bought back his studio. Had Kuhn succeeded the effect on PolyGram's production stake in the British film industry could have been momentous: its fortunes would have been tied to one of the richest entities in the film business run by a dynamic expansionist.

Kuhn's failure to convince his bosses was an early warning to him that 'the quick-moving risk-taking style required to be successful in the entertainment business was inimical to the ethos of a hardware company like Philips'. It was hardly a flash of insight; Kuhn had been depressed by the need to prove himself and his proposals to boards of unimaginative directors in Philips's gloomy Eindhoven headquarters with its ornamental water feature in the lobby that looked ominously like a pool of blood. But even he was unaware of how brutally the cup might be dashed from his lips a short time later – and, with it, hopes of a genuine British film renaissance.

PolyGram, however, established its British office amid marble and chrome inside a mansion in St James's Square in London's West End, and let folk know it was in buying mode. As a post-*Four Weddings* celebration present, the Working Title team of Bevan and Fellner were given a $30 million production fund, the sort of post-dated cheque that signifies credibility, and gets stars, agents and scriptwriters hungry for the meat they know hangs on such financial bones. They promptly paid $1 million for the film rights to a new, as yet unpublished, British novel by Philip Kerr entitled 'Gridiron', about a skyscraper that malevolently turns against the construction crew erecting it – a high-concept Stephen King-type plot. 'Gridiron: The Movie', however, was never made. The reasons remain undisclosed, despite teasing questions asked of the producers at several Cannes Film Festival luncheons over the next few years. In the euphoria of *Four Weddings*, however, it hardly mattered: a million dollars spent on a property entitled PolyGram–Working Title to take their place at the big players' table.

If *Four Wedding*'s box office had been their entrance fee, the $1 million purchase price of 'Gridiron' signified they were there to stay in the game. 'We now have offices in Los Angeles,' said Tim Bevan. 'We can negotiate directly with American talent, or with the agents who represent British talent there . . . Emma Thompson, Anthony Hopkins, Kenneth Branagh, Daniel Day-Lewis, Hugh Grant. They're stars who can now create an "environment" in their movies that makes mainstream American audiences feel comfortable with the British presence. They can "open" a movie in the States – kick start it.'

It might be questioned – indeed was – why Working Title needed to go to the US to negotiate deals for born and bred British stars; but the reality was that the latter now expected the customary fees for their status as artists in American films, even if it was doubtful that those named could 'open' or 'kick start' their new film in quite the same manner as Schwarzenegger, Redford, Stallone or even the new boy, Jim Carrey. But it helped to have the confidence of American chain-cinema operators and British stars who were at least 'names' at the US box office commanded this confidence, if only in the short term and as long as the love affair with British talent lasted. For the moment, then, one withheld judgement on the PolyGram–Working Title enthusiasm and extravagance, but at the same time held one's breath.

Considered individually, the British films premièred in 1995 provided evidence of the talent available, if only it could be harnessed to a sustainable development programme. A record number of new, or newish, British directors made their debuts, some shakily, others with surprisingly swift self-confidence. Antonia Bird's *Priest* was a melodramatic but spirited attack on pietistic hypocrisy in the Catholic Church written by one of Ken Loach's fellow subversives, Jimmy McGovern; Tim Sullivan's *Jack and Sarah*, a romantic comedy about single parenthood starring Richard E. Grant, required finer tuning by Hugh Grant. It marked Granada TV's return to film-making, though the company's enthusiasm was not sustained by the box office and relapsed quickly. This was to be Granada's pattern over the next few years: a potential 'studio' produced largely 'one-offs'.

The 'group of friends' comic template of *Four Weddings* was plain to see in *Jack and Sarah*; Justin Hardy's *A Feast at Midnight* advertised itself as 'quintessentially English', in the hope (unfulfilled) that Americans would respond to its prep-school milieu where an obsession with food has replaced pubescent sex. Darker in shading and more ingenious in its exploration of the everyday grotesque was Benjamin Ross's *The Young Poisoner's Handbook*, which revealed its German investment in a story of a schoolboy devising a 'final solution' for his dysfunctional family.

Two movies starred Hugh Grant, though not Hugh Grant as we had recently known him. The new star's arrest in Los Angeles, in June 1995, on a charge of 'public lewdness' with a Beverly Hills hooker actually turned out to be a move of considerable, if possibly unintentional, shrewdness. Gold always looks a little more natural, a bit more pedigreed, when it has had a smidgen of common wear and tear. Grant's image was in danger of looking too shining for his own good. A new way of perceiving him – however temporarily embarrassing to his personal dignity – arrived at just the right moment: women found him even more amusingly disarrayed, especially after his swift round of TV chat shows, while men found him more understandable. Stardom is formed at the interface of who an actor really is and how the public sees him. Moving from one to the other is where the trick of success, or survival, lies: altering expectations, but retaining a certain predictability. Grant did not suffer from his escapade, since the phenomenon of celebrity had effectively neutralised the threat of scandal. And people saw in him – or tried to see – something more than the diffident charmer who dithered his way in and out of *Four Weddings*. It rather helped that, at the time, he was publicising his new (American-made) film, *Nine Months* (aka *Baby*).

The two films preceding it had been contractual jobs, accepted before *Four Weddings*; his professionalism helped mitigate the knowledge that the fees he was to receive were now very small indeed in comparison with future remuneration. Mike Newell's *An Awfully Big Adventure* was the more interesting project: it showed an untypical Grant. A cynical, monocled, lank-haired, abrasive-tongued, dandyish, manipulative closet homosexual, with a nicotine talon hooked round a cigarette, casting a concupiscent eye over the male juveniles before sowing fear and loathing in the green room as an assistant stage manager at the Liverpool Rep in 1947. It was a part Daniel Day-Lewis might have played, except that this star was now firmly fixed in the American constellation, playing Hawkeye the Indian scout in Michael Mann's *The Last of the Mohicans*.

The film stretched Grant: its theme, echoed by Peter Pan in J. M. Barrie's play, was that of death – the 'awfully big adventure'. Photographed by Dick Pope, who did many of Mike Leigh's downbeat works, the film contained one of his sharpest, if depressing, impressions of post-war English austerity. A fateful collision between theatre and life, the 'never land' of people damaged by the war years, the film is probably destined to be unfairly forgotten in Grant's list of credits.

His second film, *The Englishman Who Went Up a Hill and Came Down a Mountain*, had a title suggesting tumescent sniggers, but simply referred to the territorial extension that a little Welsh hamlet added to its local protuberance in order to qualify it for mountain status in Hugh Grant's Ordnance Survey mapping reconnoitre. Christopher Monger turned it into a lightweight community comedy set in 1917, the kind Alec Guinness once turned out for Ealing. Despite period breeches, braces and grandad vest, Grant sounded and apologised much as he did in *Four Weddings*. The film's only importance lay in calling attention to the rise of regionalism, as it was now politically incorrect to speak of 'nationalism'. This was shortly to lead to totally unrealistic claims that Wales and Scotland (yes, and soon Northern Ireland, too) could be independent film-making powers. But the claims made in 1995 had some solid evidence to back them.

The vitality of Scottish writing, acting and directing had been proven with *Shallow Grave* and in 1996 was to be confirmed sensationally with *Trainspotting*. Perhaps its historical and literary pedigree diminished the Scottish chauvinism of Michael Caton-Jones's *Rob Roy* that shook the dust of ages out of Scott's pages and replaced it with a revisionist view of romanticism and a brutal commentary on British triumphalism. Though American-financed by United Artists, the film was supported by the Scottish Film Production Fund (and British Screen Finance); and its Scottish pedigree was impeccable. It withstood comparison with Kubrick's *Barry Lyndon* for its willingness to give an adventure story room to look around at society, engross us in the strangeness of behaviour and the ruthlessness of men. The politics of blue blood; the ever-ready willingness to spill the red kind; the venality of high culture; and the radical toughness of law: all this gave the film a subtext as thick as a winter kilt to an already sturdy tale starring Liam Neeson, but dominated by Tim Roth's bastard adventurer turning living tissue into deadweight carcass in duels that evoked the same horrified-fascinated intake of breath as Hannibal Lecter did at first bite.

Mel Gibson was producing, directing and starring in *Braveheart* on much the same stretch of heather; and though wholly American in format and anti-monarchical in the way it travestied history in order to project the republican sympathies of the Australian (now naturalised American) media tycoon Rupert Murdoch, whose company, 20th

Century-Fox, produced it, *Braveheart* caught Scottish nationalism with
political timeliness. The Scottish Nationalist Party co-opted Gibson's
image as the martyr-hero William Wallace for its poster campaign for
political autonomy. For a brief moment the blue cross of Scotland, the
saltire, dimmed the prominence of the Union flag – if any dared show
the latter on football terraces or electoral hustings.

It all reinforced the impression of British film-making diversifying
into the regions. *Sight and Sound*, in its October editorial, said, '. . . it's
worth considering that the received idea of British cinema might be past
its sell-by date and that it is better to think in terms of, say, English and
Scottish cinema.' The same journal added, '. . . it may well be best to
think of the autumn slew of films as examples of an English rather than
a British cinema. No one can doubt that most of them are enquiries
into the condition of England.' Well, yes – and no. Nostalgia heavily
overlaid the themes and stories from the eighteenth to the early twentieth
centuries. But few of them reflected *contemporary* England. One was
prepared to forgive them this omission because of the vigour of the new
directors who made them.

Forerunner of this 'English' wave, opening early in 1995, hot upon
its Oscar success, was *The Madness of King George*. It marked Nicholas
Hytner's apparently effortless transfer of Alan Bennett's stage play at the
Royal National Theatre to the screen, scenes opening into each other
as smartly as the invisible flunkeys flinging open the salon doors at
George III's approach and, thanks to Andrew Dunn's photography and
a Royal Command Performance of British talents, shaking off the
heritage feeling and making one feel one is *there*, contemporary with
events surrounding the sovereign's temporary lapse into apparent insanity.

'I am the King of England,' cries Nigel Hawthorne's George, con-
fronting his puritanical physician and proto-psychiatrist (Ian Holm).

'No, sir, you are the patient . . . Until you can govern yourself, you
are unfit to govern England.'

Alan Bennett's script reverberated with nudging references to contemporary royalty, anticipating the slow but inexorably rising level of
republican sentiment in Britain. The film looked full-scale, yet intimate;
crowded with idiosyncratic 'takes' on the manners of the time yet
truly and woundingly modern; endowed with energy yet holding still
courtiers and commoners long enough for us to 'read' them with profit
as instruments of drama and embodiments of English heritage. The
'heritage' aspect softened the social critique; yet, ironically, it was this

that finally persuaded the National Heritage secretary, Stephen Dorrell, to yield to those entreating him to let the film industry qualify for National Lottery patronage.

The power of costume drama succeeded where the persuasion of producers had only half convinced. Niche marketing was a concept that even politicians could grasp: it seemed within the possibilities of a shrunken British industry. When the National Heritage Select Committee had published its report on the British Film Industry in April, the illustrations on the cover might well have included a still from *The Madness of King George*, so cosily selective were the iconic images of the past that were supposed to frame recommendations for the future. Among them were a tweed-jacketed Kenneth More, the number one box-office favourite in the days when Rank was making films, a brace of runners from *Chariots of Fire*, and Alec Guinness and Dennis Price in *Kind Hearts and Coronets*.

If this was England, then indeed the past looked 'another country', where they did things very differently from 1990s Britain. Yet the committee correctly judged the selling power of this 'national gallery' of cosy stereotypes, and not only to Parliament. Sam Goldwyn Jr had gladly bought it. Goldwyn was the American 'angel' co-financing *The Madness of King George*, though he stipulated that the 'King George III' of Bennett's original title be amended, so as not to confuse Americans who might have wondered how they had come to miss parts I and II of the movie franchise. Goldwyn put up $6 million, three quarters of its budget – along with Channel 4 and Stephen Evans and David Parfitt (Branagh's partners in Renaissance Films).

Almost immediately, Nicholas Hytner left for America. He was to direct a worthy but predictably conceived version of Arthur Miller's *The Crucible* (1996); *The Object of My Desire* (1998), a sensitively made but *longueur*-filled 'relationship' comedy of mix-and-match genders among the thirty-somethings; and *Center Stage* (2000), a ballet-school 'soap'. The declining trajectory of working in an uncongenial industry eventually returned him to Britain and the stage that had launched him. His undoubted talents were thus lost to the industry at a crucial time in its attempt to revive, or at least refresh itself, with Lottery cash.

Playwright Christopher Hampton stepped into his debut directing role at short notice, having scripted *Carrington* for the producers Ronald Shedlo and John McGrath. Shedlo's earlier British films, Jack Gold's *The Reckoning* (1969) and Jim O'Brien's *The Dressmaker* (1988), both scripted by John McGrath, showed him to be one of the few US-born producers who understood that the social scene of provincial Britain could reveal the dynamics of how class formed character and precipitated tragedy. *Carrington* was a much calmer work, in obvious ways a forerunner of the 'literary heritage' films of the early twenty-first century, like *Iris*, *Possession* and *The Hours*; yet in other ways, particularly its overt emphasis on the sexuality of not long deceased historical figures, it challenged the way they had been viewed in their time.

'Post-heritage' quickly became a term in use. It focused on the bohemianism of the Bloomsbury Set, revolving around the artist Dora Carrington and her lover Lytton Strachey (Emma Thompson and Jonathan Pryce). The bizarre homo-hetero-bisexual infatuation of a relationship that could have been weighed down with the baggage of 'heritage' produced enigmatic tensions of character that suggested a meeting of minds, not bodies. Eventually, too many other bodies 'interposed' themselves between these two – to co-opt Strachey's famous choice of phrase in response to the World War One draft board testing his conscientious objector credentials with the enquiry of what he would do if the Hun were about to rape his sister. But if the perspective was 'retro', in performance and psychology it was refreshingly removed from literary embrace.

The third new director, Michael Winterbottom, preferred the American model of the 'road' movie with his calling-card work, *Butterfly Kiss*. He had clearly caught the *folie à deux* infection of murderous young women incubated by Ridley Scott's *Thelma and Louise* and spread by two of 1995's other films: Peter Jackson's *Heavenly Creatures* and Rafal Zielinski's *Fun*. Bleakly landscaped against the moral limbo of an English motorway, sado-masochistic in deed and transgressively unrepentant, *Butterfly Kiss* was American in the way its two vagrant girls become habituated to murder: it was killing to a feminist agenda, not just for a perverse kick – though in enticing a child to be a potential victim it came close to the denatured acts of a Myra Hindley. Though the geography of Middle England lacked the mythologising dimensions of *Thelma and Louise*'s America and therefore kept the film landlocked in its own sordidness, its pathology certainly served notice of provocative new talents on the loose in Winterbottom and his screenwriter Frank Cottrell-Boyce. Whether it intended to demonise women, indict lesbians or demonstrate that men are natural-born lechers and deserve death were questions one asked afterwards – the performances of Saskia

Reeves and Amanda Plummer looked like feral mutations of the cheerily irresponsible girls played by Margi Clarke and Alexandra Pigg in *Letter to Brezhnev* ten years earlier.

One awaited Winterbottom's next film: the surprise was to find it was to be Thomas Hardy's *Jude the Obscure*. Thereafter, each new film he directed, from then to the present, appears selected to afford him the self-discovery of working in new genre: literary classic, Bosnia war reportage, period Western, East End soap opera, Ulster social comedy, glam-rock clubland, overland asylum seeking. Bewildering; at the same time, curiously courageous for a British director.

Mike Leigh hadn't finished his new film, *Secrets and Lies*, in 1995; Terence Davies was in America, fulfilling his love affair with the Hollywood movies that had offered him a dreamland refuge from a violent parent when he was a child in Liverpool and experiencing his second childhood by translating his own memories of those days into the liberating epiphany of his young alter ego in *The Neon Bible*. The film's critical success was to give the genuinely retiring Davies the confidence to work triumphantly on an even larger and trickier American social scene, Edith Wharton's *The House of Mirth*, five years later – an achievement made even more notable by being shot entirely in England.

Peter Chelsom had also moved across the Atlantic, at least in nostalgia, for his new comedy *Funny Bones*, which set some of the same showbiz bones rattling in the closet that he'd opened with his fantasy biopic of the Irish tenor Josef Locke in *Hear My Song*. His trouper this time was the son of a former king of comedy (Jerry Lewis) who 'dies' on stage before his dad and seeks to redeem and reinvent himself by drawing strength (and comedy acts) from his birthplace in Blackpool – Chelsom's own home town. With American money in the film, Chelsom could afford Jerry Lewis and Leslie Caron, a wonderful assortment of old-time seaside acts, and a newcomer, Lee Evans, who proved himself a virtuoso comedian in the post-Goons style. In a better-ordered film, Evans would have been the centre of attention to which his talents as mime and acrobat entitled him, and so been positioned for stardom. But then a less freakish obsession than Chelsom's for old-time vaudeville acts might never have discovered him at all, or known what to do with him. It demonstrates the weaknesses of one-off British film-making that no second movie was developed for Evans once it was evident what talent he brought to his first: and so another choice opportunity for star making was thrown away.

Ken Loach was the most significant director who had a new film ready in 1995 to wave the flag for Britain – a Red Flag, it turned out. He did so memorably with *Land and Freedom*, set in the Spanish Civil War, but suffused with an anger that the years hadn't cooled but calibrated revealingly against the perspective of faith betrayed. The film opened in Liverpool at the deathbed of an obscure, unremarked man, then developed into one long and moving flashback to him as a youth, beginning a journey, both physical and philosophical, from a naive idealist out to change the world, then to a battle-hardened activist and finally to an embittered reject of history. Loach is at his best when the causes he adopts are lost ones. The politics of revolutionary Marxism – scripted by Jim Allen, who else? – were subsumed in human disillusionment as Ian Hart's volunteer with the British Brigade sees the *realpolitik* of Stalinism subverting the Spanish struggle for 'land and freedom', lest it generate a momentum of its own outside the Soviet orbit of influence.

Loach played to his own ideological strength, however: the film's strongest scene was one where the politics of revolution turn, with surprising naturalness, into the agenda of an impassioned parish-pump debate as the whole village, after shooting the priest and seeing off the landlords, hold an impromptu seminar on whether or not to collectivise the farms. In Spanish and English – a co-production, for once, served both languages well – the argument rages back and forth, yet always animate, never didactic. A Spanish passion was exactly what a British film needed. *Land and Freedom* was acclaimed at Cannes.

However, British gratification at Loach's reception at the festival was accompanied by mortification over one of the most embarrassing gaffes ever perpetrated by a distinguished visitor, Stephen Dorrell, the National Heritage Secretary. By now, it was a well-known superstition that Cannes seemed to put a curse on any such office holder who visited the festival. They were shifted to other jobs – occasionally sacked for some private indiscretion – shortly after they had tasted Cannes fleshpots. Stephen Dorrell, answering some innocuous question, referred to the president of that year's festival jury as 'a distinguished Frenchman, Jean Moreau'. 'He' was, in fact, the distinguished actress Jeanne Moreau, of whom Britain's culture representative had apparently never heard. News of the Minister's gaffe zipped along the Croisette like an ignited powder trail and far beyond. It reached Michael Kuhn as he was doing business in his hacienda in the luxurious Hotel du Cap at Eden Roc. He voiced the common British reaction: 'I have given up. What do comments like this make us look like to the rest of the world?' Before the year was over the 'curse' had come true. In a government reshuffle Stephen Dorrell was moved to another ministry; Virginia Bottomley, previously a Health Minister, was appointed in his place. Immediately, she was asked by the media if she knew who Mme Jeanne Moreau was. (She did.) Subsequently, the question became a mischievous 'tick the box' test for the appointee every time this government portfolio changed hands.

Some of the films already mentioned illustrated the deep-rooted British taste for costume drama. This soon precipitated an outbreak of Austen-itis, adaptations for cinema and TV of the Jane Austen canon. But even more symptomatic was British popular culture's half-appalled, half-admiring fascination with thuggery in politics, sport and films: party 'hard men', like the Tories' Michael Portillo or Labour's John Prescott; the rise of Oasis and the Gallagher brothers in the Pop charts; and even the domestic brutality of the Mitchell brothers in the *EastEnders* TV soap. The turnout at the funeral of Ronnie Kray had shown the abiding loyalties of family networks in London's so-called East End, the sentimentality attaching to 'hard cases' and a hankering for 'the good old days' when the Krays and other gangsters kept 'order' in their communities by intimidation and extortion.

Quite a number of the British film industry's craft members, and even acting professionals, came from a cultural milieu whose old neighbourhoods had suffered – as they saw it – from the post-war tide of Caribbean and African immigrants, and later wavelets of East European and Balkan refugees. Film-makers' own cultural contribution to the industry over the next few years reflected this folk-memory loyalty to tight-knit lifestyles based on coercion or even blunter methods of sorting people out. As Andy Medhurst, one of the sharpest commentators on evolving classes in Britain, put it: 'They cut through the conciliatory pieties of post-feminist man.'

The year 1995 saw the rise of yob culture on the British screen, marching in lock-step with that on the soccer pitch and the adulation of film actors who spoke and behaved like 'hard men', and sometimes even possessed the convictions to go with their performances. The *Football Pink*, the gay soccer supporters' newspaper, voted the skinhead player Vinnie Jones and the crop-haired Dennis Wise two of the sexiest players in the game. Jones was to be promoted to supporting roles and enjoy a sort of ersatz stardom as an *über*-thug, in the films that Guy Ritchie was even then devising as his calling-cards.

There had already been films – *The Krays* and *Let Him Have It*, both
referred to – which 'celebrated' East End hoodlums' lives, or made a
show of support for alleged miscarriages of justice, while not denying
audiences the vicarious thrill of watching crimes that led to the hang-
man's appointment. But a film like Philip Davis's *i.d.* was something else
again. Part-financed by BBC TV and part by EU funding, and produced
by Sally Hibbin, a Ken Loach protégée and a pillar of Loach's Parallax
Films production company, it injected its agitprop energy into a contemporary vein of public concern. To say it was about soccer hooliganism
is correct, but only half states its importance. As Medhurst put it, 'It was
about the lure of brutishness and the thinness of the line that divides
approved masculine strength from vilified male thuggishness'.

With the help of a sympathetic barmaid (Saskia Reeves), a pot belly
and bovver boots, a pair of undercover cops (Reece Dinsdale, Richard
Graham) infiltrate the hooligans who travel from match to match to
create turmoil on the stands and in the streets. The cops enjoy an away-
day with 'the firm'. 'Enjoy' is all too apposite. They see something
'more honest' in the display of emotion by the skinheads than in the
manoeuvring and jockeying for promotion among their superiors. The
fictive role turns into the reality. In the end, there's no difference between
a policeman and a born-again Nazi. The law's authoritarian zeal, it is
suggested, succumbs all too easily to the Fascist glamour of the far Right.
Its psychology was not profound and its romanticising of violence was
reprehensible. The girlfriend of one of the cops discovers that his
lovemaking gets rougher as he moves to the Right of the bed: that's as
deep as it gets.

i.d. identified a strain in British movie-making that was to swell over
the next few years until, in the aftermath of Ritchie's *Lock, Stock and
Two Smoking Barrels*, it threatened to become mainstream. If sociology
was weak in *i.d.*'s case, emulation of the genre it fitted was a lure to be
exploited – and it soon was. Channel 4, BBC Films, PolyGram and
British Screen helped finance most of these films.

The sheer range of the 1995 output, while greatly varying in quality,
is the astonishing feature of the year's production. It was the last year
before Lottery financing – and eventually tax breaks – encouraged the
output to increase to an extent that was to make the production machine
appear to be running out of control. And the more films there were, the
narrower the range of subjects and themes they covered. Whatever one
thinks of some of the 1995 releases, there is a sense of diversity about

them. They haven't yet been compressed into the genre formats that financing by a central body, the Arts Council, intent on avoiding risk was going to inflict on the industry that was all too willing to accept public money in order to encourage private investment.

Once the reason for producing a film was mainly – sometimes simply – because the money was there and it had got to be spent, the decline in quality and variety, however sporadic, was swift and dire.

14

Hit the Screen Running

The film industry had successfully lobbied MPs during 1995 to agree that their wares should be eligible for National Lottery funding. Having established the intention and seen it put into practice, producers set to work in 1996 to subvert the principle.

In the beginning, when it was a gleam in Parliament's eye, Lottery cash was to be used for films that would experience difficulty in getting made – 'art-house' films, for want of a less patronising term. This 'topping-up' concept was soon to be known by the hideously bureaucratic term 'additionality' – because it was money used 'in addition' to the inadequate sum that art alone could hope to attract. But for an entrepreneurial industry this fell far short of expectations and needs.

Changes began to be made with surprising speed. This was largely due to the inexperience of those making them. But, more so, it was due to the wily persistence of producers who were to be the beneficiaries of the changes. They had always had the incentive; now they had the means. The unexpectedly huge amounts of gamblers' money was available for recycling into a gambling industry: in its first year alone, the Lottery was to raise £7 billion. A pipe of plenty seemed to have burst; now it was vital to redirect the flow.

Within months, the idea of patronising art was converted into a strategy for subsidising commercial production. The new 'new thing' was not just handouts for individual film-makers but nothing less than the reinvention of the entire business as a miniature version of Hollywood.

The first experimental year of Lottery funding for films was due to end in April 1996. Several months earlier, the job of reconstructing it was begun. If the Arts Council was apprehensive, it must also have experienced relief. Its sole modus operandi had at first been simply to throw money at the industry and see what happened. Though this was often exactly how film-making functioned, it wasn't at all attuned to the way the Council weighed and balanced its resources to reward the

Fine Arts: music, opera, painting, sculpture and a little dabbling in films about artists' work and lives. Commercial films were a 'whole new ball game', to use one of the rackety phrases that the civil servants of Great Peter Street were having to learn to use. Films were hit-and-miss. Films were vulgar. Films were capable of costing a very great deal of money and losing even more.

In April 1996 Lord Gowrie, the Arts Council's chairman, vetoed his own advisory body which wished to give Lottery funding to a £900,000 co-production (by BBC Films and the British Film Institute Production Board) entitled *Love Is the Devil*. It asked for £360,000 of Lottery coin. It was a very freely based biography of the artist Francis Bacon, and dwelt on his homosexuality, sado-masochism and the generally raffish world in which he and his male lovers moved. Gowrie was believed to have rejected the proposed subject out of a concern for the posthumous reputation (and painterly values) of Bacon. If so, then his decision illuminates the vestigial protectionism that such proposed films brought out in the body cultural of the Arts Council. His decision was eventually revoked and the film went ahead. It was one of the few early successes; but, at the start anyhow, sexual excess and gritty social realism were not quantities handled with comfort by the Arts Council.

Its old reliable system of judging applications for funding meant absolutely nothing when film scripts had to be evaluated. In the early days, as mentioned, a ragtag group of freelance 'readers' was employed, at rates of about £5 per report, to guide the decision makers. Scripts that had been round every commercial desk in town, and been turned down over and over again, now found their way, in brand-new binders, to the Council – some actually got made. Market forces were not yet wholly taken on board. How could they be when they were not even understood? The discernible hankering after 'heritage' subjects, apparent in the first bunch of approved film projects, testifies to the Council's nervousness about abandoning its traditional remit: a Shakespeare play, a classic novel, a *tour d'horizon* of England, the English, a movie about the Boat Race, with a thriller about a serial killer thrown in as popular makeweight (perhaps even as moneymaker!) provided it was done with style. After all, hadn't *Kind Hearts and Coronets* had umpteen murders in it and wasn't it a classic?

Such was the thinking of an Establishment quango that had never conceived of the need to 'get down and dirty' – another of those common Hollywood showbiz terms. Civil servants were in charge, attempting to impose a bureaucratic template on an entrepreneurial industry, and quickly realising they had not the competence, nor even the taste for it. As the films part-financed by Lottery cash began to appear, their anxiety to bring order into the business, or better still, share the blame avoidance, was to increase. Early in February 1996 it was announced that Carolyn Lambert, described as 'a film expert from the Department of National Heritage', had been seconded to the Arts Council in order to sort out the chaos. She was wise enough not to try to lay the Midas touch of Lottery bounty on worthy projects and hope for the best. Instead, an equally hallowed, but safer, means of enlightenment was adopted: a report. The work of many hands was more in tune with Council thinking than relying on a single golden finger. The Spectrum Report, as it was to be known, had to be ready by the end of April, for the start of the Lottery's second year. It was delivered on 3 May 1996. But already its recommendations were being pre-empted by a much stronger body of lobbyists.

The Producers Alliance for Cinema and Television (PACT) now took Lottery funding and ran with it to where it wished to see it lodged – in the industry's own pockets. Among PACT's working party were Nik Powell, Simon Relph and Timothy Burrell, who had taken over from the Puttnams and Attenboroughs. They were influential in floating their ideas on to Spectrum's pages. The core proposal was to use Lottery funds to create what were called 'mini-studios', power groups of producers, distributors and sales agents. These consortiums would each be given a 'franchise', otherwise known as a wad of money, that would last them for several years. During this solvent span they could call down sums of money from it and invest them in projects of their own choice as 'soft equity' – not absolutely needing to be repaid, though hopeful enough of success not to have actually to consider the dismal prospect of losing it. After five years, they reasoned, there might be a dozen such mini-studios. The Lottery money, of course, would not be the sole means of support, but be used as seed capital capable of attracting the succulent private investment that the industry had always lacked. When the subsidy had to end, they would be well-nourished, full-blooded, flushed with success and quite capable of standing alone.

Chris Auty, then part of Jeremy Thomas's Recorded Picture Company, was quoted as saying, 'There's scarcely a producer in London who isn't expecting to form or join a consortium.' He added, 'The problem is going to be finding people with the same taste as us.' Nik

Powell, late of Palace Pictures, now incorporated with his partner, Stephen Woolley, as Scala Pictures, also showed a characteristic caution about taking partners on board: 'Scala would prefer not to have to link up with anybody. If they make it conditional for people to have to link up with each other, then we'd have to make a decision whether to make a bid at all.' This sounded rather like a man with a cigar in his mouth disdaining to pick up a cigarette butt off the street.

Duncan Kenworthy, producer of *Four Weddings* and one of the few who had drunk deeply at the box office and had no need to slake his thirst with art, was also quoted by *Variety*'s reporter Adam Dawtrey: 'The one thing we've got going for us, because of the neglect over the years, is that we are driven by market forces, and we haven't got that awful subsidy culture you see in other countries.'

If certain of these remarks sound a little ungrateful in the context of the proffered riches, it may be attributed to the natural suspicion of people welcoming unexpected riches, but wondering where the catch was – more ancient cultures had had the same trouble with Greeks who came bearing gifts.

One man not altogether enthused by the proposals was Simon Perry, head of British Screen Finance. The reason was pretty clear. Seeing other little 'film banks' being set up all around his own government-funded edifice was like seeing the neighbourhood go to pot, even if it was a money pot. Perry had a point. He foresaw how Lottery money, by inflating the possibilities of film-making, would drive off the screen the cheap, intelligent British movies that international audiences wanted to see. His early opinion is worth quoting, for it was an absolutely accurate prediction: 'What they're doing is releasing pure heroin on to the street rather than the diluted methadone that everyone's used to. So they had best be sure they get it right.'

Most of the capital's producers did not care about 'right', they wanted it 'now'. To them, the advantages were as clear as a promissory note on a bearer bond: it would speed up the whole process of getting Lottery money. It would allow a much larger bag of money to be spent more quickly than the Arts Council's unwieldy committee system; at present, fourteen nail-biting stages had to be endured before the applicant was notified whether he had got the money. Some producers argued that franchises should be given to distributors, with producers attached. It would also be an added incentive for investors, who might welcome the chance of getting their money back (and then some) more quickly if

they were linked to the side of the industry where money was traditionally made first (and kept). But few producers were so altruistic. A
lump sum in their hands would enable them to make their movies; and
since they only ate when working, that lump couldn't come soon
enough. Only one fly remained in the cream: the Arts Council would
still be empowered with the final decision on whether to greenlight a
film or not. It was prohibited by law from devolving this decision on to
the producers: it must still make the final decision itself on every film
supported by the Lottery.

One large group – the largest in the industry, actually – that failed to
make its voice heard were the British-based outposts of the major
Hollywood producer-distributor companies. To them, Lottery money
threw an element of uncertainty into the well-protected market for their
own films. They did not need it themselves, but looked askance at its
existence. What would it do if it actually did transform the British
film industry? Would it put muscle into British film-makers' arms and
embolden them to claim their entitlement to a larger share of the market
now that they had the goods to sell? Not one American company went
on record for or against the proposals. *Variety*'s headline might broadcast
the excitement in terms typical of the paper's wayward lexicon – 'WHOLE
LOTTO SHAKIN' IN BRITISH FILM FUNDING' – but the Americans in
the midst of their British brothers' new-found plenty scarcely gave it a
toss. They did not apply for a share of the windfall, since they would
then have been committed to public accountability over how they spent
it. The worst nightmare would thus happen: being obligated to open
their books and, maybe, have to answer questions about what 'net profit'
actually meant. It was tantamount to going into court and giving
evidence on oath. From Hollywood's earliest days, truth-telling was
regarded as a slapdash business practice and disclosure of commercial
information was an act of supreme folly. They already had their own
Lottery – film-making, it was called – and knew how to play the numbers
game. So they held back and, contrary to the polite protocol when
guests came to tea, allowed 'the family' to rush towards the table and
gobble their fill.

Virginia Bottomley, like earlier culture ministers, wasn't long in charge
of the arts, but it was the general election in 1997 that removed her, not
the 'curse of Cannes' that had fallen on quite a few ministers paying
courtesy calls on the 1996 film festival. Mrs Bottomley certainly cut a
more stylish figure on the Croisette than her predecessors: navy shoes,

navy stockings, navy skirt, a jacket in the Queen Mother's favourite powder blue and a small handbag co-ordinated in the same navy tone strung over her shoulder on a slender gold chain: just enough of Hermès to offset Britannia. French bystanders speculated who the tall slim blonde might be.

'C'est Emma Thompson,' said one.

'Non,' cried another excitedly, 'c'est Vanessa – Vanessa Redgrave.'

She gave no formal press conference but attended the out-of-competition screening of *Trainspotting*.

Why was she in Cannes? (Obvious question.)

To support the British film industry. (Obvious reply.) Now that it was flourishing, she added, due to Lottery money. (Not so obvious.)

Her questioner persisted, while her 'minder', Sir Sydney Samuelson, recently appointed head of the British Film Commission which had flown the Minister down to the Côte d'Azur, tried to detach her from the *Evening Standard*'s vexatious interrogator who had stalked her along the seafront.

But why was she supporting by her presence a film like *Trainspotting*, which was in trouble for advocating a soft line on hard drugs?

'My daughter told me it was the one to see. It's made £10 million, hasn't it?'

What did her daughter think of it?

Mrs Bottomley began to look as if the proposed new bill to make stalking a chargeable offence couldn't come soon enough. 'I shouldn't dream of revealing my daughter's confidence.'

Well, then, what did the Minister think?

'It was hard-hitting and harrowing. It reminded me of my past.'

Did the Minister do drugs?!

A quick correction: 'No, but I was a magistrate for twelve years and then Health Secretary. I know about these things.' Well, *that* was all right.

The TV people, drawn now by the crowds surrounding 'la vedette anglaise', asked Mrs Bottomley to stand against a palm tree, as if a touch of the exotic were needed to prove that she really had come to Cannes. A split second too late she realised there was a film poster on the tree – for *Trainspotting*. Oh well, it was British and it *had* taken £10 million.

Trainspotting (1996) was indeed the turn-of-the-year sensation in Britain. It came in on the adrenalin rush already supplied by *Shallow Grave* and the boisterous production stirring in new Scottish cinema, so much more alive, physically as well as verbally, than its restrained and tasteful neighbour south of the border. Its audacity lay not only in the violently expressionist imagery generated by drug taking – a baby crawling across the ceiling, an addict ingested bodily down a lavatory bowl while in pursuit of the suppositories ejected from his rectum and then swimming among the turds in a faecal dream-sea – but in the frankness with which its makers (director Danny Boyle, screenwriter John Hodge – from the Irvine Welsh novel – producer Andrew Macdonald) refused to condemn all such chemical experience.

They were prudent, professing to be anti-moralist rather than pro-drugs – especially when they went to New York in August to promote the film – but a film fashioned to produce the sensation of a continual 'high', which abjured the customary 'downer', was unmistakably on the side of experimentation. 'It may screw you up, but it's a hell of a ride on the way down.' This wasn't the usual language of 'youth' cinema, which gave the jolt but followed it up with the caution. In the words of Renton (Ewan McGregor in the performance that defined his talents but also set him an unmatchable standard), 'Take the best orgasm you ever had, multiply it by a thousand and you're still nowhere near it.' The movie-makers were more than that: they were lobbyists for the good times – for the pulse that quickens when the vein is pumped. *Time Out*'s Tom Charity called it, accurately, 'the first British film of the Nineties generation to speak to the way we live here and now'. He could have added '. . . and die', but didn't.

Trainspotting divided people who saw it, but then age had already done that: youth saw it as a public-service announcement that not all drug taking was a bad trip; their elders as an irresponsible incitement to drop down dead unless, of course, you had the charmed lives of Renton and his four junkie buddies whose escapades hit the street running – literally, after a spot of shoplifting – with Renton's voice-over narration jeeringly rejecting all moralistic virtues in favour of substance abuse.

Twenty-five years earlier *A Clockwork Orange* had caused a public furore for much the same anarchic defiance: *Trainspotting* pushed Kubrick's tone and style even further into the black, while short, ugly Scottish expletives – 'shite' nationalistically standing in for the Anglo-Saxon 'fuck' – kept the dialogue grounded in the dirt. Even such effluvia seemed to embody the animate malice of those who exuded them. Excrement hit a family breakfast table in a massive in-your-face assault on bourgeois conformity; ecstasy, too, in the good-times opiate of Iggy

Pop, Pulp, Blur, Primal Scream, Elastica and Underworld, carried the message to the credulous young.

Kubrick, who saw the film soon after its release, noted with wry amusement how closely it followed the trajectory of his own film, right down to Renton's last-minute 'salvation' when, in a retake of his opening manifesto, he declares his new allegiance to the values he spurned: 'I'm a bad person, but that's going to change ... I'm cleaning up ... I'm moving on ... I'm going straight and choosing life.' Such was the personal velocity of the movie up to then that this turning point wasn't viewed as a sell-out but a pit stop. But if the film had a frailty, it was here: there wasn't the slightest irony in this Pauline conversion, the way there was in *A Clockwork Orange* when another Alex – the Junior Satan of inner-city wrongdoing played by Malcolm McDowell – declares himself 'cured all right' and enlists as a government rent-a-thug to seal the alliance between the individual's love of violence and the state's espousal of it.

Kubrick's film made one think: Boyle's film simply made one puke. Kubrick and I watched *Trainspotting* together – we both came out feeling that, stirred though we might be, there were more lethal substances on which to OD than a voyeuristic tour of the drugs scene. But for the generation that came to it and returned to it for another and yet another fix of the 'extreme' life – making instant stars of McGregor and Robert Carlyle, cast as Begbie, the bar-room psychopath, never happier than in the scrum with a broken beer bottle in his hand – *Trainspotting* was one of those experiences that feel like rites as one undergoes them.

Made for a mere £1,550,000 budget and shot in seven weeks, its success almost everywhere needed no 'hype' to sustain it. It had 'cred' in every country where there was a drugs problem – in short, the world. It was neither socio-realistic, nor hyper-literary: simply rebelliously sensate. In America kids viewed the five junkies as 'hip, nihilistic and harbouring a grudge against the Man', as *New York Magazine*'s critic put it, adding, 'It looks like nothing else out of Britain in living memory.' In one word, it had 'heat'. Now all one had to do was find fuel to feed the flames.

It looked, for a brief moment anyhow, as if Scotland would provide this as *Trainspotting* coincided with Scottish nationalism peaking in politics and producing a sense of 'gael force' in popular culture too. Even a foreigner like Lars von Trier had drawn on the lack of joy in a Scottish Presbyterian town for *Breaking the Waves* and subverted it with the eroticism his strangely mystical film released in Emily Watson's raw performance as the wife-turned-whore. Scottish cinema suddenly seemed about to become the new European art-house trend.

Unfairly overshadowed by *Trainspotting*'s advance notices was the new film, *Small Faces*, directed by Gillies MacKinnon and co-written with his brother Billy. About the fortunes of three restless, fatherless boys and a widowed mother vainly trying to keep the lid on her brood's hormones. Its setting in late-Sixties Glasgow, where backstreet tailors routinely put a razor pocket in a young gent's new suit and teenage tribes mustered their forces for war in fortress tenements separated by puddles as wide as the sea, it stripped proletarian Scotland down to the raw and bleeding essentials. Where a film-maker like Terence Davies recounted his cloistered life of misery indoors, the MacKinnons, with the raw confidence of autobiography, presented a coming-of-age fable rich in details of memory and horrifying invention: the stabbed body dragged over an ice rink leaving a scarlet wake behind it; the kid biding his time with his killer's dirk at a cinema Saturday-morning sing-song while the voices rise and fall around him. The film's primitive strength came from character under pressure – Scottish character. From the perspective of South-East England, *Small Faces* felt, sounded, like a foreign film. It was produced by BBC Scotland and the Glasgow Film Fund.

In Wales, too, the Celts were rising – against their own people, the so-called Taffia, or high-culture merchants, whose view of Wales as a land of song, faux Druids and green valleys corresponded to the Scottish promotion of tartan and shortbread: export products that were past their shelf life. As well as a Welsh version of Chekhov's *Uncle Vanya*, directed by and starring Anthony Hopkins, and released in August 1996, three films were being shot in Wales that summer. Though all three were in the English language, Kim Howells, MP for Pontypridd and later a Films Minister in the second Labour administration, condemned what he called 'the very small cultural elite' that didn't speak Welsh but seemed to run the principality.

Marc Evans's *House of America* was set among the impoverished youth of South Wales. Though derived from a psycho-drama stage play by Edward Thomas, it opted for the opened-out lyricism of a Kerouac-type 'road' film, an *Easy Rider* whose heroes lose themselves in the lure of the American Dream. Kevin Allen's *Twin Town*, set in Port Talbot, with a £1.5 million budget fully financed by PolyGram, reached into American urban melodrama, family vengeance and local drop-outs doing drugs, joyriding and running rings round cops. Andrew Macdonald and Danny Boyle, the *Trainspotting* duo, served as executive producers. The film was self-confessedly cut from the same social fabric as *Trainspotting*, which had inspired Allen when he was on his fifth draft of *Twin Town*. And Julian Richards's *Darklands* laid claim to be the Welsh *Wicker Man*, with its story of serial murders, neo-pagans, revivalist conspiracies and – producer Paul Brooks hastily reassured questioners – 'the issue of Welsh nationalism'.

These films all had genre ambitions and their weakness was failing to transcend this Hollywood template; their value, though, derived from the new talents that the cultural rush of nationalism assisted. In a word that was soon to acquire an all-purpose vogue, applicable to everything from soccer to politics, it looked as if Wales had become 'sexy'. Certainly British film-making had become 'contemporary'.

It was too early – it was *always* too early – to say that costume drama was dead, but the film-making groups now stirring in the regions, stimulated by a little local financing and the promise of greater subsidies to come (maybe) from the Lottery, were anxious at all costs to be modern, to create more overtly 'entertaining' films, to include recognisable daily reality but not to seek out the miserabilism that daunted audiences and saw a downturn in box-office receipts. 'Wrap a genre envelope around social issues so that it will be understandable in Korea,' was how Adam Dawtrey summed it all up. All very well, but unless the momentum was maintained by films that made news as well as money, the nationalistic initiatives tended to dwindle, the local confidence to ebb.

Thus Pilgrim, a Newcastle-based company, was an early recipient of Lottery cash to produce an urban thriller entitled *Downtime* – rather ominously, two more planned films were entitled *Killing Time* and *Primetime* – which strove to work issues of unemployment and social breakdown into a love story about a couple who get trapped in a lift when the lift shaft catches fire. Unsurprisingly, the film did not catch fire; the prospect of fitting Geordie characters into genre plots put a dampener on regional zest.

The general euphoria around in 1996 peaked with the win of the Palme d'or at Cannes by Mike Leigh's *Secrets and Lies* – the first British film in a decade to do so. Produced by Channel 4 and the French-owned Ciby 2000, based in London, some saw it as a retreat from the radical change of emphasis and tone that his raw and violent *Naked* had represented. It was Leigh's thirteenth film – apart from Alan Bennett, no other artist had worked with such consistent success in every medium: cinema, stage and television. And save for Loach, no director had extracted from contemporary life the essential looks and feelings of the class that caught his sympathies. Leigh had earned the right to rework characteristic material – dysfunctional families and bleak lives masked by the smiles that the Lowry-like clients of Timothy Spall's commercial photographer put on their woebegone faces as he does their studio portraits. Spall, in a lower-key performance than usual, is the fulcrum of an unusually fairly balanced Mike Leigh film, neither caricatural nor patronising – a familiar charge by now, but one that Leigh's defenders convincingly dismissed as being 'the discomfort of the British confronted by the distorting mirror of their own snobberies'.

Secrets and Lies included a class divide running through Spall's family, but without class antipathies to be exploited. And it included two elements, one new and the other infrequent in Leigh's work: race and the quality of hope. Into the film's circle of lower-middle-class people concealing their pain within unfulfilled lives, it introduced a catalytic stranger, Hortense, a professionally unqualified, upwardly mobile, articulate young Caribbean-Brit (Marianne Jean-Baptiste) who's successfully traced her blood mother: she turns out to be Spall's scatterbrained but benevolent sister Cynthia (Brenda Blethyn) who somehow 'forgot' she'd had the child from a one-night stand. An unlikely event; yet such is Cynthia's transition from disbelief, rejection and grudging acceptance to genuine affection for her unlikely child that the sequence of the two meeting in a café and drawing closer physically and intimately was a rare moment of high tenderness in Leigh's oeuvre. Blethyn took the 'Best Actress' prize at Cannes, deservedly.

Mrs Bottomley's visit to Cannes was not timed to allow her to see Mike Leigh carry off the premier award of the festival. But her call to the industry to foster 'heritage films' – an exception being made for electorally useful youth-cult films like *Trainspotting* – would have been better met by Michael Winterbottom's *Jude*, which was shown in the Directors' Fortnight section. This version of Hardy's *Jude the Obscure* – 'Obscure' had been dropped since, apart from Buñuel's *That Obscure Object of Desire*, it wasn't a word that sat well on the ads – was one of the first tranche of Lottery-funded films. It attempted to lighten the deterministic pessimism of Hardy's tale of a working-class boy's cruelly defeated aspirations to better himself, yet remained an intelligent approximation to the novel. But as a cinematic experience it was a 'downer'. The sort of elective affinities that Truffaut had drawn on for *Jules et Jim* failed to work their free-spirited magic on the masochistic relationships between Christopher Eccleston's Jude and Kate Winslet as a cousin of surprisingly advanced nineteenth-century habits (cigarettes) and phrases ('Isn't that rather confrontational?'). The players lacked compatible chemistry.

The production design looked as if it had been purpose-built to please Mrs Bottomley. It was an artful jigsawing of bits and pieces of national heritage of England and Scotland into Hardy's fictitious Wessex, a place of populous country towns and isolated hamlets, though both unfortunately often in the rain belt. Socially, though, it was all vaguer, more questionable, trapped between literary fidelity and a deluded straining after modernity. It was a worthy film but a dull one. I was glad Winterbottom had had the chance to make it, for its sympathies for a loser were obviously near his own heart and mind, but the main interest it aroused was where was he going next?

Heritage cinema in 1996 fought a rearguard offensive against the contemporary explosion. Miramax's US–UK production of *Emma* gave Gwyneth Paltrow her early and (so far) enduring taste for English-accented roles and almost rounded out the Jane Austen canon, which now included the Ang Lee–Emma Thompson *Sense and Sensibility* and two BBC television productions of *Persuasion* (by Roger Michell, released as a theatrical film), and *Pride and Prejudice*.

Oliver Parker made a very unsure version of *Othello*, casting an authentic black star, Laurence Fishburne, as the Moor. Unfortunately, he came across as the wrong shade of black – ghetto blackness, more of a home boy than Venetian nobility. Kenneth Branagh's Iago was one of his best performances, a career-wise and dangerous NCO with officer-class attitude. It was certainly a change to have an Othello who looked shiftier than Iago but no help to the play.

The most radical reinvention of Shakespeare was the Richard Loncraine–Ian McKellen modern-dress version of *Richard III*, situated in a mid-Thirties England such as it might have been had Hitler's writ run across the Channel and enticed the Windsors into fascistic trappings. McKellen was superb: less deformed than the customary Crookback, more like a Goebbels who's conquered his physical disabilities (in his case a club-foot) and makes a conjuring act out of the dozens of things one dexterous arm and hand can do, his Richard sported the dashing moustaches of an inter-war Hollywood star, the charm of a dissolute

Rex Harrison and a mocking – sometimes self-mocking – malevolence. From first to last, one was caught in the grip of a demon king.

The smell of money on the wind, some of it actually blowing into film-makers' pockets, stimulated several hibernating companies with famous pasts behind them to awake, arise and walk again. The remnants of Goldcrest, salvaged in 1987 by Brent Walker, now announced plans for half a dozen films a year with budgets up to $4.5 million: property, facility rentals and film libraries were the financial collateral. HandMade Films, bought for $8.4 million by Canada's Paragon Films after the split between Denis O'Brien and ex-Beatle George Harrison, actually shot two films in 1995, its first for five years. Now it planned a period mystery-romance, *Photographing Fairies*, with Lottery money. Zenith, sold by Carlton TV, had merged with another independent production house, Portman, which in turn broke away and left Zenith owned by a financial venture capital fund called TEAM. Active again, it was readying *Velvet Goldmine* (with Ewan McGregor) and *The Wisdom of Crocodiles* (with Lottery funding). Initial Films, which had produced *Sid and Nancy*, *Hidden Agenda* and a handful of others under Eric Fellner, until he broke away and joined Working Title, had *Trojan Eddie*, an Irish-based Channel 4-financed drama about the travelling people, which Gillies MacKinnon had directed with Richard Harris and Stephen Rea. Now it had struck a deal which brought *Love and Death on Long Island* on to its slate (with Lottery funding).

Even Rank was stirring on the morgue slab where British film-makers had consigned it. Andrew Teare, its new chief executive designate, the former boss of English China Clay who was already on Rank's board, succeeded Michael Gifford when he retired in April. Fred Turner, who headed Rank Film Distributors, 'linked' a deal with Granada Films to co-produce a half-dozen low-budget ($1.5 million) comedies over the next two years. It also fully financed the new film, *Lawn Dogs*, to be produced by Duncan Kenworthy, still warm with the success of *Four Weddings*.

Several such deals suggested a hope that the film-maker's most recent success would rub off on his next potential one. A three-picture deal was also done between Rank and Orion, the rump of the former United Artists, though the subjects would scarcely enrich British film-making: *Eight Heads in a Duffle Bag*, from the producers of *Dumb and Dumber*; a comedy from the future 'gross-out' merchants, the Farrelly brothers; and a Drew Barrymore actioner. Rank's film-making reversal of attitude (if not yet of fortune) may have been encouraged by the removal of Gifford's iron hand. Moreover, its production juices had been stimulated by unexpected success: a $14 million American film in which it had taken a deep breath and invested $7 million, *Fried Green Tomatoes at the Whistle Stop Café*, a comedy-drama set in Deep South backwoods, grossed $150 million in foreign markets. Unfortunately, instead of viewing this as a lucky one-off, it became the standard against which subsequent Rank film investments were measured.

Turner said of his new policy, 'It doesn't alter the fact that our discipline [*sic*] isn't going to change. We're still not convinced that spending $40 million to $100 million on a single film makes sense. . . . It would be crazy for us to go above $25 million.' Films in this range were considered by Hollywood to lie in the Bermuda Triangle of the business; without immediately attractive production values (stars, locations, action sequences), their distribution costs usually ran ahead of their box-office grosses. Rank was keen on getting back into the business, but not mad keen. Film scripts were read by Turner in London, while a Hollywood film consultancy, the Steel Co., represented Rank for acquiring films worldwide. Philip Clement, recently appointed head of Rank's TV and Film in New York, had come from the technical side of the company's laboratory and video services in Illinois. His brief was to 'grow the company'. Whether he would have succeeded, given time, it is hard to say; for time was already now being called for the Man With the Gong on Rank's trademark logo.

Gifford had been a prodigious generator of cash in his last year at Rank, mainly through the sale of assets, and a record year in cinema-going and the related leisure industry. The film and entertainment division had a good year in 1996, with sales of $998 million and operating profit up by 24 per cent to $135 million. But industry outsiders had their eye on what they considered the underused assets of Rank Film Distributors, in particular the company's huge film library (even though large tranches of it had already been rented out to other companies) as well as its theatrical distribution and international sales arms. Michael Grade, who quit as Channel 4's chief executive in mid 1996, to run his late uncle Bernard Delfont's First Leisure empire, was tipped as a potential buyer. He denied it, having his eye on an even richer prize, Pinewood Studios.

Over at Shepperton, which Ridley and Tony Scott had bought two years earlier with consortium finance, production stages had been 'brought up to speed with California'. Studios, considered white elephants a few years before, were again hot properties. A total of 121 films were made by British and foreign (mostly US) companies using British studios or locations in 1996, compared with seventy-five the year before, fifty-three of them wholly British, three times the total in 1995. Inward investment rose by two thirds, from £394 million in 1995 to £655 million. But such growth was fuelled by the big spenders from America such as *101 Dalmatians*, *Evita*, *Mission: Impossible*, attracted by a stable dollar-sterling exchange rate. Demand for studio space was so strong that even the new James Bond had to be turned away from Leavesden studios, the converted airfield, which the new *Star Wars* was occupying, and was forced into a converted warehouse near Radlett airfield. Pinewood was booked for Kubrick's *Eyes Wide Shut* and a new version of *The Day of the Jackal*.

The plethora of new TV channels – Channel 5 began in 1996 – needing 'product' increased the demand for low-budget movies. Few noticed – or, if they did, thought it good manners to comment – that all this was encouraging an oversupply of British films. As noted, 52.5 per cent of them failed to reach the screen in 1995 within a year of completion; by mid 1996 an estimated 46 per cent looked headed for oblivion. Either the American-owned circuits were squeezing them out, or else many of them should never have been made in the first place. At this time one begins to see the increasing momentum of what would come to be, within the next five years, the biggest trend in British filmmaking – the making of films not necessarily for public entertainment but for private investors' tax write-downs. If the patient looked healthy, that flush in his cheeks was actually a high fever.

It was at this moment, on 2 August 1996, that the government published the report of an advisory committee headed by a former Treasury mandarin, Sir Thomas Middleton, which had been set up in 1995 to formulate proposals for film financing and to involve City investors. The ubiquitous Charles Denton, whose job as Head of Drama at BBC TV had fallen short of expectations, was a member; he was also a former chairman of PACT, the producers' association, and now chaired the Arts Council's Lottery Fund Advisory Panel, in effect the body which picked the films to be funded. Another PACT apparatchik, John Woodward, also sat on the Middleton committee – just three years later he would be appointed chief executive of the Film Council set up by the new Labour government. Thus the proponents of public funding were well placed to advocate it to the Department of National Heritage and, crucially, the Treasury. They carried the original Lottery initiative to new extremes of benefit to an industry and effectively drowned out any opposition that was querying why film-making should be so privileged above the other entertainment arts and crafts.

The core of the report recommended the creation of up to four film franchises which would be awarded on a commercial basis – note, no mention of cultural values – in the spring of 1997. Reports had it that some committee members urged the creation of *seven* franchises, possibly feeling that three or even four wouldn't be sufficient for the number of snouts all jostling for position round the public feeding troughs. Modesty prevailed. Charles Denton was elated. 'We now have in our hands the means to begin to reverse the fragmented and ad hoc nature of film production in this country and I am absolutely convinced that the industry will embrace this opportunity.' Like an open moneybag, he neglected to add.

15

Fool's Gold

It was as if a gold mine was being raffled. The impatiently awaited announcement came on 22 October 1996. The National Lottery was to fund four film commercial franchises, each lasting six years, awarded on a competitive basis the following spring. Winners must have a corporate basis: partnership was a key criterion. In other words not just producers, but distributors, exhibitors, financiers, sales agents should sink their historic distrust of each other: lions lie down with lambs, snakes with pussy-cats, in a cross-species amnesty of financial probity, artistic aspiration and long-term stability. Even foreign-owned companies and broadcasters might apply. Did this mean Hollywood majors? It did, if they had a British base (which they had). Did it include BBC, Channel 4, ITV? Yes, they could have a stake, too. 'We are trying to let everyone in, provided they have profit-distributing objectives,' declared an Arts Council spokesman piously, omitting, perhaps prudently, anything about 'loss-sharing obligations'.

Each consortium could name the amount it needed for its six-year business plan, though the maximum any one of them could hope for over the six-year term would be around £35 million. In case this incited applicants to go to the limit, they were required to bring 'matching finance' to the table. Even at this stage the Arts Council's secretary-general, Mary Allen, was insisting that Lottery money shouldn't replace funding for films that 'would be made anyhow'. It was about 'additionality' (that beloved bureau-speak phrase): to top up film projects that wouldn't, or couldn't, be made without public subsidy. Needless to say, this piety was among the first things to be abandoned in the subsequent gold rush.

The notion that Lottery-funded films should assist a cultural agenda – i.e. 'be good for us', as Geoff Andrew sniffed in *Time Out* – was speedily jettisoned in the unabashed leap into commercial cinema. Yet it was 'commercial' only in the sense that it was 'not (necessarily) art'. 'We have no idea', said Ms Allen, 'what kind of return we should expect to get on investments.' Even what constituted 'net profit' was to be left until later. Had a chief executive of a public company uttered such sentiments, investors might well have melted away. But the investors in this case were the British public, whose 'benefit', as defined by Lottery legislation, would ultimately be as difficult to define as 'net profit' in an industry where 'remoteness of profits due' was more likely to recur on individuals' payment statements.

By November 1996 *Variety* reported, 'Lottery franchises ignite UK film frenzy.' The entire industry seemed engaged in a mating dance, 'trying to find their ideal partners to bid for the four pots of Lottery gold ... Everyone is flirting with everyone else, and no one's yet ready to make a firm commitment.' The advantages of the franchises were more visible in the abstract than they were to prove in reality: among them was the hope that the bundles of diverse interests brought together in the hope of winning a franchise would stay together even if they lost. Not so: almost all of them held a consolation party, then reverted to their old competitive ways. Simon Perry, of British Screen Finance, said, 'If just two or three [of these "families"] become mini-majors, committed to working in Europe, providing an alternative to what Hollywood provides, that'd be a tremendous triumph.' It would indeed – except that, once constituted, the franchises would feel like 'Little Hollywoods'. Europe – Perry's favourite partner: co-financing, he said, had gone from almost nothing in 1991 to 40–50 per cent of his investments now – would not prove to be the alternative model for franchise winners. Truly independent film-makers would not wish to take cherished projects along to the franchise winners who might be out of sympathy with them and, anyhow, would have to submit them to the Arts Council's advisory panel to be second-guessed if they were to get the go-ahead.

More obvious pitfalls were the stretching of talent too thinly, creating resentful losers who would feel sidelined by their nouveaux riches competitors, inflated costs which had risen to meet instant wealth – and sheer underhandedness. *Time Out* reported that producers not involved in potential franchise bids were being canvassed to allow films they were developing to be included in the bidders' slate, 'even though there is no guarantee they will be put into production'. And then, Perry added in the tones of a man who sensed his own operation might be imperilled by the new kids on the block, 'if you analyse the Lottery franchise

scheme brutally, it's not *that* great a business opportunity, because as a
production company you don't get to keep the money. You get to apply
for it on a fast-track basis, use it, and if you're successful, you send it
back to the Lottery. You can then use it again, but that's not quite the
same thing as having it in your own company to let it grow.' True, true
... still it was nice to have it in one's own pocket for a bit. Paying it
back was, well, a matter for hope: the fact would be that losses would
be considered 'soft loans' – public money one would like to see coming
back, but not attracting the death penalty if lost.

Charles Denton's advisory panel had been awarding millions over the
past year – £22.6 million invested in forty-three films by October 1996,
to be exact. Yet the Arts Council only set up a dedicated Film Department
within its Lottery division towards the end of 1996 when 'franchise fever'
reached a pitch requiring more than a bedside visit. 'I am responsible for
managing the process of assessing the franchising applications,' Carolyn
Lambert, ex-Department of Trade and Industry, wrote to me. Industrious
though Ms Lambert undoubtedly was, it's doubtful if her capabilities had
been honed on the hard grind of a business as chancy, spendthrift,
cut-throat and irrational as film-making. In short, a great folly was being
prepared, and marketed under the auspices of a patriarchal and patrician
body unequipped to judge its effectiveness.

An American film, *Jerry Maguire*, contained one brutal line of dialogue
that became a catchphrase in the Lottery frenzy around this time as the
greedy sports star in it utters it repeatedly: 'Show me the money.'
Beneath all the fine aspirations in business plans that were now being
written and rewritten – more times, often, than film scripts were – to
catch the application deadline of 26 February 1997, this was the shibboleth shared by the contenders. By 16 December 1996, 176 groups had
registered their intention to bid for a franchise: the final tally, by the
February date, was reduced to thirty-seven, comprising well over a
hundred separate partner companies, of which eighteen went 'public'
with their intentions; the rest stayed under wraps. While the Arts
Council assessors now went into purdah until the winners' names were
announced – originally scheduled for 24 May but brought forward so as
to use the platform of the Cannes Film Festival on 14 May – the
applicants could take heart from other signs of the confidence generated
in the new era of Lottery money.

Brits who had gone to Hollywood years earlier to make their careers
there began returning: economic migrants anxious, now, to share the

zeal of the stay-at-homes and, if possible, the pickings. These 'prodigal children', as Adam Dawtrey called them, included agents, actors and producers, all seeing the 'uptight London' they remembered in the Seventies now transformed into 'a place of opportunity and creative vitality'. The invigorating new British cinema (*Trainspotting* was often named); a new generation attuned to 'commercial' subjects; 'fiscal flexibility' (aka tax breaks) were the cited reasons, though £100 million of Lottery coin going begging had its magnetic pull, too.

Charles Finch, son of the actor Peter Finch, who had left Britain in 1983, was sent back expressly by his William Morris Agency to shake up the London office, bring American tactics to production deals, and transplant the Hollywood trend of agents becoming 'packagers' and assembling all the main constituents of a deal with a major studio, from raising development funding to 'kick starting' projects, to casting from among their own writer, actor and director clients, and thus pocket what was a producer's fee in all but name. Morgan Mason, son of James Mason, arrived home to revive Korda's London Films, which had been bought by the millionaire Swedish entrepreneur (and owner of Head skis and tennis rackets) Johann Elias; David Heyman, whose father John had been agent to Burton and Taylor, spent eighteen years in the US and now was home with a 'housekeeping' deal from Warner Bros to find subjects. 'When I left Britain in 1979,' he said, 'there was this pervasive nihilism, but now in the film business and beyond there's greater optimism and openness.' Finch said, 'This is an opportunity to make and finance British movies that will play in North America,' a seemingly innocuous statement, but one with ominous undertones suggesting cultural separatism might have to conform to 'universal themes' established by the Hollywood product.

Barnaby Thompson, who had spent several useful but undistinguished years at Paramount with Lorne Michaels producing *Wayne's World* and *The Coneheads*, blamed 'the tremendous sniffiness [in England] about making films for people to see' which had driven him abroad to those populist ventures. He recalled getting a letter from a Channel 4 executive saying, 'Sorry, this project is too commercial for us.' Now 'commercial' was the touchstone word. Mason talked of London offering a 'civilised' life – he was soon installed in select Church Row, Hampstead, with a nanny for the children – while Finch admitted, 'I wanted to live in London with a nice house in the country.' These names were worth dwelling on. Their views, though self-interested (and why not?)

represented the transforming power of money on the production scene. Some of them benefited almost immediately, getting Lottery grants for individual films and, in Thompson's case, to help revive Ealing Studios; others were even more fortunate. Heyman 'found' the Harry Potter books, made the deal with Warner Bros and thus initiated a franchise that was soon vastly to exceed all the film funding put together in the various Lottery permutations. Their upbeat pronouncements on stepping off liner or aircraft were being amplified by the changes that had indeed come to the capital in the mid Nineties.

The return of the natives coincided accidentally with the return of the 'Swinging London' phenomenon of the Sixties. New architectural structures were rising after the recession at the end of the Eighties; new or newly fashionable restaurants (The Avenue in St James's, Daphne's, the Oxo Tower, Vendôme and the Zen and Café Rouge chains); new trends in 'loft living', open-plan, New York-style, if possible overlooking the Thames in Docklands; new 'boutique' hotels (Anouska Hempel's minimalist bailiwick, The Hempel, in Bayswater); an influx of new designer names in Bond Street, giants of Italian and US fashion; a millennium exposition envisaged (though still somewhat vaguely) to sit on a transformed Greenwich peninsula; a new Tate Gallery for modern British art at Southwark; a new conference centre at Heathrow; redevelopment of the Royal Opera House.

The tourist figures had recovered from the first Gulf War drop; the London Stock Exchange was winning the tug o' war with its Frankfurt rival; a new flexibility in licensing laws and pavement cafés was giving a Continental look to Soho. 'London is crackling with chic, jumping with ideas,' declared the *Telegraph Magazine* at the end of 1996, much as *Queen* magazine had once pronounced London to be the boom town of the Sixties. And, oh yes, don't forget: a general election was scheduled for May. A new party – or, at least, 'New' Labour as defined by its new leader Tony Blair – confidently expected to sweep to power this time, just two weeks before the franchise winners got their bonanzas. Blair had been the first Labour leader to make a speech on 'the cultural industries' since Harold Wilson, though culture as such hardly featured on the party's election manifesto: it came below the 'Anglers' Charter' in promises. True, Jack Cunningham, when Shadow National Heritage Secretary, spoke of 'pay what you can nights' at the theatre, but even this was far from the cultural revolution carried out by Wilson's cultural tsarina, Jennie Lee.

Blair promised to set up a National Endowment for Science, Technology and the Arts (Nesta), a fund for talented individuals; he later did so, under David Puttnam's benign but somewhat distant authority: it was not likely to do much for those who had been Puttnam's fellow film-makers. Yet the film industry's vote was already spoken for: it was fairly solidly for Labour. 'Improving the Quality of Life', the Tories' policy paper, made the ghastly error of declaring that the revival of the British film industry was already achieved and 'owed a great deal to the economic climate created by this government'. True: limited tax write-offs, Lottery cash, franchises had all been Tory presents. But the past tense in the policy promise suggested little more largesse was to come from those godfathers; whereas Labour's Shadow Arts Minister, Mark Fisher, pledged his party would do even more to help the industry. Call them ingrates, but film people's appetites worked on the Oliver Twist principle – not 'Thank you' but 'More, please'.

Tony Blair also saw the vote value in films: along with the Pop industry, they were the people's entertainment, especially *young* people and, more crucially still, young *voters*. Soon the Union flag would be flaunted (in the words of *Sight and Sound*) as a 'Pop prop', as it had been in the Bond and Beatles era; icons of Britpop would be officially invited to Downing Street, while 'Cool Britannia' would be (for a time) the password to all that was politically fashionable and plausibly Labourite.

David Puttnam was one of the most important crossover figures in the manner in which New Labour subsumed old film-makers who presented themselves as gurus to the Blair revolution. Sir David (as he was now, having been knighted by John Major) was undergoing a mid-life renewal. His new film, appositely named *My Life So Far*, was not exactly cutting-edge Socialism: it was a period piece, steeped in nostalgia for a comfortable upper-middle-class manor-house upbringing based on the early memoirs of Sir Denis Forman, a pioneer of independent television. It was in production in Scotland, with Hugh Hudson directing, and would not be released for some time, perhaps because its conservative values did not quite fit the 'Cool Britannia' mood. But its producer was certainly 'on line' in all other respects. He shrewdly realised other film-makers were in fashion. His own slate of films had dwindled after *Memphis Belle* and *Meeting Venus*, a disastrous tale of opera folk made by the Hungarian director Istvan Szabo in 1990. He had given 182 lectures in the past three years. Now rueful, indeed melancholic, he admitted to an interviewer, Nigel Farndale, that 'when I try to bring values and visions ... to the rough and tumble of the cinema, what do they do to me? They are very polite – they label me an idealist. Put me on a shelf. "Terrific guy, but don't take any notice of what he's saying because it ain't going to happen in his lifetime." '

New Labour's fresh confidence was now the draught that revived him. His politics had not been emphasised while he was a film producer, though he had joined the Labour Party at sixteen – switching briefly to the Social Democrats, then lured back to the orthodox fold by Neil Kinnock – and he had represented his branch in the old ACTT film union. But now Tony Blair fell under the persuasive tongue of a man who had convinced himself that although Europeans had lost the film war with Hollywood, a greater victory could still be theirs (or, rather, Britain's) if they embraced education in all its multiple-media and saleable audio-visual forms. 'If we move fast, we could become the Hollywood of education ... the place where educational software is developed, finessed and marketed.'

The Blairs passed the New Year before the 1997 election at the West Cork home Puttnam owned, having sold 'Chariot's Chase', as he nicknamed Kingsmead Mill, the Wiltshire house he purchased in his post-Columbia months, to James Dyson, inventor of the bagless vacuum cleaner and a proactive innovator of the kind Puttnam revered. 'Education, education, education', one of the earliest, and still most celebrated soundbites of Tony Blair, the new Prime Minister, has the unmistakable echo of Puttnam the proselytiser. Puttnam's Columbia severance also helped pay for a private 'think-tank' run by John Newbiggin, Neil Kinnock's adviser, to whom Puttnam offered the job on the day after Labour's defeat in the 1992 general election. Puttnam soon turned this influence into real power and eventual office. Immediately after Labour's win, it was Puttnam who produced the video 'mission statement' that Robin Cook, the new Foreign Secretary, sent to 223 British diplomats abroad. He was appointed to advise the government on raising standards in education and also became a member of the post-1997 election 'task force' set up to review the 'creative industries' and advise on how to make them more productive. Among these were, of course, films.

When 14 May came round, with the announcement at the Cannes Film Festival of who had won the Lottery franchises, Puttnam ascended the steps of the rather grotty cinema in the rue d'Antibes to hear Mary Allen announce the names from the stage. He looked pleased. I was sure he knew the names already. I suspected he had other reasons to be pleased. Sure enough, with Tony Blair's first honours list just over two months later he became Lord Puttnam. The days of righteous scourging of himself and others might not be over but ennoblement surely was a powerful balm. He had passed from sackcloth to ermine. Chris Smith accompanied Mary Allen to Cannes for the announcement of the franchises. He was the new Secretary of State for National Heritage. (His Ministry didn't get round to renaming itself the Department of Culture, Media and Sport until 24 July 1997: the old name was regarded as 'backward looking'. Smith's deputy, Tom Clarke, had been made Minister for Film, the first government member ever to be so designated. Chris Smith was the first openly homosexual government minister. Wicked Auberon Waugh made mischief out of this: 'I would hate to think that his appointment by Blair was an example of insensitive typecasting: because Smith has announced that he is homosexual, he must be interested in the arts. They all are, don't you know?'

Generally, though, Smith got a tolerant press. He had been Shadow Secretary of State for Health and some felt the new posting was a demotion. That is not how he saw it. His immediate aim was to double British films' share of the UK market, to 20 per cent. It was suggested to him that he could do it immediately by introducing a law compelling multiplex cinemas to show a larger percentage of British films. The proposal didn't catch fire, though six years later, in the Communications Bill, a Private Member's clause would require TV companies to do precisely that. 'I am confident that the franchises will help build the sort of lasting success for British films that we all want to see,' he said with bland confidence outside the Star cinema.

A well-read individual with a rather soft smile, who had written his university thesis on Wordsworth and gave his hobby, appropriately enough, as hill climbing, Smith had passed the unofficial 'culture test', the equivalent of asking very rich and very famous people on TV chat shows if they could say how much a pint of milk cost. He was able to name at least two recent films he'd seen: Lars von Trier's *Breaking the Waves* and Scott Hicks's *Shine*. The first was a non-UK, the second an Australian–UK co-production. Still, it was 200 per cent better than his Tory predecessor Steven Dorrell had registered. The first enquiries about 'Monsieur Jean Moreau' were met with a soft but wary smile, signifying perhaps something less than displeasure at the memory of Dorrell's monumental gaffe. 'The arts are for everyone,' Smith added, as he climbed on to the stage with Mary Allen.

Yes, but who was the money for?

'We were looking for commitment, enthusiasm and imagination as well as business sense and an eye to the box office, because we want the Lottery funding to be recouped,' Ms Allen began, covering the waterfront. Then she identified the winning all-rounders. First to be 'in the money' (£30.25 million of it, exactly what it had asked for) was the Film Consortium. This new entity comprised four production companies in association with Virgin Cinemas, a 25 per cent shareholder. They were: Greenpoint (Ann Scott); Parallax (Sally Hibbin, Ken Loach); Skreba (Simon Relph and Anne Skinner) and Scala (Nik Powell and Stephen Woolley). They had declared themselves able to make thirty-nine films over the six-year life of their franchise. The names of Powell and Woolley in the winning consortium elicited cries of 'Oh!'. The collapse of the two producers' Palace Pictures barely five years earlier, leaving debts reported to be in double-digit millions, evidently didn't disqualify them as individuals and non-bankrupts from possessing the essential 'enthusiasm, imagination and commitment as well as business sense' that had won them a share of £30.25 million of public funding. Some of those present at Cannes, who had lost money in Palace's crash, were less than enthusiastic.

Another surprise followed. Pathé Productions, a new company formed by the giant French conglomerate, won the second franchise, worth £33 million, the biggest franchise, capable (their business plan claimed) of financing thirty-five films. The shock of British funding going to a foreign-owned company was somewhat modified when Ms Allen read out the list of six 'associated producers', all British: Simon Channing-Williams (Mike Leigh's frequent partner); Jake Eberts (formerly Goldcrest's supremo); Norma Heyman; Lynda Myles; Barnaby Thompson and his partner Uri Fruchtman; Michael White, better known as a theatrical angel and impresario. Nearly all these were experienced, often successful names, who could list productions such as *Gandhi*, *The Killing Fields*, *Dangerous Liaisons*, *The Commitments*, *Sirens*, *Secrets and Lies*, *Monty Python and the Holy Grail* and *Nuns on the Run* on their production slates.

The third franchise went to Duncan Kenworthy (Toledo Productions) and Andrew Macdonald (Figment Films), partners in a new company imaginatively named DNA, an acronym that promisingly also connoted the basic structure of life itself. They got £29 million and proposed to make sixteen films. 'Our trademark', a delighted Macdonald said later, 'will be quality, energy and films for the British audience.' His partner, Kenworthy, added, 'We intend to make DNA a home for a new generation of British film-makers.' We all waited to see how the promised fourth franchise would top that. But there was to be none.

Three franchises only, said Ms Allen severely, refusing to elaborate why £63.75 million of the £156 million that had been promised to four consortia remained undistributed. She dealt brusquely indeed with the few questions possible in a crowded cinema with no microphones for questioners. 'During the second half of the third year,' she added, 'the Arts Council will evaluate franchise holders' performance and decide whether the award should be extended for the second three-year term.' Considering nearly £100 million of public money was being disbursed, the explanations of how and why the election had fallen on these winners were grudging and vague. The Arts Council and Ms Allen preferred to put things down on paper, rather than yield to the hurly-burly of public inquisition. The choice of Cannes was perhaps meant to borrow resonance for the occasion from the festival: but it usefully deflected on-the-spot, informed enquiries from the media. The questions were limited in time and number.

The tone of the responses from the platform was adversarial rather than informative. My own question about the propriety of the award to a consortium containing film-makers of unquestioned talent but dubious business sense was nearly dismissed as an impropriety – something 'not done', though it had support from others in the audience. Not until a month later did Charles Denton amplify what had gone on in the selection committee – and then in a personal letter to me. Each of the successful groups, he wrote, had submitted written material about past history and future plans; this was assessed by paid external examiners, who remained a secret at the time. Denton's letter to me stated they had been the accountancy firm, Messrs Cooper & Lybrand, appointed after open tender – 'they were required to report on the business plans and financial status (including past record) of each applicant, including their constituent companies' and yes, they had been aware of Palace Pictures' history. Their assessments were then reviewed by Arts Council staff, after which they were passed to the Film Franchise Review Committee for detailed discussion.

At first even the names of those on the committee had not been disclosed. Perhaps this was wise, but it was totally contrary to the principle of transparency. It gave rise to all sorts of suspicions. Under pressure, they eventually were named: Clare Mulholland (chairman and deputy chief executive, Independent Television Commission); David Aukin (head of film, Channel 4); Charles Denton (chairman, National Lottery Film Advisory Panel); Graham Easton (completion guarantor at Mainline Pictures, a high-risk occupation which, for a fee, insured films in the making would get finished, or else); Tim Johnson (film lawyer, S. J. Berwin); Frank Pierce (ex-vice-president, Europe, Warner Bros); Olivia Stewart (producer, Velvet Goldmine Production); Janet Walker (finance director, Granada Media Group); and John Woodward (chief executive, PACT). Mulholland and Woodward were also members of Denton's National Lottery Film Advisory Panel and had thus a powerful voice (and vote) in each camp. Given that most of the British film industry had put in for Lottery franchises, this group was about as representative and yet independent as one could reasonably hope for. Yet they gave no reasons for their choices. This was understandable for those they rejected, since it would have been invidious and legally perilous. The Film Franchise Review Committee, said Denton, then reported its finding 'to my Film Panel,' which made its final recommendations to the Arts Council.

Whew! one feels like saying, after taking in a series of what resembles steps to spiritual purity, never mind commercial acuity. And then, of course, the applicants who had passed were interviewed? No, not at all. 'We decided that there was no need to call any of the applicants to interview,' wrote Charles Denton, 'and I personally believe that to have done so would have risked introducing an element of subjective judgement based on the strength of each party's verbal pitch.' There may be something to be said for this – if so, it resides surely in the possibilities of sheer physical exhaustion rather than further enlightenment. However, millions of pounds were at stake.

I wrote back to Denton on 16 July 1997, '. . . never do I remember a time . . . when public funds were made available by return of post, without further interviewing, and without the slightest effort to give an explanation to those who . . . failed.' My letter continued, no doubt still reflecting the heat that the manner and nature of the awards had generated, albeit principally among the losers, 'You cannot run a film industry on Civil Service lines; you should know that as well as I do. The market forces will either abuse it or frustrate it; and the Arts Council of England has neither the commercial know-how, nor, I think, the ruthlessness that is necessary to defend itself in a cut-throat market place.'

No explanation of why the fourth franchise had been dropped was ever given; but guesswork wasn't hard. A late rush of reality had possibly convinced the selectors that there simply wasn't enough talent on the ground to stretch to a fourth, since all the franchises, plus other independent producers, plus BBC, Channel 4 and ITV, would be competing for much the same properties, writers, directors, actors, etc. But possibly even more decisive was the warning that even the National Lottery might be stretched thin, since the new government had decided to create a sixth benediction dedicated to 'health and education' to the original recipients of Lottery funds. This would mean a 12–16 per cent drop in Lottery awards across the board, including the Arts Council – and film funding. As Norman Lebrecht later wrote, 'the National Lottery may well go down in history as a one-off windfall for British arts, a Conservative benediction that was stinted the moment Labour took office.'

The post-Cannes Arts Council took pre-emptive action: it shelved another plan for £12 million non-commercial film franchises planned for the next six years. With dismaying speed it began to look as if Lottery payments would not match aspirations. The franchise losers were considered to be protected. But the losers, who now depended on individual Lottery grants from the Arts Council in lieu of any *pourboire* from the franchises, took mild fright, fearing that their subsidies would be cut. They were only reassured when a new post-franchise cycle of Arts Council grants resumed and it was announced that Lottery funding for film-makers would be protected in the overall cuts. Thus in the 1997–8 financial year the Council planned to invest £24 million in British films; in 1998–9 £30 million; and in 1999–2000 £35 million. At this point the Council had invested some £40 million in films since the scheme began in September 1995.

It has to be stressed that for any one of the franchises to draw money from their 'pot' for one of its member's films, or to co-finance an outside producer's film, approval still had to be obtained from the Arts Council, which generally authorised about a third of the film's total cost – never more than half – and required matching equity to be available. This was accepted as a necessary inconvenience by franchise holders who would have liked to be able to draw down sums of public money without having to submit to their patrons' scrutiny. But what stuck in their craw was the discovery that projects were to be 'vetted' by British Film Institute appointees. This emerged when the Institute asked for extra funding to cover the work of 'reading and reporting'. Being second-guessed by bureaucrats and 'non-professionals', turning in their opinions in secret, was clearly not acceptable: it was quietly dropped.

The Arts Council had expected the franchise winners to have signed contracts by the end of July: it took months longer. The Film Consortium didn't sign until mid September; Pathé until the end of October; DNA left it until 1998. Delays in the delivery of the promised manna set in. Plans to use Lottery cash to distribute films — paying for prints and advertising, though not for publicity and personal appearances by the stars — after all, there were limits though they were constantly widening — which had been recommended by BSAC's study group, had to be put on hold because of the delay in signing the contracts.

An essential requirement of winning a franchise was having a distributor for the resulting films. Pathé, whose partner in the franchise bid was the leading French production company Canal Plus, had its own long-established distribution system (and cinemas) in France and Germany, and now in the UK: its Continental leverage was one reason for the offspring of a very wealthy French parent getting British subsidies. The hope was that it would help push the home product on to European screens owned or tied to Pathé. DNA announced, 'PolyGram has guaranteed to give a UK cinema release to every film DNA produces.' This left the Film Consortium to put its trust in the group that had bought Rank Film Distributors in April 1997 for £65 million, a clear signal that big commercial TV groups were becoming a force in the film industry. With the deal went a huge haul of 740 films which Rank had produced or owned rights in. But was Carlton in it for the library, or would it continue Rank's distribution business? First cause for concern arose when Carlton Film Distributors began turning down every project suggested to it by the production arm, Carlton Films — much as the Rank Film Distributors in years gone by had rejected films its own company had produced. This is not uncommon in vertically integrated structures where one level doesn't wish its profit to depend on another level's erratic operations. By September 1997, just as the Film Consortium signed its contract and the Arts Council could start handing over the cash, Carlton announced it was pulling out of distributing films: it had clearly been in it for the old films, not the new ones. *Screen International*, describing Carlton's move as 'a purely cynical one', said, 'Theatrical distribution is the main plank of the government's film policy review which is designed to double the market share of British films at

UK cinemas.' Thus the ground was cut from under one of the franchise's feet before it even got to work.

Pathé also looked vulnerable for a time when its banking partner, Barclays, put its investment arm, Barclays de Zoete Wedd (BZW), up for sale. BZW had guaranteed equity investment in franchise films. Barclays, though – after a few queasy moments – said it would honour any commitments made to Pathé. A near shave. A deeper hole should have been visible.

By adding to production, while neglecting distribution, or leaving it to the franchises to make what arrangements they could, the Arts Council was promoting a volume of movies which, in many cases, would have nowhere to go. Warnings were ignored in the post-election rush to 'get things going'. 'What we need', wrote one ex-distributor, David Marlow, in *Screen International*, 'is an environment to support more independent distributors and exhibitors with fresh marketing initiatives designed to break the majors' [i.e. Hollywood's] stranglehold over screens.' But distribution was not glamorous, not as 'sexy' as film-making. By going for the latter, without attempting first to restructure distribution and exhibition, the governments (Tory and Labour) made the most crucial error of all the grand designs. It was one that would dog the planning over the coming years.

Mike Southwood, managing director of Film Four Distributors, commented that the market could not possibly support 'the extra traffic'. Fifty per cent of British films already being made were failing to get a domestic release. Another ninety films – all trying to be squeezed on to distributors' schedules – was 'a recipe for disaster'. But even he was against greater participation by distributors in calling the shots. 'It would be the grossest form of tail wagging the dog if you suddenly had a "suit" [an executive] in distribution dictating what films should or should not get made.' Channel 4 said it feared the franchises would lead to an 'unhealthy' increase in competition for domestic projects; some of the franchises would be looking for much the same kind of film. Channel 4 was therefore going to develop more international co-productions. This would impact, in turn, on Simon Perry's strategy at British Screen Finance, which now also administered the government-financed Green-light Fund of £5 million, available to producers of larger-budgeted films. The fund's future, now in doubt, came 'under discussion', since the Arts Council was concerned about independent funders such as Perry being largely outside its remit. It should have been a sign of troubles to come.

In a special section of *Parliamentary Review* that May, ominously
entitled 'Follywood', Perry told his interviewer, Neal Rafferty, that there
would be a failure rate among franchise films that could start to overtake
the successes 'to a dangerous degree'. Mike Ryan, of the sales company
J & M, had already warned of this in even blunter terms: 'Let's face it,
some of the stuff that is going to be made over the next few years will
be straight-to-radio material, let alone straight-to-video.' Continuing
more diplomatically, Perry said, 'If the franchise system implies a loss of
quality, it is that with a greater volume of films there will be a greater
volume of bad films . . .' He added, '. . . but more good films.'

This was to prove a fallacy. Increasing the numbers of films made did
not increase the odds on more good films being made. Though trumpeted as a rationale for the ill-conceived franchises, the results were
otherwise: about the same number of 'good' films – i.e. films deemed
critical and commercial successes – got made as before the franchises,
but they were to be overwhelmed by the exponential numbers of 'bad'
when the justification for making them was to achieve tax breaks for
investors rather than 'public benefit', or simply to pay the makers their
upfront fees because the public funding was available to make the films.

It was ironical that one of Blair's crucial appointments, Gordon
Brown, the new Chancellor of the Exchequer, poured fuel on the
production flames in his first Budget after the May election. He
announced that henceforth expenditure on producing a film could be
written off as incurred, not, as hitherto, over three years, which had
been the write-off time embedded in the 1993 Finance Act. Virginia
Bottomley had rejected this accelerated write-off. Chris Smith now
claimed the credit for it, though no one hustled Gordon Brown. He
probably listened more closely to his few intimates, of whom Smith was
not one.

Christmas had come early for the film industry. 'It is just fantastic – a
huge, huge shot in the arm,' cried PolyGram's Stewart Till. Shares in
film companies rose. 'Terrific news,' said Lynda Myles, now of the Film
Consortium, 'the major breakthrough we have wanted.' But the people
the tax change was to enrich were not film-makers. Indeed, like an
answered prayer, it was to prove a woeful, indeed destructive, element
in the deterioration of British film-making from 1997 onwards. A 100
per cent write-off in the first year would certainly benefit film-makers
by an estimated 6 per cent of the average budget and it might encourage
Hollywood film-makers to make films in the UK, though the tax break

was limited to productions budgeted at under £15 million and most US blockbusters made in Britain were well over that.

The biggest windfall went to the investment market, which now had a guaranteed, gilt-edged, Chancellor-approved tax deferral opportunity to offer the richer investors – those with in excess of £100,000 – who would not necessarily be the ones most interested in producing quality entertainment, simply useful 'loadsamoney' packages beyond reach of the Inland Revenue for many years. City analysts were delighted, calculating it would add 11,000 more jobs to their industry and boost investment in British films by 30 per cent. Premila Hoon, of Guinness Mahon and one of the members of a losing consortium in the franchise gold rush as well as a member of the British Screen Advisory Council, estimated that the write-off would generate enough increased economic activity to compensate the Treasury for loss of tax revenues. She was probably thinking it would encourage the sale-and-leaseback industry, whereby a finished film was sold to a bank or other institution that had large taxes to pay and could write off the purchase of the film against tax – the bank then leased it back to the distributors-producers for annual rent, which the latter then set off against *their* taxes. This was to become enormous business in New Labour's film industry assistance; but it did not help to create a well-structured film industry. Hoon's belief was never to be proved and is probably unquantifiable. Estimates varied from £30 million to £60 million a year in deferred revenues.

Theoretically, it would now be possible for a producer to make a film, never have it released, yet enter a profit for himself and his investors on the strength of the write-off value and the sale-and-leaseback deal. 'Coming soon: the tax-free British film,' said the *Daily Telegraph*'s Nigel Reynolds. He was only wrong in one thing: such a product was already here – for those with money to buy it. As Anthony Hilton, City editor of the *Evening Standard*, wrote, 'The history of trying to grow industries by giving them favourable treatment demonstrates that a bad idea does not become a good idea just because it attracts a tax break.'

What escaped most people's attention in the run-up to the franchises was an article contributed to *Parliamentary Review* in May by Wilf Stevenson, then director of the British Film Institute but, more important perhaps, an old crony of Gordon Brown, who had been best man at Stevenson's wedding. In it, Stevenson recommended setting up 'a stand-alone Lottery distributor for film – provided it has the correct statutory framework which allows it to work in harness with the existing film bodies in the UK'. The company could invest in production, too. Already, even before the franchises got started, a political agenda was being drawn up to remove control of the Lottery funding from the Arts Council and have it administered by some kind of 'stand-alone' body with 'the correct statutory framework'. Chris Smith echoed this idea within weeks of taking office. He asked PACT, the producers' lobby group of which John Woodward was chief executive, to consider plans for bringing all film-related activities under a single agency, thus avoiding overlap and lack of accountability to central government. This was to become the outline of the Film Council that, in 2000, finally secured control for (if not exactly by) the film industry of a huge segment of funding from a Lottery that had been expressly set up to benefit the needs of the public, not to add to the privileges that the film industry had collected under Labour. He not only floated the idea of a single body with a large fund but added, 'If this fund could be combined with some kind of tax break (which the industry and the Department of National Heritage have been arguing for over the past few years, although the idea has been consistently rebuffed by the Treasury), then Britain could be on to a winner.' Just two months after this article appeared, Gordon Brown rebuffed his own Treasury mandarins and gave the industry its tax break. Clearly, Stevenson was well informed.

Not all the principal players in this defining event ended the year happily. Some did not even end it in their jobs. Mary Allen, having handed out the gifts, left her post as secretary-general of the Arts Council of England almost the next day for a job (unadvertised) as chief executive of the Royal Opera House, which was in crisis, so debt-ridden and short of money that even £78 million of Lottery money (not much less than the entire film franchise awards) might not bail it out without top-to-bottom reconstruction. Unfortunately, it was a case of frying pan to fire: she resigned within a very short period.

With her departure Lord Gowrie, the Council's chairman, found his part-time job was turning into a full-time crisis management one – he was already a director of Sotheby's, the auction house, and chairman of a property company which had just announced a 50 per cent profits rise. Gowrie tendered his resignation (effective in 1998) to spend more time with his company. He admitted, with his characteristic blend of rueful charm which had often won over the Council's hostile critics, that the Arts Council's usefulness was perhaps over. When the government came in through the door, patronage had to take its orders from the new occupants. It had less and less say in how to hand out the money when the 'good causes' were already written on the bills presented to the paymaster. 'Whole days', Gowrie sighed, 'are spent trying to get people out of impossible holes.' Being allowed to use public money, for example, to pay for capital projects but not running costs – 'as if you installed gold taps in a bathroom, but had no bath plugs'.

If it occurred to him that this precisely summed up the condition of the newly gold-plated film industry he did not mention it. But the oversight in providing waste plugs was to prove expensive.

16

Thrown Away

Chris Smith, the new Culture Secretary, was one of the busiest ministers in the new Labour government. Barely had he got the sea air inhaled while treading the Croisette with the great and the glamorous at Cannes in May 1997 than he did what became almost a staple of his department's strategy – he set up a new committee.

The Film Policy Review Group was its grand name. It was chaired by Tom Clarke, the first-ever specially designated Minister for Film, along with Stewart Till, head of international activities at PolyGram Filmed Entertainment, which Smith described in a slightly defensive letter to the *Sunday Times* as 'probably Europe's biggest current success story . . .' That word 'current' had an ominous tone: it was not to be the only time Smith's enthusiasm for a 'success story' was to be proved premature. The new 'working party' – which sounded plainer and more industrious than 'committee': such semantics would be built into the various reports issued over the next eighteen months, like mantras to be chanted in the hope that their prayers would come true – would be 'more focused' than the Middleton committee. It would conjure up a new, workable definition of what was a 'British' film – necessary, if tax benefits were to go to the right parties – and form strong bonds with City institutions. This, in turn, envisaged yet another committee, a 'Forum for Film'.

The review group, numbering some fourteen members, would also examine the viability of the accelerated write-off for film costs in the first year. Smith made it known he was in favour of this; his predecessor, Virginia Bottomley, had not been. Actually, much of this was 'spin'. The 100 per cent tax write-off had already been agreed to by the only Minister who really mattered, Gordon Brown, the Chancellor of the Exchequer, and it was generally believed his old college crony, Wilf Stevenson, had helped him make up his mind.

Smith's main instruction to the working party was: come up with policies that will double the share of the UK market that British films have at the moment – from 10 to 20 per cent. It was ordered to report by March 1998. It passed, if not unnoticed, then without comment, that BSAC already had a committee, set up in October 1996 under Simon Perry, to do exactly the same work by advising the Arts Council on ironing out the kinks in its Lottery debacle. It suggested that distributors, as well as producers, ought to have a bite at the carrot by enjoying Lottery support. This was an idea which was to gain support in the next few years. The trouble was that no one then – or, indeed, later – could think of how it could be done. Another suggestion – paying stars to attend provincial premières of movies that qualified as British – would have been easily adopted, but no one was quite shameless enough to take it up. Many heads were put together, many minds focused, generally over lunch tables, in the intervening months. Such focus-group zeal was to become one of the most relied on – if not always reliable – tools of Labour's first term in office. It was an unabashed return to corporatism and intervention, which in more structured industries might (just might) have been appropriate, but was not remotely applicable to a film industry whose essence was competition and whose 'product' was individual talents. But ideologues are unstoppable (until stopped).

Other committees were called into being, related to the working party. Some were strictly utilitarian: PACT was asked to form a committee and advise on the viability of bringing all film-making activities under a single agency. This was clearly Smith's vision. He felt there was too much overlap between some well-established institutions, like the BFI and British Screen Finance, and the multiplying new ones, like the Arts Council's film advisory panel, and the up-and-coming film franchises. A firm appositely named Hydra Associates was in turn commissioned to report. Simon Perry, at British Screen Finance, must have felt his own position growing weaker by the week as each new Labour initiative seemed to second-guess his pro-Europe production policy and undermine its confidence.

Some of the new committees Labour created in these heady months were ostentatiously glamorous and looked designed deliberately to link the part with, well, 'creativity'. Virgin's Richard Branson, the clothes designer Paul Smith, Oasis manager Alan McGhee, publisher Gail Rebuck, media consultant Janet Hughes and the soon to be ennobled David Puttnam, and others, formed a Creative Standards Committee to supplement Smith's culture ministry by devising new strategies at home and abroad for 'the creative industries'. Puttnam was already serving on a Standards Task Force to foster 'good teaching' in the UK: he announced he was gradually withdrawing from film-making. Indeed, so many members of the film community had now been co-opted on to quangos and task forces that it was a marvel they found time to turn out films.

Yet the years 1997–8 saw an unprecedented number of British movies, running into triple digits, partly due to Lottery funding, but also to the sense of optimism, or opportunism, in the creative cosmos. Hearts, minds and (particularly) purses were bursting, for a change, with 'can do' pride instead of 'couldn't quite' apology. New Labour, new miracle! It passed, maybe not unnoticed but certainly unremarked, that many of those who sat on these committees also held down jobs in the very Hollywood companies whose hold over the distribution and exhibition economy in Britain were part of the problem they'd been set up to solve. As *Variety* put it pithily in September 1997, 'HOLLYWOOD MUSCLE PUSHES BRITISH PIX BLITZ'. Their own agendas were self-serving ones: always the first and only rule of British-based Hollywood majors – protect the HQ. They weren't in the business to put anyone else's cinema culture on its own two feet again, though they were shrewd enough to know that self-interest requires Samaritan-like assistance to the weak and ailing – if only to guard against the possibility of the latter becoming rich and strong. Hollywood's values were always those of the market place – and, in Britain, they effectively controlled the market. Some sensed, in retrospect, a fifth column at work in the deliberations over Smith's grand design to double the British share of the market. But for the moment no evidence of this was tangible: it was all in the minds of the Cassandras.

The industry had a fright, along with the cultural agencies, at the end of 1997 when the Arts Council's grant was cut in what seemed a forerunner of volatile Lottery money being used to replace stable Treasury grants. But reassurances were given, as has been noted; handouts went on and the partying continued in 1998.

The film industry was then caught up in one of the most ludicrous emanations of over-hype that any British government had sponsored: the short-lived but extremely silly phenomenon nicknamed 'Cool Britannia'. It was a label that perfectly reflected the 'identity rebranding' of a generation that had taken to e-mailing, on-lining and (slightly later) text-messaging, and was nothing less than spin-doctoring under a more populist name, and nothing more than a refashioning of the national image to enhance the Labour government's aura of political success. Labour held 417 seats in the Commons, against the Conservatives' 162 – a three-to-one majority that gave sanction to the most extravagant attempts to turn perception into reality. Tony Blair, who had taken to calling Britain 'The Young Country', modern, upbeat and energetic, cast in his own image, now applied the 'Cool Britannia' label, with its more diffused connotations and less ageist vulnerability, to all kinds of creation, particularly Pop and films. Both were 'sexy'. The Union flag was taken out of the closet where Labour had consigned it for several generations, had the dust shaken from its folds, and was unfurled as the symbol of national striving and artistic success.

A wretched Foreign Office Minister, one Derek Fatchett who owned a Paul Smith tie, was put in charge of telling British embassies how to promote the 'cool' culture of the UK. 'If designers want our embassies to promote their clothes, I'm sure we can oblige,' he said, 'I'm the Minister for Cool.' Yes, he did like cricket, and gardening was his hobby, but recovering himself with aplomb, he excused this lapse in coolness by admitting that he preferred the Spice Girls to bagpipes.

Panel 2000, with thirty-nine members, was set up (aka the Committee of Cool), on which sat Sir Colin Marshall (BA chairman), Stella McCartney (designer), Waheed Alli (TV executive whose company produced *The Big Breakfast Show*), Zeinab Banawi (C4 newsreader), Martin Bell (ex-BBC TV reporter turned Independent MP), Judy Simpson (ex-Olympics athlete who now played Nightshade in ITV's *Gladiators*) and Peter Mandelson (Minister Without Portfolio and promoter of the great dome designed to arise on the peninsula of poisoned land in North Greenwich in time for the millennium celebrations). Plastic 'igloos' on Horse Guards Parade housed design products, including an orthopaedic overshoe for cattle and a device for entrapping cockroaches; scenes of imperial grandeur were removed from the walls of government buildings and replaced by abstract canvases; 'Dolly', the first cloned sheep, lay down with the British lion, so to speak, in the newly configured symbols of 'cool' Britannia; while Indian cuisine – the favourite dish of the Blairites, at least until government offered them a more upmarket menu – was praised for having a higher turnover than what remained of the coal, steel and shipbuilding industries. Boris Johnson (later to edit *The Spectator* and become a Tory MP), interviewing Mark Leonard, the publicist of 'cool', was informed that policemen's helmets should be abolished, 'though he is prepared to grant the red double-decker bus a stay of execution'.

The cash now being munificently doled out to film-makers was matched by talk of cuts in archaic ceremonies of state that had long pre-dated the invention of the cinematograph. It was suddenly a Monty Python world, which Tony Blair, a one-time guitar player at university with an artistic crush on Mick Jagger, wished to be seen as 'a vibrant, modern place, since countries steeped in nostalgia cannot build a strong future'. As Philip Norman commented shrewdly, 'New Labour is trying to duplicate a recycled Swinging London, with Oasis taking over the role of the Beatles, Alexander McQueen and John Galliano that of Mary Quant and Ossie Clark, Jodie Kidd that of Jean Shrimpton, Kate Winslet that of Julie Christie, Damien Hirst that of David Hockney.' If perception was reality then, even more so, surface was depth. The film community's members were caught up in this created euphoria: 'Never in eighteen years of Tory rule – and barely within living memory – have British film-makers found themselves with so much to do, so little to complain about,' said a *Sight and Sound* editorial in August that year.

Cool Britannia, of course, could not last long – and did not. The first to turn against it were the ones who realised they were being conscripted into it for their 'youth cred' – the Pop artists, traditionally expected to be outsiders, who now drank champagne with Tony and Cherie at Downing Street; Liam Gallagher, to his eternal credit, was a holdout who refused the gilt-edged invitation card. *New Musical Express* published an article in which a dozen leading bands laid into Tony Blair for cutting welfare handouts to young people; Richard Benson, editor of *The Face*, the leading generational magazine at the time, wrote, 'Artists, writers and designers, if they're any good, aren't in the mainstream. They're outsiders and troublemakers. They don't conform.' And it took only another strong puff from an unexpected source, the *Radio Times*, to blow 'cool' to bits. Ben Elton, the comedian, in an article headlined 'COOL BRITANNIA? I DON'T THINK SO', described cool as 'a deeply destructive force ... the most gruesome aspect ... is the way politicians are trying to latch on to it. I can do without the Labour Party trying to strut its funky stuff.' His deepest cut went into Chris Smith for encour-aging television drama full of crinolines, instead of gritty dramas like *Trainspotting*. His polemic was reported as if it were an account of a split in the Cabinet.

When Chumbawamba's Danbert Nobacon poured a jug of iced water over the head of John Prescott, Deputy Prime Minister, at the Brit Awards, the 'C' word, as it had become known in the lexicon of unmentionables, was banished from official communiqués. By April 1998 it had become a 'naff embarrassment'. Even Ben and Jerry, the ice-cream men, replaced its 'cool Britannia' flavour with one called 'Coffee, Coffee, Buzz, Buzz' and issued their own communiqué: 'All flavours have a shelf life and we are sorry to say goodbye to an old favourite.' Few others in Blair's so uncool Britain were.

It is useful to recall this period of preposterous spin-doctoring, since it helps to understand why there was at first so little protest about the early and accumulating disasters of Lottery-funded film production. When 'cool' was banned by Labour spokesmen as unfitting a nation dedicated to creative realities – or so they hoped – it was gradually replaced by the word 'sorted', which became associated with the *achievement* of things. 'I've got it "sorted" ' began to be heard. And if one shut one's eyes to the realities of the film-making boom from 1997 onwards, and the sheer numbers of movies now being made, it was possible to credit that New Labour's film policy makers had it 'sorted'. It was very quickly evident they had not, but ministers had a vested interest in what their generosity had wrought and film-makers certainly didn't want to turn off the tap. In the hubbub of 'creativity', what *Sight and Sound* was to call the 'vast tangle of unwatched celluloid' seemed its own jus-tification, if only because at some point or other quantity has to turn into quality.

The first tranche of films funded from the National Lottery began appearing in the autumn of 1996. They immediately justified the mis-givings: they were, in the main, a poor collection with only their diversity to commend them. Some should never have been made under Arts Council patronage: they were certainly not art – and most proved not to be box office, either. *Crimetime* (Lottery grant £300,000, total project cost a high £4.3 million) was a sleazy slasher movie starring Pete Postlethwaite as a serial killer who puts the knife into women in back alleys, cuts out their left eye and keeps the orbs in his ice-cube tray. The dubious 'intellectual' justification for a gruesome but commonplace shocker was the symbiotic relationship between a tabloid TV show in-volving police reconstructions that makes him into a hero and that confirms him in his killing spree in order to promote his on-screen surro-gate's stardom. It aped decadent but superior North American genre models. Later, it was pitched that its Dutch director George Sluizer's

well-received *The Vanishing* was what had commended it to the Arts
Council; no one had apparently informed its advisory panel that Sluizer's
own Hollywood remake of his Franco-Dutch movie had somewhat
invalidated his artistic integrity. *True Blue* carried more hopes – and even
more public money (£1 million of funding, total project cost £3.5
million). It was picked as that year's royal film performance. Surely a
story inspired by the 1987 Oxford and Cambridge Boat Race and the
bad feeling between the resident Oxford Brits and the Yankee jocks
specially imported to give their boat oar power had the makings of a
Chariots of Fire on water? It might, but that earlier film, involving one
in the spiritual and personal dilemmas of the competitors which shaped
their will to win, gave one something to cheer for. *True Blue* simply
offered bad-tempered argy-bargy, bluster and ill manners before the
predictable moment of glory. As two of its co-financiers were Channel
4 and Booker Entertainment, both well-heeled companies, particularly
as the former now had money to spend from the abolition of the yearly
stipend it had had to pay ITV, such a film had no need at all for a public
windfall from the Lottery.

Adrian Noble's *A Midsummer Night's Dream* (Lottery funding,
£750,000, total project cost £2.5 million) was 'art', certainly, but not
very good art, nor inspired, being mainly an archival record of his stage
production, now vulgarised beyond belief, in which people floated in
Mary Poppins-style on giant umbrellas, the Athenian woods resembled a
long-life light-bulb departmental display, the 'rude mechanicals' were
like *Dad's Army* in civvies, and the fairies resembled waiters in a gay and
lesbian-themed restaurant. The quality of verse speaking was variable,
to say the least. 'I am amazed and know not what to say,' a character
declaimed – nor even how to say it. Philip French's comment in the
Observer was cruel but just: 'The final credits list a group of "Principle
Fairies", presumably to distinguish them from unprincipled fairies.' The
film took an estimated £9,156 at the British box office; though its
producers were reported to have repaid £78,000 of their Lottery award,
this was understood to have followed a sale to Miramax.

An American sale also enabled the £6 million *Land Girls* to start
repaying some of its £1.5 million Lottery award made through the
British Screen Finance-administered Greenlight Fund. Produced by
Simon Relph (who was a member of the winning Film Consortium
franchise) and directed by David Leland, it was a disappointment from
the man whose 1987 social comedy, *Wish You Were Here*, precisely fixed

the mood of youthful rebelliousness in the Fifties against convention-conscious, middle-class Britain. *Land Girls* might have been more appropriately called 'Mills and Boon Go to War' or 'The Ploughman's Lunch Box'. Its three city lasses who volunteer to help with the sowing, mowing and general mucking out in wartime Britain serve their country only until opportunity allows them to serve themselves with the farmer's son, after which war was forgotten in favour of a sketchy valentine to the liberties that girls at that time could take when freed from the constraints of family and in possession of the one able-bodied member of a Dorset farmstead. Although elbow grease is applied early on, at least to the sexy bits of farm life like the cows' udders, it is facials that matter most of the time. Despite its large budget, it had the dimensional feel of a made-for-TV movie.

As the Lottery-funded films rolled out, quantity sometimes did eventually turn into quality – but it was rare. Phil Agland's sturdy version of Thomas Hardy's *The Woodlanders* (Lottery grant £1.4 million; total cost £4.3 million); Richard Kwietniowski's *Love and Death on Long Island* (Lottery grant £750,000, total cost £2,300,874), from Gilbert Adair's literate satire on boyish American innocence assailed by a reclusive old English queen (John Hurt) with a crush on a US pin-up: it felt like a more tender parody of *Death in Venice*. A film of William Golding's *The Spire* seemed perfect Arts Council material, but Anthony Hopkins proved too expensive, even with Lottery money, and then Roger Spottiswoode opted instead to direct the next James Bond film. Golding's work remains unfilmed.

Other films, hastily prepared with scripts that still needed rewrites but put into premature production because the Lottery money came through, began to pile up the heap of duds. Even more dismaying was that the critical reception many of this jumble of films got was the public's disdain of them – when given the choice, that is.

By mid 1997, of the sixty-six projects so far part-funded by Lottery money, two only, *Crimetime* and *True Blue*, had gained general release throughout the UK. Very quickly the Arts Council perceived its Lottery generosity had created a 'film mountain' – movies that could not find space on British screens either quickly or widely because Hollywood's product was the sitting tenant. Expecting exhibitors, with product ties to American distributors in Britain, to move these wares off screen and obligingly make way for British-funded movies was a triumph of patriotic hope over oligopoly practice. Increasing the volume of production, which Chris Smith continued to claim was an 'achievement' of Lottery funding, was only tantamount to increasing the number of corpses for which there were not sufficient graves. The Arts Council weren't foolish enough not to have foreseen this. But the Council was a delivery chute for government policy on the arts. Generally, this was to do with an aristocratic discrimination – in the best sense – and the funding of ostensibly artistic projects.

When funding films became a major part of its remit, the Council very soon realised it was getting into big business, and rather 'dirty' big business at that, never mind a nose for sharp practices to supervise its policies through to the box office and beyond. Its advisory panel put its imprimatur on the projects viewed favourably, but their responsibility ended there, too. Conflicts of interest on the panel were a clear danger, despite a general observance of Civil Service rules about declaring them or disqualifying oneself from voting, or even attending the judgemental process (cursory at best) a proposed film was put through by the panel. As a result, its members had to be selected from parts of the film community that varied widely in film-making experience, so that this would be reflected in their intuitive suspiciousness of projects submitted.

The panel's early membership consisted of Charles Denton (chairman); Mike Dibb (director-producer); Lyn Goldy (film lawyer); Keith Griffiths (producer); Hilary King (managing director of Little Theatre, Bath); Colin Leventhal (Channel 4 film lawyer); Clare Mulholland (deputy chief executive, Independent Television Commission); Ann Pointon (TV producer-director); Roger Shannon (director of Moving Image Development Agency, Liverpool); Alex Lisborne (producer, Picture Palace North, Sheffield); and John Woodward (chief executive, PACT). Denton, Mulholland and Woodward were also members of the nine-member Film Franchise Review Committee (whose make-up was only revealed after the franchises had been awarded), and hence had a voice and votes in both crucial decision-making bodies. Such talents are obvious; what is not so obvious is the skill needed to judge a film's likely box-office success, never mind artistic worth, from the bare 'coverage' report of the screenplay, etc. submitted by the early body of readers. 'The Lottery may be a devil in disguise,' said one (unnamed) British executive quoted in *Variety*. The same man then confessed that he, too, was putting his film forward for a Lottery grant. The moral was clear. One shakes hands with the devil, if he's got money in his grip.

Much – predictably overmuch – was made of Stefan Schwartz's *Shooting Fish* (Lottery fund £980,000, total project cost £2,135,000), a scam story of two young con men mulcting rich mugs, which was shrewdly marketed at Cannes in 1997. It took *Four Weddings and a Funeral* as its template, with smartish one-liners, a desertion at the altar, a last-reel double wedding, and even a hero with a mentally challenged brother recalling the hero's deaf brother of *Four Weddings*. Its agenda of social envy masquerading as class anarchy seemed set in an England of forty years ago. But the hope of repeating a *Four Weddings* success sold it instantly to the distributors in major territories who had the promotional muscle to make it succeed. 'Our first big one,' crowed the Arts Council spokesman, as Chris Smith was presented with an enlarged cheque for £280,000 by its distributor – who claimed the film would become the first one to recoup and repay its Lottery award. But it was a very small fish. What made it a box-office success was the ability of its distributors in the respective territories – Polygram, Pathé, Entertainment and Fox Searchlight – to make it succeed: they could afford the prints and advertising.

Few other Lottery-funded films had such rich godfathers. In Britain, *Shooting Fish* was shown on 205 screens and grossed £4,023,825. *An Ideal Husband* (Lottery grant £1 million, total project cost £6,350,000) also opened 'big' and grossed £2,891,515. *Plunkett and Macleane* (Lottery grant £1 million, total project cost, £8,490,000) was shown on 345 screens and grossed £2,757,485. These three examples suggest that when producers were prepared to back their films with substantial amounts of their own funding, these films were distributed with a serious and expensive promotional budget, and did excellent to reasonable business most times. The average Lottery-backed film, however, withered swiftly through lack of money to distribute and advertise it, lack of talent to have made it, or lack of interest among the public to see it – all three were common features of the scheme. Even badly made big-budget successes like *Plunkett and Macleane*, an abortive attempt to turn an eighteenth-century highwayman melodrama into a caper for the Pop-video generation's short attention span, did well because of its star, Robert Carlyle, and a heavy promotion budget. Disappointment came particularly hard on those young film-makers whose receipt of Lottery money for their projects had seemed especially benevolent, but who lacked the follow-up nourishment of prints and advertising – as well as the time for their talents to mature.

The Welsh New Wave directors who had boasted of their cultural iconoclasm were revealed as Hollywood wannabes, and did not enjoy the breakthrough of the *Shallow Grave/Trainspotting* set of Scottish radicals. Kevin Allen's *Twin Town* (1997, Lottery grant £500,000, total cost £1.7 million), certainly possessed what a *Time Out* reviewer called appreciatively 'a louche, rude boy energy' in its depiction of joyriding, solvent abuse and vandalism in Port Talbot, but was basically a grossed-out mafiosi parody in which a couple of glue-sniffing slackers brought a little lawless cheer into their joyless existence, exploiting their nihilism for no perceptible social revelations, but simply a yobbish kick.

Like *Twin Town*, Marc Evans's *House of America* was anxious to disown traditional Welshness, but it moved further and further from any approximate Celtic identity with its brother and sister characters, both high on drugs and drink, playing at being the author and Beat poet Jack Kerouac and his girlfriend Joyce Johnson, and roaring around on a Harley Davidson to bring a touch of *The Wild One* to the sodden valleys. 'If you're a teenager in Wales, where we've always lived somewhat in the shadow of England,' Evans said, 'there's a tendency to leapfrog and look towards the romantic idea of wide-open spaces, which comes to us from America, through the Beats, Bruce Springsteen songs, movies, etc . . .' True, but the palimpsest of imposing one culture on another was tortuous. Once again, British initiative had been subverted by the allure of generic Hollywood. Evans was fully aware of the problem: 'The challenge for Welsh film-makers is somehow to find a budget level that will make our films accessible to a wider audience, but which doesn't force us to lose our own voice.' He stated the problem, but without solving it. At least *House of America* gave honest notice of its intentions in the title, and was 'accessible', if only film-goers had 'accessed' it.

In contrast, *The Slab Boys* (Lottery cost *c.* £125,000, total project cost £2.5 million), 'accessible' to few beyond the Glasgow community who didn't speak in the impenetrable vernacular of the young carpet-factory boys of the title, worked. It hardly got shown in the UK, and was subtitled when sent round selected cities in the US in a selection of Lottery-financed films. An expensive tribute to Scottish nationalism. Julian Richards's *Darklands* (total cost £500,000) fell back derivatively on an earlier cult template: it took the 1973 classic *The Wicker Man* as starting and finishing point for its journalist hero's investigation into a steelworker's death that is tied in with pagan rites, sacrificial pigs and revivalist right-wing politics. A heady mix; but energy, once again, was not enough. *Darklands* and *House of America* together took less than £11,000 at the box office.

While such figures do not signal the end of a film's revenue-earning potential – TV and video sales are still to come – and may have risen since first promulgated in the trade papers, they do suggest that the 'public benefit', which Lottery funding of films was intended to supply, might be served by the 'spend' on location and in post-production, but signifies public indifference where it should matter most to film-makers: the cinema box office. The Arts Council members in charge of Lottery funding were not necessarily stung by the almost continuous outpouring of bad reviews – they were hardened to that. It was not this that proved crucial in 1996–7 in deciding to assign more and more control of Lottery funding to the very industry that was jettisoning the original cultural remit that attracted such funding in the first place. It was the evidence piling up that the Arts Council was being damaged by association with an industry of which it knew little, had small competence in monitoring and was being drawn into book-keeping of a kind totally alien to its core philosophy of patronage.

The trickle of Lottery-funded films increased to a flood in 1997; but midway through that year it was plain that the scheme was an extravagant disaster. Subsidy was essential to the British – or any – film industry, either in direct grants or tax relief, but subsidy on this scale, applied by people lacking time and judgement, and utilised by others lacking talent and commitment to anything but paying their own salaries upfront, was bound to fail. A member (unnamed) of the Film Policy Review Group set up by Chris Smith immediately after Labour came to power was quoted in January 1998 as saying, 'We are considering switching subsidies from film to distribution, perhaps paying for more prints of a film to be duplicated, or offering cinemas a levy to show more British films for longer than two weeks. This will create time for word to get around ...' Grants for distribution, prints and advertising did increase slightly, but to no noticeable improvement.

Multiplexes committed to an even supply of Hollywood films, and some even owned by American companies connected by computer directly to their British box offices, were not going to behave altruistically, even with modest financial inducement, and keep flops on their screens. As soon as the British box offices registered poor ticket sales the controllers back in the US had them off the screen and substituted another film – generally American – with proven or potential crowd-pulling power. Not to own the money box of the cinema, and hence control exhibition time, left the Lottery-funding project a hostage to the business ethics of those who did.

Even some of the three franchise holders, about to come on stream in 1998 with Lottery-subsidised films, were critical about their forerunners whose individual producers had taken the Lottery coin. In *Talking Pictures: Interviews with Contemporary British Filmmakers*, published by the BFI in 1997, Andrew Macdonald, co-partner in the £29.3 million DNA franchise, declared, 'Look at the films that are being made with Lottery money ... it's ridiculous, they're just more of the same.' It wasn't exactly a case of pot calling kettle black: though DNA had been awarded their franchise eight months before, its partners still had not produced a single film. Perhaps this was a negative virtue, seeing what films *had* been produced with public money.

The Arts Council grants supposedly boosted production from £400 million worth of films in 1995 to £770 million worth in 1997; but as John Harlow, in the *Sunday Times*, accurately noted, 'The typical British movie is neither commercially nor critically more successful than it was in 1994.' About the same number of films that were one or the other got made, with or without Lottery money: only the volume of films that were neither increased exponentially.

About a third of the Lottery-funded films were period pieces, or literary adaptations. Non-Lottery films also reflected the industry's abiding love affair with the national heritage: not only did we have three Jane Austen adaptations in 1997 alone, but BBC Films had a box-office and critical hit with *Mrs Brown*, directed by John Madden, which, thanks to Judi Dench and the unlikely Billy Connolly cast as Queen Victoria and her Scottish groom John Brown, squeezed a huge amount of lifestyle and unstated love (as the English prefer it) into a royal miniature. It instantly established Madden as a favoured Miramax director, a privilege he justified by delivering *Shakespeare in Love* to that American patron the following year.

For obvious reasons, Lottery films with historical antecedents in their storyline tended to have a better critical reception, and sometimes did better business than the general run. Brian Gilbert's *Wilde* (1997, Lottery grant £1.5 million, total project cost £5.6 million from the Greenlight Fund), scripted by Julian Mitchell and produced by Peter and Marc Samuelson was, to its credit, not an overtly gay polemic. It did take a highly elective view of Wilde's vanity and vices – omitting entirely the witness-box faux pas about not kissing a boy because he was singularly ugly, which damned him out of his own mouth in his libel action against the Marquess of Queensberry. But it touched true heights of personal tragedy with Stephen Fry's performance whose own intelligence and quicksilver tongue, that turned epigrams into easy conversation, took care of the poet-playwright's humanity as well as his gifts: this was Oscar in the round. Wilde's vanity, lust and, above all, need for an audience (fatally so in the courtroom) were caught in the net of Jude Law's alarming Lord Alfred Douglas. If Fry made Wilde's flesh weak, Law made Bosie's temperament wild. It established him as a leading British star. For once, every pound and penny of public money was well spent and seen to be.

Films Minister Tom Clarke attended *Wilde*'s première at the 1997 Venice Film Festival – perhaps Chris Smith would have caused too much excitement – where no fewer than seven other British films had been honoured with a special sidebar event: evidence of the talent that was around. Though six were co-financed by BBC Films, some benefited from additional Lottery finance – otherwise, they might never have got made: this was the original intention of the fund. Among them were Gillies MacKinnon's *Regeneration*, a study of post-battlefield pathology among shellshocked World War One soldiers and the relationship between two of them, Siegfried Sassoon and Wilfred Owen; Philip Saville's *Metroland*, based on Julian Barnes's novel, a rather shaky recap of how dreams die among the Sixties generation when they turn into nine-to-five commuters; Alan Rickman's *The Winter Guest*, following four couples through a long afternoon in a frost-bound Scottish seaside town: a radio play with pictures; and Iain Softley's *The Wings of the Dove*, from Henry James's story of thwarted love now updated to the Edwardian age but still finely attuned to the cruel deceits that rebound on the deceiver and condemn her to the Jamesian punishment of guilt and loneliness.

Shane Meadows's *24/7*, a reference to the bleak sameness of life twenty-four hours a day, seven days a week, shot in raw black and white as Bob Hoskins encourages violent teenagers to work with each other in a boxing club, instead of aggressively against the community, supplied what most of the films in this British mini-renaissance signally lacked: a prickling feeling of contemporary relevance. *Fever Pitch*, adapted from Nick Hornby's novel that had become required reading about soccer by Britain's better-educated classes – 'It's now more intellectually credible

... to watch Ian Wright play at Highbury than Ralph Fiennes at the nearby Almeida Theatre,' declared Adam Dawtrey in *Variety* – also released a spate of male confessional writing. But David Evans's film of it, for Channel 4, simply turned the author's obsession with football teams and results into a 'mismatched couples' sitcom with Colin Firth as the arrested adolescent with a one-track mind for scores and players, and Ruth Gemmell as a starchy fiancée who finds even his underpants are in Arsenal colours.

Mike Leigh's new film, *Career Girls*, was a small-scale study shot back-to-back with his more ambitious *Secrets and Lies* about how time changes friendships, with Katrin Cartlidge and Linda Steadman as two girls whose youthful uncertainties and rough edges have been smoothed by their new roles as businesswomen. Flashbacks didn't suit Leigh's style of accumulating social detail; but it was honest and touching (and more so, after Cartlidge's tragically early death barely five years later). 'For all its jokes and its spirit of female solidarity,' wrote David Denby in *New York Magazine*, 'the movie has an overall melancholy.' Ken Loach was in uncharacteristically romantic mood with *My Name Is Joe*, about a recovering alcoholic trying to keep his job and win the love of his health service worker. After the strained revolutionary dialectic of *Carla's Song*, the year before, which took Loach to Latin America, this Glasgow-set study of edge, love and desperation had more sexuality than Loach had allowed himself ever before; it proved his most accessible and popular work. Peter Mullan as the irascible but emotionally vulnerable Joe, was catapulted to stardom, the way his Scottish compatriot Robert Carlyle had been by *Trainspotting*.

One of the few films that isolated the changes going on in Britain, rather than simply repeating their makers' well-established concerns with class idiosyncrasies and social injustices, was *My Son the Fanatic* (1998, Lottery funding £750,000, total project cost £2,134,800). Hanif Kureishi's screenplay, directed by Udayan Prasad, had the bite of relevance to the New (rather than the 'cool') Britain: a place where immigrant Asian fathers are more liberal than their native-born fundamentalist children. At the time, this tragi-comedy set in Bradford got scant attention. In view of the growth of Muslim fundamentalism and the civic violence of the early years of the twenty-first century, it can have just claim to have been the most far-sighted film of the Nineties. Its protagonist is a Pakistani cab driver (Om Puri) who bears racist gibes with good humour, loves his adopted country and strikes up an extramarital relationship with the tart he drives daily to her evening's work. His son (Akbar Kurtha) upsets the delicate balance between the two cultures when he celebrates his coming of age by rediscovering his Islamic roots and inciting his extremist brethren to a clean-up campaign against 'loose' women, especially his dad's mistress. Though it doesn't dig very deeply into Islamic fundamentalism – not to the point, anyhow, of promoting a fatwah – the funny-pathetic collapse of the bridge that Puri had built between the two worlds is wryly expressed. It raised questions – finally evaded by the film – which were the divisive issues of life and faith to Britain's races in Bradford's streets a few years later. We should have paid more attention to this not so distant early-warning signal. Its box office was disappointing: it took about £123,000 in its initial, very restricted, distribution.

Channel 4, its producer, had hit a more responsive social nerve and box office with *Brassed Off* (1996), not a Lottery-financed film, an Ealingesque comedy made over into an explicit anti-Tory polemic that made refreshing entertainment for much of its length out of the traditional North Country mix of muck and brass. The 'muck' was a Yorkshire colliery whose miners were being compelled to vote for redundancy (and their own extinction as a community). The 'brass' was the colliery band, whose success when it toured the pit towns and gritty cities offered the consolation of still being 'listened to' by an otherwise distant and indifferent world. Pete Postlethwaite was the spartan bandmaster; Tara Fitzgerald the girl in this all-male world – and one, moreover, working for 't' management'. An American social comedy would have had no trouble crossing the demarcation line between 'them' and 'us', but, true to history, this British comedy showed how committed it was to the past, like the community itself, by keeping the mutual attraction these two felt for each other until they could make music of an asexual kind. Ken Loach wouldn't have missed the class confrontation opportunity; but the film literally used band practice to drown out the politics of redundancy when union and bosses lock horns. The bitterness of the 1994 miners' strike against the Tory government permeated the film, as well as the hopelessness of defeat – 'Ten years ago, you were full of fight,' one band member is scolded by his disgruntled wife, 'now you just blow your bloody trumpet' – was excoriated in a speech from the conductor's podium. In voice and spirit, if not in victory, the film's miners had the last word – or last note – at the film's metropolitan climax at the brass bands finals in the Albert Hall when Tory heartlessness was denounced from the conductor's podium. It was a sentimental victory, though, rather than a dialectical one – another punch that Loach would not have pulled. No matter (or not much). The pits might have closed; in the rousing music their brass bands made, the myth of a deeper, darker England lingered on. One could shed an honest tear. The film cost £2.8 million to make and took £3 million.

The aftermath of this modest success for Channel 4, however, was to prove baleful for David Aukin, in charge of film production there since taking over David Rose's job in 1990. Channel 4 had advanced a modest sum – under £15,000 – to develop a project brought to it by Uberto Pasolini, a relative of Luchino Visconti, who had begun as a runner, the lowest rank in a film unit, then assisted David Puttnam on *The Killing Fields* and now worked both sides of the Atlantic as a fully fledged producer: his last US-made film, *Paolookaville*, had inventively transposed to New Jersey Mario Monicelli's 1958 comedy of disorganised crime, *I Soliti Ignoti*. Pasolini seemed to have inherited the neo-realist gift, evident in De Sica's early films, for mixing social comment with human comedy and a feeling that the film-maker actually liked the characters in them and empathised with their plight: *The Full Monty*, in this respect, was to turn out the best Italian film ever made in Britain. But when the screenplay by Simon Beaufoy was deemed ready for production, Channel 4 passed on it. Its story of redundant steelworkers in Sheffield who recover their dignity and sense of worth by shedding their clothes seemed too close to the theme of *Brassed Off*. Both films observed the same community, had the same concerns about unemployment and self-worth, and shared much the same geographical setting. This was true: but most films are formulaic. Anyhow, the budget was reasonable and the basic premise of men stripping to the buff was probably more intriguing in box-office terms than that of men making music, so it is hard to see why the argument of similarity carried the decisive weight.

Aukin graciously allowed Pasolini to place it elsewhere, if he could. The Italian left Channel 4's Horseferry Road offices and took a cab to Soho Square, where Lindsay Law, for whom he had made *Paolookaville*, was only one month in his new job as UK production chief for Fox Searchlight, the 'boutique' division of 20th Century-Fox. Law had arrived with the influx of Americans drawn to the UK by the Lottery millions. He put up the entire budget of *The Full Monty* – under £3 million – in return for world rights. And thus the British film industry lost the biggest moneymaker in its post-war history, for the film became a global sensation, took £40 million in the UK alone, outgrossing the US blockbusters *Men in Black* and *Independence Day*, took over £134 million worldwide and was recycled (and Americanised) as a stage musical which Lindsay Law supervised like a devoted godfather when it had produced successfully in several continents.

If Channel 4 had held on to it for the very modest sum it cost, it would have earned enough to cover its annual film-making budget (£19 million) twice over and given a tremendous boost to the broadcaster and a moral one to the industry. This, though, assumes Channel 4 would have promoted it as robustly as Fox Searchlight, which is less certain: the US-owned company spent £9 million to release it in America, £16 million in Britain and the rest of the world, and finished up probably making an estimated £40 million net profit. Once again, the minute that the potential was perceived, the US distributor had the means to make it succeed and used them. It is less likely that a British company could have duplicated this financial success. Nevertheless ... like the recording company that turned down the Beatles, the loss lingered like an unhealed wound in Channel 4's collective psyche.

The Full Monty (1997) differed in one signal respect from *Brassed Off*: it was not overtly political. It did not attack any particular government, yet came closest to showing how worklessness saps the will, disrupts the home, depresses self-esteem − and does it by rude comedy. No one makes revolution in the film. The comedy mined from folk in miserable straits comes to their social rescue without violence. 'Workers of the world, unite: you have nothing to lose but your chains,' the old Marxist call to arms is transmuted. The men united all right, but they have nothing to lose but their pants. And, paradoxically, they regain their manhood. Beaufoy's script also appealed, covertly as well as in its uncovered state, to a wide female audience. It knocks men's sexual pride in ways unrelated to the unemployment statistics. At one point Robert Carlyle, the monstrous psychopath of *Trainspotting*, is trapped along with his mates in the men's lavatory of their bingo club that's been taken over for a one-night, women-only act of male strippers. A woman bursts in to use the urinal. Can female liberation hit male pride a lower blow than this? The comedy thus established its credentials as a crossover film, with appeal to both sexes, and one that *closed* the gap between them. It appeals to the propensity of menfolk to behave like blokes and of womenfolk (when the men are not around) to behave like girls. It is comedy born of disjuncture − when the men, preparing to give their all or at least show it, are greeted by the cheers of the other sex, not their jeers. Carlyle's explosive nature lights the fuse that gives the film its indignation, its sense of people living at the extremes of their society, yet tempered by the affectionate bond between his divorced dad and his small son – a togetherness like that of De Sica's classic comedy of a family unit surviving unemployment in *Bicycle Thieves*.

There were, of course, a multitude of interpretations of the film: this, too, suggests its latent appeal. 'It is a social drama about post-industrial Britain.' No, 'It taps male vulnerability to gender-role reversal.' No, 'It is about men deprived of economic utility and finding fulfilment only in displaying their bodies for money.' No, 'It is about breaking the dependency cycle: only through co-operative enterprise can the unemployed regenerate community ties.' These heavy-duty inter-pretations – particularly the last, which could be put into a Tory election manifesto – were quoted by Simon Jenkins, that astute social com-mentator who enjoyed it, but saw the film as an 'economic blind alley'. 'The "full monty" forges no steel and pays no salary.' One can lay one's bet on so many 'meanings'. Yet Robert Carlyle, whose edgy, working-class belligerency as a lapsed Socialist himself was tempered by the exposure, in every sense, his character accepted in the pecking order of survival, saw its appeal in the simplest, and hence the likeliest terms: 'Suddenly these guys were forced to look at themselves the way they had always looked at women.'

In its 16 September 1997 issue, *Screen International* celebrated fifteen years of Channel 4's film division, from its first acquisition (*My Beautiful Laundrette*), its first production (*Angel*), David Aukin's taking over from David Rose, and its developing international sales and UK distribution arms (both under Colin Leventhal). The glory was real enough and should have been gratifying. But it must have been soured by the article's mentioning 'the one that got away' – *The Full Monty*. 'The whole policy is based on taking risks and gambling on talent,' Aukin was quoted as saying. Allowing the biggest box-office film of the year – the runner-up was *Bean*, a Rowan Atkinson comedy financed by PFE's Working Title subsidiary – to go to an American major, 20th Century-Fox, showed the downside of 'risks' and 'gambling'. It was desperately sad. Aukin continued, 'The problem with much UK money is that when they get involved in a UK film, they want to turn it [the film] into something comfortable for a US audience.' But *The Full Monty* was British to the core, yet US audiences felt comfortable with it, and indeed US reception helped make stars of Tom Wilkinson and Mark Addy – who soon were appearing in independent US movies they would possibly never have been considered for in pre-*Monty* days.

Aukin, however, had kind words for Miramax, the Weinsteins' production-distribution operation which, despite being wholly owned by Walt Disney, had set up its own London base; in mid 1998 it was to apply for Lottery financing for its revisionist British version of *Mansfield Park* that imported some unpleasant economic realities, such as the American slave trade, into Jane Austen's comfortably insulated world of marriage-broking and manners. This £6,162,000 production, which Miramax could certainly have financed alone, qualified for British subsidy and got it – £1 million. Wardour Street referred to this coup, somewhat enviously, as a 'flyer', but had to applaud the company's 'chutzpah'. Aukin spoke warmly of the quality of Miramax's risk taking, though it was rumoured that the company had leaned heavily (and unsuccessfully) to have such US-friendly stars as Woody Harrelson and Marisa Tomei head the cast of Michael Winterbottom's new film for Channel 4, *Welcome to Sarajevo*.

Hardly had the anniversary been celebrated than reports appeared that Aukin was quitting his job as head of film production and, along with Colin Leventhal, was forming a joint venture with . . . Miramax. Whether the timing was coincidental, or it was primed by the *Full Monty* affair, the news created a sensation. Channel 4 was thrown into turmoil. It had lost Michael Grade as chief executive when he resigned in January 1997; now his successor, Michael Jackson, was losing its two top film people, as well as Allon Reich, the channel's deputy commissioning editor, who was set to join Miramax UK's new outfit – and all this at a time when the channel was committing to spend more on film-making. Aukin said he had felt frustrated at not being able to invest in bigger movies: he had a £5 million cap on each Channel 4 production. Miramax budgets would go as high as $25 million. He anticipated producing up to six films a year for his new partners. Their outfit was officially designated HAL-Miramax. The acronym stood for Hoving, Aukin, Leventhal.

Trea Hoving, daughter of the distinguished Metropolitan Museum curator Dr Thomas Hoving, had been acquisitions executive for Miramax before her retirement to spend more time on family life, where she was known as Mrs Colin Leventhal. Harvey Weinstein called her his most trusted talent spotter: she had 'brought' *Cinema Paradiso* to

Miramax, one of their earliest US box-office hits. Aukin, then fifty-five, immediately ceased to be pitied by his peers for losing *The Full Monty* and, overnight, was envied for the 'dream team' he had helped form. 'His new post confirms [him] as the most important player in British cinema,' declared David Gritten. 'It is the first time a US company has made a significant investment in film production here and left the control of that money in the hands of a British management team.' This is to be doubted, but it's true to say it was the perception surrounding the new HAL team.

The three film franchises had barely got under way and here, in one stroke, Aukin and co. controlled a budget ($50 million, it was credibly estimated) as big as any one of them *and* had an advantage none of the franchise holders had: a US release for films they might acquire as well as access to Miramax's worldwide distribution network. Channel 4 swallowed its disappointment, announced that a 'stand-alone' film division was still on its agenda and, by the end of 1997, had appointed Paul Wester to head it from 1 February 1998: he had been senior executive vice-president for production at ... Miramax. The game of musical chairs got under way again.

For others, though, the music stopped in 1997 and left them without anywhere to sit. One unfortunate was the Films Minister, Tom Clarke, whom the new Culture Secretary, Chris Smith, had put in charge of the Film Policy Review Group. It published its proposals on the dot, on 25 March 1998, in a glossy brochure entitled 'The Bigger Picture' – in which the word 'culture' never once appeared. It was strictly functional. Its principal recommendation was a levy on all sections of the film industry which was estimated to make £18 million available annually through voluntary contributions based on a 0.5 per cent levy on revenues from every sector, including video stores and 'visiting' Hollywood block-busters. This would allow film development to get £5 million a year and provide a £3 million training fund. It would be topped up by a Lottery contribution of £7 million. Although voluntary, only companies contributing to the levy would be eligible to receive Lottery funding through the Arts Council or British Screen. Tax breaks would also be linked to levy contributions. Old industry hands smiled, particularly if they worked for US-owned companies.

In June the backlash they anticipated came – from Jack Valenti, the most powerful figure in the American motion picture industry. He saw the red light. And just as Lew Wasserman, in the previous decade, had told Mrs Thatcher of the benefits to the British film industry if the Eady Levy were abolished, Valenti's words were interpreted as a warning shot to the British government not to mess with his people. Even a 0.5 per cent levy would add six figures on to budgets of blockbusters American producers were intending to film in the UK. Steven Spielberg was even then preparing *Saving Private Ryan* for filming in Britain; this £50 million film would thus pay £150,000 in levy. No deal! Hollywood, said Valenti, was ready to pump millions into British films, provided the Blair government didn't 'interfere'. 'Governments', he said, 'cannot be the prime force which ignited the creative flame, nor can they command superior films to be made.' Though the diminutive Valenti may have lacked stature, his voice carried at full blast into the inner sanctums of Chris Smith's culture ministry. What had they done! Who had allowed this to happen! Smith was already being forced to contemplate cuts in Lottery funding for the arts: he argued against them, successfully. But the price was a clampdown on inefficiency and a positive response from the film industry which would let the proposed levy make up for any cuts in government grants to film-making.

The government hastened to distance itself from the Bigger Picture proposals. Tom Clarke's was the head of choice for decapitation. The first-ever Films Minister was sacked at the end of July; he was replaced by Janet Anderson, whose knowledge of films was problematic and who was only a parliamentary under-secretary, one rung down from a minister. At a film industry awards meeting in October, Ms Anderson let no mention of a levy slip through her lips. The official reason was the slight but predictable drop in cinema admissions following the huge success of *The Full Monty*. Few were convinced by this: Valenti had been prepared to go along with the measure if everyone else did. It was, in fact, the British television industry that blocked it.

Clarke, a popular man who knew something about the cinema, was not given any reason for his dismissal. Chris Smith carried on, his easy smile betraying no outward dismay at the complete collapse of his review body's year-long work – no committee was ever set up to liaise with City institutions. He had weathered worse crises – the Royal Opera House's soaring cost of reconstruction – and would do so in the months ahead over the Millennium Dome debacle. He had even survived the worst reviews in living memory for his collection of essays that was published in May 1998, entitled *Creative Britain*. 'Sanctimonious bilge,' was George Walden's opening judgement on this 'Mr Pooter of the arts'

in the *Sunday Telegraph* and it got worse: 'Is it elitist to expect a modicum
of intellectual self-respect in a Secretary of State for Culture? The fact
that neither Smith nor his civil servants understood that his book was
unpublishable maudlin trash tells us everything about our true cultural
dilemmas.'

However damaging to the ego such extreme criticism might be, Smith
nobly forbore to complain. Indeed, his bruised *amour propre* was probably
less painful than the blow that fate, at the start of 1998, dealt an even
bigger player in the film business's attempt to reconcile art and box
office. Suddenly, Michael Kuhn saw his dream of an alternative to
Hollywood's domination of the market place brutally interrupted. Poly-
Gram Filmed Entertainment, the giant distribution and production
outfit he had been carefully constructing since 1986, was sold from under
him – by his own boss.

17

Ends and Beginnings

Throughout 1997, Michael Kuhn continued to extend PolyGram Filmed Entertainment into Europe. He set up distribution networks in Germany, Austria, Italy, Switzerland and elsewhere. These were low-intensity operations. They attracted little attention in the boardroom of Philips, the parent company, back in Eindhoven. It was a much bigger risk when he opened up the company's full distribution operation in the US, in May 1997. This was taking the war to 'the enemy'. It was Hollywood's battleground, a much more expensive one. The upside was being 'in charge', marketing one's own goods, not having to cut others in on the deal: in a phrase, becoming 'a player' at the big boys' table. The downside was surrendering the safety net of selling rights to a film to a US buyer in a deal worth, maybe, up to half its budget. And then, of course, one had to put up one's own prints and advertising costs. But the *perceived* view that the Hollywood majors had of PFE was worth it: 'Suddenly, we had arrived ... never before had a European-based studio had its own US distribution as well as distribution in all major territories in the world,' Kuhn wrote later in an allowable exaggeration.

Rank in its prime, and even Thorn-EMI in its decline, had accomplished some of these goals, though certainly not on PFE's scale. Kuhn was still under fifty; it had been an eventful eight years. He was now learning how to pick and manage a slate of movies with more shrewdness than in the early stages of his learning curve. Remember, as long as the figures added up, he was willing to do the deal without too much heartburn over the content (or sometimes quality) of what he financed and sold, nor was PFE's 'product' all-British. He part-financed or picked up US-made movies like the Coen Brothers' *Fargo* and *The Big Lebowski* and Brian Singer's *The Usual Suspects*; foreign-language art-house fare such as Jaco van Dormael's *Le Huitième Jour*, a follow-up to *Toto le Héros*; Patrice Leconte's eighteenth-century satire, *Ridicule*; international hits like *Bean* and *Notting Hill*; even Leon Gast's documentary, *When We*

Were Kings, about the Muhammad Ali–George Foreman title fight in Zaire in 1974. He could say, with justice, that not only was his company's marketing of this mixed slate as efficient as any Hollywood studio's, but it was probably more 'talent friendly'.

Kuhn's account of his success, *A Hundred Films and a Funeral*, more a memorandum than a celebration and very cautious in revealing the behind-the-scene manoeuvring that was to bring tragedy to his enterprise, doesn't shy away from acknowledging the risks all this involved him in. 'If you make fifteen to twenty Hollywood movies a year and market them professionally on a worldwide basis you will have enough hits to justify who's in charge.' Yes, but 'to justify this blanket investment every year, the historic record is that there will be a big hit every three years, and a *Titanic* or similar every five years'. This is where the balance sheet shades into the gambling slip. So long as you are backed by a friendly patron with deep pockets, it is a gamble to be taken with reasonable equanimity. But making sure this indulgence continues is as important as ensuring you are getting and giving value for it.

It may be that Kuhn, in his deserved glow of achievement, took his eye off his patrons – Philips. In retrospect, he seems to have recognised the signals changing from financial greenlighting to anxious amber. 'The quick-moving, risk-taking style required to be successful in the entertainment business was inimical to the ethos of a hardware company like Philips, with their ponderous committee-driven ways.'

The Philips boardroom, comprising solid Calvinist Dutchmen, penny-cautious and attuned to calculable risks and policies as scrupulously adjusted to profit-and-loss as the printed circuits on their electrical products, shared few characteristics with Hollywood's boardrooms, with their mindset of manageable risk taking balanced by decades of actuarial experience and, at worst, the collateral of hugely valuable film libraries. In short, Kuhn's backers were businessmen, most of them austere in outlook and practice, attuned to the hardware of factory production, not the software of fantasy. 'History meant little to them,' Kuhn wrote. The bottom line meant everything.

Here, Kuhn was vulnerable. The one division of PFE that was consistently profitable was Working Title. Bevan and Fellner, both of them protégés of Kuhn, supported by him in the early years of loss making, then, elevated to importance by the giddy grosses of *Four Weddings*, had cultivated the talent while Kuhn was acquiring the territories. It paid off handsomely. They had a discretionary development fund of £6.5 million a year and support of PFE's now worldwide distribution network. Their hearts and minds – souls, too, on occasion – were as much in developing films to the point of production as in producing them.

By 1998 they had fostered popular hits like _Elizabeth_, Shekhar Kapur's sixteenth-century conspiracy movie set in the labyrinthine plotting of the Tudor court, which owed so much structurally to the _Godfather_ trilogy of Puzzo and Coppola. _The Hi-Lo Country_, a modern Western, made in the US but directed by Stephen Frears almost as a homage to Sam Peckinpah, was coming up on the 1998 horizon. This was officially a US–British co-production, due to the canny allocation of 'spend' in pre- and post-production inside the UK tax break parameters. So, too, was another apparently all-American film, an anti-death penalty drama, Frank Darabont's _The Green Mile_ (PolyGram and Castle Rock). One could (and would) argue about 'British identity', but Working Title could confront those who accused them of stretching it to invisibility in the product on screen with such indigenous British productions as the delightful scaled-down world of Mary Norton's 'Little Folk' who lived beneath the floorboards in Peter Hewitt's _The Borrowers_ – one of the three PFE-financed British films (the others were _Spice World_ and _Bean_) at the UK box office in 1997. Fellner and Bevan were now preparing a financially grandiose SF entertainment based on the highly successful TV serial _Thunderbirds_. In fact, they shelved it – it was not to go into production until 2003 – as they did other in-house projects. But this by itself was proof of the financial confidence (and profit) they enjoyed as a PFE founder member. They could afford to put projects on hold.

Adam Dawtrey reported in _Variety_, '[They] say they are more confident to push ahead with more expensive pictures now that they do not have to submit themselves to the mercy of a major [American] studio for co-financing and US release, as they did with Fox on their first $40 million picture, _French Kiss_, back in 1994.' _French Kiss_ was a disappointment: it was simply too expensive. That was the price Working Title had had to pay to get 'access' to 'A' list names. But it had taught Working Title the value of having stars (Meg Ryan, Kevin Kline) in a film to buy it 'protection'. The fact that it made over $100 million worldwide confirmed Kuhn's trust in PFE's global distribution network – and this was _before_ he had expanded into the US.

Ironically, some of his US purchases were the troublesome ones. In 1992 PFE had paid $35 million for 51 per cent of the US production company, Interscope, hoping for a flow of blockbuster product. Instead, it got a string of disasters. 'We reached the quantity of movies we were supposed to make, and the proportion which worked was about right, but the degree to which they worked wasn't enough,' Kuhn had said in 1996, laying the groundwork for 'selling' Philips on the need to set up his own US distribution network. But Dawtrey commented at the time, 'There are only so many times that he can explain to the engineers at Philips, which owns 75 per cent of PolyGram [PFE's parent company], why building a Hollywood studio brick by brick always costs more than originally promised.'

By 1998, PolyGram's profits were being hit by a recession in its own engine room, the international music and recording business. The company had had to issue a profits warning for 1997, foreseeing an end to double-digit profitability. This was due to the delayed release of some potential best-selling music albums, but also to the fact that PFE's own results were below expectations. During the first half of 1997 PFE saw its losses increase from $18.9 million to $46.9 million, reflecting a slow first-half release schedule. Kuhn put his hopes in David Fincher's *The Game*, starring Michael Douglas and Sean Penn, a Kafkaesque entertainment about a control-freak executive being loosened up by accepting a degree of orchestrated chaos in his life. It did well, but not well enough. Too sophisticated, it was said: PFE needed to lower its aim to hit the blockbuster target. Philips announced that its confidence in PFE's slow but steady haul into profitability was unshaken, but the very fact of the announcement was ominous. Such words of support, not infrequently, simply delayed the withdrawal of it.

PFE made one more 'acquisition' before the day of reckoning. Early in April 1998, it announced it would distribute worldwide all films produced by DNA, the £29.3 million Lottery franchise headed by Macdonald and Kenworthy. It would also put up a development fund for DNA – whose original £200,000 earmarked for this was now appreciably enhanced. PFE was already in place as DNA's UK distributor. In Kenworthy and Macdonald, Kuhn may have believed, he had a second-string Fellner and Bevan.

On 6 May 1998 the blow fell. Philips Electronics announced it was 'evaluating various strategic options with respect to its stake in Poly-Gram'. On 7 May 1998 Kuhn recalls opening *Daily Variety* and seeing the headline, 'POLYGRAM UP FOR GRABS'. It was his forty-ninth birthday. Cor Boonstra, Philips's chairman, said he wanted to concentrate on the core electrical business of the conglomerate and, as he put it, 'weed out the bleeders'. It would be a mistake to identify film-making as the principal haemophiliac element. PolyGram's music division, its powerhouse, with Alain Levy as its president, was probably Boonstra's main concern: profitability had slowed. Like other conglomerates, EMI and Sony for instance, that had placed their belief in the magical properties of combining hardware and software, machinery and artists, Philips had found that such synergy was illusory. Their individual properties did not combine in enhanced profitability. For some time the compact disc boom had sustained PolyGram but that had slowed. Levy, a cautious chief executive, had been unwilling to gamble on aggressive acquisitions – unlike Kuhn, who had made it his shibboleth. Stockholders were making impatient noises. Philips's share price was moving south. But film-making had played its decisive part in Boonstra's ultimatum. Even such a 'minor' item as an expense account enjoyed by a PFE executive, running to several hundreds of thousands of pounds annually, was hard for Dutch Calvinists to swallow; the very elevators at their Eindhoven HQ did not move until stepped on, thus saving power and guilders.

Philips had had a net loss of \$2.47 billion in 1990, and when Cor Boonstra took over in 1996 he had immediately begun reducing the group's non-electronic subsidiaries and sold off about thirty of them over the next two years. That should have warned Kuhn. 'Our bosses', Kuhn wrote, 'were interested in one thing and one thing only – the various businesses of the hardware company Philips . . . The will to grow PolyGram into a worldwide leader among media groups was not in their blood.' That was said sadly; and pretty well said it all.

A rumour arose quickly, however, and persists to this day, that Philips had somehow been approached by those shadowy 'elder statesmen' of Hollywood, who feared the growing success of Kuhn's operation would eventually reduce their territorial grip on the global film industry, and their persuasiveness had tipped the balance with the Dutch conglomerate. If so – and no evidence for it has ever been seen – the very approach of such men may well have caused Boonstra to draw back a little further, seeing the ruthless faces of people who worshipped only one god, show business, and not the preferred deity of the Netherlands at that.

The news shocked the UK film community – and beyond. 'To many figures in the Euro film industry [the sale of PolyGram] represents the biggest setback since the invention of the auteur theory,' *Variety* reported. Alain Levy and Kuhn tried to allay Boonstra's nervousness and regain his confidence. He agreed to meet them at a country-house hotel outside London. He admitted he was not impressed by the entertainment industry, did not understand it and was unwilling to try. He wanted out. As Levy and Kuhn headed back to London, trying benignly to develop an 'exit strategy' for their disillusioned parent company, they did not know that Boonstra's team had already opened negotiations with Swiss banks to sell PolyGram to the Seagram Corporation, headed by the Canadian-born heir to the liquor-distilling empire, Edgar Bronfman Jr.

Seagram already owned Universal Pictures but needed to put muscle on Universal's music divisions. Buying PolyGram's vast music library, arts and futures contracts was Seagram's real desire; but with the music came Kuhn's film division. The true implication of the sell-off soon became apparent. Everything that Kuhn had laboured to do over eight years, by building PFE into a European production and distribution entity with global reach that had the potential to rival Hollywood's age-old empire, was now going to be delivered to the enemy 'like a vassal state', as Kuhn had once declared. 'Instead of achieving a Hollywood ending,' wrote Neil Watson, a researcher and collaborator on David Puttnam's book *The Undeclared War*, '[PFE] has ended up as part of the Hollywood locomotive it set out to derail.'

At first, Levy and Kuhn could not believe Philips would be so blind to its self-interest. As they saw it, PolyGram could have been leveraged into a larger alliance, perhaps with the French film-financing and pro-duction outfit Canal Plus, to create a super-group of movies, TV and music interests that would benefit Philips's core interests in electronics. It was not to be. The deal was done – more or less – for a reported $10.6 billion, about $2 billion of it in Seagram stock and the rest in cash. One hope remained: a management buyout by PFE, or a 'Euro-rescue' operation of several Continental powers opposed to Hollywood's cul-tural and economic domination. Seagram didn't seem opposed to this. It wanted the music division. Kuhn's film operation was, frankly, an 'inconvenience'.

Universal Pictures already had its own distribution operation, United International Pictures, an umbrella group distributing the product of Universal, Paramount and MGM–UA. PFE's foreign distribution network, confusingly named Universal Pictures International, would unnecessarily replicate UIP's work. But even here there were complications. The European Union executive in Brussels was, at this very moment, threatening to withdraw UIP's exemption from European monopoly laws, alleging that its operation in Europe was tantamount to a cartel. If it did, it would be highly opportune for Universal to have a fall-back position in its ownership of the authentically European network such as Kuhn had built up over the years. A third risk was that US majors like Disney or Sony-Columbia, casting covetous eyes on PFE's film library, might trump any offer Kuhn and co. could raise for PFE and the company (or parts of it) would finish up in simply a different pair of Hollywood hands.

What frustrated everyone was the difficulty of establishing a realistic value for PolyGram (and hence PFE). Its library, comprising approximately 1,500 feature films and 10,000 hours of television programming, was the third largest post-1948 independent catalogue in the world: its value could be calculated. But what was Working Title worth? Its value lay principally in the 'talent and good will' of its two top executives. Bevan's and Fellner's contracts with PFE had a year to run: would they renew? When a figure was at last articulated, it was $1 billion. That cooled potential Euro-bidders' ardour. Pathé's chief, Jerome Seydoux, immediately announced his company's uninterest. Canal Plus's Pierre Lescure was doubtful. So were the Kirch and Bertelsmann broadcasting and publishing groups in Germany. Wall Street's wisest put a 'reasonable' price for PolyGram at $500–700 million. Seagram shook its head at that. The predatory wolf of Hollywood, Kirk Kerkorian, from whom Kuhn had at one time tried to buy MGM, complicated matters by seeking to buy PFE's film library.

Britain's EMI, which had been out of films as a major player ever since its own crash, looked interested – for a minute or two, anyhow, until institutional investors reacted with pain and dismay: they had been burned once before. 'They are diluting a highly cash-generative business with a very capital-intensive business. They are also heightening the risk profile of the stock,' said one analyst. Even so, EMI put a value of $600 million on PFE, though Goldman Sachs, the merchant bank handling the transaction, had indicated a target area nearer $750 million. Alain Levy was believed to be behind EMI's 'sympathetic' approach: he would probably have become chief executive if it made a successful offer. Final bids were due in by 18 September 1999. Kuhn's buyout plan required a cash injection of $376 million just to cover PFE's cash-flow loss in 1999 – its overhead was currently running at an average rate of $170 million and another $118 million in 2000 to finance a full slate of sixteen movies. EMI decided at the last minute not to bid. Result: no one came up with what Seagram was asking.

The consequence was clear: Universal, which had bitten off more than it could digest with its parent company's acquisition of PolyGram's film business, now had to absorb it somehow or other, take on the sixteen to eighteen PFE productions awaiting release (which alone would require an enormous additional financial commitment in marketing and distribution) and decide what to do about Universal Pictures International. Its one compensation for this unwieldy mouthful was acquiring Working Title, since Bevan and Fellner decided to go with Universal, provided they got their required degree of autonomy. They were in a very strong position: they had *Notting Hill* ready for release, and would make *Captain Corelli's Mandolin* and *Bridget Jones's Diary* – at least two of these turned out to be substantial box-office hits. In seeking to protect their independence of operation, though knowing that success was the best safeguard, they are believed to have insisted that Canal Plus be brought into the deal, as a European balancing factor against the overweening power of their Hollywood parent.

Stewart Till, PFE's president, was retained to draft a blueprint that, he hoped, would save the company from destruction by Universal by retaining a separate production-distribution operation in Europe. He predictably failed; UPI was eventually shut down. Till would later attempt to set up his own European-based finance and production company under the Signpost banner, but his efforts coincided with severe recession in several major territories, which caused potential partners to pull back. Ironically, he would then become chief executive of UIP, the company that had 'swallowed' UPI, while still participating as Alan Parker's deputy chairman in the Film Council; thus the head of a major Hollywood-owned corporation 'doubled' as the deputy head of the new entity called into being to sustain the British film industry.

As for Michael Kuhn, on 11 December 1998 he sent this memo to all PFE staff: 'Subject: Farewell. The whole PFE ride has been really great.'

That was all. It scarcely needed saying that the outright loser in all this was the UK film industry. Kuhn came closer than any other single individual to putting in place an alternative to Hollywood. Kuhn, it's important to understand, was not anti-Hollywood – he was a businessman, for heaven's sake. He brought PFE to the brink of success: he 'grew' the company to the point where its accumulated assets in terms of library, expertise and working talents, as well as its outreach to fourteen countries, created a realistic 'studio' of a size and power that Hollywood's establishment would respect in market place and boardroom. While the UK continued to busy itself with bureaucratic strategies to retrieve or, failing that, to repudiate the hugely expensive public subsidies already expended on its film industry to little effect, Kuhn's efforts and Philips's cash effectively engaged in a show of strength and determination with the foot soldiers of Hollywood's empire at home and abroad. Kuhn took the reversal of his fortunes with a lighter heart than one would have imagined. But then his heart had always been in the deal, not the artistry. Artists might be broken-hearted by such a setback, dealers live to play another day. They cannot afford to get emotional.

Over the next year Kuhn saw even the omnipotent Seagram selling Universal to the French-owned conglomerate Vivendi, headed by the international entrepreneur Jean-Marie Messier, a man of Napoleonic ambitions who might have come swaggering out of Tom Wolfe's satire of boom-time America, *Bonfire of the Vanities*, as one of its 'Masters of the Universe'. 'Who knows what may happen to Vivendi in the years ahead?' Kuhn wrote in his memoirs. He did not have to wait 'years'. Within the twelvemonth Messier, the self-styled 'maître du monde', was toppled by shareholders and Vivendi plunged into financial chaos.

By October 1999 Kuhn was in business again, seeking to raise £32.6 million capital from investors in Europe to build up another PFE, with a modest base of thirty or so employees, offices in London, Paris or Berlin, but relying on a network of local distributors 'who know their markets best'. He described himself, in an interview with the *Financial Times*, as 'an idealist with a romantic notion of Europe'.

The collapse of PFE had an immediate effect on the franchise experiment. It left DNA, the studio run by Duncan Kenworthy and Andrew Macdonald, without anyone to distribute its films, though eventually Universal, PFE's successor, stepped into the breach. Not that this was very serious, yet. In two and a half years since winning its £29.3 million Lottery funding, DNA had not got a single film ready for screening. It was only now, in mid 1999, putting *Beautiful Creatures*, its first candidate for profit and acclaim, into production. Its opening kept on being announced, then delayed. When it was premièred, late in 2000, it turned out to be a bungled attempt at a female buddy-buddy black comedy, with Rachel Weisz and Susan Lynch cast as agents of female empowerment, who relish killing men (and a dog, without making much distinction) amid escalating mayhem. The film cost a reported £4 million, of which roughly half was Lottery funding. The box-office returns were very disappointing; the reviews were devastating.

Macdonald and Kenworthy had certainly been in no hurry to kick start their franchise. To critics of tardiness, Macdonald retorted that they wouldn't begin making a single film until the scripts were 'right'. He had earlier said, in a BFI collection of interviews with contemporary film-makers, 'Look at the films that are being made with Lottery money . . . it's ridiculous, just more of the same.' Words that, perhaps, were returning to haunt their speaker now that they had taken DNA's coin. He added defensively, reiterating the concern he and his partner now had about the degree of public scrutiny involved in accepting public subsidy, in late 1999, 'Ripping up our roots to inspect our growth is not a good idea.' This would have rung truer had such 'growth' been apparent. Both he and Kenworthy, with commendable post-franchise zeal, had applied their talents to 'growing' other companies' successes: Kenworthy produced *Notting Hill*, Richard Curtis's 'sequel' to *Four Weddings*, which eloquently paired Hugh Grant and Julia Roberts; Macdonald fulfilled the same function for his old *Trainspotting* partner, Danny Boyle, on *The Beach*, starring Leonardo DiCaprio. The first was for Sony-Columbia, the second for Warner Bros. It had maybe sunk in that producing films under the DNA franchise took a great deal of time and commitment, and made less financial sense than the fees for producing American-financed films.

Working Title had put in a franchise bid but been rejected, possibly because they were already under PFE's patronage. Fellner and Bevan soon thanked God that they had not succeeded: it would have meant deflecting their full and rewarding attention from building up PFE, and possibly for little money and less praise. By March 1999 Working Title were emerging from new ownership with their integrity intact and their finances enhanced. Under a five-year pact with Universal Pictures they had the right to greenlight up to five modestly budgeted films a year, and for the first time would see some 'back end', as profit-sharing was called, in their own pictures. *Variety* terms this 'an unprecedented declaration of faith by a Hollywood studio in a European production company'. Against these deals the British franchises looked decidedly mingy.

As DNA managed to ready its subsequent two productions – small-scale comedies like *Strictly Sinatra* and *The Parole Officer*, both built around a TV personality, Steve Coogan – observers concluded that the franchise holders would have been better off pursuing their individual routes, even if these led to Hollywood, than attempting to fulfil a business plan – sixteen films over six years – that was now clearly overambitious. The results of a half-term franchise review, due in 2001, were anticipated, by some with relish.

Not that the other two franchises, Pathé and the Film Consortium, were acclaimed successes. Both, though, were priming the production pumps with more alacrity, though their films were only starting to trickle out. Pathé's franchise was now regarded as a friendly gesture of self-interest to a company whose ownership by the biggest French film conglomerate rendered any begging-bowl alms unnecessary, (though nice to have). It was hoped Pathé would help British-made franchise films get a wider showing in Continental Europe.

Hideous Kinky (1999, Lottery funding £1,070,000, total budget £3.2 million) was the first of the Film Consortium's productions to be premièred. A story set in the 1970s, from Esther Freud's semi-auto-biographical account of a mother and two children taking off on a *sine die* sabbatical in Morocco, it was an enjoyable, if bland and cautiously radical, 'adventure'. Gillies MacKinnon and his screenwriting brother Billy, both skilful intuitors of child–parent relationships, laid on the irony of infant conservatism defeating parental irresponsibility like a grace note rather than an exclamation mark. Kate Winslet made Mum a free spirit, but scarcely a reckless one. Mum's Arab lover, a muscular pet of a man who toiled in the stone quarries, played proxy spouse and surrogate father to the English trio. The ingredients evoked no alarm for middle-class, middle-ageing film-goers grown out of their own gap-year hankering. It drew a line in the sand which such transgressive events as sex and drugs were not permitted to cross. It exuded the trust of strangers, far easier in its retro setting than nowadays, and maternal duties were put before nomadic liberation. In a word, it was 'safe'. A disappointment from a director hitherto shaping into a richer, darker Ken Loach, yet honourable. But not the 'big bang' it had been hoped the franchise would supply with the star of *Titanic*.

Chris Auty left Jeremy Thomas's Recorded Picture Co. to take over as the Film Consortium's chief executive in June 1999. To observers, it seemed that the various components of the franchise were experiencing much the same strain between personal projects and consortium obligations as the DNA partners had done. Ken Loach (Parallax Pictures) had enjoyed his greatest box-office success with *My Name Is Joe*, which eventually took over £1 million at the UK box office.

Virgin Entertainment's contribution to the consortium was of the financial kind; in the first flush of enthusiasm it seemed a strong supporter. But by 1999 Richard Branson was finding a need for additional capital and the chain of cinemas he had bought for £190 million in 1995 no longer seemed a gold mine: cinema-going had dipped sharply due to consumer fatigue after *Titanic*, though releases such as *Star Wars* and *Shakespeare in Love* might correct that. All the same, from being one of the 'under-screened' territories outside the US, the UK was now looking as if it had more screens than it needed and any increase in their number would simply mean one multiplex cannibalising another's patrons. Virgin put its cinema chain on the market in October 1999 and sold it to the French group, UGC, for £215 million. Virgin's US venture-capital backers were said to be very happy. This was to have a knock-on effect on Virgin's loyalty to the Film Consortium. Its other members, Skreba (Simon Relph) and Scala (Powell and Woolley), were proven deliverers of film projects, but maybe not always for their consortium. Auty would have found it difficult to mobilise such inveterate freelancers. Some of them still enjoyed American financial patronage on a 'first look' basis at any likely project they developed. Some now viewed the franchises as if what had seemed 'a good idea at the time' was not turning out too well. Others among the new film-financing groups even then coming into prominence late in 1999 were to take a more aggressive view. They saw them as ripe for a takeover bid. The Film Consortium, in particular, looked a candidate. Meanwhile the proponents of the Film Council felt they could well have done with the additional £100 million that the franchises were enjoying, if not successfully exploiting.

The franchises were indeed privileged. They were now able to draw down Lottery money not only for film production, but for development and even for resources to market the films. As a notable distributor, Mike Southworth, a director of the Feature Film Co., put it, 'It now comes to light that one particular line of "funded" product will be propped up with what amounts to no less than a free handout to buy the prints and advertising ... To me, and many like me, this smacks of the Lottery trying to buy an audience in the vain hope of covering up all the original bad investment decisions.' Southworth's company had distributed *My Son the Fanatic* and no doubt he bitterly reflected what a help 'P & A' subsidy would have been to him then. The status of the franchises could not be altered, however, at least not until the half-term review due in 2001. All that the Film Council, and its designated chiefs, Alan Parker and John Woodward, could do at present was lay plans for their own stewardship of the film industry, implore the Arts Council to go steady with its non-franchise handouts to individual producers and try to move the bar in favour of making fewer films, but bigger and better ones. This is the political theme running through the pre-Council period of 1999–2000. For tactical reasons, so as not to seem to criticise the Arts Council and its Maecenases on the Lottery advisory panel, it was described as 'moving towards more responsibility to the audience', which, translated, meant, 'making films people will go to see'.

The past four years had seen eighty-six films part-financed by the Lottery, with some gain to the industry's infrastructure and great gain to investors drawing on all the tax breaks available that even accountancy firms were now structuring around scripts written at their dictation so as to provide a vessel for investors. But very few such productions had drawn audiences, good notices and even substantial box-office returns. None of the first-time directors had graduated to a second film by mid 1999. Just two Lottery-assisted directors had gone on to make their next films. Barely £5.5 million had been recouped by the Arts Council from a Lottery investment in film funding more than ten times that. But don't forget DVD and video fees and overseas sales are still to come, was the Council's stony-faced reply to its critics. Yes, but such residuals *generally* reflect a film's initial success or lack of it. In fact, after seven years of Lottery funding, recoupment would still be less than £10 million on a total investment getting on for £200 million.

The big money was still being made by the independently financed – i.e. non-Lottery – films: blockbusters like Miramax's *Shakespeare in Love* (1999), after a prolonged feeding frenzy in the US and UK media on Gwyneth Paltrow, young Will Shakespeare's muse who sets his creative juices running again. It was she who converted its early, uneasy resemblance to a sophomoric pantomime into a dazzling entertainment rewritten by Tom Stoppard's ironic reworking of literary history replete with linguistic conceits, 'in' jokes and Eng. Lit. gamesmanship. With this role stardom fell on Paltrow like a coronation robe. British craftsmanship once again – how many times, oh God! – was called into being by American venture capital and repaid the risk with compound interest.

Everyone came out of it looking well, feeling richer. John Madden, following up his stiff but well-received Victorian chamber play, *Mrs*

Brown, had his style loosened by the fleet tongues and robust temper of Elizabethan rowdiness. Joseph Fiennes, as young Shakespeare, made one feel the passionate fluids of ink and semen that animated the man before the receding hairline and graveyard mask of history were thrust on him. No later British film ever allowed him to build on his success.

The film's solidly carpentered construction – attributed to its original writer Marc Norman – expensive *mise-en-scène* and multitudinous Anglo-US cast all signified the hallmark of Miramax's Harvey Weinstein. One felt like hiring him for a year or two to work the same miracle on the indigenous British scene. A bulldozer like Weinstein would always be preferable to the strimmers that were trying to reshape the film landscape in the UK.

Raymond Snoddy, interviewing Alan Parker, the Film Council's chairman designate, late in 1999, found a man who spoke with something of Weinstein's candour. 'Additionality', he began – spitting out the word devised by civil servants to cover grants to films that would possibly not be made (and with good reason) unless they were propped up by 'additional' funding – 'was meant to enable the disenfranchised. Yet it has often fostered work that is not good enough. In my opinion, unskilled directors have been able to make films that they should not have.' No one would disagree with that, except maybe the entrenched, now embattled, Arts Council, which could scarcely wait to hand over the whole mess to the Film Council. Parker acknowledged his own work in the US – where Universal Pictures funded his in-house development operation – might take him out of the country, keep him for lengthy periods of time away from his remit. This consideration of self-interest might have deterred less committed public servants than Parker. But he saw one compensation. It was more fun than having to deal with 'stroppy film-makers'. Somehow, one cannot hear Harvey Weinstein, a pugnacious creative talent, articulating that thought.

Film Four, freed of the obligation to remit profits to ITV and now able to reinvest them in film-making, dominated Cannes in 1999 with nine titles in the official selection – several of them American like David Lynch's *The Straight Story* and Jim Jarmusch's *Ghost Dog*. In part, this was the late flowering of David Aukin's production and acquisitions policy. Paul Webster, his successor, now formed partnerships with other companies, including Miramax, to develop the 'studio' idea. Projects being readied included the Butterworth Brothers' *Birthday Girl* (with HAL-Miramax), Jonathan Glazer's *Sexy Beast* (with the Recorded

Picture Co. and Fox Searchlight) and Paul McGuigan's *Gangster No. 1* (for Norma Heyman's Pagoda Films). 'We now have a truly integrated operation,' said Webster. He added, however, a caveat: 'We are not making movies to satisfy movie-makers' desire to make statements.' He was looking, he said, 'for quality entertainment with a cutting edge'. This was the familiar refrain of almost every new executive beginning his reign with a vow of commercial aspiration. How many of the films Channel 4 'opened' at Cannes in 1999 would have been picked by Webster – in fact, most of them had necessarily been on his predecessor's slate – it's hard to say. But it was recalled that the poster for Ken Loach's *My Name Is Joe* had omitted mention of Robert Carlyle's win of the 'Best Actor' award at the 1998 Cannes Festival – lest it signified 'art house', perhaps? Webster knew he had a lot of leeway to make up.

Despite Channel 4's diversity of product, its films accounted for no more than 1 per cent of UK revenues in 1998. *East Is East* (1999), previewed at Cannes, turned into 1999's new *Full Monty* and started Webster's remake of the channel's film policy with a box-office bang. It also exposed the hefty millions to be made from Britain's Asian community and may thus be said to have seeded the ground for the success of *Bend It Like Beckham* three years later. Adapted from Ayub Khan Din's stage play, and picking up more expanded exuberance from the rebelliousness of a Pakistani family in Northern England whose young British-born children seek an escape route from their Genghis Khan-type father, the £2.5 million production was directed by an Irishman, Damien O'Donnell, and seemed to bottle up the civil wars of Ireland and the Indian subcontinent within the walls of a Salford terrace house. The air is filled with the shattering of taboos; secular shibboleths have replaced the diktats of the mosque; and the novelty of hearing homely words not usually heard issuing on the screen from immigrant lips in local accents forced an enriching double take on characters who would be thought stereotyped if they were white and spoke plain North Country. This brought the zest of foreign spice to a home-cooked sitcom.

Despite the emphasis on Muslim traditions being enforced (by dad) and flouted (by his seven mixed-race children) the film had little of the impact, and none of the prophetic accuracy, of Hanif Kureishi's *My Son the Fanatic*: it was as much about the generation gap as Muslim fundamentalism. But it asserted its own ethnicity boisterously and rib-aldly. A small film, its huge box-office success gave it an importance: it proved to be a giant leap over the threshold of multicultural cinema in Britain. It travelled well, too. Miramax, possibly sensing the elements of a Jewish sitcom in its patriarchal rebellion, snapped it up for North America.

Ken Loach's was the perceptible influence on several notable films presented at Cannes. One was Lynne Ramsay's *Ratcatcher* (1999), a bleak but impressively engaging story of a twelve-year-old Glasgow boy, with pale, pinched, yet alert features, facing life with a dad whose cheeks are a tramway junction of knife scars. His pals, neighbours and grungy existence beside a brackish canal on wasteland were transfigured by an imagination that invested everything with the mood of a magic kingdom. It made manifest the secret life of a child with the same empathy as Loach's *Kes* and the power to look straight at one and set one wondering what he is thinking; its final image, when the lad turns towards the camera of John De Borman – the veteran photographer selflessly helping newcomers like Ramsay into the commercial world – and smiles for the first time had the Cannes audience completely on his side – the way a tormented young Jean-Pierre Léaud had done in *Les 400 Coups* exactly forty years earlier. *Ratcatcher* was part-financed (£615,000) from Pathé's Lottery franchise. For once, it had produced a film that stood up as 'art', even if it was a hard sell as 'box office'.

Tim Roth, actor turned director, made *The War Zone*, Loach-driven also in style and content and comparable to his fellow actor Gary Oldman's *Nil by Mouth*. Both films were set in the 'war zone' also known as family life. This time incest was added to the list of parental abuses with the father, played by Ray Winstone in both films, again being the domestic threat. Whereas *Ratcatcher*'s kid views his family's move to a rural housing estate as his hope of salvation, the fifteen-year-old alienated hero of *The War Zone* finds relocation to Devon an uprooting experience that exacerbates his growing pains. The sexual climax of the father's rape of a daughter while his concealed son looks on was tough viewing – as it should be. Neither Roth nor Oldman immediately followed up his debut as director, as if their highly personal films had purged them without engaging them. A loss, since both had made the right moves, bonding with life as well as art.

Michael Winterbottom's *Wonderland* was a Loach-like slice of life that followed the misfortunes of three London-based sisters, their husbands (separated or about to desert) and parents (mismatched) through a long weekend over Guy Fawkes night. For some, it remains Winterbottom's most achieved venture into Realityville; for others, its very ordinariness looked assumed, falling somewhere between Ken Loach and Mike Leigh and, in the end, resembling a week's editions of TV's *EastEnders*. Bringing the kitchen sink back to the screen pays diminishing rewards when it is filled with well-worn crockery.

Social realism on the 1999 screen still profited from the phenomenon of *Trainspotting* and *The Full Monty* and the appetites of producers and distributors that it had whetted. Few of the new films, however, re-created the shock value of their models, Justin Kerrigan's *Human Traffic*, a comedy about teenage clubbers named Jipp, Nina, Coop, Lulu and Moff larking over a weekend in Cardiff, clearly looked back to *Train-spotting*'s feverish rush. Drugs and drug dealing didn't feature in it; the euphoria of clubland stood in for them. Peter Bradshaw's review in the *Guardian* showed the gulf that separated a film that set out simply to please – and did so by its refreshing honesty – from one that had set out to change things. '*Trainspotting* was a gut-wrenchingly angry and despairing film which was a product of John Major's Britain, but whose unflinchingly bleak representation of drug use was sufficient for an obtuse "Just Say No" interpretation which earned it an endorsement from Mrs Virginia Bottomley. ... *Human Traffic* is higher up the socio-economic scale of Blair's Britain at the middle-class student-loan level ... It makes for a strangely depthless film.'

Everyone, in particular British exhibitors, wanted the successor to *Monty*. Sadly, it was not to be the same writer Simon Beaufoy's *Among Giants*, instantly nicknamed 'The Monty Pylon Show'. It reflected Beaufoy's fascination with masculinity and the changing roles of men and women, both well rooted in the Yorkshire moors, where tough gangs of men (and the heroine) scale the giant electricity pylons to repaint them, perching amid vertiginous steel struts and sometimes drifting into a Pop ballad like a cage of songbirds. But this time the men weren't social victims: they were scroungers, with cash-in-hand jobs, uninsured and cheap labour, but spared the ignominy of shuffling forward in the dole queue or heading for the human scrap heap like *Monty*'s boys. The edge of desperation was absent; and it all softened into a conventional English romance about the girl who breaks up the buddy-buddy group of pylon monkeys. It cost £2,479,000 (including £665,000 Lottery money). Significantly, perhaps, Fox Searchlight, the boutique company of 20th Century-Fox which had taken the risk of backing *The Full Monty* when Channel 4 passed on it and thereby scooped the biggest jackpot in British film-making history, decided this time not to foot the full bill out of its own ample pockets.

If any of 1999's releases could be regarded as the rightful 'sleeper' – unexpected hit – and *Full Monty* follow-up, it was *Waking Ned*, a black comedy set in Ireland though filmed in the Isle of Man, under that semi-detached part of the UK's highly successful policy of attracting film-makers from the mainland (and elsewhere) with a clever system of loans and tax breaks whereby film-makers were lent a quarter of their budget costs in return for 50 per cent of the film being shot there. (One soon became tired of seeing a certain particularly attractive sea-coast cottage appearing again and again in qualifying films.) This policy was enunciated on the Croisette on the very day Chris Smith in 1997 declared the UK franchise winners at Cannes; at the time it was a little regarded initiative but arguably the more commercially successful of the two.

Waking Ned's slight plot – a scam among the shamrocks, about a couple of elderly fly 'boys' stepping into the shoes of a corpse that's inconveniently expired holding a winning Lottery ticket – need not concern one long. Its producer was Richard Holmes, an engineering graduate who had begun film-making in 1992 with *Soft Top, Hard Shoulder*, a road film strongly influenced by Bill Forsyth's whimsical comedies; he then produced *Shooting Fish* in 1997, the film that Chris Smith singled out for a pat on the head for swift repayment of its £971,000 Lottery money. Holmes was shortly to assume more prominence (and enhanced spending power) thanks, indirectly, to the extraordinary cycle of British-made gangster films that had been sparked off by *Lock, Stock and Two Smoking Barrels* (1998) and its director Guy Ritchie.

Ritchie was without formal film-school training – it is doubtful if it would have done much for a talent already well annealed in the cut-and-thrust of the Pop industry. Though he adopted a 'mockney' accent as protective coloration for his early activity, shooting promos for rave bands under contract to Island Records, thus thoroughly honing the impatient, gimmicky style *Lock, Stock* exhibited every minute of its rampaging plot, his origins were comfortably middle class (a titled stepfather, too) and Home Counties manor house rather than council estate. Later, as Madonna's husband, Ritchie came to occupy the status of a celebrity consort. He had financed a short film, *The Hard Case*, about four yuppies taking on the underworld's hard men at a poker game and running into the predictable trouble; it was the template for

Lock, Stock. Ritchie made the same impact on young British film-makers
that Tarantino did on his generational wannabes with *Reservoir Dogs* in
1992: after its British première, in 1994, they wanted to make films like
it. The ecstatic greeting Tarantino received at the National Film Theatre,
on London's South Bank, in January 1997 reflected the heady mix of
criminal cool and casual violence his film inspired. And once something
like this had entered the commercial system it travelled fast. PFE advertised *Lock, Stock* on 1,500 sites and released it on over 200 screens.

As Moya Luckett, an academic at the University of Pittsburgh, noted,
Ritchie's film coincided with the 'rediscovery' and commercial reissue
of films like *Performance* (1970), *Get Carter* (1971), *The Long Good Friday*
(1980) and the formation of 'an alternative canon' to the traditional
heritage cinema of Merchant Ivory. Professor Luckett also pinpointed
how new, scatological magazines, aimed at the 'lad' culture fed by Nick
Hornby's novels and the rise of football to be the new 'rock'n'roll' of
affluent middle-class culture, spearheaded the market saturation of *Lock,
Stock* and its imitators.

The few traditional British genres, horror and comedy, now acquired
a third that focused on violence and sexuality while incorporating some
of the other two in the horror-comic form of Vinnie Jones, a one-time
star footballer who had earned a conviction for failing to manage his
anger off the field, who played a zombie bagman and instantly became
an iconic figure of this new brand of unrestrained violence with an edge
of black humour. Not a great man with the verbals, Jones resembled
Boris Karloff in his most celebrated role, when Dr Frankenstein's creation, lacking a nimble tongue to explain his inner urges, would give
vent to his atavistic instinct and throw the little girl in the river. Jones's
success as a man with a face set in concrete and a heart of natural stone
created a demand for his services in other British productions that drew
on the hooliganism of street and football terrace. His act didn't require
literacy, simply the immediacy of the hard man who would slam a car
door on a rival's skull without a flicker of emotion.

Ritchie capitalised on this transgressive element, boasting that his film
had employed as 'adviser' East End gangsters whose criminal convictions
might be 'spent', but whose 'form' could still be used to design the
film's new laddism. For all the skill of its interlocking narrative, *Lock,
Stock* was signally short on Tarantino's macabre, funny insights into how
language diverges from livelihood in the profession of violence. Everyone
in it was gainfully immoral. Their cockney wit (sometimes subtitled for

comic effect, as if they formed a separate state of the British nation) was flaunted like a cut-throat razor; it caught the eardrum but that was all. The plot lost itself in a limbo land of revengers' tragedies. The film cosies up to its own violence, half in awe of it, half in love with it. The statement made by its makers and their cast – 'We know these types and they have a real lust for life' – is as cretinous as the explicit intentions of Ritchie's entertainment – 'What's going to sell this film to the audience is that they'll recognise humorous situations out of everyday life which they can identify with' – are cynically indecent. It wasn't exactly trash – its huge box-office success validated Ritchie's detection of a tabloid appetite for brutality in its target audience – but not art, either. It is best categorised as a cold-blooded artificial construct for a generation raised without moral judgement who would treat its depiction of the most grotesque deeds as if they were simply the comic meat in a slice-of-life sandwich.

By October 1999 a crime wave swamped film production. No fewer than seven British gangster films were being made at speed, such was the effect of *Lock, Stock*, which had grossed £11 million in the UK by this time. Former members of the East End underworld had never had it so good in their old age. Some, like Bruce Reynolds, one of the Great Train Robbery bandits, acted as adviser on *Gangster No. 1* and proclaimed, 'Certain types of criminal do extraordinary things, and for people who don't do extraordinary things that's very attractive.' No professional film critic got nearer it.

Public enemies *were* public favourites, it appeared, looking at the roster. Among them (and the only one to repeat Ritchie's success) was *Sexy Beast*, a ballsy drama directed overemphatically by Jonathan Glazer, whose best half featured a bald, beady-eyed Ben Kingsley putting dynamite under Ray Winstone's reluctant ex-safecracker who's understandably reluctant to be winkled out of his Spanish villa to return to London for one last job. Its first sequence of a huge boulder, dislodged by natural forces, hurtling past sunbathing Winstone's head by inches to splash down in his swimming pool was one of those 'shock and awe' openings that producers like Jeremy Thomas dream of – the rest of the story could not match it but, for once, a British genre film succeeded without Hollywood stars and hit the European box office hard.

Each succeeding annal of British gangster land grew paler and more self-parodic. *Honest* (Dave A. Stewart, 2000) starred three quarters of the All Saints Pop group (Nicole and Natalie Appleton and Melanie Blatt, looking like refugees from commercials for the cheaper brands of shampoo) who cross-dressed in boyz kit, taped down their boobs, glued on facial hair and headed up West to rob the rich and sleazy. A retro-crime caper – though tossing in anachronistic references to Women's Lib, it was fit only for a jumble sale of Sixties leftovers.

A look at the supporting cast confirmed the impression that Equity's ugliest card-carrying members were living well on the Gangster fetish initiated by Guy Ritchie. *Love, Honour and Obey* (Dominic Anciano, Ray Burdess, 2000) was an unredeemable mess, a slack, lazy romper-room movie featuring Jude Law, Jonny Lee Miller, Sadie Frost, Sean Pertwee and Rhys Ifans playing East End gangster scum of the sort that the lower ranks of show business and the film industry turns out to support at weddings and funerals of underworld celebrities – Ray Winstone appeared again, this time as a North London hoodlum and karaoke king. (Someone calculated that Winstone had appeared in sixteen movies over three years: not all of them gangsters.) It was violent, pornographic, incoherent and sickeningly narcissistic. *Essex Boys* (Terry Winsor, 2000) put the accent on little else but graphic thuggery, verbal and bodily abuse and pseudo-tough dialogue like 'Jason needed a new shirt, the bloke needed a new face'. Like all these films, it had a heavy cargo of misogyny – the Essex girls did little more than let their knickers fall round their ankles and obediently turn themselves into mattresses for the boys. It was produced by Granada, the film, TV and motorway café conglomerate, whose then boss supplied the Arts Council with its part-time chairman.

The odd-mobster-out in this bunch was *Gangster No. 1* (2000) directed by Paul McGuigan, who had coped with Irvine Welsh's devils in the Scottish writer's nauseous *Acid House* follow-up to *Trainspotting*. *Gangster No. 1*, a UK–German co-production, differed in its degree of violence – one notorious scene depicting a gruesome murder done with the dispassionate despatch of a surgeon has probably not been matched for cruelty in any film since. But it could claim, more reputably, that it had higher pretensions to an existentialism than were commonly to be found in the estuarine breeding ground of Essex crooks, or the Soho ghettos. In its concentration on the dynamics of personality, its nearest kith or kin was the Butterworth Brothers' *Mojo*, itself a Pinteresque psychodrama conceived as bloody comedy: the characters in both films belonged to the same nightmare milieu.

Gangster No. 1 recounted the rise and rise of an amoral young blood, the eponymous enforcer (Paul Bettany), in the 1960s underworld, his role model being a fashion-plate capo Freddie Mays, aka 'The Butcher of Mayfair' (David Thewlis). He quickly learns to terminate Freddie's enemies while notching up his own grudges and grooming himself and his psychotic drives for a takeover of the business. The scene that became notorious records at deliberative length and in ritualistic detail the torture of a loutish rival and his physical dismemberment while still alive. The event is depicted from the victim's viewpoint. A subjective camera looks up at Bettany, stripped of his Jermyn Street finery down to prosaic underpants and vest, soon turned blood red, as he axes, hammers and saws off the man's limbs while Peter Sova's camera fades into black and back again to replicate, with alarming empathy, the unseen victim's spells of fainting and revival. Adapted, like *Mojo*, from a stage play, this cinematic tour de force overwhelms the somewhat tired theatrical device of subsequent abdication and penitence by a reformed Freddie Mays that allows Gangster No. 1 – played in present-day scenes by a raddled Malcolm McDowell – to rule an empty roost. It has been compared with *A Clockwork Orange* and *American Psycho* for its exorcising of the demons that psychopathy has let loose. The picture was preceded by strong word-of-mouth, not least because it was thought vulnerable to heavy censorship (it wasn't), and caught the attention of one of the new financial groups looking for a 'way in' to the burgeoning Lottery-enhanced film industry. The old century was coming to an end; investment in films had less and less to do with the films themselves.

WhiteCliff Film and TV had been engaged in servicing football clubs and actually owned a team; it then went into meat rendering. It was headed by the multimillionaire Richard Thompson, an entrepreneur whose family was a powerful name in the horse-racing industry. Films, perhaps, were regarded as 'sexier' bloodstock. WhiteCliff bought Pagoda, the company that produced *Gangster No. 1*, and had announced *Kiss, Kiss, Bang, Bang* as its next production. Richard Holmes, the successful producer of two money-making comedies, whose company, owned by him and the director of the two earlier hits, Stefan Schwartz, had been acquired by WhiteCliff on its way to the big time in the film industry, joined the board as chief executive. Tax breaks and related advantages were undoubtedly a factor; but then this is what was driving the industry more and more in these years.

As the decade closed, the rush of new money into films had become a torrent; even accountants like Ernst and Young were now bankrolling films for their write-offs and sale-and-leaseback deals. Every week a new group announced itself. The one with the most apposite title was Alchymie (then occupying four floors above a Soho sandwich shop and bankrolled by a financial set-up called Flashpoint, which had promised to invest $250 million over five years). It later occurred to some people that 'Flashpoint' and 'Alchymie' were perhaps ill-chosen names for an industry that required long-term patience and solid experience. But if so, it was forgotten in the high fever of financial wheeling and dealing that *Variety* characterised with typical succinctness as 'Lucre Lends Life'.

And so the millennium came to a close. Essentially the British film industry was in the same state that it had always been – or at least for the last forty years. The switchback of (occasionally extreme, though much more frequently qualified) success and that of abysmal failure. The exhilaration of boom, then the all too common reality of bust. The making of films in Britain has never been easy, though if misplaced tax breaks and Lottery funding should continue to proliferate, all that may be said for certain is that there will be more and that more will inevitably mean worse. The pity is that by the year 2000 there was no sign at all that anything would change. The industry, the critic and the cinema-goer, though, surely have one thing in common: we all of us continue to live in hope.

Notes on sources

Reading for this book included the weekly trade journals on both sides of the Atlantic including *Screen International* (UK) and *Variety* (US); also the monthly magazines, *Sight and Sound* and the AIP Newsletters. Usually in the text I have indicated specific issues of newspapers and magazines.

A.W.

Index